Democracy in America

Democracy
IN AMERICA

By *ALEXIS DE TOCQUEVILLE*

THE HENRY REEVE TEXT
AS REVISED BY FRANCIS BOWEN
NOW FURTHER CORRECTED AND EDITED
WITH A HISTORICAL ESSAY, EDITORIAL
NOTES, AND BIBLIOGRAPHIES BY

PHILLIPS BRADLEY

Volume I

VINTAGE BOOKS NEW YORK
A Division of Random House

THE ATTENTION OF THE READER
is called to the extensive historical essay by
the editor which begins on page 389 of Volume II of the present edition, and which discusses in detail Tocqueville and his work.

VINTAGE BOOKS

are published by ALFRED A. KNOPF, INC.

and RANDOM HOUSE, INC.

Reprinted by arrangement with ALFRED A. KNOPF, INC.

Manufactured in the United States of America

Author's Preface to the Twelfth Edition

HOWEVER SUDDEN AND MOMENTOUS the events which we have just beheld so swiftly accomplished, the author of this book has a right to say that they have not taken him by surprise. His work was written fifteen years ago, with a mind constantly occupied by a single thought—that the advent of democracy as a governing power in the world's affairs, universal and irresistible, was at hand. Let it be read over again and there will be found on every page a solemn warning that society changes its forms, humanity its condition, and that new destinies are impending. It was stated in the very Introduction to the work that "the gradual development of the principle of equality is a providential fact. It has all the chief characteristics of such a fact: it is universal, it is durable, it constantly eludes all human interference, and all events as well as all men contribute to its progress. Would it be wise to imagine that a social movement the causes of which lie so far back can be checked by the efforts of one generation? Can it be believed that the democracy which has overthrown the feudal system and vanquished kings will retreat before tradesmen and capitalists? Will it stop now that it is grown so strong and its adversaries so weak?"

He who wrote these lines in the presence of a monarchy which had been rather confirmed than shaken by the Revolution of 1830 may now fearlessly ask again the attention of the public to his work. And he may be permitted to add that the present state of affairs gives to his book an immediate interest and a practical utility that it had not when it was first published. Royalty was then in power; it has now been overthrown. The institutions of America, which were a subject only of curiosity to monarchical France, ought to be a subject of study for republican France. It is not force alone, but good laws, that give stability to a new government. After the combatant comes the legislator; the one has pulled down, the other builds up; each has his office. Though it is no longer a question whether we shall have a monarchy or a republic in France, we are yet to learn whether we shall have a convulsed or a tranquil republic, whether it shall be regular or irregular, pacific or warlike, liberal or oppressive, a republic that menaces the sacred rights of property and family, or one that honors and protects them both. It is a fearful problem, the solution of which concerns not France alone, but the whole civilized world. If we save ourselves, we save at the same time all the nations which surround us. If we perish, we shall cause all of them to perish with us. According as democratic liberty or democratic tyranny is established here, the destiny of the world will be different; and it may be said that this day it depends upon us whether the republic shall be everywhere finally established or everywhere finally overthrown.

Now, this problem, which among us has but just been proposed for solution, was solved by America more than sixty years ago. The principle of the sovereignty of the people, which we enthroned in France but yesterday, has there held undivided sway for over sixty years. It is there reduced to practice in the most direct, the most unlimited, and the most absolute manner. For sixty years the people who have made it the common source of all their laws have increased continually in population, in territory, and in opulence; and— consider it well—it is found to have been, during that period, not only the most prosperous, but the most stable, of all the nations of the earth. While all the nations of Europe have been devastated by war or torn by civil discord, the American people alone in the civilized world have remained at peace. Almost all Europe was convulsed by revolutions; America has not had even a revolt. The republic there has not been the assailant, but the guardian, of all vested rights; the property of individuals has had better guarantees there than in any other country of the world; anarchy has there been as unknown as despotism.

Where else could we find greater causes of hope, or more instructive lessons? Let us look to America, not in order to make a servile copy of the institutions that she has established, but to gain a clearer view of the polity that will be the best for us; let us look there less to find examples than instruction; let us borrow from her the principles, rather than the details, of her laws. The laws of the French republic may be, and ought to be in many cases, different from those which govern the United States; but the principles on which the American constitutions rest, those principles of order, of the balance of powers, of true liberty, of deep and sincere respect for right, are indispensable to all republics; they ought to be common to all; and it may be said beforehand that wherever they are not found, the republic will soon have ceased to exist. 1848

Synoptic Table of Contents

VOLUME I

VOLUME II

Contents of VOLUME I

Chapter I

Chapter II

Contents of Volume I

Chapter IX

Chapter X

xv Contents of Volume 1

Chapter XVIII

Democracy in America

FIRST PART

Author's Introduction

AMONG the novel objects that attracted my attention during my stay in the United States, nothing struck me more forcibly than the general equality of condition among the people. I readily discovered the prodigious influence that this primary fact exercises on the whole course of society; it gives a peculiar direction to public opinion and a peculiar tenor to the laws; it imparts new maxims to the governing authorities and peculiar habits to the governed.

I soon perceived that the influence of this fact extends far beyond the political character and the laws of the country, and that it has no less effect on civil society than on the government; it creates opinions, gives birth to new sentiments, founds novel customs, and modifies whatever it does not produce. The more I advanced in the study of American society, the more I perceived that this equality of condition is the fundamental fact from which all others seem to be derived and the central point at which all my observations constantly terminated.

I then turned my thoughts to our own hemisphere, and thought that I discerned there something analogous to the spectacle which the New World presented to me. I observed that equality of condition, though it has not there reached the extreme limit which it seems to have attained in the United States, is constantly approaching it; and that the democracy which governs the American communities appears to be rapidly rising into power in Europe.

Hence I conceived the idea of the book that is now before the reader.

It is evident to all alike that a great democratic revolution is going on among us, but all do not look at it in the same light. To some it appears to be novel but accidental, and, as such, they hope it may still be checked; to others it seems irresistible, because it is the most uniform, the most ancient, and the most permanent tendency that is to be found in history.

I look back for a moment on the situation of France seven hundred years ago, when the territory was divided among a small number of families, who were the owners of the soil and the rulers of the inhabitants; the right of governing descended with the family inheritance from generation to generation; force was the only means by which man could act on man; and landed property was the sole source of power.

Soon, however, the political power of the clergy was founded and began to increase: the clergy opened their ranks to all classes, to the poor and the rich, the commoner and the noble; through the church, equality penetrated into the government, and he who as a serf must have vegetated in perpetual bondage took his place as a priest in the midst of nobles, and not infrequently above the heads of kings.

The different relations of men with one another became more complicated and numerous as society gradually became more stable and civilized. Hence the want of civil laws was felt; and the ministers of law soon rose from the obscurity of the tribunals and their dusty chambers to appear at the court of the monarch, by the side of the feudal barons clothed in their ermine and their mail.

While the kings were ruining themselves by their great enterprises, and the nobles exhausting their resources by private wars, the lower orders were enriching themselves by commerce. The influence of money began to be perceptible in state affairs. The transactions of business opened a new road to power, and the financier rose to a station of political influence in which he was at once flattered and despised.

Gradually enlightenment spread, a reawakening of taste for literature and the arts became evident; intellect and will contributed to success; knowledge became an attribute of government, intelligence a social force; the educated man took part in affairs of state.

The value attached to high birth declined just as fast as new avenues to power were discovered. In the eleventh century, nobility was beyond all price; in the thirteenth, it might be purchased. Nobility was first conferred by gift in 1270, and equality was thus introduced into the government by the aristocracy itself.

In the course of these seven hundred years it sometimes happened that the nobles, in order to resist the authority of the crown or to diminish the power of their rivals, granted some political power to the common people. Or, more frequently, the king permitted the lower orders to have a share in the government, with the intention of limiting the power of the aristocracy.

In France the kings have always been the most active and the most constant of levelers. When they were strong and ambitious, they spared no pains to raise the people to the level of the nobles; when they were temperate and feeble, they allowed the people to rise above themselves. Some assisted democracy by their talents, others by their vices. Louis XI and Louis XIV reduced all ranks beneath the throne to the same degree of subjection; and finally Louis XV descended, himself and all his court, into the dust.

As soon as land began to be held on any other than a feudal tenure, and personal property could in its turn confer influence and power, every discovery in the arts, every improvement in commerce of manufactures, created so many new elements of equality among men. Henceforward every new invention, every new want which it occasioned, and every new desire which craved satisfaction were steps towards a general leveling. The taste for luxury, the love of war, the rule of fashion, and the most superficial as well as the deepest passions of the human heart seemed to cooperate to enrich the poor and to impoverish the rich.

From the time when the exercise of the intellect became a source of strength and of wealth, we see that every addition to science, every fresh truth, and every new idea became a germ of power placed within the reach of the people. Poetry, eloquence, and memory, the graces of the mind, the fire of imagination, depth of thought, and all the gifts which Heaven scatters at a venture turned to the advantage of democracy; and even when they were in the possession of its adversaries, they still served its cause by throwing into bold relief the natural greatness of man. Its conquests spread, therefore, with those of civilization and knowledge; and literature became an arsenal open to all, where the poor and the weak daily resorted for arms.

In running over the pages of our history, we shall scarcely find a single great event of the last seven hundred years that has not promoted equality of condition.

The Crusades and the English wars decimated the nobles and divided their possessions: the municipal corporations introduced democratic liberty into the bosom of feudal monarchy; the invention of firearms equalized the vassal and the noble on the field of battle; the art of printing opened the same resources to the minds of all classes; the post brought knowledge alike to the door of the cottage and to the gate of the palace; and Protestantism proclaimed that all men are equally able to find the road to heaven. The discovery of America opened a thousand new paths to fortune and led obscure adventurers to wealth and power.

If, beginning with the eleventh century, we examine what has happened in France from one half-century to another, we shall not fail to perceive that at the end of each of these periods a twofold revolution has taken place in the state of society. The noble has gone down the social ladder, and the commoner has gone up; the one descends as the other rises. Every half-century brings them nearer to each other, and they will soon meet.

Nor is this peculiar to France. Wherever we look, we perceive the same revolution going on throughout the Christian world.

The various occurrences of national existence have everywhere turned to the advantage of democracy: all men have aided it by their exertions, both those who have intentionally labored in its cause and those who have served it unwittingly; those who have fought for it and even those who have declared themselves its opponents have all been driven along in the same direction, have all labored to one end; some unknowingly and some despite themselves, all have been blind instruments in the hands of God.

The gradual development of the principle of equality is, therefore, a providential fact. It has all the chief characteristics of such a fact: it is universal, it is lasting, it constantly eludes all human interference, and all events as well as all men contribute to its progress.

Would it, then, be wise to imagine that a social movement the causes of which lie so far back can be checked by the efforts of one generation? Can it be believed that the democracy which has overthrown the feudal system and vanquished kings will retreat before tradesmen and capitalists? Will it stop now that it has grown so strong and its adversaries so weak?

Whither, then, are we tending? No one can say, for terms of comparison already fail us. There is greater equality of condition in Christian countries at the present day than there has been at any previous time, in any part of the world, so that the magnitude of what already has been done prevents us from foreseeing what is yet to be accomplished.

The whole book that is here offered to the public has been written under the influence of a kind of religious awe produced in the author's mind by the view of that irresistible revolution which has advanced for centuries in spite of every obstacle and which is still advancing in the midst of the ruins it has caused.

It is not necessary that God himself should speak in order that we may discover the unquestionable signs of his will. It is enough to ascertain what is the habitual course of nature and the constant tendency of events. I know, without special revelation, that the planets move in the orbits traced by the Creator's hand.

If the men of our time should be convinced, by attentive observation and sincere reflection, that the gradual and progressive development of social equality is at once the past and the future of their history, this discovery alone would confer upon the change the sacred character of a divine decree. To attempt to check democracy would be in that case to resist the will of God; and the nations would then be constrained to make the best of the social lot awarded to them by Providence.

The Christian nations of our day seem to me to present a most alarming spectacle; the movement which impels them is already so strong that it cannot be stopped, but it is not yet so rapid that it cannot be guided. Their fate is still in their own hands; but very soon they may lose control.

The first of the duties that are at this time imposed upon those who direct our affairs is to educate democracy, to reawaken, if possible, its religious beliefs; to purify its morals; to mold its actions; to substitute a knowledge of statecraft for its inexperience, and an awareness of its true interest for its blind instincts, to adapt its government to time and place, and to modify it according to men and to conditions. A new science of politics is needed for a new world.

This, however, is what we think of least; placed in the middle of a rapid stream, we obstinately fix our eyes on the ruins that may still be descried upon the shore we have left, while the current hurries us away and drags us backward towards the abyss.

In no country in Europe has the great social revolution that I have just described made such rapid progress as in France; but it has always advanced without guidance. The heads of the state have made no preparation for it, and it has advanced without their consent or without their knowledge. The most powerful, the most intelligent, and the most moral classes of the nation have never attempted to control it in order to guide it. Democracy has consequently been abandoned to its wild instincts, and it has grown up like those children who have no parental guidance, who receive their education in the public streets, and who are acquainted only with the vices and wretchedness of society. Its existence was seemingly unknown when suddenly it acquired supreme power. All then servilely submitted to its caprices; it was worshipped as the idol of strength; and when afterwards it was enfeebled by its own excesses, the legislator conceived the rash project of destroying it, instead of instructing it and correcting its vices. No attempt was made to fit it to govern, but all were bent on excluding it from the government.

The result has been that the democratic revolution has taken place in the body of society without that concomitant change in the laws, ideas, customs, and morals which was necessary to render such a revolution beneficial. Thus we have a democracy without anything to lessen its vices and bring out its natural advantages; and although we already perceive the evils it brings, we are ignorant of the benefits it may confer.

While the power of the crown, supported by the aristocracy, peaceably governed the nations of Europe, society, in the midst of its wretchedness, had several sources of happiness which can now scarcely be conceived or appreciated. The power of a few of his subjects was an insurmountable barrier to the tyranny of the prince; and the monarch, who felt the almost divine character which he enjoyed in the eyes of the multitude, derived a motive for the just use of his power from the respect which he inspired. The nobles, placed high as they were above the people, could take that calm and benevolent interest in their fate which the shepherd feels towards his flock; and without acknowledging the poor as their equals, they watched over the destiny of those whose welfare Providence had entrusted to their care. The people, never having conceived the idea of a social condition different from their own, and never expecting to become equal to their leaders, received benefits from them without discussing their rights. They became attached to them when they were clement and just and submitted to their exactions without resistance or servility, as to the inevitable visitations of the Deity. Custom and usage, moreover, had established certain limits to oppression and founded a sort of law in the very midst of violence.

As the noble never suspected that anyone would attempt to deprive him of the privileges which he believed to be legitimate, and as the serf looked upon his own inferiority as a consequence of the immutable order of nature, it is easy to imagine that some mutual exchange of goodwill took place between two classes so differently endowed by fate. Inequality and wretchedness were then to be found in society, but the souls of neither rank of men were degraded.

Men are not corrupted by the exercise of power or debased by the habit of obedience, but by the exercise of a power which they believe to be illegitimate, and by obedience to a rule which they consider to be usurped and oppressive.

On the one side were wealth, strength, and leisure, accompanied by the pursuit of luxury, the refinements of taste, the pleasures of wit, and the cultivation of the arts; on the other were labor, clownishness, and ignorance. But in the midst of this coarse and ignorant multitude it was not uncommon to meet with energetic passions, generous sentiments, profound religious convictions, and wild virtues.

The social state thus organized might boast of its stability, its power, and, above all, its glory.

But the scene is now changed. Gradually the distinctions of rank are done away with; the barriers that once severed mankind are falling; property is divided, power is shared by many, the light of intelligence spreads, and the capacities of all classes tend towards equality. Society becomes democratic, and the empire of democracy is slowly and peaceably introduced into institutions and customs.

I can conceive of a society in which all men would feel an equal love and respect for the laws of which they consider themselves the authors; in which the authority of the government would be respected as necessary, and not divine; and in which the loyalty of the subject to the chief magistrate would not be a passion, but a quiet and rational persuasion. With every individual in the possession of rights which he is sure to retain, a kind of manly confidence and reciprocal courtesy would arise between all classes, removed alike from pride and servility. The people, well acquainted with their own true interests, would understand that, in order to profit from the advantages of the state, it is necessary to satisfy its requirements. The voluntary association of the citizens might then take the place of the individual authority of the nobles, and the community would be protected from tyranny and license.

I admit that, in a democratic state thus constituted, society would not be stationary. But the impulses of the social body might there be regulated and made progressive. If there were less splendor than in an aristocracy, misery would also be less prevalent; the pleasures of enjoyment might be less excessive, but those of comfort would be more general; the sciences might be less perfectly cultivated, but ignorance would be less common; the ardor of the feelings would be constrained, and the habits of the nation softened; there would be more vices and fewer crimes.

In the absence of enthusiasm and ardent faith, great sacrifices may be obtained from the members of a commonwealth by an appeal to their understanding and their experience; each individual will feel the same necessity of union with his fellows to protect his own weakness; and as he knows that he can obtain their help only on condition of helping them, he will readily perceive that his personal interest is identified with the interests of the whole community. The nation, taken as a whole, will be less brilliant, less glorious, and perhaps less strong; but the majority of the citizens will enjoy a greater degree of prosperity, and the people will remain peaceable, not because they despair of a change for the better, but because they are conscious that they are well off already.

If all the consequences of this state of things were not good or useful, society would at least have appropriated all such as were useful and good; and having once and forever renounced the social advantages of aristocracy, mankind would enter into possession of all the benefits that democracy can offer.

But here it may be asked what we have adopted in the

place of those institutions, those ideas, and those customs of our forefathers which we have abandoned.

The spell of royalty is broken, but it has not been succeeded by the majesty of the laws. The people have learned to despise all authority, but they still fear it; and fear now extorts more than was formerly paid from reverence and love.

I perceive that we have destroyed those individual powers which were able, single-handed, to cope with tyranny; but it is the government alone that has inherited all the privileges of which families, guilds, and individuals have been deprived; to the power of a small number of persons, which if it was sometimes oppressive was often conservative, has succeeded the weakness of the whole community.

The division of property has lessened the distance which separated the rich from the poor; but it would seem that, the nearer they draw to each other, the greater is their mutual hatred and the more vehement the envy and the dread with which they resist each other's claims to power; the idea of right does not exist for either party, and force affords to both the only argument for the present and the only guarantee for the future.

The poor man retains the prejudices of his forefathers without their faith, and their ignorance without their virtues; he has adopted the doctrine of self-interest as the rule of his actions without understanding the science that puts it to use; and his selfishness is no less blind than was formerly his devotion to others.

If society is tranquil, it is not because it is conscious of its strength and its well-being, but because it fears its weakness and its infirmities; a single effort may cost it its life. Everybody feels the evil, but no one has courage or energy enough to seek the cure. The desires, the repinings, the sorrows, and the joys of the present time lead to nothing visible or permanent, like the passions of old men, which terminate in impotence.

We have, then, abandoned whatever advantages the old state of things afforded, without receiving any compensation from our present condition; we have destroyed an aristocracy, and we seem inclined to survey its ruins with complacency and to accept them.

The phenomena which the intellectual world presents are

not less deplorable. The democracy of France, hampered in its course or abandoned to its lawless passions, has overthrown whatever crossed its path and has shaken all that it has not destroyed. Its empire has not been gradually introduced or peaceably established, but it has constantly advanced in the midst of the disorders and the agitations of a conflict. In the heat of the struggle each partisan is hurried beyond the natural limits of his opinions by the doctrines and the excesses of his opponents, until he loses sight of the end of his exertions, and holds forth in a way which does not correspond to his real sentiments or secret instincts. Hence arises the strange confusion that we are compelled to witness.

I can recall nothing in history more worthy of sorrow and pity than the scenes which are passing before our eyes. It is as if the natural bond that unites the opinions of man to his tastes, and his actions to his principles, was now broken; the harmony that has always been observed between the feelings and the ideas of mankind appears to be dissolved and all the laws of moral analogy to be abolished.

Zealous Christians are still found among us, whose minds are nurtured on the thoughts that pertain to a future life, and who readily espouse the cause of human liberty as the source of all moral greatness. Christianity, which has declared that all men are equal in the sight of God, will not refuse to acknowledge that all citizens are equal in the eye of the law. But, by a strange coincidence of events, religion has been for a time entangled with those institutions which democracy destroys; and it is not infrequently brought to reject the equality which it loves, and to curse as a foe that cause of liberty whose efforts it might hallow by its alliance.

By the side of these religious men I discern others whose thoughts are turned to earth rather than to heaven. These are the partisans of liberty, not only as the source of the noblest virtues, but more especially as the root of all solid advantages; and they sincerely desire to secure its authority, and to impart its blessings to mankind. It is natural that they should hasten to invoke the assistance of religion, for they must know that liberty cannot be established without morality, nor morality without faith. But they have seen religion in the ranks of their adversaries, and they inquire no further; some of them attack it openly, and the rest are afraid to defend it.

In former ages slavery was advocated by the venal and slavish-minded, while the independent and the warm-hearted were struggling without hope to save the liberties of mankind. But men of high and generous character are now to be met with, whose opinions are directly at variance with their inclinations, and who praise that servility and meanness which they have themselves never known. Others, on the contrary, speak of liberty as if they were able to feel its sanctity and its majesty, and loudly claim for humanity those rights which they have always refused to acknowledge.

There are virtuous and peaceful individuals whose pure morality, quiet habits, opulence, and talents fit them to be the leaders of their fellow men. Their love of country is sincere, and they are ready to make the greatest sacrifices for its welfare. But civilization often finds them among its opponents; they confound its abuses with its benefits, and the idea of evil is inseparable in their minds from that of novelty.

Near these I find others whose object is to materialize mankind, to hit upon what is expedient without heeding what is just, to acquire knowledge without faith, and prosperity apart from virtue; claiming to be the champions of modern civilization, they place themselves arrogantly at its head, usurping a place which is abandoned to them, and of which they are wholly unworthy.

Where are we, then?

The religionists are the enemies of liberty, and the friends of liberty attack religion; the high-minded and the noble advocate bondage, and the meanest and most servile preach independence; honest and enlightened citizens are opposed to all progress, while men without patriotism and without principle put themselves forward as the apostles of civilization and intelligence.

Has such been the fate of the centuries which have preceded our own? and has man always inhabited a world like the present, where all things are not in their proper relationships, where virtue is without genius, and genius without honor; where the love of order is confused with a taste for oppression, and the holy cult of freedom with a contempt of law; where the light thrown by conscience on human actions is dim, and where nothing seems to be any longer forbidden or allowed, honorable or shameful, false or true?

I cannot believe that the Creator made man to leave him in an endless struggle with the intellectual wretchedness that surrounds us. God destines a calmer and a more certain future to the communities of Europe. I am ignorant of his designs, but I shall not cease to believe in them because I cannot fathom them, and I had rather mistrust my own capacity than his justice.

There is one country in the world where the great social revolution that I am speaking of seems to have nearly reached its natural limits. It has been effected with ease and simplicity; say rather that this country is reaping the fruits of the democratic revolution which we are undergoing, without having had the revolution itself.

The emigrants who colonized the shores of America in the beginning of the seventeenth century somehow separated the democratic principle from all the principles that it had to contend with in the old communities of Europe, and transplanted it alone to the New World. It has there been able to spread in perfect freedom and peaceably to determine the character of the laws by influencing the manners of the country.

It appears to me beyond a doubt that, sooner or later, we shall arrive, like the Americans, at an almost complete equality of condition. But I do not conclude from this that we shall ever be necessarily led to draw the same political consequences which the Americans have derived from a similar social organization. I am far from supposing that they have chosen the only form of government which a democracy may adopt; but as the generating cause of laws and manners in the two countries is the same, it is of immense interest for us to know what it has produced in each of them.

It is not, then, merely to satisfy a curiosity, however legitimate, that I have examined America; my wish has been to find there instruction by which we may ourselves profit. Whoever should imagine that I have intended to write a panegyric would be strangely mistaken, and on reading this book he will perceive that such was not my design; nor has it been my object to advocate any form of government in particular, for I am of the opinion that absolute perfection is rarely to be found in any system of laws. I have not even pretended to judge whether the social revolution, which I believe to be irresistible, is advantageous or prejudicial to mankind. I have acknowledged this revolution as a fact already accomplished, or on the eve of its accomplishment; and I have selected the nation, from among those which have undergone it, in which its development has been the most peaceful and the most complete, in order to discern its natural consequences and to find out, if possible, the means of rendering it profitable to mankind. I confess that in America I saw more than America; I sought there the image of democracy itself, with its inclinations, its character, its prejudices, and its passions, in order to learn what we have to fear or to hope from its progress.

In the first part of this work I have attempted to show the distinction that democracy, dedicated to its inclinations and tendencies and abandoned almost without restraint to its instincts, gave to the laws the course it impressed on the government, and in general the control which it exercised over affairs of state. I have sought to discover the evils and the advantages which it brings. I have examined the safeguards used by the Americans to direct it, as well as those that they have not adopted, and I have undertaken to point out the factors which enable it to govern society.

My object was to portray, in a second part, the influence which the equality of conditions and democratic government in America exercised on civil society, on habits, ideas, and customs; but I grew less enthusiastic about carrying out this plan. Before I could have completed the task which I set for myself, my work would have become purposeless. Someone else would before long set forth to the public the principal traits of the American character and, delicately cloaking a serious picture, lend to the truth a charm which I should not have been able to equal.[1]

---

[1] At the time I published the first edition of this work, M. Gustave de Beaumont, my traveling-companion in America, was still working on his book entitled *Marie, ou l'Esclavage aux Etats-Unis,* which has since appeared. M. de Beaumont's primary purpose was to portray clearly and accurately the position of Negroes in Anglo-American society. His work will throw a new and vivid light on the question of slavery, a vital one for all united republics. I am not certain whether I am mistaken, but it

I do not know whether I have succeeded in making known what I saw in America, but I am certain that such has been my sincere desire, and that I have never, knowingly, molded facts to ideas, instead of ideas to facts.

Whenever a point could be established by the aid of written documents, I have had recourse to the original text, and to the most authentic and reputable works.[2] I have cited my authorities in the notes, and anyone may verify them. Whenever opinions, political customs, or remarks on the manners of the country were concerned, I have endeavored to consult the most informed men I met with. If the point in question was important or doubtful, I was not satisfied with one witness, but I formed my opinion on the evidence of several witnesses. Here the reader must necessarily rely upon my word. I could frequently have cited names which either are known to him or deserve to be so in support of my assertions; but I have carefully abstained from this practice. A stranger frequently hears important truths at the fireside of his host, which the latter would perhaps conceal from the ear of friendship; he consoles himself with his guest for the silence to which he is restricted, and the shortness of the traveler's stay takes away all fear of an indiscretion. I carefully noted every conversation of this nature as soon as it occurred, but these notes will never leave my writing-case. I had rather injure the success of my statements than add my name to the list of those strangers who repay generous hospitality they have received by subsequent chagrin and annoyance.

I am aware that, notwithstanding my care, nothing will

---

seems to me that M. de Beaumont's book, after having vitally interested those who will put aside their emotions and regard his descriptions dispassionately, should have a surer and more lasting success among those readers who, above all else, desire a true picture of actual conditions.

[2] Legislative and executive documents have been furnished to me with a kindness which I shall always remember with gratitude. Among the American statesmen who have thus helped my researches, I will mention particularly Mr. Edward Livingston, then Secretary of State, afterwards Minister Plenipotentiary at Paris. During my stay in Washington, he was kind enough to give me most of the documents which I possess relating to the Federal government. Mr. Livingston is one of the few men whose writings cause us to conceive an affection for them, whom we admire and respect even before we come to know them personally, and to whom it is a pleasure to give recognition.

be easier than to criticize this book should anyone care to do so.

Those readers who may examine it closely will discover, I think, in the whole work a dominant thought that binds, so to speak, its several parts together. But the diversity of the subjects I have had to treat is exceedingly great, and it will not be difficult to oppose an isolated fact to the body of facts which I cite, or an isolated idea to the body of ideas I put forth. I hope to be read in the spirit which has guided my labors, and that my book may be judged by the general impression it leaves, as I have formed my own judgment not on any single consideration, but upon the mass of evidence.

It must not be forgotten that the author who wishes to be understood is obliged to carry all his ideas to their utmost theoretical conclusions, and often to the verge of what is false or impracticable; for if it be necessary sometimes to depart in action from the rules of logic, such is not the case in discourse, and a man finds it almost as difficult to be inconsistent in his language as to be consistent in his conduct.

I conclude by pointing out myself what many readers will consider the principal defect of the work. This book is written to favor no particular views, and in composing it I have entertained no design of serving or attacking any party. I have not undertaken to see differently from others, but to look further, and while they are busied for the morrow only, I have turned my thoughts to the whole future.

Chapter I

EXTERIOR FORM OF NORTH AMERICA

North america divided into two vast regions, one inclining towards the Pole, the other towards the Equator—Valley of the Mississippi—Traces found there of the revolutions of the globe—Shore of the Atlantic Ocean, on which the English colonies were founded—Different aspects of North and of South America at the time of their discovery—Forests of North America—Prairies—Wandering tribes of natives—Their outward appearance, customs, and languages—Traces of an unknown people.

North America presents in its external form certain general features which it is easy to distinguish at the first glance.

A sort of methodical order seems to have regulated the separation of land and water, mountains and valleys. A simple but grand arrangement is discoverable amid the confusion of objects and the prodigious variety of scenes.

This continent is almost equally divided into two vast regions. One is bounded on the north by the Arctic Pole, and on the east and west by the two great oceans. It stretches towards the south, forming a triangle, whose irregular sides meet at length above the great lakes of Canada. The second region begins where the other terminates, and includes all the remainder of the continent. The one slopes gently towards the Pole, the other towards the Equator.

The territory included in the first region descends towards the north with a slope so imperceptible that it may almost be said to form a plain. Within the bounds of this immense level tract there are neither high mountains nor deep valleys. Streams meander through it irregularly; great rivers intertwine, separate, and meet again, spread into vast marshes, losing all trace of their channels in the labyrinth of waters they have themselves created, and thus at length, after innumerable windings, fall into the Polar seas. The great lakes which bound this first region are not walled in, like most of those in the Old World, between hills and rocks. Their banks are flat and rise but a few feet above the level of their waters, each thus forming a vast bowl filled to the brim. The slightest change in the structure of the globe would cause their waters to rush either towards the Pole or to the tropical seas.

The second region has a more broken surface and is better suited for the habitation of man. Two long chains of mountains divide it, from one to the other: one, named the Allegheny, follows the direction of the shore of the Atlantic Ocean; the other is parallel with the Pacific.

The space that lies between these two chains of mountains contains 228,843 square leagues.[1] Its surface is therefore about six times as great as that of France.[2]

This vast territory, however, forms a single valley, one side of which descends from the rounded summits of the Alleghenies, while the other rises in an uninterrupted course to the tops of the Rocky Mountains. At the bottom of the valley flows an immense river, into which you can see, flowing from all directions, the waters that come down from the mountains. In memory of their native land, the French formerly called this river the St. Louis. The Indians, in their pompous language, have named it the Father of Waters, or the Mississippi.

The Mississippi takes its source at the boundary of the two great regions of which I have spoken, not far from the highest point of the plateau that separates them. Near the same spot rises another river,[3] which empties into the Polar seas. The course of the Mississippi is at first uncertain: it winds several times towards the north, whence it rose, and only at length, after having been delayed in lakes and marshes, does it assume its definite direction and flow slowly onward to the south.

Sometimes quietly gliding along the chalky bed that nature has assigned to it, sometimes swollen by freshets, the Mississippi waters over 1,032 leagues in its course.[4] At the

[1] 1,341,649 miles. See Darby's *View of the United States*, p. 499. I have reduced these miles to leagues of 2,000 toises.

[2] France is 35,181 square leagues.

[3] Red River [of the North].

[4] 2,500 miles, 1,032 leagues. See *Description of the United States*, by Warden, Vol. I, p. 169.

distance of 600 leagues[5] from its mouth this river attains an average depth of 15 feet; and it is navigated by vessels of 300 tons for a course of nearly 200 leagues. One counts, among the tributaries of the Mississippi, one river of 1,300 leagues,[6] one of 900,[7] one of 600,[8] one of 500,[9] four of 200,[10] not to speak of a countless multitude of small streams that rush from all directions to mingle in its flow.

The valley which is watered by the Mississippi seems to have been created for it alone, and there, like a god of antiquity, the river dispenses both good and evil. Near the stream nature displays an inexhaustible fertility; the farther you get from its banks, the more sparse the vegetation, the poorer the soil, and everything weakens or dies. Nowhere have the great convulsions of the globe left more evident traces than in the valley of the Mississippi. The whole aspect of the country shows the powerful effects of water, both by its fertility and by its barrenness. The waters of the primeval ocean accumulated enormous beds of vegetable mold in the valley, which they leveled as they retired. Upon the right bank of the river are found immense plains, as smooth as if the tiller had passed over them with his roller. As you approach the mountains, the soil becomes more and more unequal and sterile; the ground is, as it were, pierced in a thousand places by primitive rocks, which appear like the bones of a skeleton whose flesh has been consumed by time. The surface of the earth is covered with a granitic sand and irregular masses of stone, among which a few plants force their growth and give the appearance of a green field covered with the ruins of a vast edifice. These stones and this sand disclose, on examination, a perfect analogy with those that compose the arid and broken summits of the Rocky Mountains. The flood of waters which washed the soil to the bottom of the valley afterwards carried away portions of the rocks themselves; and these, dashed and bruised against

[5] 1,364 miles, 563 leagues. See ibid., Vol. I, p. 169.
[6] The Missouri. See ibid., Vol. I, p. 132 (1,278 leagues).
[7] The Arkansas. See ibid., Vol. I, p. 188 (877 leagues).
[8] The Red River. See ibid., Vol. I, p. 190 (598 leagues).
[9] The Ohio. See ibid., Vol. I, p. 192 (490 leagues).
[10] The Illinois, St. Pierre, St. Francis, Des Moines. The above measurements are based on the legal mile (statute mile) and on the postal league of 2,000 toises.

the neighboring cliffs, were left scattered like wrecks at their feet.[11]

The valley of the Mississippi is, on the whole, the most magnificent dwelling-place prepared by God for man's abode; and yet it may be said that at present it is but a mighty desert.

On the eastern side of the Alleghenies, between the base of these mountains and the Atlantic Ocean, lies a long ridge of rocks and sand, which the sea appears to have left behind as it retired. The average breadth of this territory does not exceed 48 leagues;[12] but it is about 300 leagues in length.[13] This part of the American continent has a soil that offers every obstacle to the husbandman, and its vegetation is scanty and unvaried.

Upon this inhospitable coast the first united efforts of human industry were made. This tongue of arid land was the cradle of those English colonies which were destined one day to become the United States of America. The center of power still remains here; while to the west of it the true elements of the great people to whom the future control of the continent belongs are gathering together almost in secrecy.

When Europeans first landed on the shores of the West Indies, and afterwards on the coast of South America, they thought themselves transported into those fabulous regions of which poets had sung. The sea sparkled with phosphoric light, and the extraordinary transparency of its waters disclosed to the view of the navigator all the depths of the ocean.[14] Here and there appeared little islands perfumed with odoriferous plants, and resembling baskets of flowers floating on the tranquil surface of the ocean. Every object that met the sight in this enchanting region seemed prepared to satisfy the wants or contribute to the pleasures of man. Almost all the trees were loaded with nourishing fruits, and those which were useless as food delighted the eye by the

[11] See Appendix A.
[12] 100 miles.
[13] About 900 miles.
[14] Malte-Brun tells us (Vol. III, p. 726) that the water of the Caribbean Sea is so transparent that corals and fish are discernible at a depth of sixty fathoms. The ship seemed to float in air, the navigator became giddy as his eye penetrated through the crystal flood and beheld submarine gardens, or beds of shells, or gilded fishes gliding among tufts and thickets of seaweed.

brilliance and variety of their colors. In groves of fragrant lemon trees, wild figs, flowering myrtles, acacias, and oleanders, which were hung with festoons of various climbing plants, covered with flowers, a multitude of birds unknown in Europe displayed their bright plumage, glittering with purple and azure, and mingled their warbling with the harmony of a world teeming with life and motion.[15]

Underneath this brilliant exterior death was concealed. But this fact was not then known, and the air of these climates had an indefinably enervating influence, which made man cling to the present, heedless of the future.

North America appeared under a very different aspect: there everything was grave, serious, and solemn; it seemed created to be the domain of intelligence, as the South was that of sensual delight. A turbulent and foggy ocean washed its shores. It was girt round by a belt of granitic rocks or by wide tracts of sand. The foliage of its woods was dark and gloomy, for they were composed of firs, larches, evergreen oaks, wild olive trees, and laurels.

Beyond this outer belt lay the thick shades of the central forests, where the largest trees which are produced in the two hemispheres grow side by side. The plane, the catalpa, the sugar maple, and the Virginian poplar mingled their branches with those of the oak, the beech, and the lime.

In these, as in the forests of the Old World, destruction was perpetually going on. The ruins of vegetation were heaped upon one another; but there was no laboring hand to remove them, and their decay was not rapid enough to make room for the continual work of reproduction. Climbing plants, grasses, and other herbs forced their way through the mass of dying trees; they crept along their bending trunks, found nourishment in their dusty cavities, and a passage beneath the lifeless bark. Thus decay gave its assistance to life, and their respective productions were mingled together. The depths of these forests were gloomy and obscure, and a thousand rivulets, undirected in their course by human industry, preserved in them a constant moisture. It was rare to meet with flowers, wild fruits, or birds beneath their shades. The fall of a tree overthrown by age, the rushing torrent of a cataract, the lowing of the buffalo, and the howl-

[15] See Appendix B.

ing of the wind were the only sounds that broke the silence of nature.

To the east of the great river the woods almost disappeared; in their stead were seen prairies of immense extent. Whether Nature in her infinite variety had denied the germs of trees to these fertile plains, or whether they had once been covered with forests, subsequently destroyed by the hand of man, is a question which neither tradition nor scientific research has been able to answer.

These immense deserts were not, however, wholly untenanted by men. Some wandering tribes had been for ages scattered among the forest shades or on the green pastures of the prairie. From the mouth of the St. Lawrence to the Delta of the Mississippi, and from the Atlantic to the Pacific Ocean, these savages possessed certain points of resemblance that bore witness to their common origin; but at the same time they differed from all other known races of men;[16] they were neither white like the Europeans, nor yellow like most of the Asiatics, nor black like the Negroes. Their skin was reddish brown, their hair long and shining, their lips thin, and their cheekbones very prominent. The languages spoken by the North American tribes had different vocabularies, but all obeyed the same rules of grammar. These rules differed in several points from such as had been observed to govern the origin of language. The idiom of the Americans seemed to be the product of new combinations, and bespoke an effort of the understanding of which the Indians of our days would be incapable.[17]

The social state of these tribes differed also in many respects from all that was seen in the Old World. They seem to have multiplied freely in the midst of their deserts, with-

[16] With the progress of discovery, some resemblance has been found to exist between the physical conformation, the language, and the habits of the Indians of North America, and those of the Tungus, Manchus, Mongols, Tatars, and other wandering tribes of Asia. The land occupied by these tribes is not very distant from Behring's Strait, which allows of the supposition that at a remote period they gave inhabitants to the desert continent of America. But this is a point which has not yet been clearly elucidated by science. See Malte-Brun, Vol. V; the works of Humboldt; Fischer: *Conjecture sur l'origine des Américains:* Adair: *History of the American Indians.*

[17] See Appendix C.

out coming in contact with other races more civilized than their own. Accordingly, they exhibited none of those indistinct, incoherent notions of right and wrong, none of that deep corruption of manners, which is usually joined with ignorance and rudeness among nations who, after advancing to civilization, have relapsed into a state of barbarism. The Indian was indebted to no one but himself; his virtues, his vices, and his prejudices were his own work; he had grown up in the wild independence of his nature.

If in polished countries the lowest of the people are rude and uncivil, it is not merely because they are poor and ignorant, but because, being so, they are in daily contact with rich and enlightened men. The sight of their own hard lot and their weakness, which is daily contrasted with the happiness and power of some of their fellow creatures, excites in their hearts at the same time the sentiments of anger and of fear: the consciousness of their inferiority and their dependence irritates while it humiliates them. This state of mind displays itself in their manners and language; they are at once insolent and servile. The truth of this is easily proved by observation: the people are more rude in aristocratic countries than elsewhere; in opulent cities than in rural districts. In those places where the rich and powerful are assembled together, the weak and the indigent feel themselves oppressed by their inferior condition. Unable to perceive a single chance of regaining their equality, they give up to despair and allow themselves to fall below the dignity of human nature.

This unfortunate effect of the disparity of conditions is not observable in savage life: the Indians, although they are ignorant and poor, are equal and free.

When Europeans first came among them, the natives of North America were ignorant of the value of riches, and indifferent to the enjoyments that civilized man procures for himself by their means. Nevertheless there was nothing coarse in their demeanor; they practiced habitual reserve and a kind of aristocratic politeness.

Mild and hospitable when at peace, though merciless in war beyond any known degree of human ferocity, the Indian would expose himself to die of hunger in order to succor the stranger who asked admittance by night at the door of his hut; yet he could tear in pieces with his hands the still quivering limbs of his prisoner. The famous republics of antiquity never gave examples of more unshaken courage, more haughty spirit, or more intractable love of independence than were hidden in former times among the wild forests of the New World.[18] The Europeans produced no great impression when they landed upon the shores of North America; their presence engendered neither envy nor fear. What influence could they possess over such men as I have described? The Indian could live without wants, suffer without complaint, and pour out his death-song at the stake.[19] Like all the other members of the great human family, these savages believed in the existence of a better world, and adored, under different names, God, the Creator of the universe. Their notions on the great intellectual truths were in general simple and philosophical.[20]

Although we have here traced the character of a primitive people, yet it cannot be doubted that another people, more civilized and more advanced in all respects, had preceded it in the same regions.

An obscure tradition which prevailed among the Indians on the borders of the Atlantic informs us that these very tribes formerly dwelt on the west side of the Mississippi. Along the banks of the Ohio, and throughout the central valley, there are frequently found, at this day, tumuli raised by the hands of men. On exploring these heaps of earth to their center, it is usual to meet with human bones, strange instruments, arms and utensils of all kinds, made of metal, and destined for purposes unknown to the present race.

The Indians of our time are unable to give any informa-

[18] We learn from President Jefferson (*Notes on Virginia,* p. 148), that among the Iroquois, when attacked by a superior force, aged men refused to fly, or to survive the destruction of their country; and they braved death like the ancient Romans when their capital was sacked by the Gauls. Further on (p. 150), he tells us that "there is no example of an Indian, who, having fallen into the hands of his enemies, begged for his life; on the contrary, the captive sought to obtain death at the hands of his conquerors by the use of insult and provocation."

[19] See *Histoire de la Louisiane,* by Lepage Dupratz; Charlevoix: *Histoire de la Nouvelle France;* Lettres du Rev. G. Heckewelder, *Transactions of the American Philosophical Society,* Vol. I; Jefferson: *Notes on Virginia,* pp. 135–90. What is said by Jefferson is of special weight on account of the personal merit of the writer, of his peculiar position, and of the matter-of-fact age in which he lived.

[20] See Appendix D.

tion relative to the history of this unknown people. Neither did those who lived three hundred years ago, when America was first discovered, leave any accounts from which even a hypothesis could be formed. Traditions, those perishable yet ever recurrent monuments of the primitive world, do not provide any light. There, however, thousands of our fellow men have lived; one cannot doubt that. When did they go there, what was their origin, their destiny, their history? When and how did they disappear? No one can possibly tell.

How strange it appears that nations have existed and afterwards so completely disappeared from the earth that the memory even of their names is effaced! Their languages are lost; their glory is vanished like a sound without an echo; though perhaps there is not one which has not left behind it some tomb in memory of its passage. Thus the most durable monument of human labor is that which recalls the wretchedness and nothingness of man.

Although the vast country that I have been describing was inhabited by many indigenous tribes, it may justly be said, at the time of its discovery by Europeans, to have formed one great desert. The Indians occupied without possessing it. It is by agricultural labor that man appropriates the soil, and the early inhabitants of North America lived by the produce of the chase. Their implacable prejudices, their uncontrolled passions, their vices, and still more, perhaps, their savage virtues, consigned them to inevitable destruction. The ruin of these tribes began from the day when Europeans landed on their shores; it has proceeded ever since, and we are now witnessing its completion. They seem to have been placed by Providence amid the riches of the New World only to enjoy them for a season; they were there merely to wait till others came. Those coasts, so admirably adapted for commerce and industry; those wide and deep rivers; that inexhaustible valley of the Mississippi; the whole continent, in short, seemed prepared to be the abode of a great nation yet unborn.

In that land the great experiment of the attempt to construct society upon a new basis was to be made by civilized man; and it was there, for the first time, that theories hitherto unknown, or deemed impracticable, were to exhibit a spectacle for which the world had not been prepared by the history of the past.

Chapter II

ORIGIN OF THE ANGLO-AMERICANS, AND IMPORTANCE OF THIS ORIGIN IN RELATION TO THEIR FUTURE CONDITION

UTILITY *of knowing the origin of nations, in order to understand their social condition and their laws—America the only country in which the starting-point of a great people has been clearly observable—In what respects all who emigrated to British America were similar—In what they differed—Remark applicable to all the Europeans who established themselves on the shores of the New World—Colonization of Virginia—Colonization of New England—Original character of the first inhabitants of New England—Their arrival—Their first laws—Their social contract—Penal code borrowed from the Hebrew legislation—Religious Fervor—Republican spirit—Intimate union of the spirit of religion with the spirit of liberty.*

A MAN has come into the world; his early years are spent without notice in the pleasures and activities of childhood. As he grows up, the world receives him when his manhood begins, and he enters into contact with his fellows. He is then studied for the first time, and it is imagined that the germ of the vices and the virtues of his maturer years is then formed.

This, if I am not mistaken, is a great error. We must begin higher up; we must watch the infant in his mother's arms; we must see the first images which the external world casts upon the dark mirror of his mind, the first occurrences that he witnesses; we must hear the first words which awaken the sleeping powers of thought, and stand by his earliest efforts if we would understand the prejudices, the habits, and the passions which will rule his life. The entire man is, so to speak, to be seen in the cradle of the child.

The growth of nations presents something analogous to this; they all bear some marks of their origin. The circumstances that accompanied their birth and contributed to their development affected the whole term of their being.

If we were able to go back to the elements of states and to examine the oldest monuments of their history, I doubt not that we should discover in them the primal cause of the prejudices, the habits, the ruling passions, and, in short, all that constitutes what is called the national character. We should there find the explanation of certain customs which now seem at variance with the prevailing manners; of such laws as conflict with established principles; and of such incoherent opinions as are here and there to be met with in society, like those fragments of broken chains which we sometimes see hanging from the vaults of an old edifice, supporting nothing. This might explain the destinies of certain nations which seem borne on by an unknown force to ends of which they themselves are ignorant. But hitherto facts have been lacking for such a study: the spirit of analysis has come upon nations only as they matured; and when they at last conceived of contemplating their origin, time had already obscured it, or ignorance and pride had surrounded it with fables behind which the truth was hidden.

America is the only country in which it has been possible to witness the natural and tranquil growth of society, and where the influence exercised on the future condition of states by their origin is clearly distinguishable.

At the period when the peoples of Europe landed in the New World, their national characteristics were already completely formed; each of them had a physiognomy of its own; and as they had already attained that stage of civilization at which men are led to study themselves, they have transmitted to us a faithful picture of their opinions, their manners, and their laws. The men of the sixteenth century are almost as well known to us as our contemporaries. America, consequently, exhibits in the broad light of day the phenomena which the ignorance or rudeness of earlier ages conceals from our researches. The men of our day seem destined to see further than their predecessors into human events; they are close enough to the founding of the American settlements to know in detail their elements, and far enough away from that time already to be able to judge what these beginnings have produced. Providence has given us a torch which our forefathers did not possess, and has allowed us to discern fundamental causes in the history of the world which the obscurity of the past concealed from them.

If we carefully examine the social and political state of America, after having studied its history, we shall remain perfectly convinced that not an opinion, not a custom, not a law, I may even say not an event is upon record which the origin of that people will not explain. The readers of this book will find in the present chapter the germ of all that is to follow and the key to almost the whole work.

The emigrants who came at different periods to occupy the territory now covered by the American Union differed from each other in many respects; their aim was not the same, and they governed themselves on different principles.

These men had, however, certain features in common, and they were all placed in an analogous situation. The tie of language is, perhaps, the strongest and the most durable that can unite mankind. All the emigrants spoke the same language; they were all children of the same people. Born in a country which had been agitated for centuries by the struggles of faction, and in which all parties had been obliged in their turn to place themselves under the protection of the laws, their political education had been perfected in this rude school; and they were more conversant with the notions of right and the principles of true freedom than the greater part of their European contemporaries. At the period of the first emigrations the township system, that fruitful germ of free institutions, was deeply rooted in the habits of the English; and with it the doctrine of the sovereignty of the people had been introduced into the very bosom of the monarchy of the house of Tudor.

The religious quarrels which have agitated the Christian world were then rife. England had plunged into the new order of things with headlong vehemence. The character of its inhabitants, which had always been sedate and reflective, became argumentative and austere. General information had been increased by intellectual contests, and the mind had received in them a deeper cultivation. While religion was the topic of discussion, the morals of the people became more pure. All these national features are more or less discoverable in the physiognomy of those Englishmen who came to seek a new home on the opposite shores of the Atlantic.

Another observation, moreover, to which we shall have occasion to return later, is applicable not only to the English, but to the French, the Spaniards, and all the Europeans who successively established themselves in the New World. All these European colonies contained the elements, if not the development, of a complete democracy. Two causes led to this result. It may be said that on leaving the mother country the emigrants had, in general, no notion of superiority one over another. The happy and the powerful do not go into exile, and there are no surer guarantees of equality among men than poverty and misfortune. It happened, however, on several occasions, that persons of rank were driven to America by political and religious quarrels. Laws were made to establish a gradation of ranks; but it was soon found that the soil of America was opposed to a territorial aristocracy. It was realized that in order to clear this land, nothing less than the constant and self-interested efforts of the owner himself was essential; the ground prepared, it became evident that its produce was not sufficient to enrich at the same time both an owner and a farmer. The land was then naturally broken up into small portions, which the proprietor cultivated for himself. Land is the basis of an aristocracy, which clings to the soil that supports it; for it is not by privileges alone, nor by birth, but by landed property handed down from generation to generation that an aristocracy is constituted. A nation may present immense fortunes and extreme wretchedness; but unless those fortunes are territorial, there is no true aristocracy, but simply the class of the rich and that of the poor.

All the British colonies had striking similarities at the time of their origin. All of them, from their beginning, seemed destined to witness the growth, not of the aristocratic liberty of their mother country, but of that freedom of the middle and lower orders of which the history of the world had as yet furnished no complete example.

In this general uniformity, however, several marked divergences could be observed, which it is necessary to point out. Two branches may be distinguished in the great Anglo-

American family, which have hitherto grown up without entirely commingling; the one in the South, the other in the North.

Virginia received the first English colony; the immigrants took possession of it in 1607. The idea that mines of gold and silver are the sources of national wealth was at that time singularly prevalent in Europe; a fatal delusion, which has done more to impoverish the European nations who adopted it, and has cost more lives in America, than the united influence of war and bad laws. The men sent to Virginia[1] were seekers of gold, adventurers without resources and without character, whose turbulent and restless spirit endangered the infant colony[2] and rendered its progress uncertain. Artisans and agriculturists arrived afterwards; and, although they were a more moral and orderly race of men, they were hardly in any respect above the level of the inferior classes in England.[3] No lofty views, no spiritual conception, presided over the foundation of these new settlements. The colony was scarcely established when slavery was introduced;[4] this was the capital fact which was to exercise an immense influence on the character, the laws, and the whole future of the South. Slavery, as I shall afterwards show, dishonors labor; it introduces idleness into society, and with idleness, ignorance and pride, luxury and distress. It enervates the powers of the mind and benumbs the activ-

[1] The charter granted by the crown of England in 1609 stipulated, among other conditions, that the adventurers should pay to the crown a fifth of the produce of all gold and silver mines. See *Life of Washington,* by Marshall, Vol. I, pp. 18–66.

[2] A large portion of the adventurers, says Stith (*History of Virginia*), were unprincipled young men of family, whom their parents were glad to ship off in order to save them from an ignominious fate, discharged servants, fraudulent bankrupts, debauchees, and others of the same class, people more apt to pillage and destroy than to promote the welfare of the settlement. Seditious leaders easily enticed this band into every kind of extravagance and excess. See for the history of Virginia the following works: *History of Virginia, from the First Settlements in the Year 1624,* by Smith; *History of Virginia,* by William Stith; *History of Virginia, from the Earliest Period,* by Beverley, translated into French in 1807.

[3] It was not till some time later that a certain number of rich English landholders came to establish themselves in the colony.

[4] Slavery was introduced about the year 1620, by a Dutch vessel, which landed twenty Negroes on the banks of the James River. See Chalmer.

ity of man. The influence of slavery, united to the English
character, explains the manners and the social condition of
the Southern states.

On this same English foundation there developed in the
North very different characteristics. Here I may be allowed
to enter into some details.

In the English colonies of the North, more generally
known as the New England states,[5] the two or three main
ideas that now constitute the basis of the social theory of the
United States were first combined. The principles of New
England spread at first to the neighboring states; they then
passed successively to the more distant ones; and at last, if I
may so speak, they *interpenetrated* the whole confederation.
They now extend their influence beyond its limits, over the
whole American world. The civilization of New England has
been like a beacon lit upon a hill, which, after it has diffused
its warmth immediately around it, also tinges the distant
horizon with its glow.

The foundation of New England was a novel spectacle,
and all the circumstances attending it were singulaı and
original. Nearly all colonies have been first inhabited either
by men without education and without resources, driven by
their poverty and their misconduct from the land which gave
them birth, or by speculators and adventurers greedy of
gain. Some settlements cannot even boast so honorable an
origin; Santo Domingo was founded by buccaneers; and at
the present day the criminal courts of England supply the
population of Australia.

The settlers who established themselves on the shores of
New England all belonged to the more independent classes
of their native country. Their union on the soil of America
at once presented the singular phenomenon of a society con-
tıining neither lords nor common people, and we may almost say neither rich nor poor. These men possessed, in proportion to their number, a greater mass of intelligence than
is to be found in any European nation of our own time. All,
perhaps without a single exception, had received a good education, and many of them were known in Europe for their

[5] The New England states are those situated to the east of the
Hudson. They are now six in number: (1) Connecticut, (2)
Rhode Island, (3) Massachusetts, (4) New Hampshire, (5)
Vermont, (6) Maine.

talents and their acquirements. The other colonies had been founded by adventurers without families; the immigrants of New England brought with them the best elements of order and morality; they landed on the desert coast accompanied by their wives and children. But what especially distinguished them from all others was the aim of their undertaking. They had not been obliged by necessity to leave their country; the social position they abandoned was one to be regretted, and their means of subsistence were certain. Nor did they cross the Atlantic to improve their situation or to increase their wealth; it was a purely intellectual craving that called them from the comforts of their former homes; and in facing the inevitable sufferings of exile their object was the triumph of an idea.

The immigrants, or, as they deservedly styled themselves, the Pilgrims, belonged to that English sect the austerity of whose principles had acquired for them the name of Puritans. Puritanism was not merely a religious doctrine, but corresponded in many points with the most absolute democratic and republican theories. It was this tendency that had aroused its most dangerous adversaries. Persecuted by the government of the mother country, and disgusted by the habits of a society which the rigor of their own principles condemned, the Puritans went forth to seek some rude and unfrequented part of the world where they could live according to their own opinions and worship God in freedom.

A few quotations will throw more light upon the spirit of these pious adventurers than all that we can say of them. Nathaniel Morton,[6] the historian of the first years of the settlement, thus opens his subject:

"Gentle Reader, I have for some lengths of time looked upon it as a duty incumbent especially on the immediate successors of those that have had so large experience of those many memorable and signal demonstrations of God's goodness, viz. the first beginners of this Plantation in New England, to commit to writing his gracious dispensations on that behalf; having so many inducements thereunto, not only otherwise, but so plentifully in the Sacred Scriptures: that so, what we have seen, and what our fathers have told us (Psalm lxxviii. 3, 4), we may not hide from our children,

---

[6] *New England's Memorial* (Boston, 1826), p. 14. See also Hutchinson's *History,* Vol. II, p. 440.

showing to the generations to come the praises of the Lord; that especially the seed of Abraham his servant, and the children of Jacob his chosen (Psalm cv. 5, 6), may remember his marvellous works in the beginning and progress of the planting of New England, his wonders and the judgments of his mouth; how that God brought a vine into this wilderness; that he cast out the heathen, and planted it; that he made room for it and caused it to take deep root; and it filled the land (Psalm lxxx. 8, 9). And not only so, but also that he hath guided his people by his strength to his holy habitation, and planted them in the mountain of his inheritance in respect of precious Gospel enjoyments: and that as especially God may have the glory of all unto whom it is most due; so also some rays of glory may reach the names of those blessed Saints, that were the main instruments and the beginning of this happy enterprise."

It is impossible to read this opening paragraph without an involuntary feeling of religious awe; it breathes the very savor of Gospel antiquity. The sincerity of the author heightens his power of language. In our eyes, as well as in his own, it was not a mere party of adventurers gone forth to seek their fortune beyond seas, but the germ of a great nation wafted by Providence to a predestined shore.

The author continues, and thus describes the departure of the first Pilgrims:[7]

"So they left that goodly and pleasant city of Leyden, which had been their resting-place for above eleven years; but they knew that they were pilgrims and strangers here below, and looked not much on these things, but lifted up their eyes to heaven, their dearest country, where God hath prepared for them a city (Heb. xi. 16), and therein quieted their spirits. When they came to Delfs-Haven they found the ship and all things ready; and such of their friends as could not come with them followed after them, and sundry came from Amsterdam to see them shipt, and to take their leaves of them. One night was spent with little sleep with the most, but with friendly entertainment and Christian discourse, and other real expressions of true Christian love. The next day they went on board, and their friends with them, where truly doleful was the sight of that sad and mournful parting, to hear what sighs and sobs and prayers did sound amongst

[7] *New England's Memorial,* p. 22.

them; what tears did gush from every eye, and pithy speeches pierced each other's heart, that sundry of the Dutch strangers that stood on the Key as spectators could not refrain from tears. But the tide (which stays for no man) calling them away, that were thus loth to depart, their Reverend Pastor, falling down on his knees, and they all with him, with watery cheeks commended them with most fervent prayers unto the Lord and his blessing; and then with mutual embraces and many tears they took their leaves one of another, which proved to be the last leave to many of them."

The emigrants were about 150 in number, including the women and the children. Their object was to plant a colony on the shores of the Hudson; but after having been driven about for some time in the Atlantic Ocean, they were forced to land on the arid coast of New England, at the spot which is now the town of Plymouth. The rock is still shown on which the Pilgrims disembarked.[8]

"But before we pass on," continues our historian,[9] "let the reader with me make a pause, and seriously consider this poor people's present condition, the more to be raised up to admiration of God's goodness towards them in their preservation: for being now passed the vast ocean, and a sea of troubles before them in expectation, they had now no friends to welcome them, no inns to entertain or refresh them, no houses, or much less towns, to repair unto to seek for succour: and for the season it was winter, and they that know the winters of the country know them to be sharp and violent, subject to cruel and fierce storms, dangerous to travel to known places, much more to search unknown coasts. Besides, what could they see but a hideous and desolate wilderness, full of wilde beasts, and wilde men? and what multitudes of them there were, they then knew not: for which way soever they turned their eyes (save upward to Heaven) they could have but little solace or content in re-

[8] This rock has become an object of veneration in the United States. I have seen bits of it carefully preserved in several towns of the Union. Does not this sufficiently show how all human power and greatness are entirely in the soul? Here is a stone which the feet of a few poor fugitives pressed for an instant, and this stone becomes famous; it is treasured by a great nation, a fragment is prized as a relic. But what has become of the doorsteps of a thousand palaces? Who troubles himself about them?

[9] *New England's Memorial*, p. 35.

spect of any outward object; for summer being ended, all things stand in appearance with a weather-beaten face, and the whole country, full of woods and thickets, represented a wild and savage hew; if they looked behind them, there was the mighty ocean which they had passed, and was now as a main bar or gulph to separate them from all the civil parts of the world."

It must not be imagined that the piety of the Puritans was merely speculative, or that it took no cognizance of the course of worldly affairs. Puritanism, as I have already remarked, was almost as much a political theory as a religious doctrine. No sooner had the immigrants landed on the barren coast described by Nathaniel Morton than it was their first care to constitute a society, by subscribing the following Act:[10]

"IN THE NAME OF GOD. AMEN. We, whose names are underwritten, the loyal subjects of our dread Sovereign Lord King James, &c. &c., Having undertaken for the glory of God, and advancement of the Christian Faith, and the honour of our King and country, a voyage to plant the first colony in the northern parts of Virginia; Do by these presents solemnly and mutually, in the presence of God and one another, covenant and combine ourselves together into a civil body politick, for our better ordering and preservation, and furtherance of the ends aforesaid: and by virtue hereof do enact, constitute, and frame such just and equal laws, ordinances, acts, constitutions, and offices, from time to time, as shall be thought most meet and convenient for the general good of the Colony; unto which we promise all due submission and obedience," etc.

This happened in 1620, and from that time forwards the emigration went on. The religious and political passion which ravaged the British Empire during the whole reign of Charles I drove fresh crowds of sectarians every year to the shores of America. In England the stronghold of Puritanism continued to be in the middle classes; and it was from the middle classes that most of the emigrants came. The popu-

---

[10] The emigrants who founded the state of Rhode Island in 1638, those who landed at New Haven in 1637, the first settlers in Connecticut in 1639, and the founders of Providence in 1640 began in like manner by drawing up a social contract, which was acceded to by all the interested parties. See Pitkin's *History,* pp. 42 and 47.

lation of New England increased rapidly; and while the
hierarchy of rank despotically classed the inhabitants of the
mother country, the colony approximated more and more
the novel spectacle of a community homogeneous in all its
parts. A democracy more perfect than antiquity had dared
to dream of started in full size and panoply from the midst
of an ancient feudal society.

The English government was not dissatisfied with a large
emigration which removed the elements of fresh discord and
further revolutions. On the contrary, it did everything to encourage it and seemed to have no anxiety about the destiny
of those who sought a shelter from the rigor of their laws
on the soil of America. It appeared as if New England was a
region given up to the dreams of fancy and the unrestrained
experiments of innovators.

The English colonies (and this is one of the main causes
of their prosperity) have always enjoyed more internal freedom and more political independence than the colonies of
other nations; and this principle of liberty was nowhere
more extensively applied than in the New England states.

It was generally allowed at that period that the territories
of the New World belonged to that European nation which
had been the first to discover them. Nearly the whole coast
of North America thus became a British possession towards
the end of the sixteenth century. The means used by the
English government to people these new domains were of
several kinds: the king sometimes appointed a governor of
his own choice, who ruled a portion of the New World in
the name and under the immediate orders of the crown;[11]
this is the colonial system adopted by the other countries of
Europe. Sometimes grants of certain tracts were made by
the crown to an individual or to a company,[12] in which
case all the civil and political power fell into the hands of
one or more persons, who, under the inspection and control
of the crown, sold the lands and governed the inhabitants.
Lastly, a third system consisted in allowing a certain number of emigrants to form themselves into a political society
under the protection of the mother country and to govern
themselves in whatever was not contrary to her laws. This

[11] This was the case in the state of New York.
[12] Maryland, the Carolinas, Pennsylvania, and New Jersey were
in this situation. See Pitkin's *History*, Vol. I, pp. 11–31.

mode of colonization, so favorable to liberty, was adopted only in New England.[13]

In 1628 [14] a charter of this kind was granted by Charles I to the emigrants who went to form the colony of Massachusetts. But, in general, charters were not given to the colonies of New England till their existence had become an established fact. Plymouth, Providence, New Haven, Connecticut, and Rhode Island [15] were founded without the help and almost without the knowledge of the mother country. The new settlers did not derive their powers from the head of the empire, although they did not deny its supremacy; they constituted themselves into a society, and it was not till thirty or forty years afterwards, under Charles II, that their existence was legally recognized by a royal charter.

This frequently renders it difficult, in studying the earliest historical and legislative records of New England, to detect the link that connected the emigrants with the land of their forefathers. They continually exercised the rights of sovereignty; they named their magistrates, concluded peace or declared war, made police regulations, and enacted laws, as if their allegiance was due only to God.[16] Nothing can be more curious and at the same time more instructive than the legislation of that period; it is there that the solution of

[13] See the work entitled *Historical Collection of State Papers and Other Authentic Documents Intended as Materials for a History of the United States of America,* by Ebenezer Hazard, printed at Philadelphia, 1792, for a great number of documents relating to the commencement of the colonies, which are valuable for their contents and their authenticity; among them are the various charters granted by the English crown, and the first acts of the local governments.

See also the analysis of all these charters given by Mr. Story, Judge of the Supreme Court of the United States, in the Introduction to his *Commentaries on the Constitution of the United States.* It is proved by these documents that the principles of representative government and the external forms of political liberty were introduced into all the colonies almost from their origin. These principles were more fully acted upon in the North than in the South, but they existed everywhere.

[14] See Pitkin's *History,* p. 35. Also, the *History of the Colony of Massachusetts Bay,* by Hutchinson, Vol. I, p. 9.

[15] See ibid., pp. 42, 47.

[16] The inhabitants of Massachusetts had deviated from the forms that are preserved in the criminal and civil procedure of England; in 1650 the name of the king was not yet put at the head of the decrees of justice. See Hutchinson, Vol. I, p. 452.

the great social problem which the United States now presents to the world is to be found.

Among these documents we shall notice as especially characteristic the code of laws promulgated by the little state of Connecticut in 1650.[17]

The legislators of Connecticut[18] begin with the penal laws, and, strange to say, they borrow their provisions from the text of Holy Writ.

"Whosoever shall worship any other God than the Lord," says the preamble of the Code, "shall surely be put to death." This is followed by ten or twelve enactments of the same kind, copied verbatim from the books of Exodus, Leviticus, and Deuteronomy. Blasphemy, sorcery, adultery,[19] and rape were punished with death; an outrage offered by a son to his parents was to be expiated by the same penalty. The legislation of a rude and half-civilized people was thus applied to an enlightened and moral community. The consequence was, that the punishment of death was never more frequently prescribed by statute, and never more rarely enforced.

The chief care of the legislators in this body of penal laws was the maintenance of orderly conduct and good morals in the community; thus they constantly invaded the domain of conscience, and there was scarcely a sin which was not subject to magisterial censure. The reader is aware of the rigor with which these laws punished rape and adultery; intercourse between unmarried persons was likewise severely repressed. The judge was empowered to inflict either a pecuniary penalty, a whipping, or marriage[20] on the mis-

[17] *Code* of 1650, p. 28 (Hartford, 1830).

[18] See also in Hutchinson's *History,* Vol. I, pp. 435–6, the analysis of the penal code adopted in 1648 by the colony of Massachusetts. This code is drawn up on the same principles as that of Connecticut.

[19] Adultery was also punished with death by the law of Massachusetts; and Hutchinson (Vol. I, p. 441) says that several persons actually suffered for this crime. On this subject he quotes a curious anecdote of what took place in the year 1663. A married woman had had criminal intercourse with a young man; her husband died, and she married the lover. Several years had elapsed when the public began to suspect the previous intercourse of this couple; they were thrown into prison, put to trial, and very narrowly escaped capital punishment.

[20] *Code* of 1650, p. 48. It appears sometimes to have happened that the judges inflicted these punishments cumulatively, as is

demeanants, and if the records of the old courts of New
Haven may be believed, prosecutions of this kind were not
infrequent. We find a sentence, bearing the date of May 1,
1660, inflicting a fine and reprimand on a young woman
who was accused of using improper language and of allowing herself to be kissed.[21] The Code of 1650 abounds in preventive measures. It punishes idleness and drunkenness with
severity.[22] Innkeepers were forbidden to furnish more than
a certain quantity of liquor to each consumer; and simple
lying, whenever it may be injurious,[23] is checked by a fine
or a flogging. In other places the legislator, entirely for-
getting the great principles of religious toleration that he
had himself demanded in Europe, makes attendance on
divine service compulsory,[24] and goes so far as to visit with
severe punishment,[25] and even with death, Christians who
chose to worship God according to a ritual differing from
his own.[26] Sometimes, indeed, the zeal for regulation induces him to descend to the most frivolous particulars: thus
a law is to be found in the same code which prohibits the
use of tobacco.[27] It must not be forgotten that these fantastic
and oppressive laws were not imposed by authority, but that

---

seen in a sentence pronounced in 1643 (*New Haven Antiquities,*
p. 114), by which Margaret Bedford, convicted of loose conduct,
was condemned to be whipped and afterwards to marry Nicolas
Jemmings, her accomplice.

[21] *New Haven Antiquities,* p. 104. See also Hutchinson's *History,* Vol. I, p. 435, for several causes equally extraordinary.

[22] *Code* of 1650, pp. 50, 57.

[23] Ibid., p. 64.

[24] Ibid., p. 44.

[25] This was not peculiar to Connecticut. See, for instance, the
law which, on September 13, 1644, banished the Anabaptists
from Massachusetts (*Historical Collection of State Papers,* Vol.
I, p. 538). See also the law against the Quakers, passed on October 14, 1656. "Whereas," says the preamble, "an accursed race
of heretics called Quakers has sprung up," etc. The clauses of the
statute inflict a heavy fine on all captains of ships who should
import Quakers into the country. The Quakers who may be
found there shall be whipped and imprisoned with hard labor.
Those members of the sect who should defend their opinions
shall be first fined, then imprisoned, and finally driven out of the
province. *Historical Collection of State Papers,* Vol. I, p. 630.

[26] By the penal law of Massachusetts, any Catholic priest who
should set foot in the colony after having been once driven out
of it was liable to capital punishment.

[27] *Code* of 1650, p. 96.

they were freely voted by all the persons interested in them, and that the customs of the community were even more austere and puritanical than the laws. In 1649 a solemn association was formed in Boston to check the worldly luxury of long hair.[28]

These errors are no doubt discreditable to human reason; they attest the inferiority of our nature, which is incapable of laying firm hold upon what is true and just and is often reduced to the alternative of two excesses. In strict connection with this penal legislation, which bears such striking marks of a narrow, sectarian spirit and of those religious passions which had been warmed by persecution and were still fermenting among the people, a body of political laws is to be found which, though written two hundred years ago, is still in advance of the liberties of our age.

The general principles which are the groundwork of modern constitutions, principles which, in the seventeenth century, were imperfectly known in Europe, and not completely triumphant even in Great Britain, were all recognized and established by the laws of New England: the intervention of the people in public affairs, the free voting of taxes, the responsibility of the agents of power, personal liberty, and trial by jury were all positively established without discussion.

These fruitful principles were there applied and developed to an extent such as no nation in Europe has yet ventured to attempt.

In Connecticut the electoral body consisted, from its origin, of the whole number of citizens; and this is readily to be understood.[29] In this young community there was an almost perfect equality of fortune, and a still greater uniformity of opinions.[30] In Connecticut at this period all the executive officials were elected, including the governor of the state.[31] The citizens above the age of sixteen were

[28] *New England's Memorial*, p. 316. See Appendix E.

[29] Constitution of 1638, p. 17.

[30] In 1641 the General Assembly of Rhode Island unanimously declared that the government of the state was a democracy, and that the power was vested in the body of free citizens, who alone had the right to make the laws and to watch their execution *Code* of 1650, p. 70.

[31] Pitkin's *History*, p. 47.

obliged to bear arms; they formed a national militia, which appointed its own officers, and was to hold itself at all times in readiness to march for the defense of the country.[32]

In the laws of Connecticut, as well as in all those of New England, we find the germ and gradual development of that township independence which is the life and mainspring of American liberty at the present day. The political existence of the majority of the nations of Europe commenced in the superior ranks of society and was gradually and imperfectly communicated to the different members of the social body. In America, on the contrary, it may be said that the township was organized before the county, the county before the state, the state before the union.

In New England, townships were completely and definitely constituted as early as 1650. The independence of the township was the nucleus round which the local interests, passions, rights, and duties collected and clung. It gave scope to the activity of a real political life, thoroughly democratic and republican. The colonies still recognized the supremacy of the mother country; monarchy was still the law of the state; but the republic was already established in every township.

The towns named their own magistrates of every kind, assessed themselves, and levied their own taxes.[33] In the New England town the law of representation was not adopted; but the affairs of the community were discussed, as at Athens, in the marketplace, by a general assembly of the citizens.

In studying the laws that were promulgated at this early era of the American republics, it is impossible not to be struck by the legislator's knowledge of government and advanced theories. The ideas there formed of the duties of society towards its members are evidently much loftier and more comprehensive than those of European legislators at that time; obligations were there imposed upon it which it elsewhere slighted. In the states of New England, from the first, the condition of the poor was provided for;[34] strict measures were taken for the maintenance of roads, and surveyors were appointed to attend to them;[35] records were

[32] Constitution of 1638, p. 12.
[33] *Code* of 1650, p. 80.
[34] Ibid., p. 78.
[35] Ibid., p. 49.

established in every town, in which the results of public deliberations and the births, deaths, and marriages of the citizens were entered; [36] clerks were directed to keep these records; [37] officers were appointed to administer the properties having no claimants, and others to determine the boundaries of inherited lands, and still others whose principal functions were to maintain public order in the community.[38] The law enters into a thousand various details to anticipate and satisfy a crowd of social wants that are even now very inadequately felt in France.

But it is by the mandates relating to public education that the original character of American civilization is at once placed in the clearest light.[39] "Whereas," says the law, "Satan, the enemy of mankind, finds his strongest weapons in the ignorance of men, and whereas it is important that the wisdom of our fathers shall not remain buried in their tombs, and whereas the education of children is one of the prime concerns of the state, with the aid of the Lord. . . ." Here follow clauses establishing schools in every township and obliging the inhabitants, under pain of heavy fines, to support them. Schools of a superior kind were founded in the same manner in the more populous districts. The municipal authorities were bound to enforce the sending of children to school by their parents; they were empowered to inflict fines upon all who refused compliance; and in cases of continued resistance, society assumed the place of the parent, took possession of the child, and deprived the father of those natural rights which he used to so bad a purpose.[40] The reader will undoubtedly have remarked the preamble of these enactments: in America religion is the road to knowledge, and the observance of the divine laws leads man to civil freedom.

If, after having cast a rapid glance over the state of American society in 1650, we turn to the condition of Europe, and more especially to that of the Continent, at the same period, we cannot fail to be struck with astonishment. On the continent of Europe at the beginning of the

---

[36] See Hutchinson's *History,* Vol. I, p. 455.
[37] *Code* of 1650, p. 86.
[38] Ibid., p. 40.
[39] Ibid., p. 90.
[40] Ibid., p. 83.

seventeenth century absolute monarchy had everywhere triumphed over the ruins of the oligarchical and feudal liberties of the Middle Ages. Never perhaps were the ideas of right more completely overlooked than in the midst of the splendor and literature of Europe; never was there less political activity among the people; never were the principles of true freedom less widely circulated; and at that very time those principles which were scorned or unknown by the nations of Europe were proclaimed in the deserts of the New World and were accepted as the future creed of a great people. The boldest theories of the human mind were reduced to practice by a community so humble that not a statesman condescended to attend to it; and a system of legislation without a precedent was produced offhand by the natural originality of men's imaginations. In the bosom of this obscure democracy, which had as yet brought forth neither generals nor philosophers nor authors, a man might stand up in the face of a free people, and pronounce with general applause the following fine definition of liberty:

"Concerning liberty, I observe a great mistake in the country about that. There is a twofold liberty, natural (I mean as our nature is now corrupt) and civil or federal. The first is common to man with beasts and other creatures. By this, man, as he stands in relation to man simply, hath liberty to do what he lists; it is a liberty to evil as well as to good. This liberty is incompatible and inconsistent with authority, and cannot endure the least restraint of the most just authority. The exercise and maintaining of this liberty makes men grow more evil, and in time to be worse than brute beasts: *omnes sumus licentiâ deteriores*. This is that great enemy of truth and peace, that wild beast, which all the ordinances of God are bent against, to restrain and subdue it. The other kind of liberty I call civil or federal; it may also be termed moral, in reference to the covenant between God and man, in the moral law, and the politic covenants and constitutions, among men themselves. This liberty is the proper end and object of authority, and cannot subsist without it; and it is a liberty to that only which is good, just, and honest. This liberty you are to stand for, with the hazard not only of your goods, but of your lives, if need be. Whatsoever crosseth this, is not authority, but a distemper thereof. This liberty is maintained and exercised in a way of subjection to authority; it is of the same kind of liberty wherewith Christ hath made us free." [41]

I have said enough to put the character of Anglo-American civilization in its true light. It is the result (and this should be constantly kept in mind) of two distinct elements, which in other places have been in frequent disagreement, but which the Americans have succeeded in incorporating to some extent one with the other and combining admirably. I allude to the *spirit of religion* and the *spirit of liberty*.

The settlers of New England were at the same time ardent sectarians and daring innovators. Narrow as the limits of some of their religious opinions were, they were free from all political prejudices.

Hence arose two tendencies, distinct but not opposite, which are everywhere discernible in the manners as well as the laws of the country.

Men sacrifice for a religious opinion their friends, their family, and their country; one can consider them devoted to the pursuit of intellectual goals which they came to purchase at so high a price. One sees them, however, seeking with almost equal eagerness material wealth and moral satisfaction; heaven in the world beyond, and well-being and liberty in this one.

Under their hand, political principles, laws, and human institutions seem malleable, capable of being shaped and combined at will. As they go forward, the barriers which imprisoned society and behind which they were born are lowered; old opinions, which for centuries had been controlling the world, vanish; a course almost without limits, a field without horizon, is revealed: the human spirit rushes forward and traverses them in every direction. But having reached the limits of the political world, the human spirit stops of itself; in fear it relinquishes the need of exploration; it even abstains from lifting the veil of the sanctuary; it bows with respect before truths which it accepts without discussion.

[41] Mather's *Magnalia Christi Americana,* Vol. II, p. 13. This speech was made by Winthrop; he was accused of having committed arbitrary actions during his magistracy, but after having made the speech, of which the above is a fragment, he was acquitted by acclamation, and from that time forwards he was always re-elected Governor of the state. See Marshall, Vol. I, p. 166.

Thus in the moral world everything is classified, systematized, foreseen, and decided beforehand; in the political world everything is agitated, disputed, and uncertain. In the one is a passive though a voluntary obedience; in the other, an independence scornful of experience, and jealous of all authority. These two tendencies, apparently so discrepant, are far from conflicting; they advance together and support each other.

Religion perceives that civil liberty affords a noble exercise to the faculties of man and that the political world is a field prepared by the Creator for the efforts of mind. Free and powerful in its own sphere, satisfied with the place reserved for it, religion never more surely establishes its empire than when it reigns in the hearts of men unsupported by aught beside its native strength.

Liberty regards religion as its companion in all its battles and its triumphs, as the cradle of its infancy and the divine source of its claims. It considers religion as the safeguard of morality, and morality as the best security of law and the surest pledge of the duration of freedom.[42]

REASONS FOR CERTAIN ANOMALIES WHICH THE LAWS AND CUSTOMS OF THE ANGLO-AMERICANS PRESENT. *Remains of aristocratic institutions amid the most complete democracy—Why?—Careful distinction to be drawn between what is of Puritanical and what of English origin.*

THE reader is cautioned not to draw too general or too absolute an inference from what has been said. The social condition, the religion, and the customs of the first immigrants undoubtedly exercised an immense influence on the destiny of their new country. Nevertheless, they could not found a state of things originating solely in themselves: no man can entirely shake off the influence of the past; and the settlers, intentionally or not, mingled habits and notions derived from their education and the traditions of their country with those habits and notions that were exclusively their own. To know and to judge the Anglo-Americans of the present day, it is therefore necessary to distinguish what is of Puritanical and what of English origin.

Laws and customs are frequently to be met with in the United States which contrast strongly with all that surrounds them. There laws seem to be drawn up in a spirit contrary

[42] See Appendix F.

to the prevailing tenor of American legislation; and these customs are no less opposed to the general tone of society. If the English colonies had been founded in an age of darkness, or if their origin was already lost in the lapse of years, the problem would be insoluble.

I shall quote a single example to illustrate my meaning. The civil and criminal procedure of the Americans has only two means of action, committal or bail. The first act of the magistrate is to exact security from the defendant or, in case of refusal, to incarcerate him; the ground of the accusation and the importance of the charges against him are then discussed.

It is evident that such a legislation is hostile to the poor and favorable only to the rich. The poor man has not always security to produce, even in a civil case; and if he is obliged to wait for justice in prison, he is speedily reduced to distress. A wealthy person, on the contrary, always escapes imprisonment in civil cases; nay, more, if he has committed a crime, he may readily elude punishment by breaking his bail. Thus all the penalties of the law are, for him, reduced to fines.[43] Nothing can be more aristocratic than this system of legislation. Yet in America it is the poor who make the law, and they usually reserve the greatest advantages of society to themselves. The explanation of the phenomenon is to be found in England; the laws of which I speak are English,[44] and the Americans have retained them, although repugnant to the general tenor of their legislation and the mass of their ideas.

Next to its habits the thing which a nation is least apt to change is its civil legislation. Civil laws are familiarly known only to lawyers, whose direct interest it is to maintain them as they are, whether good or bad, simply because they themselves are conversant with them. The bulk of the nation is scarcely acquainted with them; it sees their action only in particular cases, can with difficulty detect their tendency, and obeys them without thought.

I have quoted one instance where it would have been easy to adduce many others. The picture of American society has, if I may so speak, a surface covering of democracy, beneath which the old aristocratic colors sometimes peep out

---

[43] Crimes no doubt exist for which bail is inadmissible, but they are few in number.

[44] See Blackstone and Delolme, Bk. I, ch. 10.

Chapter III

SOCIAL CONDITION OF THE ANGLO-AMERICANS

Social condition is commonly the result of circumstances, sometimes of laws, oftener still of these two causes united; but when once established, it may justly be considered as itself the source of almost all the laws, the usages, and the ideas which regulate the conduct of nations: whatever it does not produce, it modifies.

If we would become acquainted with the legislation and the manners of a nation, therefore, we must begin by the study of its social condition.

The striking characteristic of the social condition of the anglo-americans is its essential democracy. *The first immigrants of New England—Their equality—Aristocratic laws introduced in the South—Period of the Revolution—Change in the laws of inheritance—effects produced by this change—Democracy carried to its utmost limits in the new states of the West—Equality of mental endowments.*

Many important observations suggest themselves upon the social condition of the Anglo-Americans; but there is one that takes precedence of all the rest. The social condition of the Americans is eminently democratic; this was its character at the foundation of the colonies, and it is still more strongly marked at the present day.

I have stated in the preceding chapter that great equality existed among the immigrants who settled on the shores of New England. Even the germs of aristocracy were never planted in that part of the Union. The only influence which obtained there was that of intellect; the people became accustomed to revere certain names as representatives of knowledge and virtue. Some of their fellow citizens acquired a power over the others that might truly have been called aristocratic if it had been capable of transmission from father to son.

This was the state of things to the east of the Hudson: to the southwest of that river, and as far as the Floridas, the case was different. In most of the states situated to the southwest of the Hudson some great English proprietors had settled who had imported with them aristocratic principles and the English law of inheritance. I have explained the reasons why it was impossible ever to establish a powerful aristocracy in America; these reasons existed with less force to the southwest of the Hudson. In the South one man, aided by slaves, could cultivate a great extent of country; it was therefore common to see rich landed proprietors. But their influence was not altogether aristocratic, as that term is understood in Europe, since they possessed no privileges; and the cultivation of their estates being carried on by slaves, they had no tenants depending on them, and consequently no patronage. Still, the great proprietors south of the Hudson constituted a superior class, having ideas and tastes of its own and forming the center of political action. This kind of aristocracy sympathized with the body of the people, whose passions and interests it easily embraced; but it was too weak and too shortlived to excite either love or hatred. This was the class which headed the insurrection in the South and furnished the best leaders of the American Revolution.

At this period society was shaken to its center. The people, in whose name the struggle had taken place, conceived the desire of exercising the authority that it had acquired; its democratic tendencies were awakened; and having thrown off the yoke of the mother country, it aspired to independence of every kind. The influence of individuals gradually ceased to be felt, and custom and law united to produce the same result.

But the law of inheritance was the last step to equality. I am surprised that ancient and modern jurists have not attributed to this law a greater influence on human affairs.[1]

---

[1] I understand by the law of inheritance all those laws whose principal object it is to regulate the distribution of property after the death of its owner. The law of entail is of this number; it certainly prevents the owner from disposing of his possessions before his death; but this is solely with the view of preserving them entire for the heir. The principal object, therefore, of the law of entail is to regulate the descent of property after the death of its owner; its other provisions are merely means to this end.

It is true that these laws belong to civil affairs; but they ought, nevertheless, to be placed at the head of all political institutions; for they exercise an incredible influence upon the social state of a people, while political laws show only what this state already is. They have, moreover, a sure and uniform manner of operating upon society, affecting, as it were, generations yet unborn. Through their means man acquires a kind of preternatural power over the future lot of his fellow creatures. When the legislator has once regulated the law of inheritance, he may rest from his labor. The machine once put in motion will go on for ages, and advance, as if self-guided, towards a point indicated beforehand. When framed in a particular manner, this law unites, draws together, and vests property and power in a few hands; it causes an aristocracy, so to speak, to spring out of the ground. If formed on opposite principles, its action is still more rapid; it divides, distributes, and disperses both property and power. Alarmed by the rapidity of its progress, those who despair of arresting its motion endeavor at least to obstruct it by difficulties and impediments. They vainly seek to counteract its effect by contrary efforts; but it shatters and reduces to powder every obstacle, until we can no longer see anything but a moving and impalpable cloud of dust, which signals the coming of the Democracy. When the law of inheritance permits, still more when it decrees, the equal division of a father's property among all his children, its effects are of two kinds: it is important to distinguish them from each other, although they tend to the same end.

As a result of the law of inheritance, the death of each owner brings about a revolution in property; not only do his possessions change hands, but their very nature is altered, since they are parceled into shares, which become smaller and smaller at each division. This is the direct and as it were the physical effect of the law. In the countries where legislation establishes the equality of division, property, and particularly landed fortunes, have a permanent tendency to diminish. The effects of such legislation, however, would be perceptible only after a lapse of time if the law were abandoned to its own working; for, supposing the family to consist of only two children (and in a country peopled as France is, the average number is not above three), these children, sharing between them the fortune of both parents, would not be poorer than their father or mother.

But the law of equal division exercises its influence not merely upon the property itself, but it affects the minds of the heirs and brings their passions into play. These indirect consequences tend powerfully to the destruction of large fortunes, and especially of large domains.

Among nations whose law of descent is founded upon the right of primogeniture, landed estates often pass from generation to generation without undergoing division; the consequence of this is that family feeling is to a certain degree incorporated with the estate. The family represents the estate, the estate the family, whose name, together with its origin, its glory, its power, and its virtues, is thus perpetuated in an imperishable memorial of the past and as a sure pledge of the future.

When the equal partition of property is established by law, the intimate connection is destroyed between family feeling and the preservation of the paternal estate; the property ceases to represent the family; for, as it must inevitably be divided after one or two generations, it has evidently a constant tendency to diminish and must in the end be completely dispersed. The sons of the great landed proprietor, if they are few in number, or if fortune befriends them, may indeed entertain the hope of being as wealthy as their father, but not of possessing the same property that he did; their riches must be composed of other elements than his. Now, as soon as you divest the landowner of that interest in the preservation of his estate which he derives from association, from tradition, and from family pride, you may be certain that, sooner or later, he will dispose of it; for there is a strong pecuniary interest in favor of selling, as floating capital produces higher interest than real property and is more readily available to gratify the passions of the moment.

Great landed estates which have once been divided never come together again; for the small proprietor draws from his land a better revenue, in proportion, than the large owner from his; and of course he sells it at a higher rate.[2]

---

[2] I do not mean to say that the small proprietor cultivates his land better, but he cultivates it with more ardor and care; so that he makes up by his labor for his want of skill.

The reasons of economy, therefore, which have led the rich man to sell vast estates will prevent him all the more from buying little ones in order to form a large one.

What is called family pride is often founded upon an illusion of self-love. A man wishes to perpetuate and immortalize himself, as it were, in his great-grandchildren. Where family pride ceases to act, individual selfishness comes into play. When the idea of family becomes vague, indeterminate, and uncertain, a man thinks of his present convenience; he provides for the establishment of his next succeeding generation and no more. Either a man gives up the idea of perpetuating his family, or at any rate he seeks to accomplish it by other means than by a landed estate.

Thus, not only does the law of partible inheritance render it difficult for families to preserve their ancestral domains entire, but it deprives them of the inclination to attempt it and compels them in some measure to co-operate with the law in their own extinction. The law of equal distribution proceeds by two methods: by acting upon things, it acts upon persons; by influencing persons, it affects things. By both these means the law succeeds in striking at the root of landed property, and dispersing rapidly both families and fortunes.[3]

Most certainly it is not for us, Frenchmen of the nineteenth century, who daily witness the political and social changes that the law of partition is bringing to pass, to question its influence. It is perpetually conspicuous in our country, overthrowing the walls of our dwellings, and removing the landmarks of our fields. But although it has produced

---

[3] Land being the most stable kind of property, we find from time to time rich individuals who are disposed to make great sacrifices in order to obtain it and who willingly forfeit a considerable part of their income to make sure of the rest. But these are accidental cases. The preference for landed property is no longer found habitually in any class except among the poor. The small landowner, who has less information, less imagination, and less prejudice than the great one, is generally occupied with the desire of increasing his estate: and it often happens that by inheritance, by marriage, or by the chances of trade he is gradually furnished with the means. Thus, to balance the tendency that leads men to divide their estates, there exists another, which incites them to add to them. This tendency, which is sufficient to prevent estates from being divided *ad infinitum,* is not strong enough to create great territorial possessions, certainly not to keep them up in the same family.

great effects in France, much still remains for it to do. Our recollections, opinions, and habits present powerful obstacles to its progress.

In the United States it has nearly completed its work of destruction, and there we can best study its results. The English laws concerning the transmission of property were abolished in almost all the states at the time of the Revolution. The law of entail was so modified as not materially to interrupt the free circulation of property.[4] The first generation having passed away, estates began to be parceled out; and the change became more and more rapid with the progress of time. And now, after a lapse of a little more than sixty years, the aspect of society is totally altered; the families of the great landed proprietors are almost all commingled with the general mass. In the state of New York, which formerly contained many of these, there are but two who still keep their heads above the stream; and they must shortly disappear. The sons of these opulent citizens have become merchants, lawyers, or physicians. Most of them have lapsed into obscurity. The last trace of hereditary ranks and distinctions is destroyed; the law of partition has reduced all to one level.

I do not mean that there is any lack of wealthy individuals in the United States; I know of no country, indeed, where the love of money has taken stronger hold on the affections of men and where a profounder contempt is expressed for the theory of the permanent equality of property. But wealth circulates with inconceivable rapidity, and experience shows that it is rare to find two succeeding generations in the full enjoyment of it.

This picture, which may, perhaps, be thought to be overcharged, still gives a very imperfect idea of what is taking place in the new states of the West and Southwest. At the end of the last century a few bold adventurers began to penetrate into the valley of the Mississippi, and the mass of the population very soon began to move in that direction: communities unheard of till then suddenly appeared in the desert. States whose names were not in existence a few years before, claimed their place in the American Union; and in the Western settlements we may behold democracy arrived at its utmost limits. In these states, founded offhand and as it

[4] See Appendix G.

were by chance, the inhabitants are but of yesterday. Scarcely known to one another, the nearest neighbors are ignorant of each other's history. In this part of the American continent, therefore, the population has escaped the influence not only of great names and great wealth, but even of the natural aristocracy of knowledge and virtue. None is there able to wield that respectable power which men willingly grant to the remembrance of a life spent in doing good before their eyes. The new states of the West are already inhabited, but society has no existence among them.

It is not only the fortunes of men that are equal in America; even their acquirements partake in some degree of the same uniformity. I do not believe that there is a country in the world where, in proportion to the population, there are so few ignorant and at the same time so few learned individuals. Primary instruction is within the reach of everybody; superior instruction is scarcely to be obtained by any. This is not surprising; it is, in fact, the necessary consequence of what I have advanced above. Almost all the Americans are in easy circumstances and can therefore obtain the first elements of human knowledge.

In America there are but few wealthy persons; nearly all Americans have to take a profession. Now, every profession requires an apprenticeship. The Americans can devote to general education only the early years of life. At fifteen they enter upon their calling, and thus their education generally ends at the age when ours begins. If it is continued beyond that point, it aims only towards a particular specialized and profitable purpose; one studies science as one takes up a business; and one takes up only those applications whose immediate practicality is recognized.

In America most of the rich men were formerly poor; most of those who now enjoy leisure were absorbed in business during their youth; the consequence of this is that when they might have had a taste for study, they had no time for it, and when the time is at their disposal, they have no longer the inclination.

There is no class, then, in America, in which the taste for intellectual pleasures is transmitted with hereditary fortune and leisure and by which the labors of the intellect are held in honor. Accordingly, there is an equal want of the desire and the power of application to these objects.

55 *Social Condition of the Anglo-Americans*

A middling standard is fixed in America for human knowledge. All approach as near to it as they can; some as they rise, others as they descend. Of course, a multitude of persons are to be found who entertain the same number of ideas on religion, history, science, political economy, legislation, and government. The gifts of intellect proceed directly from God, and man cannot prevent their unequal distribution. But it is at least a consequence of what I have just said that although the capacities of men are different, as the Creator intended they should be, the means that Americans find for putting them to use are equal.

In America the aristocratic element has always been feeble from its birth; and if at the present day it is not actually destroyed, it is at any rate so completely disabled that we can scarcely assign to it any degree of influence on the course of affairs.

The democratic principle, on the contrary, has gained so much strength by time, by events, and by legislation, as to have become not only predominant, but all-powerful. No family or corporate authority can be perceived; very often one cannot even discover in it any very lasting individual influen.

America, then, exhibits in her social state an extraordinary phenomenon. Men are there seen on a greater equality in point of fortune and intellect, or, in other words, more equal in their strength, than in any other country of the world, or in any age of which history has preserved the remembrance.

POLITICAL CONSEQUENCES OF THE SOCIAL CONDITION OF THE ANGLO-AMERICANS

THE POLITICAL consequences of such a social condition as this are easily deducible.

It is impossible to believe that equality will not eventually find its way into the political world, as it does everywhere else. To conceive of men remaining forever unequal upon a single point, yet equal on all others, is impossible; they must come in the end to be equal upon all.

Now, I know of only two methods of establishing equality in the political world; rights must be given to every citizen, or none at all to anyone. For nations which are arrived at the same stage of social existence as the Anglo-Americans, it is, therefore, very difficult to discover a medium between the sovereignty of all and the absolute power of one man: and it would be vain to deny that the social condition which I have been describing is just as liable to one of these consequences as to the other.

There is, in fact, a manly and lawful passion for equality that incites men to wish all to be powerful and honored. This passion tends to elevate the humble to the rank of the great; but there exists also in the human heart a depraved taste for equality, which impels the weak to attempt to lower the powerful to their own level and reduces men to prefer equality in slavery to inequality with freedom. Not that those nations whose social condition is democratic naturally despise liberty; on the contrary, they have an instinctive love of it. But liberty is not the chief and constant object of their desires; equality is their idol: they make rapid and sudden efforts to obtain liberty and, if they miss their aim, resign themselves to their disappointment; but nothing can satisfy them without equality, and they would rather perish than lose it.

On the other hand, in a state where the citizens are all practically equal, it becomes difficult for them to preserve their independence against the aggressions of power. No one among them being strong enough to engage in the struggle alone with advantage, nothing but a general combination can protect their liberty. Now, such a union is not always possible.

From the same social position, then, nations may derive one or the other of two great political results; these results are extremely different from each other, but they both proceed from the same cause.

The Anglo-Americans are the first nation who, having been exposed to this formidable alternative, have been happy enough to escape the dominion of absolute power. They have been allowed by their circumstances, their origin, their intelligence, and especially by their morals to establish and maintain the sovereignty of the people.

Chapter IV

THE PRINCIPLE OF THE SOVEREIGNTY OF THE PEOPLE OF AMERICA

It DOMINATES the whole society in America—Application made of this principle by the Americans even before their Revolution—Development given to it by that Revolution—Gradual and irresistible extension of the elective qualification.

WHENEVER the political laws of the United States are to be discussed, it is with the doctrine of the sovereignty of the people that we must begin.

The principle of the sovereignty of the people, which is always to be found, more or less, at the bottom of almost all human institutions, generally remains there concealed from view. It is obeyed without being recognized, or if for a moment it is brought to light, it is hastily cast back into the gloom of the sanctuary.

"The will of the nation" is one of those phrases that have been most largely abused by the wily and the despotic of every age. Some have seen the expression of it in the purchased suffrages of a few of the satellites of power; others, in the votes of a timid or an interested minority; and some have even discovered it in the silence of a people, on the supposition that the fact of submission established the right to command.

In America the principle of the sovereignty of the people is neither barren nor concealed, as it is with some other nations; it is recognized by the customs and proclaimed by the laws; it spreads freely, and arrives without impediment at its most remote consequences. If there is a country in the world where the doctrine of the sovereignty of the people can be fairly appreciated, where it can be studied in its application to the affairs of society, and where its dangers and its advantages may be judged, that country is assuredly America.

I have already observed that, from their origin, the sovereignty of the people was the fundamental principle of most of the British colonies in America. It was far, however, from then exercising as much influence on the government of society as it now does. Two obstacles, the one external, the other internal, checked its invasive progress.

It could not ostensibly disclose itself in the laws of colonies which were still forced to obey the mother country; it was therefore obliged to rule secretly in the provincial assemblies, and especially in the townships.

American society at that time was not yet prepared to adopt it with all its consequences. Intelligence in New England and wealth in the country to the south of the Hudson (as I have shown in the preceding chapter) long exercised a sort of aristocratic influence, which tended to keep the exercise of social power in the hands of a few. Not all the public functionaries were chosen by popular vote, nor were all the citizens voters. The electoral franchise was everywhere somewhat restricted and made dependent on a certain qualification, which was very low in the North and more considerable in the South.

The American Revolution broke out, and the doctrine of the sovereignty of the people came out of the townships and took possession of the state. Every class was enlisted in its cause; battles were fought and victories obtained for it; it became the law of laws.

A change almost as rapid was effected in the interior of society, where the law of inheritance completed the abolition of local influences.

As soon as this effect of the laws and of the Revolution became apparent to every eye, victory was irrevocably pronounced in favor of the democratic cause. All power was, in fact, in its hands, and resistance was no longer possible. The higher orders submitted without a murmur and without a struggle to an evil that was thenceforth inevitable. The ordinary fate of falling powers awaited them: each of their members followed his own interest; and as it was impossible to wring the power from the hands of a people whom they did not detest sufficiently to brave, their only aim was to secure its goodwill at any price. The most democratic laws were consequently voted by the very men whose interests they impaired: and thus, although the higher classes did not excite the passions of the people against their order, they themselves accelerated the triumph of the new state of things; so that, by a singular change, the democratic impulse was found to be most irresistible in the very states where the aristocracy had the firmest hold. The state of Maryland, which had been founded by men of rank, was the first to proclaim universal suffrage[1] and to introduce the most democratic forms into the whole of its government.

When a nation begins to modify the elective qualification, it may easily be foreseen that, sooner or later, that qualification will be entirely abolished. There is no more invariable rule in the history of society: the further electoral rights are extended, the greater is the need of extending them; for after each concession the strength of the democracy increases, and its demands increase with its strength. The ambition of those who are below the appointed rate is irritated in exact proportion to the great number of those who are above it. The exception at last becomes the rule, concession follows concession, and no stop can be made short of universal suffrage.

At the present day the principle of the sovereignty of the people has acquired in the United States all the practical development that the imagination can conceive. It is unencumbered by those fictions that are thrown over it in other countries, and it appears in every possible form, according to the exigency of the occasion. Sometimes the laws are made by the people in a body, as at Athens; and sometimes its representatives, chosen by universal suffrage, transact business in its name and under its immediate supervision.

In some countries a power exists which, though it is in a degree foreign to the social body, directs it, and forces it to pursue a certain track. In others the ruling force is divided, being partly within and partly without the ranks of the people. But nothing of the kind is to be seen in the United States; there society governs itself for itself. All power centers in its bosom, and scarcely an individual is to be met with who would venture to conceive or, still less, to express the idea of seeking it elsewhere. The nation participates in the making of its laws by the choice of its legislators, and in the execution of them by the choice of the

[1] Amendment made to the Constitution of Maryland in 1801 and 1809.

agents of the executive government; it may almost be said to govern itself, so feeble and so restricted is the share left to the administration, so little do the authorities forget their popular origin and the power from which they emanate. The people reign in the American political world as the Deity does in the universe. They are the cause and the aim of all things; everything comes from them, and everything is absorbed in them.[2]

[2] See Appendix H.

Chapter V

NECESSITY OF EXAMINING THE CONDITION OF THE STATES BEFORE THAT OF THE UNION AT LARGE

IN THE following chapter the form of government established in America on the principle of the sovereignty of the people will be examined; what are its means of action, its hindrances, its advantages, and its dangers. The first difficulty that presents itself arises from the complex nature of the Constitution of the United States, which consists of two distinct social structures, connected, and, as it were, encased one within the other; two governments, completely separate and almost independent, the one fulfilling the ordinary duties and responding to the daily and indefinite calls of a community, the other circumscribed within certain limits and only exercising an exceptional authority over the general interests of the country. In short, there are twenty-four small sovereign nations, whose agglomeration constitutes the body of the Union. To examine the Union before we have studied the states, would be to adopt a method filled with obstacles. The form of the Federal government of the United States was the last to be adopted; and it is in fact nothing more than a summary of those republican principles which were current in the whole community before it existed, and independently of its existence. Moreover, the Federal government, as I have just observed, is the exception; the government of the states is the rule. The author who should attempt to exhibit the picture as a whole before he had explained its details would necessarily fall into obscurity and repetition.

The great political principles which now govern American society undoubtedly took their origin and their growth in the state. We must know the state, then, in order to gain a clue to the rest. The states that now compose the American Union all present the same features, as regards the external aspect of their institutions. Their political or administrative life is centered in three focuses of action, which may be compared to the different nervous centers that give motion to the human body. The township is the first in order, then the county, and lastly the state.

THE AMERICAN SYSTEM OF TOWNSHIPS. *Why the author begins the examination of the political institutions with the township—Its existence in all nations—Difficulty of establishing and preserving municipal independence—Its importance—Why the author has selected the township system of New England as the main topic of his discussion.*

IT is not without intention that I begin this subject with the township. The village or township is the only association which is so perfectly natural that, wherever a number of men are collected, it seems to constitute itself.

The town or tithing, then, exists in all nations, whatever their laws and customs may be: it is man who makes monarchies and establishes republics, but the township seems to come directly from the hand of God. But although the existence of the township is coeval with that of man, its freedom is an infrequent and fragile thing. A nation can always establish great political assemblies, because it habitually contains a certain number of individuals fitted by their talents, if not by their habits, for the direction of affairs. The township, on the contrary, is composed of coarser materials, which are less easily fashioned by the legislator. The difficulty of establishing its independence rather augments than diminishes with the increasing intelligence of the people. A highly civilized community can hardly tolerate a local independence, is disgusted at its numerous blunders, and is apt to despair of success before the experiment is completed. Again, the immunities of townships, which have been obtained with so much difficulty, are least of all protected against the encroachments of the supreme power. They are unable to struggle, single-handed, against a strong and enterprising government, and they cannot defend themselves with success unless they are identified with the customs of the nation and supported by public opinion. Thus until the independence of townships is amalgamated with the manners of a people, it is easily destroyed; and it is only after a long existence in the laws that it can be thus amalgamated. Municipal freedom is not the fruit of human efforts; it is rarely created by others, but is, as it were, secretly self-produced in the midst of a semi-barbarous state of society. The constant action of the laws and the national habits, peculiar circumstances, and, above all, time, may consolidate it; but there is certainly no nation on the continent of Europe that has experienced its advantages. Yet municipal institutions constitute the strength of free nations. Town meetings ar to liberty what primary schools are to science; they bring it within the people's reach, they teach men how to use and how to enjoy it. A nation may establish a free government, but without municipal institutions it cannot have the spirit of liberty. Transient passions, the interests of an hour, or the chance of circumstances may create the external forms of independence, but the despotic tendency which has been driven into the interior of the social system will sooner or later reappear on the surface.

To make the reader understand the general principles on which the political organization of the counties and townships in the United States rests, I have thought it expedient to choose one of the states of New England as an example, to examine in detail the mechanism of its constitution, and then to cast a general glance over the rest of the country.

The township and the county are not organized in the same manner in every part of the Union; it is easy to perceive, however, that nearly the same principles have guided the formation of both of them throughout the Union. I am inclined to believe that these principles have been carried further and have produced greater results in New England than elsewhere. Consequently they stand out there in higher relief and offer greater facilities to the observations of a stranger.

The township institutions of New England form a complete and regular whole; they are old; they have the support of the laws and the still stronger support of the manners of the community, over which they exercise a prodigious influence. For all these reasons they deserve our special attention.

LIMITS OF THE TOWNSHIP

THE TOWNSHIP of New England holds a middle place between the *commune* and the *canton* of France. Its average population is from two to three thousand,[1] so that it is not so large, on the one hand, that the interests of its inhabitants would be likely to conflict, and not so small, on the other, but that men capable of conducting its affairs may always be found among its citizens.

POWERS OF THE TOWNSHIP IN NEW ENGLAND. *The people the source of all power in the township as elsewhere— Manages its own affairs—No municipal council—The greater part of the authority vested in the selectmen —How the selectmen act—Town meeting—Enumeration of the officers of the township—Obligatory and remunerated functions.*

IN the township, as well as everywhere else, the people are the source of power; but nowhere do they exercise their power more immediately. In America the people form a master who must be obeyed to the utmost limits of possibility.

In New England the majority act by representatives in conducting the general business of the state. It is necessary that it should be so. But in the townships, where the legislative and administrative action of the government is nearer to the governed, the system of representation is not adopted. There is no municipal council; but the body of voters, after having chosen its magistrates, directs them in everything that exceeds the simple and ordinary execution of the laws of the state.[2]

This state of things is so contrary to our ideas, and so

[1] In 1830 there were 305 townships in the state of Massachusetts, and 610,014 inhabitants; which gives an average of about 2,000 inhabitants to each township.

[2] The same rules are not applicable to the cities, which generally have a mayor, and a corporation divided into two bodies; this, however, is an exception that requires the sanction of a law. —See the Act of February 22, 1822, regulating the powers of the city of Boston. *Laws of Massachusetts,* Vol. II, p. 588. It frequently happens that small towns, as well as cities, are subject to a peculiar administration. In 1832, 104 townships in the state of New York were governed in this manner. Williams's *Register.*

different from our customs that I must furnish some examples to make it intelligible.

The public duties in the township are extremely numerous and minutely divided, as we shall see farther on; but most of the administrative power is vested in a few persons, chosen annually, called "the selectmen." [3]

The general laws of the state impose certain duties on the selectmen, which they may fulfill without the authority of their townsmen, but which they can neglect only on their own responsibility. The state law requires them, for instance, to draw up a list of voters in their townships; and if they omit this duty, they are guilty of a misdemeanor. In all the affairs that are voted in town meeting, however, the selectmen carry into effect the popular mandate, as in France the *maire* executes the decree of the municipal council. They usually act upon their own responsibility and merely put in practice principles that have been previously recognized by the majority. But if they wish to make any change in the existing state of things or to undertake any new enterprise, they must refer to the source of their power. If, for instance, a school is to be established, the selectmen call a meeting of the voters on a certain day at an appointed place. They explain the urgency of the case; they make known the means of satisfying it, the probable expense, and the site that seems to be most favorable. The meeting is consulted on these several points; it adopts the principle, marks out the site, votes the tax, and confides the execution of its resolution to the selectmen.

The selectmen alone have the right of calling a town meeting; but they may be required to do so. If ten citizens wish to submit a new project to the assent of the town, they may demand a town meeting; the selectmen are obliged to comply and have only the right of presiding at the meeting.[4] These political forms, these social customs, doubtless seem strange to us in France. I do not here undertake to judge

[3] Three selectmen are appointed in the small townships, and nine in the large ones.—See *The Town Officer*, p. 186. See also the principal laws of Massachusetts relating to selectmen: law of February 20, 1786, Vol. I, p. 219; February 24, 1796, Vol. I, p. 488; March 7, 1801, Vol. II, p. 45; June 16, 1795, Vol. I, p. 475; March 12, 1808, Vol. II, p. 186; February 28, 1787, Vol. I, p. 302; June 22, 1797, Vol. I, p. 539.

[4] See *Laws of Massachusetts*, Vol. I, p. 150. Law of March 25, 1786

them or to make known the secret causes by which they are produced and maintained. I only describe them.

The selectmen are elected every year, in the month of March or April. The town meeting chooses at the same time a multitude of other town officers,[5] who are entrusted with important administrative functions. The assessors rate the township; the collectors receive the tax. A constable is appointed to keep the peace, to watch the streets, and to execute the laws; the town clerk records the town votes, orders, and grants. The treasurer keeps the funds. The overseers of the poor perform the difficult task of carrying out the poor-laws. Committee-men are appointed to attend to the schools and public instruction; and the surveyors of highways, who take care of the greater and lesser roads of the township, complete the list of the principal functionaries. But there are other petty officers still; such as the parish committee, who audit the expenses of public worship; fire wardens, who direct the efforts of the citizens in case of fire; tithing-men, hog-reeves, fence-viewers, timber-measurers, and sealers of weights and measures.[6]

There are, in all, nineteen principal offices in a township. Every inhabitant is required, on pain of being fined, to undertake these different functions, which, however, are almost all paid, in order that the poorer citizens may give time to them without loss. In general, each official act has its price, and the officers are remunerated in proportion to what they have done.

LIFE IN THE TOWNSHIP. *Everyone the best judge of his own interest—Corollary of the principle of the sovereignty of the people—Application of these doctrines in the townships of America—The township of New England is sovereign in all that concerns itself alone, and subject to the state in all other matters—Duties of the township to the state—In France the government lends its agents to the commune—In America it is the reverse.*

I HAVE already observed that the principle of the sovereignty of the people governs the whole political system of

[5] Ibid.

[6] All these magistrates actually exist; their different functions are all detailed in a book called *The Town Officer,* by Isaac Goodwin (Worcester, 1827), and the *General Laws of Massachusetts* in 3 vols. (Boston, 1823).

the Anglo-Americans. Every page of this book will afford new applications of the same doctrine. In the nations by which the sovereignty of the people is recognized, every individual has an equal share of power and participates equally in the government of the state. Why, then, does he obey society, and what are the natural limits of this obedience? Every individual is always supposed to be as well informed, as virtuous, and as strong as any of his fellow citizens. He obeys society, not because he is inferior to those who conduct it or because he is less capable than any other of governing himself, but because he acknowledges the utility of an association with his fellow men and he knows that no such association can exist without a regulating force. He is a subject in all that concerns the duties of citizens to each other; he is free, and responsible to God alone, for all that concerns himself. Hence arises the maxim, that everyone is the best and sole judge of his own private interest, and that society has no right to control a man's actions unless they are prejudicial to the common weal or unless the common weal demands his help. This doctrine is universally admitted in the United States. I shall hereafter examine the general influence that it exercises on the ordinary actions of life: I am now speaking of the municipal bodies.

The township, taken as a whole, and in relation to the central government, is only an individual, like any other to whom the theory I have just described is applicable. Municipal independence in the United States is therefore a natural consequence of this very principle of the sovereignty of the people. All the American republics recognize it more or less, but circumstances have peculiarly favored its growth in New England.

In this part of the Union political life had its origin in the townships; and it may almost be said that each of them originally formed an independent nation. When the kings of England afterwards asserted their supremacy, they were content to assume the central power of the state. They left the townships where they were before; and although they are now subject to the state, they were not at first, or were hardly so. They did not receive their powers from the central authority, but, on the contrary, they gave up a portion of their independence to the state. This is an important distinction and one that the reader must constantly recollect. The

townships are generally subordinate to the state only in those
interests which I shall term *social,* as they are common to
all the others. They are independent in all that concerns
themselves alone; and among the inhabitants of New England I believe that not a man is to be found who would
acknowledge that the state has any right to interfere in their
town affairs. The towns of New England buy and sell, sue
and are sued, augment or diminish their budgets, and no
administrative authority ever thinks of offering any opposition.[7]

There are certain social duties, however, that they are
bound to fulfill. If the state is in need of money, a town
cannot withhold the supplies;[8] if the state projects a road,
the township cannot refuse to let it cross its territory; if a
police regulation is made by the state, it must be enforced
by the town; if a uniform system of public instruction is
enacted, every town is bound to establish the schools which
the law ordains.[9] When I come to speak of the administration of the laws in the United States, I shall point out how
and by what means the townships are compelled to obey in
these different cases; I here merely show the existence of the
obligation. Strict as this obligation is, the government of the
state imposes it in principle only, and in its performance
the township resumes all its independent rights. Thus, taxes
are voted by the state, but they are levied and collected by
the township; the establishment of a school is obligatory,
but the township builds, pays for, and superintends it. In
France the state collector receives the local imposts; in
America the town collector receives the taxes of the state.
Thus the French government lends its agents to the *commune;* in America the township lends its agents to the government. This fact alone shows how widely the two nations
differ.

Spirit of the townships of New England. *How the township of New England wins the affections of its inhabitants—Difficulty of creating local public spirit in
Europe—The rights and duties of the American town-*

[7] See *Laws of Massachusetts,* law of March 23, 1786, Vol. 1,
p. 250.
[8] Ibid., law of February 20, 1786, Vol. I, p. 217.
[9] Ibid., law of June 25, 1789, Vol. I, p. 367, and of March 8,
1827. Vol. III, p. 179.

*ship favorable to it—Sources of local attachment in the
United States—How town spirit shows itself in New
England—Its happy effects.*

In America not only do municipal bodies exist, but they are
kept alive and supported by town spirit. The township of
New England possesses two advantages which strongly
excite the interest of mankind: namely, independence and
authority. Its sphere is limited, indeed; but within that
sphere its action is unrestrained. This independence alone
gives it a real importance, which its extent and population
would not ensure.

It is to be remembered, too, that the affections of men
generally turn towards power. Patriotism is not durable in
a conquered nation. The New Englander is attached to his
township not so much because he was born in it, but because
it is a free and strong community, of which he is a member, and which deserves the care spent in managing it. In
Europe the absence of local public spirit is a frequent subject of regret to those who are in power; everyone agrees
that there is no surer guarantee of order and tranquillity,
and yet nothing is more difficult to create. If the municipal
bodies were made powerful and independent, it is feared
that they would become too strong and expose the state to
anarchy. Yet without power and independence a town may
contain good subjects, but it can have no active citizens.
Another important fact is that the township of New England
is so constituted as to excite the warmest of human affections without arousing the ambitious passions of the heart
of man. The officers of the county are not elected, and their
authority is very limited. Even the state is only a second-
rate community whose tranquil and obscure administration
offers no inducement sufficient to draw men away from the
home of their interests into the turmoil of public affairs.
The Federal government confers power and honor on the
men who conduct it, but these individuals can never be very
numerous. The high station of the Presidency can only be
reached at an advanced period of life; and the other Federal
functionaries of a high class are generally men who have
been favored by good luck or have been distinguished in
some other career. Such cannot be the permanent aim of
the ambitious. But the township, at the center of the ordinary relations of life, serves as a field for the desire of public

esteem, the want of exciting interest, and the taste for authority and popularity; and the passions that commonly embroil society change their character when they find a vent so near the domestic hearth and the family circle.

In the American townships power has been distributed with admirable skill, for the purpose of interesting the greatest possible number of persons in the common weal. Independently of the voters, who are from time to time called into action, the power is divided among innumerable functionaries and officers, who all, in their several spheres, represent the powerful community in whose name they act. The local administration thus affords an unfailing source of profit and interest to a vast number of individuals.

The American system, which divides the local authority among so many citizens, does not scruple to multiply the functions of the town officers. For in the United States it is believed, and with truth, that patriotism is a kind of devotion which is strengthened by ritual observance. In this manner the activity of the township is continually perceptible; it is daily manifested in the fulfillment of a duty or the exercise of a right; and a constant though gentle motion is thus kept up in society, which animates without disturbing it. The American attaches himself to his little community for the same reason that the mountaineer clings to his hills, because the characteristic features of his country are there more distinctly marked; it has a more striking physiognomy.

The existence of the townships of New England is, in general, a happy one. Their government is suited to their tastes, and chosen by themselves. In the midst of the profound peace and general comfort that reign in America, the commotions of municipal life are infrequent. The conduct of local business is easy. The political education of the people has long been complete; say rather that it was complete when the people first set foot upon the soil. In New England no tradition exists of a distinction of rank; no portion of the community is tempted to oppress the remainder; and the wrongs that may injure isolated individuals are forgotten in the general contentment that prevails. If the government has faults (and it would no doubt be easy to point out some), they do not attract notice, for the government really emanates from those it governs, and whether it acts ill or well, this fact casts the protecting spell of a

parental pride over its demerits. Besides, they have nothing
wherewith to compare it. England formerly governed the
mass of the colonies; but the people was always sovereign in
the township, where its rule is not only an ancient, but a
primitive state.

The native of New England is attached to his township
because it is independent and free: his co-operation in its
affairs ensures his attachment to its interests; the well-being
it affords him secures his affection; and its welfare is the
aim of his ambition and of his future exertions. He takes a
part in every occurrence in the place; he practices the art of
government in the small sphere within his reach; he accustoms himself to those forms without which liberty can
only advance by revolutions; he imbibes their spirit; he
acquires a taste for order, comprehends the balance of
powers, and collects clear practical notions on the nature of
his duties and the extent of his rights.

THE COUNTIES OF NEW ENGLAND

THE DIVISION of the counties in America has considerable
analogy with that of the *arrondissements* of France. The
limits of both are arbitrarily laid down, and the various
districts which they contain have no necessary connection,
no common tradition or natural sympathy, no community of
existence; their object is simply to facilitate the administration.

The extent of the township was too small to contain a system of judicial institutions; the county, therefore, is the first
center of judicial action. Each county has a court of justice,[10] a sheriff to execute its decrees, and a prison for
criminals. There are certain wants which are felt alike by
all the townships of a county; it is therefore natural that
they should be satisfied by a central authority. In Massachusetts this authority is vested in the hands of several
magistrates, who are appointed by the governor of the state,
with the advice[11] of his council.[12] The county commissioners have only a limited and exceptional authority, which
can be used only in certain predetermined cases. The state

[10] See *Laws of Massachusetts,* law of February 14, 1821, Vol.
I, p. 551.
[11] Ibid., law of February 20, 1819, Vol. II, p. 494.
[12] The council of the governor is an elective body.

and the townships possess all the power requisite for ordinary and public business. The county commissioners can only prepare the budget; it is voted by the legislature;[13] there is no assembly that directly or indirectly represents the county. It has, therefore, properly speaking, no political existence.

A twofold tendency may be discerned in most of the American constitutions, which impels the legislator to concentrate the legislative and to divide the executive power. The township of New England has in itself an indestructible principle of life; but this distinct existence could only be fictitiously introduced into the county, where the want of it has not been felt. All the townships united have but one representation, which is the state, the center of all national authority; beyond the action of the township and that of the state, it may be said that there is nothing but individual action.

THE ADMINISTRATION OF GOVERNMENT IN NEW ENGLAND. *Administration not perceived in America—Why?—The Europeans believe that liberty is promoted by depriving the social authority of some of its rights; the Americans, by dividing its exercise—Almost all the administration confined to the township, and divided among the town officers—No trace of an administrative hierarchy perceived, either in the township or above it— Why this is the case—How it happens that the administration of the state is uniform—Who is empowered to enforce the obedience of the township and the county to the law—The introduction of judicial power into the administration—Consequence of the extension of the elective principle to all functionaries—The justice of the peace in New England—By whom appointed— County officer: ensures the administration of the townships—Court of sessions—Its mode of action—Who brings matters before this court for action—Right of inspection and indictment parceled out like the other administrative functions—Informers encouraged by the division of fines.*

NOTHING is more striking to a European traveler in the United States than the absence of what we term the govern-

[13] See *Laws of Massachusetts,* law of November 2, 1791, Vol. I, p. 61.

ment, or the administration. Written laws exist in America, and one sees the daily execution of them; but although everything moves regularly, the mover can nowhere be discovered. The hand that directs the social machine is invisible. Nevertheless, as all persons must have recourse to certain grammatical forms, which are the foundation of human language, in order to express their thoughts; so all communities are obliged to secure their existence by submitting to a certain amount of authority, without which they fall into anarchy. This authority may be distributed in several ways, but it must always exist somewhere.

There are two methods of diminishing the force of authority in a nation. The first is to weaken the supreme power in its very principle, by forbidding or preventing society from acting in its own defense under certain circumstances. To weaken authority in this manner is the European way of establishing freedom.

The second manner of diminishing the influence of authority does not consist in stripping society of some of its rights, nor in paralyzing its efforts, but in distributing the exercise of its powers among various hands and in multiplying functionaries, to each of whom is given the degree of power necessary for him to perform his duty. There may be nations whom this distribution of social powers might lead to anarchy, but in itself it is not anarchical. The authority thus divided is, indeed, rendered less irresistible and less perilous, but it is not destroyed.

The Revolution of the United States was the result of a mature and reflecting preference for freedom, and not of a vague or ill-defined craving for independence. It contracted no alliance with the turbulent passions of anarchy, but its course was marked, on the contrary, by a love of order and law.

It was never assumed in the United States that the citizen of a free country has a right to do whatever he pleases; on the contrary, more social obligations were there imposed upon him than anywhere else. No idea was ever entertained of attacking the principle or contesting the rights of society; but the exercise of its authority was divided, in order that the office might be powerful and the officer insignificant, and that the community should be at once regulated and free. In no country in the world does the law hold so absolute a language as in America; and in no country is the right of applying it vested in so many hands. The administrative power in the United States presents nothing either centralized or hierarchical in its constitution; this accounts for its passing unperceived. The power exists, but its representative is nowhere to be seen.

I have already mentioned that the independent townships of New England were not under guardianship, but took care of their own private interests; and the municipal magistrates are the persons who either execute the laws of the state or see that they are executed.[14] Besides the general laws the state sometimes passes general police regulations; but more commonly the townships and town officers, conjointly with the justices of the peace, regulate the minor details of social life, according to the necessities of the different localities, and promulgate such orders as concern the health of the community and the peace as well as morality of the citizens.[15] Lastly, these town magistrates provide, of their own accord and without any impulse from without, for those unforeseen emergencies which frequently occur in society.[16]

It results from what I have said that in the state of Massachusetts the administrative authority is almost entirely restricted to the township,[17] and that it is there distributed among a great number of individuals. In the French commune there is properly but one official functionary—namely,

---

[14] See *The Town Officer,* especially at the words SELECTMEN, ASSESSORS, COLLECTORS, SCHOOLS, SURVEYORS OF HIGHWAYS. I take one example in a thousand: the state prohibits traveling on Sunday without good reason; the tithing-men, who are town officers, are required to keep watch and to execute the law. See *Laws of Massachusetts,* law of March 8, 1792, Vol. I, p. 410.

The selectmen draw up the lists of voters for the election of the governor, and transmit the result of the ballot to the state secretary of state. Ibid., law of February 24, 1796, Vol. I, p. 488.

[15] Thus, for instance, the selectmen authorize the construction of drains, and point out the proper sites for slaughterhouses and other trades which are a nuisance to the neighborhood. See ibid., law of June 7, 1785, Vol. I, p. 193.

[16] For example, the selectmen, conjointly with the justices of the peace, take measures for the security of the public in case of contagious diseases. Ibid., law of June 22, 1797, Vol. I, p. 539.

[17] I say *almost,* for there are many incidents in town life which are regulated by the justices of peace in their individual capacity, or by an assembly of them in the chief town of the county; thus, licenses are granted by the justices. See ibid., law of February 28, 1797, Vol. I, p. 297.

the *maire;* and in New England we have seen that there are nineteen. These nineteen functionaries do not, in general, depend one upon another. The law carefully prescribes a circle of action to each of these magistrates; within that circle they are all-powerful to perform their functions independently of any other authority. If one looks higher than the township, one can find scarcely a trace of an administrative hierarchy. It sometimes happens that the county officers alter a decision of the townships or town magistrates,[18] but in general the authorities of the county have no right to interfere with the authorities of the township[19] except in such matters as concern the county.

The magistrates of the township, as well as those of the county, are bound in a small number of predetermined cases to communicate their acts to the central government.[20] But the central government is not represented by an agent whose business it is to publish police regulations and ordinances for the execution of the laws, or to keep up a regular communication with the officers of the township and the county, or to inspect their conduct, direct their actions, or reprimand their faults. There is no point that serves as a center to the radii of the administration.

How, then, can the government be conducted on a uniform plan? And how is the compliance of the counties and their magistrates or the townships and their officers enforced? In the New England states the legislative authority embraces more subjects than it does in France; the legislator penetrates to the very core of the administration; the law descends to minute details; the same enactment prescribes

---

[18] Thus, licenses are granted only to such persons as can produce a certificate of good conduct from the selectmen. If the selectmen refuse to give the certificate, the party may appeal to the justices assembled in the court of sessions, and they may grant the license. See ibid., law of March 12, 1808, Vol. II, p. 186. The townships have the right to make by-laws, and to enforce them by fines, which are fixed by law; but these by-laws must be approved by the court of sessions. Ibid., law of March 25, 1786, Vol. I, p. 254.

[19] In Massachusetts the county magistrates are frequently called upon to investigate the acts of the town magistrates; but it will be shown farther on that this investigation is a consequence, not of their administrative, but of their judicial power.

[20] Thus, the town school committees are obliged to make an annual report to the secretary of the state on the condition of the schools. See ibid., law of March 10, 1827, Vol. III, p. 183.

the principle and the method of its application, and thus imposes a multitude of strict and rigorously defined obligations on the secondary bodies and functionaries of the state. The consequence of this is that if all the secondary functionaries of the administration conform to the law, society in all its branches proceeds with the greatest uniformity. The difficulty remains, how to compel the secondary bodies and administrative officials to conform to the law. It may be affirmed in general that society has only two methods of enforcing the execution of the laws: a discretionary power may be entrusted to one of them of directing all the others and of removing them in case of disobedience; or the courts of justice may be required to inflict judicial penalties on the offender. But these two methods are not always available.

The right of directing a civil officer presupposes that of cashiering him if he does not obey orders, and of rewarding him by promotion if he fulfills his duties with propriety. But an elected magistrate cannot be cashiered or promoted. All elective functions are inalienable until their term expires. In fact, the elected magistrate has nothing to expect or to fear except from his constituents; and when all public offices are filled by ballot, there can be no series of official dignities, because the double right of commanding and of enforcing obedience can never be vested in the same person, and because the power of issuing an order can never be joined to that of inflicting a punishment or bestowing a reward.

The communities, therefore, in which the secondary officials of the government are elected are inevitably obliged to make great use of judicial penalties as a means of administration. This is not evident at first sight; for those in power are apt to look upon the institution of elective officials as one concession, and the subjection of the elected magistrate to the judges of the land as another. They are equally averse to both these innovations; and as they are more pressingly solicited to grant the former than the latter, they accede to the election of the magistrate and leave him independent of the judicial power. Nevertheless, the second of these measures is the only thing that can possibly counterbalance the first; and it will be found that an elective authority that is not subject to judicial power will sooner or later either elude all control or be destroyed. The courts of justice are the only possible medium between the central power and the administrative bodies; they alone can compel the elected functionary to obey, without violating the rights of the elector. The extension of judicial power in the political world ought therefore to be in the exact ratio of the extension of elective power; if these two institutions do not go hand in hand, the state must fall into anarchy or into servitude.

It has always been remarked that judicial habits do not render men especially fitted for the exercise of administrative authority. The Americans have borrowed from their fathers, the English, the idea of an institution that is unknown on the continent of Europe: I allude to that of justices of the peace.

The justice of the peace is a sort of middle term between the magistrate and the man of the world, between the civil officer and the judge. A justice of the peace is a well-informed citizen, though he is not necessarily learned in the law. His office simply obliges him to execute the police regulations of society, a task in which good sense and integrity are of more avail than legal science. The justice introduces into the administration, when he takes part in it, a certain taste for established forms and publicity, which renders him a most unserviceable instrument for despotism; and, on the other hand, he is not a slave of those legal superstitions which render judges unfit members of a government. The Americans have adopted the English system of justices of the peace, depriving it of the aristocratic character that distinguishes it in the mother country. The governor of Massachusetts[21] appoints a certain number of justices of the peace in every county, whose functions last seven years.[22] He further designates three individuals from the whole body of justices, who form in each county what is called the court of sessions. The justices take a personal share in the public administration; they are sometimes entrusted with administrative functions in conjunction with elected officers;[23] they sometimes constitute a tribunal before

[21] Later on we shall see the nature of the governor's functions; here it is enough to note that the governor represents the entire executive power of the state.

[22] See Constitution of Massachusetts, Chap. II, section 1, paragraph 9; Chap. II, paragraph 3.

[23] Thus, as one example among many others, a stranger arrives in a township from a country where a contagious disease prevails, and he falls ill. Two justices of the peace can, with the assent of the selectmen, order the sheriff of the county to remove and take

which the magistrates summarily prosecute a refractory citizen, or the citizens inform against the abuses of the magistrate. But it is in the court of sessions that they exercise their most important functions. This court meets twice a year, in the county town; in Massachusetts it is empowered to enforce the obedience of most[24] of the public officers.[25] It must be observed that in Massachusetts the court of sessions is at the same time an administrative body, properly so called, and a political tribunal. It has been mentioned that the county is a purely administrative division. The court of sessions presides over that small number of affairs which, as they concern several townships, or all the townships of the county in common, cannot be entrusted to any one of them in particular. In all that concerns county business the duties of the court of sessions are purely administrative; and if in its procedure it occasionally introduces judicial forms, it is only with a view to its own information,[26] or as a guarantee to those for whom it acts. But when the administration of the township is brought before it, it acts as a judicial body and only in some few cases as an administrative body.[27]

The first difficulty is to make the township itself, an almost independent power, obey the general laws of the state.

---

care of him. *Laws of Massachusetts*, law of June 22, 1797, Vol. I, p. 540. In general the justices interfere in all the important acts of the administration and give them a semi-judicial character.

[24] I say *most* of them because certain administrative misdemeanors are brought before the ordinary tribunals. If, for instance, a township refuses to make the necessary expenditure for its schools, or to name a school committee, it is liable to a heavy fine. But this penalty is pronounced by the supreme judicial court or the court of common pleas. See ibid., law of March 10, 1827, Vol. III, p. 190. For the failure of the town to make provision for military supplies, see ibid., law of February 21, 1822, Vol. II, p. 570.

[25] In their individual capacity the justices of the peace take a part in the business of the counties and townships. In general the most important acts of the town can be performed only with the concurrence of some one of them.

[26] These affairs may be brought under the following heads: (1) the erection of prisons and courts of justice; (2) the county budget, which is afterwards voted by the state legislature; (3) the distribution of the taxes so voted; (4) grants of certain patents; (5) the building and repair of the county roads.

[27] Thus, when a road is under consideration, the court of sessions decides almost all questions regarding the execution of the project with the aid of a jury.

I have stated that assessors are annually named by the town meetings to levy the taxes. If a township attempts to evade the payment of the taxes by neglecting to name its assessors, the court of sessions condemns it to a heavy fine.[28] The fine is levied on each of the inhabitants; and the sheriff of the county, who is the officer of justice, executes the mandate. Thus in the United States, government authority, anxious to keep out of sight, hides itself under the forms of a judicial sentence; and its influence is at the same time fortified by that irresistible power which men attribute to the formalities of law.

These proceedings are easy to follow and to understand. The demands made upon a township are, in general, plain and accurately defined; they consist in a simple fact, or in a principle without its application in detail.[29] But the difficulty begins when it is not the obedience of the township, but that of the town officers, that is to be enforced. All the reprehensible actions which a public functionary can commit are reducible to the following heads:

He may execute the law without energy or zeal;

He may neglect what the law requires;

He may do what the law forbids.

Only the last two violations of duty can come before a legal tribunal; a positive and appreciable fact is the indispensable foundation of an action at law. Thus, if the selectmen omit the legal formalities usual at town elections, they may be fined.[30] But when the officer performs his duty unskillfully, or obeys the letter of the law without zeal or energy, he is out of the reach of judicial interference. The court of sessions, even when clothed with administrative powers, is in this case unable to enforce a more satisfactory obedience. The fear of removal is the only check to these

[28] See *Laws of Massachusetts,* law of February 20, 1786, Vol. I, p. 217.

[29] There is an indirect method of enforcing the obedience of a township. Suppose that the funds which the law demands for the maintenance of the roads have not been voted; the town surveyor is then authorized, *ex officio,* to levy the supplies. As he is personally responsible to private individuals for the state of the roads, and indictable before the court of sessions, he is sure to employ the extraordinary right which the law gives him against the township. Thus, by threatening the officer, the court of sessions exacts compliance from the town. See ibid., law of March 5, 1787, Vol. I, p. 305.

[30] *Laws of Massachusetts,* Vol. II, p. 45.

quasi-offenses, and the court of sessions does not originate the town authorities; it cannot remove functionaries whom it does not appoint. Moreover, a perpetual supervision would be necessary to convict the officer of negligence or luke-warmness. Now, the court of sessions sits but twice a year, and then only judges such offenses as are brought to its notice. The only security for that active and enlightened obedience which a court of justice cannot enforce upon pub-lic functionaries lies in their arbitrary removal from office. In France this final security is exercised by the *heads of the administration;* in America it is obtained through the prin-ciple of *election.*

Thus, to recapitulate in a few words what I have described:

If a public officer in New England commits a *crime* in the exercise of his functions, the ordinary courts of justice are *always* called upon to punish him.

If he commits a *fault in his administrative capacity,* a purely administrative tribunal is empowered to punish him; and if the affair is important or urgent, the judge does what the functionary should have done.[31]

Lastly, if the same individual is guilty of one of those in-tangible offenses which human justice can neither define nor appreciate, he annually appears before a tribunal from which there is no appeal, which can at once reduce him to insignificance and deprive him of his charge. This system undoubtedly possesses great advantages, but its execution is attended with a practical difficulty, which it is important to point out.

I have already observed that the administrative tribunal which is called the court of sessions has no right of inspec-tion over the town officers. It can interfere only when the conduct of a magistrate is specially brought under its notice; and this is the delicate part of the system. The Americans of New England have no public prosecutor for the court of sessions,[32] and it may readily be perceived that it would be

[31] If, for instance, a township persists in refusing to name its assessors, the court of sessions nominates them; and the magis-trates thus appointed are invested with the same authority as elected officers. See ibid., the law of February 20, 1787, previ-ously cited.

[32] I say the court of sessions because in common courts there is an officer who exercises some of the functions of a public prose-cutor.

difficult to create one. If an accusing magistrate had merely been appointed in the chief town of each county and had been unassisted by agents in the townships, he would not have been better acquainted with what was going on in the county than the members of the court of sessions. But to appoint his agents in each township would have been to center in his person the most formidable of powers, that of a judicial administration. Moreover, laws are the children of habit, and nothing of the kind exists in the legislation of England. The Americans have therefore divided the offices of inspection and complaint, as well as all the other functions of the administration. Grand jurors are bound by the law to apprise the court to which they belong of all the misdemeanors which may have been committed in their county.[33] There are certain great offenses that are officially prosecuted by the state;[34] but more frequently the task of punishing delinquents devolves upon the fiscal officer, whose province it is to receive the fine; thus the treasurer of the township is charged with the prosecution of such administrative offenses as fall under his notice. But a more especial appeal is made by American legislation to the private interest of each citizen;[35] and this great principle is constantly to be met with in studying the laws of the United States. American legislators are more apt to give men credit for intelligence than for honesty; and they rely not a little on personal interest for the execution of the laws. When an individual is really and sensibly injured by an administrative abuse, his personal interest is a guarantee that he will prosecute. But if a legal formality be required which, however advantageous to the community, is of small importance to individuals, plaintiffs may be less easily found; and thus, by a tacit agreement, the laws may fall into disuse. Reduced by their system to this extremity, the Americans are obliged to encourage informers by bestowing on them a portion of the

[33] The grand jurors are, for instance, bound to inform the court of the bad state of the roads. *Laws of Massachusetts,* Vol. I, p. 308.

[34] If, for instance, the treasurer of the county holds back his accounts. Ibid., Vol. I, p. 400.

[35] Thus, to take one example out of a thousand, if a private individual breaks his carriage or is injured in consequence of the badness of a road, he can sue the township or the county for damages at the sessions. Ibid., Vol. I, p. 309.

penalty in certain cases;[36] and they thus ensure the execution of the laws by the dangerous expedient of degrading the morals of the people.

Above the county magistrates there is, properly speaking, no administrative power, but only a power of government.

GENERAL REMARKS ON ADMINISTRATION IN THE UNITED STATES.

Differences of the states of the Union in their systems of administration—Activity and perfection of the town authorities decreases towards the South—Power of the magistrates increases; that of the voter diminishes—Administration passes from the township to the county—States of New York; Ohio; Pennsylvania—Principles of administration applicable to the whole Union—Election of public officers, and inalienability of their functions—Absence of gradation of ranks—Introduction of judicial procedures into the administration.

I HAVE already said that, after examining the constitution of the township and the county of New England in detail, I should take a general view of the remainder of the Union. Townships and town arrangements exist in every state, but in no other part of the Union is a township to be met with precisely similar to those of New England. The farther we go towards the South, the less active does the business of the township or parish become; it has fewer magistrates, duties, and rights; the population exercises a less immediate influence on affairs; town meetings are less frequent, and the subjects of debate less numerous. The power of the elected magistrate is augmented and that of the voter diminished, while the public spirit of the local communities

[36] In cases of invasion or insurrection, if the town officers neglect to furnish the necessary stores and ammunition for the militia, the township may be condemned to a fine of from 1,000 to 2,700 francs. It may readily be imagined that, in such a case, it might happen that no one would care to prosecute. Hence the law adds that "any citizen may enter a complaint for offences of this kind, and that half the fine shall belong to the prosecutor." See ibid., law of March 6, 1810, Vol. II, p. 236. The same clause is frequently found in the *Laws of Massachusetts*. Not only are private individuals thus incited to prosecute the public officers, but the public officers are encouraged in the same manner to bring the disobedience of private individuals to justice. If a citizen refuses to perform the work which has been assigned to him upon a road, the road-surveyor may prosecute him, and, if he is convicted, the surveyor receives half the penalty for himself. See the law previously cited, Vol. I, p. 308.

is less excited and less influential.[37] These differences may be perceived to a certain extent in the state of New York; they are very evident in Pennsylvania; but they become less striking as we advance to the Northwest. The majority of the immigrants who settle in the Northwestern states are natives of New England, and they carry the administrative habits of their mother country with them into the country which they adopt. A township in Ohio is not unlike a township in Massachusetts.

We have seen that in Massachusetts the mainspring of public administration lies in the township. It forms the common center of the interests and affections of the citizens. But this ceases to be the case as we descend to the states in which knowledge is less generally diffused, and where the township consequently offers fewer guarantees of a wise and active administrative. As we leave New England, therefore, we find that the importance of the town is gradually transferred to the county, which becomes the center of administration and the intermediate power between the government and the citizen. In Massachusetts the business of the county is conducted by the court of sessions, which is composed of a quorum appointed by the governor and his council; but the county has no representative assembly, and its expenditure is voted by the state legislature. In the great state of New York, on the contrary, and in those of Ohio and Pennsylvania, the inhabitants of each county choose a certain number of representatives, who constitute the assembly of the county.[38] The county assembly has the right of

[37] For details, see the *Revised Statutes of the State of New York,* Part I, chap. xi, "Of the powers, duties and privileges of towns," Vol. I, pp. 336–64.

See, in the *Digest of the Laws of Pennsylvania,* the words ASSESSORS, COLLECTOR, CONSTABLES, OVERSEER OF THE POOR, SUPERVISORS OF HIGHWAYS. And in the *Acts of a General Nature of the State of Ohio,* the Act of February 25, 1834, relating to townships, p. 412. And note the special provisions relating to various town officials such as TOWNSHIP'S CLERKS, TRUSTEES, OVERSEERS OF THE POOR, FENCE-VIEWERS, APPRAISERS OF PROPERTY, TOWNSHIP'S TREASURER, SUPERVISORS OF HIGHWAYS.

[38] See the *Revised Statutes of the State of New York,* Part I, chap. xi, Vol. I, p. 340; ibid., chap. xii, p. 366; also in the *Acts of the State of Ohio,* an act relating to county commissioners, February 25, 1824, p. 263. See the *Digest of the Laws of Pennsylvania,* at the words COUNTY-RATES and LEVIES, p. 170.

In the state of New York each township elects a representative, who has a share in the administration of the county as well as in that of the township.

taxing the inhabitants to a certain extent; and it is in this respect a real legislative body. At the same time it exercises an executive power in the county, frequently directs the administration of the townships, and restricts their authority within much narrower bounds than in Massachusetts.

Such are the principal differences which the systems of county and town administration present in the Federal states. Were it my intention to examine the subject in detail, I should have to point out still further differences in the executive details of the several communities. But I have said enough to show the general principles on which the administration in the United States rests. These principles are differently applied; their consequences are more or less numerous in various localities, but they are always substantially the same. The laws differ and their outward features change, but the same spirit animates them. If the township and the county are not everywhere organized in the same manner, it is at least true that in the United States the county and the township are always based upon the same principle: namely, that everyone is the best judge of what concerns himself alone, and the most proper person to supply his own wants. The township and the county are therefore bound to take care of their special interests; the state governs, but does not execute the laws. Exceptions to this principle may be met with, but not a contrary principle.

The first result of this doctrine has been to cause all the magistrates to be chosen either by the inhabitants or at least from among them. As the officers are everywhere elected or appointed for a certain period, it has been impossible to establish the rules of a hierarchy of authorities; there are almost as many independent functionaries as there are functions, and the executive power is disseminated in a multitude of hands. Hence arose the necessity of introducing the control of the courts of justice over the administration, and the system of pecuniary penalties, by which the secondary bodies and their representatives are constrained to obey the laws. One finds this system from one end of the Union to the other. The power of punishing administrative misconduct, or of performing, in urgent cases, administrative acts, has not, however, been bestowed on the same judges in all the states. The Anglo-Americans derived the institution of justices of the peace from a common source; but although it exists in all the states, it is not always turned to the same use. The justices of the peace everywhere participate in the administration of the townships and the counties,[39] either as public officers or as the judges of public misdemeanors; but in most of the states the more important public offenses come under the cognizance of the ordinary tribunals.

Thus the election of public officers, or the inalienability of their functions, the absence of a gradation of powers, and the introduction of judicial action over the secondary branches of the administration are the principal and universal characteristics of the American system from Maine to the Floridas. In some states (and that of New York has advanced most in this direction) traces of a centralized administration begin to be discernible. In the state of New York the officers of the central government exercise, in certain cases, a sort of inspection or control over the secondary bodies.[40] At other times they constitute a sort of court of appeal for the decision of affairs.[41] In the state of New

[39] In some of the Southern states the county courts are charged with all the detail of the administration. See the *Statutes of the State of Tennessee,* at Arts. JUDICIARY, TAXES, etc.

[40] For instance, the direction of public instruction is centralized in the hands of the government. The legislature names the members of the university, who are denominated regents; the governor and lieutenant governor of the state are necessarily of the number. (*Revised Statutes [of the state of New York],* Vol. I, p. 456.) The regents of the university annually visit the colleges and academies and make their report to the legislature. Their superintendence is not inefficient, for several reasons: the colleges, in order to become corporations, stand in need of a charter, which is only granted on the recommendation of the regents; every year funds are distributed by the state, for the encouragement of learning, and the regents are the distributors of this money. See *Revised Statutes,* chap. xv, "Public Instruction," Vol. I, p. 455. The school commissioners are obliged to send an annual report to the general superintendent of the schools. Ibid., p. 488. A similar report is annually made to the same person on the number and condition of the poor. Ibid., p. 631.

[41] If anyone conceives himself to be wronged by the school commissioners (who are town officers), he can appeal to the superintendent of the primary schools, whose decision is final. *Revised Statutes,* Vol. I, p. 487.

Provisions similar to those above cited are to be met with from time to time in the laws of the state of New York; but in general these attempts at centralization are feeble and unproductive. The great authorities of the state have the right of watching and controlling the subordinate agents, without that of rewarding or punishing them. The same individual is never empowered to give an order and to punish disobedience; he has, therefore, the right

York judicial penalties are less used than in other places as a means of administration; and the right of prosecuting the offenses of public officers is vested in fewer hands.[42] The same tendency is faintly observable in some other states;[43] but in general the prominent feature of the administration in the United States is its excessive decentralization.

OF THE STATE

I HAVE described the townships and the administration; it now remains for me to speak of the state and the government. This is ground I may pass over rapidly without fear of being misunderstood, for all I have to say is to be found in the various written constitutions, copies of which are easily to be procured. These constitutions rest upon a simple and rational theory; most of their forms have been adopted by all constitutional nations, and have become familiar to us.

Here, then, I have only to give a brief account; I shall endeavor afterwards to pass judgment upon what I now describe.

LEGISLATIVE POWER OF THE STATE. *Division of the legislative body into two houses—Senate—House of Representatives—Different functions of these two bodies.*

THE LEGISLATIVE power of the state is vested in two assemblies, the first of which generally bears the name of the Senate.

The Senate is commonly a legislative body, but it sometimes becomes an executive and judicial one. It takes part in the government in several ways, according to the consti-

---

of commanding without the means of exacting compliance. In 1830 the Superintendent of Schools, in his annual report to the legislature, complained that several school commissioners, notwithstanding his application, had neglected to furnish him with the accounts which were due. He added that "if this omission continues, I shall be obliged to prosecute them, as the law directs, before the proper tribunals."

[42] Thus, the district attorney is directed to recover all fines below the sum of fifty dollars, unless such a right has been specially awarded to another magistrate. *Revised Statutes,* Part I, chap. x, Vol. I, p. 383.

[43] Several traces of centralization may be discovered in Massachusetts; for instance, the committees of the town schools are directed to make an annual report to the secretary of state. *Laws of Massachusetts,* Vol. I, p. 367.

tution of the different states;[44] but it is in the nomination of public functionaries that it most commonly assumes an executive power. It partakes of judicial power in the trial of certain political offenses, and sometimes also in the decision of certain civil cases.[45] The number of its members is always small.

The other branch of the legislature, which is usually called the House of Representatives, has no share whatever in the administration and takes a part in the judicial power only as it impeaches public functionaries before the Senate.

The members of the two houses are nearly everywhere subject to the same conditions of eligibility. They are chosen in the same manner, and by the same citizens. The only difference which exists between them is that the term for which the Senate is chosen is, in general, longer than that of the House of Representatives. The latter seldom remain in office longer than a year; the former usually sit two or three years.

By granting to the senators the privilege of being chosen for several years, and being renewed seriatim, the law takes care to preserve in the legislative body a nucleus of men already accustomed to public business, and capable of exercising a salutary influence upon the new-comers.

By this separation of the legislative body into two branches, the Americans plainly did not desire to make one house hereditary and the other elective, one aristocratic and the other democratic. It was not their object to create in the one a bulwark to power, while the other represented the interests and passions of the people. The only advantages that result from the present constitution of the two houses in the United States are the division of the legislative power, and the consequent check upon political movements; together with the creation of a tribunal of appeal for the revision of the laws.

Time and experience, however, have convinced the Americans that, even if these are its only advantages, the division of the legislative power is still a principle of the greatest necessity. Pennsylvania was the only one of the United States which at first attempted to establish a single

[44] In Massachusetts the senate is not invested with any administrative functions.

[45] As in the state of New York.

House of Assembly, and Franklin himself was so far carried
away by the logical consequences of the principle of the
sovereignty of the people as to have concurred in the measure; but the Pennsylvanians were soon obliged to change the
law and to create two houses. Thus the principle of the division of the legislative power was finally established, and
its necessity may henceforward be regarded as a demonstrated truth. This theory, nearly unknown to the republics
of antiquity, first introduced into the world almost by accident, like so many other great truths, and misunderstood by
several modern nations, has at length become an axiom in
the political science of the present age.

THE EXECUTIVE POWER OF THE STATE. *Office of governor in
an American state—His relation to the legislature—His
rights and his duties—His dependence on the people.*

THE EXECUTIVE power of the state is *represented* by the governor. It is not by accident that I have used this word; the
governor *represents* this power, although he enjoys but a
portion of its rights. The supreme magistrate, under the
title of governor, is the official moderator and counselor of
the legislature. He is armed with a veto or suspensive power,
which allows him to stop, or at least to retard, its movements at pleasure. He lays the wants of the country before
the legislative body, and points out the means that he thinks
may be usefully employed in providing for them; he is the
natural executor of its decrees in all the undertakings that
interest the nation at large.[46] In the absence of the legislature, the governor is bound to take all necessary steps to
guard the state against violent shocks and unforeseen dangers.

The whole military power of the state is at the disposal
of the governor. He is the commander of the militia and
head of the armed force. When the authority which is by
general consent awarded to the laws is disregarded, the governor puts himself at the head of the armed force of the
state, to quell resistance and restore order.

---

[46] Practically speaking, it is not always the governor who executes the plans of the legislature; it often happens that the latter,
in voting a measure, names special agents to superintend its
execution.

Lastly, the governor takes no share in the administration of the townships and counties, except through the appointment of justices of the peace, whom he cannot afterwards dismiss.[47]

The governor is an elected magistrate, and is generally chosen for one or two years only, so that he always continues to be strictly dependent upon the majority who returned him.

POLITICAL EFFECTS OF DECENTRALIZED ADMINISTRATION IN THE UNITED STATES. *Necessary distinction between a centralized government and a centralized administration—Administration not centralized in the United States: great centralization of the government—Some bad consequences resulting to the United States from the extremely decentralized administration—Administrative advantages of this order of things—The power that administers is less regular, less enlightened, less learned, but much greater than in Europe—Political advantages of this order of things—In the United States the country makes itself felt everywhere—Support given to the government by the community—Provincial institutions more necessary in proportion as the social condition becomes more democratic—Reason for this.*

"CENTRALIZATION" is a word in general and daily use, without any precise meaning being attached to it. Nevertheless, there exist two distinct kinds of centralization, which it is necessary to discriminate with accuracy.

Certain interests are common to all parts of a nation, such as the enactment of its general laws and the maintenance of its foreign relations. Other interests are peculiar to certain parts of the nation, such, for instance, as the business of the several townships. When the power that directs the former or general interests is concentrated in one place or in the same persons, it constitutes a centralized government. To concentrate in like manner in one place the direction of the latter or local interests, constitutes what may be termed a centralized administration.

Upon some points these two kinds of centralization coin-

[47] In some of the states justices of the peace are not appointed by the governor.

cide, but by classifying the objects which fall more particularly within the province of each, they may easily be distinguished.

It is evident that a centralized government acquires immense power when united to centralized administration. Thus combined, it accustoms men to set their own will habitually and completely aside; to submit, not only for once, or upon one point, but in every respect, and at all times. Not only, therefore, does this union of power subdue them compulsorily, but it affects their ordinary habits; it isolates them and then influences each separately.

These two kinds of centralization assist and attract each other, but they must not be supposed to be inseparable. It is impossible to imagine a more completely centralized government than that which existed in France under Louis XIV; when the same individual was the author and the interpreter of the laws, and the representative of France at home and abroad, he was justified in asserting that he constituted the state. Nevertheless, the administration was much less centralized under Louis XIV than it is at the present day.

In England the centralization of the government is carried to great perfection; the state has the compact vigor of one man, and its will puts immense masses in motion and turns its whole power where it pleases. But England, which has done such great things for the last fifty years, has never centralized its administration. Indeed, I cannot conceive that a nation can live and prosper without a powerful centralization of government. But I am of the opinion that a centralized administration is fit only to enervate the nations in which it exists, by incessantly diminishing their local spirit. Although such an administration can bring together at a given moment, on a given point, all the disposable resources of a people, it injures the renewal of those resources. It may ensure a victory in the hour of strife, but it gradually relaxes the sinews of strength. It may help admirably the transient greatness of a man, but not the durable prosperity of a nation.

Observe that whenever it is said that a state cannot act because it is not centralized, it is the centralization of the government that is spoken of. It is frequently asserted, and I assent to the proposition, that the German Empire has never been able to bring all its powers into action. But the

reason is that the state has never been able to enforce obedience to its general laws; the several members of that great
body always claimed the right, or found the means, of refusing their co-operation to the representatives of the common authority, even in the affairs that concerned the mass
of the people; in other words, there was no centralization
of government. The same remark is applicable to the Middle Ages; the cause of all the miseries of feudal society was
that the control, not only of administration, but of government, was divided among a thousand hands and broken up
in a thousand different ways. The want of a centralized government prevented the nations of Europe from advancing
with energy in any straightforward course.

I have shown that in the United States there is no centralized administration and no hierarchy of public functionaries. Local authority has been carried farther than any
European nation could endure without great inconvenience,
and it has even produced some disadvantageous consequences in America. But in the United States the centralization of the government is perfect; and it would be easy to
prove that the national power is more concentrated there
than it has ever been in the old nations of Europe. Not only
is there but one legislative body in each state, not only does
there exist but one source of political authority, but numerous assemblies in districts or counties have not, in general,
been multiplied lest they should be tempted to leave their
administrative duties and interfere with the government. In
America the legislature of each state is supreme; nothing can
impede its authority, neither privileges, nor local immunities, nor personal influence, nor even the empire of reason,
since it represents that majority which claims to be the sole
organ of reason. Its own determination is therefore the only
limit to its action. In juxtaposition with it, and under its
immediate control, is the representative of the executive
power, whose duty it is to constrain the refractory to submit by superior force. The only symptom of weakness lies
in certain details of the action of the government. The
American republics have no standing armies to intimidate
a discontented minority; but as no minority has as yet been
reduced to declare open war, the necessity of an army has
not been felt. The state usually employs the officers of the
township or the county to deal with the citizens. Thus, for

instance, in New England the town assessor fixes the rate of taxes; the town collector receives them; the town treasurer transmits the amount to the public treasury; and the disputes that may arise are brought before the ordinary courts of justice. This method of collecting taxes is slow as well as inconvenient, and it would prove a perpetual hindrance to a government whose pecuniary demands were large. It is desirable that, in whatever materially affects its existence, the government should be served by officers of its own, appointed by itself, removable at its pleasure, and accustomed to rapid methods of proceeding. But it will always be easy for the central government, organized as it is in America, to introduce more energetic and efficacious modes of action according to its wants.

The want of a centralized government will not, then, as has often been asserted, prove the destruction of the republics of the New World; far from the American governments being not sufficiently centralized, I shall prove hereafter that they are too much so. The legislative bodies daily encroach upon the authority of the government, and their tendency, like that of the French Convention, is to appropriate it entirely to themselves. The social power thus centralized is constantly changing hands, because it is subordinate to the power of the people. It often forgets the maxims of wisdom and foresight in the consciousness of its strength. Hence arises its danger. Its vigor, and not its impotence, will probably be the cause of its ultimate destruction.

The system of decentralized administration produces several different effects in America. The Americans seem to me to have overstepped the limits of sound policy in isolating the administration of the government; for order, even in secondary affairs, is a matter of national importance.[48] As the state has no administrative functionaries of its own, sta-

---

[48] The authority that represents the state ought not, I think, to waive the right of inspecting the local administration, even when it does not itself administer. Suppose, for instance, that an agent of the government was stationed at some appointed spot in each county to prosecute the misdemeanors of the town and county officers, would not a more uniform order be the result, without in any way compromising the independence of the township? Nothing of the kind, however, exists in America: there is nothing above the county courts, which have, as it were, only an incidental knowledge of the administrative offenses they ought to repress.

tioned on different points of its territory, to whom it can give a common impulse, the consequence is that it rarely attempts to issue any general police regulations. The want of these regulations is severely felt and is frequently observed by Europeans. The appearance of disorder which prevails on the surface leads one at first to imagine that society is in a state of anarchy; nor does one perceive one's mistake till one has gone deeper into the subject. Certain undertakings are of importance to the whole state; but they cannot be put in execution, because there is no state administration to direct them. Abandoned to the exertions of the towns or counties, under the care of elected and temporary agents, they lead to no result, or at least to no durable benefit.

The partisans of centralization in Europe are wont to maintain that the government can administer the affairs of each locality better than the citizens can do it for themselves. This may be true when the central power is enlightened and the local authorities are ignorant; when it is alert and they are slow; when it is accustomed to act and they to obey. Indeed, it is evident that this double tendency must augment with the increase of centralization, and that the readiness of the one and the incapacity of the others must become more and more prominent. But I deny that it is so when the people are as enlightened, as awake to their interests, and as accustomed to reflect on them as the Americans are. I am persuaded, on the contrary, that in this case the collective strength of the citizens will always conduce more efficaciously to the public welfare than the authority of the government. I know it is difficult to point out with certainty the means of arousing a sleeping population and of giving it passions and knowledge which it does not possess; it is, I am well aware, an arduous task to persuade men to busy themselves about their own affairs. It would frequently be easier to interest them in the punctilios of court etiquette than in the repairs of their common dwelling. But whenever a central administration affects completely to supersede the persons most interested, I believe that it is either misled or desirous to mislead. However enlightened and skillful a central power may be, it cannot of itself embrace all the details of the life of a great nation. Such vigilance exceeds the powers of man. And when it attempts unaided to create and set in motion so many complicated springs, it must submit to a very imperfect result or exhaust itself in bootless efforts.

Centralization easily succeeds, indeed, in subjecting the external actions of men to a certain uniformity, which we come at last to love for its own sake, independently of the objects to which it is applied, like those devotees who worship the statue and forget the deity it represents. Centralization imparts without difficulty an admirable regularity to the routine of business; provides skillfully for the details of the social police; represses small disorders and petty misdemeanors; maintains society in a *status quo* alike secure from improvement and decline; and perpetuates a drowsy regularity in the conduct of affairs which the heads of the administration are wont to call good order and public tranquillity;[49] in short, it excels in prevention, but not in action. Its force deserts it when society is to be profoundly moved, or accelerated in its course; and if once the co-operation of private citizens is necessary to the furtherance of its measures, the secret of its impotence is disclosed. Even while the centralized power, in its despair, invokes the assistance of the citizens, it says to them: "You shall act just as I please, as much as I please, and in the direction which I please. You are to take charge of the details without aspiring to guide the system; you are to work in darkness; and afterwards you may judge my work by its results." These are not the conditions on which the alliance of the human will is to be obtained; it must be free in its gait and responsible for its acts, or (such is the constitution of man) the citizen had rather remain a passive spectator than a dependent actor in schemes with which he is unacquainted.

It is undeniable that the want of those uniform regulations which control the conduct of every inhabitant of France is not infrequently felt in the United States. Gross instances of social indifference and neglect are to be met with; and from time to time disgraceful blemishes are seen,

[49] China appears to me to present the most perfect instance of that species of well-being which a highly centralized administration may furnish to its subjects. Travelers assure us that the Chinese have tranquillity without happiness, industry without improvement, stability without strength, and public order without public morality. The condition of society there is always tolerable, never excellent. I imagine that when China is opened to European observation, it will be found to contain the most perfect model of a centralized administration that exists in the universe.

in complete contrast with the surrounding civilization. Useful undertakings which cannot succeed without perpetual attention and rigorous exactitude are frequently abandoned; for in America, as well as in other countries, the people proceed by sudden impulses and momentary exertions. The European, accustomed to find a functionary always at hand to interfere with all he undertakes, reconciles himself with difficulty to the complex mechanism of the administration of the townships. In general it may be affirmed that the lesser details of the police, which render life easy and comfortable, are neglected in America, but that the essential guarantees of man in society are as strong there as elsewhere. In America the power that conducts the administration is far less regular, less enlightened, and less skillful, but a hundredfold greater than in Europe. In no country in the world do the citizens make such exertions for the common weal. I know of no people who have established schools so numerous and efficacious, places of public worship better suited to the wants of the inhabitants, or roads kept in better repair. Uniformity or permanence of design, the minute arrangement of details,[50] and the perfection of administrative system must not be sought for in the United States;

[50] A writer of talent who, in a comparison of the finances of France with those of the United States, has proved that ingenuity cannot always supply the place of the knowledge of facts, justly reproaches the Americans for the sort of confusion that exists in the accounts of the expenditure in the townships; and after giving the model of a departmental budget in France, he adds: "We are indebted to centralization, that admirable invention of a great man, for the order and method which prevail alike in all the municipal budgets, from the largest city to the humblest commune." Whatever may be my admiration of this result, when I see the communes of France, with their excellent system of accounts, plunged into the grossest ignorance of their true interests, and abandoned to so incorrigible an apathy that they seem to vegetate rather than to live; when, on the other hand, I observe the activity, the information, and the spirit of enterprise in those American townships whose budgets are neither methodical nor uniform, I see that society there is always at work. I am struck by the spectacle; for, to my mind, the end of a good government is to ensure the welfare of a people, and not merely to establish order in the midst of its misery. I am therefore led to suppose that the prosperity of the American townships and the apparent confusion of their finances, the distress of the French communes and the perfection of their budget, may be attributable to the same cause. At any rate, I am suspicious of a good that is united with so many evils, and I am not averse to an evil that is compensated by so many benefits.

what we find there is the presence of a power which, if it is somewhat wild, is at least robust, and an existence checkered with accidents, indeed, but full of animation and effort.

Granting, for an instant, that the villages and counties of the United States would be more usefully governed by a central authority which they had never seen than by functionaries taken from among them; admitting, for the sake of argument, that there would be more security in America, and the resources of society would be better employed there, if the whole administration centered in a single arm—still the *political* advantages which the Americans derive from their decentralized system would induce me to prefer it to the contrary plan. It profits me but little, after all, that a vigilant authority always protects the tranquillity of my pleasures and constantly averts all dangers from my path, without my care or concern, if this same authority is the absolute master of my liberty and my life, and if it so monopolizes movement and life that when it languishes everything languishes around it, that when it sleeps everything must sleep, and that when it dies the state itself must perish.

There are countries in Europe where the native considers himself as a kind of settler, indifferent to the fate of the spot which he inhabits. The greatest changes are effected there without his concurrence, and (unless chance may have apprised him of the event) without his knowledge; nay, more, the condition of his village, the police of his street, the repairs of the church or the parsonage, do not concern him; for he looks upon all these things as unconnected with himself and as the property of a powerful stranger whom he calls the government. He has only a life interest in these possessions, without the spirit of ownership or any ideas of improvement. This want of interest in his own affairs goes so far that if his own safety or that of his children is at last endangered, instead of trying to avert the peril, he will fold his arms and wait till the whole nation comes to his aid. This man who has so completely sacrificed his own free will does not, more than any other person, love obedience; he cowers, it is true, before the pettiest officer, but he braves the law with the spirit of a conquered foe as soon as its superior force is withdrawn; he perpetually oscillates between servitude and license.

When a nation has arrived at this state, it must either

change its customs and its laws, or perish; for the source of public virtues is dried up; and though it may contain subjects, it has no citizens. Such communities are a natural prey to foreign conquests; and if they do not wholly disappear from the scene, it is only because they are surrounded by other nations similar or inferior to themselves; it is because they still have an indefinable instinct of patriotism; and an involuntary pride in the name of their country, or a vague reminiscence of its bygone fame, suffices to give them an impulse of self-preservation.

Nor can the prodigious exertions made by certain nations to defend a country in which they had lived, so to speak, as strangers be adduced in favor of such a system; for it will be found that in these cases their main incitement was religion. The permanence, the glory, or the prosperity of the nation had become parts of their faith, and in defending their country, they defended also that Holy City of which they were all citizens. The Turkish tribes have never taken an active share in the conduct of their affairs, but they accomplished stupendous enterprises as long as the victories of the Sultan were triumphs of the Mohammedan faith. In the present age they are in rapid decay because their religion is departing and despotism only remains. Montesquieu, who attributed to absolute power an authority peculiar to itself, did it, as I conceive, an undeserved honor; for despotism, taken by itself, can maintain nothing durable. On close inspection we shall find that religion, and not fear, has ever been the cause of the long-lived prosperity of an absolute government. Do what you may, there is no true power among men except in the free union of their will; and patriotism and religion are the only two motives in the world that can long urge all the people towards the same end.

Laws cannot rekindle an extinguished faith, but men may be interested by the laws in the fate of their country. It depends upon the laws to awaken and direct the vague impulse of patriotism, which never abandons the human heart; and if it be connected with the thoughts, the passions, and the daily habits of life, it may be consolidated into a durable and rational sentiment. Let it not be said that it is too late to make the experiment; for nations do not grow old as men do, and every fresh generation is a new people ready for the care of the legislator.

It is not the *administrative,* but the *political* effects of de-centralization that I most admire in America. In the United States the interests of the country are everywhere kept in view; they are an object of solicitude to the people of the whole Union, and every citizen is as warmly attached to them as if they were his own. He takes pride in the glory of his nation; he boasts of its success, to which he conceives himself to have contributed; and he rejoices in the general prosperity by which he profits. The feeling he entertains towards the state is analogous to that which unites him to his family, and it is by a kind of selfishness that he interests himself in the welfare of his country.

To the European, a public officer represents a superior force; to an American, he represents a right. In America, then, it may be said that no one renders obedience to man, but to justice and to law. If the opinion that the citizen entertains of himself is exaggerated, it is at least salutary; he unhesitatingly confides in his own powers, which appear to him to be all-sufficient. When a private individual meditates an undertaking, however directly connected it may be with the welfare of society, he never thinks of soliciting the co-operation of the government; but he publishes his plan, offers to execute it, courts the assistance of other individuals, and struggles manfully against all obstacles. Undoubtedly he is often less successful than the state might have been in his position; but in the end the sum of these private undertakings far exceeds all that the government could have done.

As the administrative authority is within the reach of the citizens, whom in some degree it represents, it excites neither their jealousy nor hatred; as its resources are limited, everyone feels that he must not rely solely on its aid. Thus when the administration thinks fit to act within its own limits, it is not abandoned to itself, as in Europe; the duties of private citizens are not supposed to have lapsed because the state has come into action, but everyone is ready, on the contrary, to guide and support it. This action of individuals, joined to that of the public authorities, frequently accomplishes what the most energetic centralized administration would be unable to do.[51]

It would be easy to adduce several facts in proof of what I advance, but I had rather give only one, with which I am

[51] See Appendix I.

best acquainted. In America the means that the authorities have at their disposal for the discovery of crimes and the arrest of criminals are few. A state police does not exist, and passports are unknown. The criminal police of the United States cannot be compared with that of France; the magistrates and public agents are not numerous; they do not always initiate the measures for arresting the guilty; and the examinations of prisoners are rapid and oral. Yet I believe that in no country does crime more rarely elude punishment. The reason is that everyone conceives himself to be interested in furnishing evidence of the crime and in seizing the delinquent. During my stay in the United States I witnessed the spontaneous formation of committees in a county for the pursuit and prosecution of a man who had committed a great crime. In Europe a criminal is an unhappy man who is struggling for his life against the agents of power, while the people are merely a spectator of the conflict; in America he is looked upon as an enemy of the human race, and the whole of mankind is against him.

I believe that provincial institutions are useful to all nations, but nowhere do they appear to me to be more necessary than among a democratic people. In an aristocracy order can always be maintained in the midst of liberty; and as the rulers have a great deal to lose, order is to them a matter of great interest. In like manner an aristocracy protects the people from the excesses of despotism, because it always possesses an organized power ready to resist a despot. But a democracy without provincial institutions has no security against these evils. How can a populace unaccustomed to freedom in small concerns learn to use it temperately in great affairs? What resistance can be offered to tyranny in a country where each individual is weak and where the citizens are not united by any common interest? Those who dread the license of the mob and those who fear absolute power ought alike to desire the gradual development of provincial liberties.

I am also convinced that democratic nations are most likely to fall beneath the yoke of a centralized administration, for several reasons, among which is the following:

The constant tendency of these nations is to concentrate all the strength of the government in the hands of the only power that directly represents the people; because beyond the people nothing is to be perceived but a mass of equal individuals. But when the same power already has all the attributes of government, it can scarcely refrain from penetrating into the details of the administration, and an opportunity of doing so is sure to present itself in the long run, as was the case in France. In the French Revolution there were two impulses in opposite directions, which must never be confounded; the one was favorable to liberty, the other to despotism. Under the ancient monarchy the king was the sole author of the laws; and below the power of the sovereign certain vestiges of provincial institutions, half destroyed, were still distinguishable. These provincial institutions were incoherent, ill arranged, and frequently absurd; in the hands of the aristocracy they had sometimes been converted into instruments of oppression. The Revolution declared itself the enemy at once of royalty and of provincial institutions; it confounded in indiscriminate hatred all that had preceded it, despotic power and the checks to its abuses; and its tendency was at once to republicanize and to centralize. This double character of the French Revolution is a fact which has been adroitly handled by the friends of absolute power. Can they be accused of laboring in the cause of despotism when they are defending that centralized administration which was one of the great innovations of the Revolution? [52] In this manner popularity may be united with hostility to the rights of the people, and the secret slave of tyranny may be the professed lover of freedom.

I have visited the two nations in which the system of provincial liberty has been most perfectly established, and I have listened to the opinions of different parties in those countries. In America I met with men who secretly aspired to destroy the democratic institutions of the Union; in England I found others who openly attacked the aristocracy; but I found no one who did not regard provincial independence as a great good. In both countries I heard a thousand different causes assigned for the evils of the state, but the local system was never mentioned among them. I heard citizens attribute the power and prosperity of their country to a multitude of reasons, but they *all* placed the advantages of local institutions in the foremost rank.

Am I to suppose that when men who are naturally so

[52] See Appendix K.

divided on religious opinions and on political theories agree on one point (and that one which they can best judge, as it is one of which they have daily experience) they are all in error? The only nations which deny the ultility of provincial liberties are those which have fewest of them; in other words, only those censure the institution who do not know it.

Chapter VI

JUDICIAL POWER IN THE UNITED STATES, AND ITS INFLUENCE ON POLITICAL SOCIETY

THE ANGLO-AMERICANS have retained the characteristics of judicial power which are common to other nations— They have, however, made it a powerful political organ —How—In what the judicial system of the Anglo-Americans differs from that of all other nations—Why the American judges have the right of declaring laws to be unconstitutional—How they use this right—Precautions taken by the legislator to prevent its abuse.

I HAVE thought it right to devote a separate chapter to the judicial authorities of the United States, lest their great political importance should be lessened in the reader's eyes by merely incidental mention of them. Confederations have existed in other countries besides America; I have seen republics elsewhere than upon the shores of the New World alone: the representative system of government has been adopted in several states of Europe; but I am not aware that any nation of the globe has hitherto organized a judicial power in the same manner as the Americans. The judicial organization of the United States is the institution which a stranger has the greatest difficulty in understanding. He hears the authority of a judge invoked in the political occurrences of every day, and he naturally concludes that in the United States the judges are important political functionaries; nevertheless, when he examines the nature of the tribunals, they offer at the first glance nothing that is contrary to the usual habits and privileges of those bodies; and the magistrates seem to him to interfere in public affairs only by chance, but by a chance that recurs every day.

When the Parliament of Paris remonstrated, or refused to register an edict, or when it summoned a functionary accused of malversation to its bar, its political influence as a judicial body was clearly visible; but nothing of the kind is to be seen in the United States. The Americans have retained all the ordinary characteristics of judicial authority and have carefully restricted its action to the ordinary circle of its functions.

The first characteristic of judicial power in all nations is the duty of arbitration. But rights must be contested in order to warrant the interference of a tribunal; and an action must be brought before the decision of a judge can be had. As long, therefore, as a law is uncontested, the judicial authority is not called upon to discuss it, and it may exist without being perceived. When a judge in a given case attacks a law relating to that case, he extends the circle of his customary duties, without, however, stepping beyond it, since he is in some measure obliged to decide upon the law in order to decide the case. But if he pronounces upon a law without proceeding from a case, he clearly steps beyond his sphere and invades that of the legislative authority.

The second characteristic of judicial power is that it pronounces on special cases, and not upon general principles. If a judge, in deciding a particular point, destroys a general principle by passing a judgment which tends to reject all the inferences from that principle, and consequently to annul it, he remains within the ordinary limits of his functions. But if he directly attacks a general principle without having a particular case in view, he leaves the circle in which all nations have agreed to confine his authority; he assumes a more important and perhaps a more useful influence than that of the magistrate, but he ceases to represent the judicial power.

The third characteristic of the judicial power is that it can act only when it is called upon, or when, in legal phrase, it has taken cognizance of an affair. This characteristic is less general than the other two; but, notwithstanding the exceptions, I think it may be regarded as essential. The judicial power is, by its nature, devoid of action; it must be put in motion in order to produce a result. When it is called upon to repress a crime, it punishes the criminal; when a wrong is to be redressed, it is ready to redress it; when an act requires interpretation, it is prepared to interpret it; but it does not pursue criminals, hunt out wrongs, or examine evidence of its own accord. A judicial functionary who should take the initiative and usurp the censureship of the laws would in some measure do violence to the passive nature of his authority.

The Americans have retained these three distinguishing characteristics of the judicial power: an American judge can pronounce a decision only when litigation has arisen, he is conversant only with special cases, and he cannot act until the cause has been duly brought before the court. His position is therefore exactly the same as that of the magistrates of other nations; and yet he is invested with immense political power. How does this come about? If the sphere of his authority and his means of action are the same as those of other judges, whence does he derive a power which they do not possess? The cause of this difference lies in the simple fact that the Americans have acknowledged the right of judges to found their decisions on the *Constitution* rather than on the *laws*. In other words, they have permitted them not to apply such laws as may appear to them to be unconstitutional.

I am aware that a similar right has been sometimes claimed, but claimed in vain, by courts of justice in other countries; but in America it is recognized by all the authorities; and not a party, not so much as an individual, is found to contest it. This fact can be explained only by the principles of the American constitutions. In France the constitution is, or at least is supposed to be, immutable; and the received theory is that no power has the right of changing any part of it.[1] In England the constitution may change continually,[2] or rather it does not in reality exist; the Parliament is at once a legislative and a constituent assembly. The political theories of America are more simple and more rational An American constitution is not supposed to be immutable, as in France; nor is it susceptible of modification by the ordinary powers of society, as in England. It constitutes a detached whole, which, as it represents the will of the whole people, is no less binding on the legislator than on the private citizen, but which may be altered by the will of the people in predetermined cases, according to established rules. In America the Constitution may therefore vary; but

[1] See Appendix L.
[2] See Appendix M.

as long as it exists, it is the origin of all authority, and the sole vehicle of the predominating force.

It is easy to perceive how these differences must act upon the position and the rights of the judicial bodies in the three countries I have cited. If in France the tribunals were authorized to disobey the laws on the ground of their being opposed to the constitution, the constituent power would in fact be placed in their hands, since they alone would have the right of interpreting a constitution of which no authority could change the terms. They would therefore take the place of the nation and exercise as absolute a sway over society as the inherent weakness of judicial power would allow them to do. Undoubtedly, as the French judges are incompetent to declare a law to be unconstitutional, the power of changing the constitution is indirectly given to the legislative body, since no legal barrier would oppose the alterations that it might prescribe. But it is still better to grant the power of changing the constitution of the people to men who represent (however imperfectly) the will of the people than to men who represent no one but themselves.

It would be still more unreasonable to invest the English judges with the right of resisting the decisions of the legislative body, since the Parliament which makes the laws also makes the constitution; and consequently a law emanating from the three estates of the realm can in no case be unconstitutional. But neither of these remarks is applicable to America.

In the United States the Constitution governs the legislator as much as the private citizen: as it is the first of laws, it cannot be modified by a law; and it is therefore just that the tribunals should obey the Constitution in preference to any law. This condition belongs to the very essence of the judicature; for to select that legal obligation by which he is most strictly bound is in some sort the natural right of every magistrate.

In France the constitution is also the first of laws, and the judges have the same right to take it as the ground of their decisions; but were they to exercise this right, they must perforce encroach on rights more sacred than their own: namely, on those of society, in whose name they are acting. In this case reasons of state clearly prevail over ordinary motives. In America, where the nation can always reduce its magistrates to obedience by changing its Constitution, no danger of this kind is to be feared. Upon this point, therefore, the political and the logical reason agree, and the people as well as the judges preserve their privileges.

Whenever a law that the judge holds to be unconstitutional is invoked in a tribunal of the United States, he may refuse to admit it as a rule; this power is the only one peculiar to the American magistrate, but it gives rise to immense political influence. In truth, few laws can escape the searching analysis of the judicial power for any length of time, for there are few that are not prejudicial to some private interest or other, and none that may not be brought before a court of justice by the choice of parties or by the necessity of the case. But as soon as a judge has refused to apply any given law in a case, that law immediately loses a portion of its moral force. Those to whom it is prejudicial learn that means exist of overcoming its authority, and similar suits are multiplied until it becomes powerless. The alternative, then, is, that the people must alter the Constitution or the legislature must repeal the law. The political power which the Americans have entrusted to their courts of justice is therefore immense, but the evils of this power are considerably diminished by the impossibility of attacking the laws except through the courts of justice. If the judge had been empowered to contest the law on the ground of theoretical generalities, if he were able to take the initiative and to censure the legislator, he would play a prominent political part; and as the champion or the antagonist of a party, he would have brought the hostile passions of the nation into the conflict. But when a judge contests a law in an obscure debate on some particular case, the importance of his attack is concealed from public notice; his decision bears upon the interest of an individual, and the law is slighted only incidentally. Moreover, although it is censured, it is not abolished; its moral force may be diminished, but its authority is not taken away; and its final destruction can be accomplished only by the reiterated attacks of judicial functionaries. It will be seen, also, that by leaving it to private interest to censure the law, and by intimately uniting the trial of the law with the trial of an individual, legislation is protected from wanton assaults and from the daily aggressions of party spirit. The errors of the legislator are exposed only to meet a real want; and it is always a positive and appreciable fact that must serve as the basis of a prosecution.

I am inclined to believe this practice of the American courts to be at once most favorable to liberty and to public order. If the judge could attack the legislator only openly and directly, he would sometimes be afraid to oppose him; and at other times party spirit might encourage him to brave it at every turn. The laws would consequently be attacked when the power from which they emanated was weak, and obeyed when it was strong; that is to say, when it would be useful to respect them, they would often be contested; and when it would be easy to convert them into an instrument of oppression, they would be respected. But the American judge is brought into the political arena independently of his own will. He judges the law only because he is obliged to judge a case. The political question that he is called upon to resolve is connected with the interests of the parties, and he cannot refuse to decide it without a denial of justice. He performs his functions as a citizen by fulfilling the precise duties which belong to his profession as a magistrate. It is true that, upon this system, the judicial censorship of the courts of justice over the legislature cannot extend to all laws indiscriminately, inasmuch as some of them can never give rise to that precise species of contest which is termed a lawsuit; and even when such a contest is possible, it may happen that no one cares to bring it before a court of justice. The Americans have often felt this inconvenience; but they have left the remedy incomplete, lest they should give it an efficacy that might in some cases prove dangerous. Within these limits the power vested in the American courts of justice of pronouncing a statute to be unconstitutional forms one of the most powerful barriers that have ever been devised against the tyranny of political assemblies.

OTHER POWERS GRANTED TO AMERICAN JUDGES. *In the United States all the citizens have the right of indicting the public functionaries before the ordinary tribunals— How they use this right—Art. 75 of the French Constitution of the year VIII—The Americans and the English cannot understand the purport of this article.*

IT is hardly necessary to say that in a free country like America all the citizens have the right of indicting public functionaries before the ordinary tribunals, and that all the judges have the power of convicting public officers. The right granted to the courts of justice of punishing the agents of the executive government when they violate the laws is so natural a one that it cannot be looked upon as an extraordinary privilege. Nor do the springs of government appear to me to be weakened in the United States by rendering all public officers responsible to the tribunals. The Americans seem, on the contrary, to have increased by this means that respect which is due to the authorities, and at the same time to have made these authorities more careful not to offend. I was struck by the small number of political trials that occur in the United States, but I had no difficulty in accounting for this circumstance. A prosecution, of whatever nature it may be, is always a difficult and expensive undertaking. It is easy to attack a public man in the journals, but the motives for bringing him before the tribunals must be serious. A solid ground of complaint must exist before anyone thinks of prosecuting a public officer, and these officers are careful not to furnish such grounds of complaint when they are afraid of being prosecuted.

This does not depend upon the republican form of American institutions, for the same thing happens in England. These two nations do not regard the impeachment of the principal officers of state as the guarantee of their independence. But they hold that it is rather by minor prosecutions, which the humblest citizen can institute at any time, that liberty is protected, and not by those great judicial procedures which are rarely employed until it is too late.

In the Middle Ages, when it was very difficult to reach offenders, the judges inflicted frightful punishments on the few who were arrested; but this did not diminish the number of crimes. It has since been discovered that when justice is more certain and more mild, it is more efficacious. The English and the Americans hold that tyranny and oppression are to be treated like any other crime, by lessening the penalty and facilitating conviction.

In the year VIII of the French Republic a constitution was drawn up in which the following clause was introduced: "Art. 75. All the agents of the government below the rank of ministers can be prosecuted for offenses relating to their several functions only by virtue of a decree of the council of state; in which case the prosecution takes place before the ordinary tribunals." This clause survived the Constitution of the year VIII and is still maintained, in spite of the just complaints of the nation. I have always found a difficulty in explaining its meaning to Englishmen or Americans, and have hardly understood it myself. They at once perceived that, the council of state in France being a great tribunal established in the center of the kingdom, it was a sort of tyranny to send all complainants before it as a preliminary step. But when I told them that the council of state was not a judicial body in the common sense of the term, but an administrative council composed of men dependent on the crown, so that the king, after having ordered one of his servants, called a prefect, to commit an injustice, has the power of commanding another of his servants, called a councillor of state, to prevent the former from being punished. When I showed them that the citizen who has been injured by an order of the sovereign is obliged to ask the sovereign's permission to obtain redress, they refused to credit so flagrant an abuse and were tempted to accuse me of falsehood or ignorance. It frequently happened before the Revolution that a parliament issued a warrant against a public officer who had committed an offense. Sometimes the royal authority intervened and quashed the proceedings. Despotism then showed itself openly, and men obeyed it only by submitting to superior force. It is painful to perceive how much lower we are sunk than our forefathers, since we allow things to pass, under the color of justice and the sanction of law, which violence alone imposed upon them.

Chapter VII

POLITICAL JURISDICTION IN THE UNITED STATES

DEFINITION of political jurisdiction—What is understood by political jurisdiction in France, in England, and in the United States—In America the political judge has to do only with public officers—He more frequently decrees removal from office than an ordinary penalty —Political jurisdiction as it exists in the United States is, notwithstanding its mildness, and perhaps in consequence of that mildness, a most powerful instrument in the hands of the majority.

I UNDERSTAND by political jurisdiction that temporary right of pronouncing a legal decision with which a political body may be invested.

In absolute governments it is useless to introduce any extraordinary forms of procedure; the prince, in whose name an offender is prosecuted, is as much the sovereign of the courts of justice as of everything else, and the idea that is entertained of his power is of itself a sufficient security. The only thing he has to fear is that the external formalities of justice should be neglected and that his authority should be dishonored, from a wish to strengthen it. But in most free countries, in which the majority can never have the same influence over the tribunals as an absolute monarch, the judicial power has occasionally been vested for a time in the representatives of the people. It has been thought better temporarily to merge the functions of the different authorities than to violate the necessary principle of the unity of government.

England, France, and the United States have established this political jurisdiction by law; and it is curious to see the different use that these three great nations have made of it. In England and in France the House of Lords and the

Chamber of Peers constitute the highest criminal court[1] of their respective nations; and although they do not habitually try all political offenses, they are competent to try them all. Another political body has the right of bringing the accusation before the Peers; the only difference which exists between the two countries in this respect is that in England the Commons may impeach whomsoever they please before the Lords, while in France the Deputies can employ this mode of prosecution only against the ministers of the crown. In both countries the upper house may make use of all the existing penal laws of the nation to punish the delinquents.

In the United States as well as in Europe one branch of the legislature is authorized to impeach and the other to judge: the House of Representatives arraigns the offender, and the Senate punishes him. But the Senate can try only such persons as are brought before it by the House of Representatives, and those persons must belong to the class of public functionaries. Thus the jurisdiction of the Senate is less extensive than that of the Peers of France, while the right of impeachment by the Representatives is more general than that of the Deputies. But the great difference which exists between Europe and America is that in Europe the political tribunals can apply all the enactments of the penal code, while in America, when they have deprived the offender of his official rank and have declared him incapable of filling any political office for the future, their jurisdiction terminates and that of the ordinary tribunals begins.

Suppose, for instance, that the President of the United States has committed the crime of high treason; the House of Representatives impeaches him, and the Senate degrades him from office; he must then be tried by a jury, which alone can deprive him of liberty or life. This accurately illustrates the subject we are treating. The political jurisdiction that is established by the laws of Europe is intended to reach great offenders, whatever may be their birth, their rank, or their power in the state; and to this end all the privileges of a court of justice are temporarily given to a great political assembly. The legislator is then transformed into a magistrate; he is called upon to prove, to classify,

---

[1] The House of Lords in England is also the court of last resort in certain civil cases. See Blackstone, Bk. III, ch. 4.

and to punish the offense; and as he exercises all the authority of a judge, the law imposes upon him all the duties of that high office and requires all the formalities of justice. When a public functionary is impeached before an English or a French political tribunal and is found guilty, the sentence deprives him *ipso facto* of his functions and may pronounce him incapable of resuming them or any others for the future. But in this case the political interdict is a consequence of the sentence, and not the sentence itself. In Europe, then, the sentence of a political tribunal is a judicial verdict rather than an administrative measure. In the United States the contrary takes place; and although the decision of the Senate is judicial in its form, since the Senators are obliged to comply with the rules and formalities of a court of justice; although it is, judicial also, in respect to the motives on which it is founded, since the Senate is generally obliged to take an offense at common law as the basis of its sentence; yet the political judgment is rather an administrative than a judicial act. If it had been the intention of the American legislator really to invest a political body with great judicial authority, its action would not have been limited to public functionaries, since the most dangerous enemies of the state may not have any public functions; and this is especially true in republics, where party influence has the most force and where the strength of many a leader is increased by his exercising no legitimate power.

If the American legislator had wished to give society itself the means of preventing great offenses by the fear of punishment, according to the practice of ordinary justice, all the resources of the penal code would have been given to the political tribunals. But he gave them only an imperfect weapon, which can never reach the most dangerous offenders, since men who aim at the entire subversion of the laws are not likely to murmur at a political interdict.

The main object of the political jurisdiction that obtains in the United States is therefore to take away the power from him who would make a bad use of it and to prevent him from ever acquiring it again. This is evidently an administrative measure, sanctioned by the formalities of a judicial decision. In this matter the Americans have created a mixed system; they have surrounded the act that removes a public functionary with all the securities of a political trial, and they have deprived political condemnations of their severest penalties. Every link of the system may easily be traced from this point; we at once perceive why the American constitutions subject all the civil functionaries to the jurisdiction of the Senate, while the military, whose crimes are nevertheless more formidable, are exempted from that tribunal. In the civil service none of the American functionaries can be said to be removable; the places that some of them occupy are inalienable, and the others are chosen for a term which cannot be shortened. It is therefore necessary to try them all in order to deprive them of their authority. But military officers are dependent on the chief magistrate of the state, who is himself a civil functionary; and the decision that condemns him is a blow to them all.[2]

If we now compare the American and the European systems, we shall meet with differences no less striking in the effects which each of them produces or may produce. In France and England the jurisdiction of political bodies is looked upon as an extraordinary resource, which is only to be employed in order to rescue society from unwonted dangers. It is not to be denied that these tribunals, as they are constituted in Europe, violate the conservative principle of the division of powers in the state and threaten incessantly the lives and liberties of the subject. The same political jurisdiction in the United States is only indirectly hostile to the division of powers; it cannot menace the lives of the citizens, and it does not hover, as in Europe, over the heads of the whole community, since it reaches those only who have voluntarily submitted to its authority by accepting office. It is at the same time less formidable and less efficacious; indeed, it has not been considered by the legislators of the United States as an extreme remedy for the more violent evils of society, but as an ordinary means of government. In this respect it probably exercises more real influence on the social body in America than in Europe. We must not be misled by the apparent mildness of American legislation in all that relates to political jurisdiction. It is to be observed, in the first place, that in the United States the tribunal that passes judgment is composed of the same ele-

---

[2] An officer cannot be removed from his grade, but he can be relieved of his command.

ments, and subject to the same influences, as the body which impeaches the offender, and that this gives an almost irresistible impulse to the vindictive passions of parties. If political judges in the United States cannot inflict such heavy penalties as those in Europe, there is the less chance of their acquitting an offender; the conviction, if it is less formidable, is more certain. The principal object of the political tribunals of Europe is to punish the offender; of those in America, to deprive him of his power. A political sentence in the United States may therefore be looked upon as a preventive measure; and there is no reason for tying down the judges to the exact definitions of criminal law. Nothing can be more alarming than the vagueness with which political offenses, properly so called, are described in the laws of America. Article II, Section 4 of the Constitution of the United States runs thus: "The President, Vice President, and all civil officers of the United States shall be removed from office on impeachment for, and conviction of, treason, bribery, *or other high crimes and misdemeanors.*" Many of the constitutions of the states are even less explicit. "Public officers," says the Constitution of Massachusetts, "shall be impeached for misconduct or maladministration." [3] The Constitution of Virginia declares that "all the civil officers who shall have offended against the State by maladministration, corruption, or other high crimes, may be impeached by the House of Delegates." In some of the states the constitutions do not specify any offenses, in order to subject the public functionaries to an unlimited responsibility. [4] I venture to affirm that it is precisely their mildness that renders the American laws so formidable in this respect. I have shown that in Europe the removal of a functionary and his political disqualification are the consequences of the penalty he is to undergo, and that in America they constitute the penalty itself. The consequence is that in Europe political tribunals are invested with terrible powers which they are afraid to use, and the fear of punishing too much hinders them from punishing at all. But in America no one hesitates to inflict a penalty from which humanity does not recoil. To condemn a political opponent to death in order to deprive

[3] Chap. I, section 2, § 8.
[4] See the Constitutions of Illinois, Maine, Connecticut, and Georgia.

him of his power is to commit what all the world would execrate as a horrible assassination, but to declare that opponent unworthy to exercise that authority and to deprive him of it, leaving him uninjured in life and limb, may seem to be the fair issue of the struggle. But this sentence, which it is so easy to pronounce, is not the less fatally severe to most of those upon whom it is inflicted. Great criminals may undoubtedly brave its vain rigor, but ordinary offenders will dread it as a condemnation that destroys their position in the world, casts a blight upon their honor, and condemns them to a shameful inactivity worse than death. In the United States the influence exercised upon the progress of society by the jurisdiction of political bodies is the more powerful in proportion as it seems less frightful. It does not directly coerce the subject, but it renders the majority more absolute over those in power; it does not give to the legislature an unbounded authority that can be exerted only at some great crisis, but it establishes a temperate and regular influence, which is at all times available. If the power is decreased, it can, on the other hand, be more conveniently employed, and more easily abused. By preventing political tribunals from inflicting judicial punishments, the Americans seem to have eluded the worst consequences of legislative tyranny rather than tyranny itself; and I am not sure that political jurisdiction, as it is constituted in the United States, is not, all things considered, the most formidable weapon that has ever been placed in the grasp of a majority. When the American republics begin to degenerate, it will be easy to verify the truth of this observation by remarking whether the number of political impeachments is increased.[5]

[5] See Appendix N.

Chapter VIII

THE FEDERAL CONSTITUTION

I HAVE hitherto considered each state as a separate whole and have explained the different springs which the people there put in motion, and the different means of action which it employs. But all the states which I have considered as independent are yet forced to submit, in certain cases, to the supreme authority of the Union. The time has now come to examine the portion of sovereignty that has been granted to the Union, and to cast a rapid glance over the Federal Constitution.

HISTORY OF THE FEDERAL CONSTITUTION. *Origin of the first Union—Its weakness—Congress appeals to the constituent authority—Interval of two years between this appeal and the promulgation of the new Constitution.*

THE THIRTEEN colonies, which simultaneously threw off the yoke of England towards the end of the last century, had, as I have already said, the same religion, the same language, the same customs, and almost the same laws; they were struggling against a common enemy; and these reasons were sufficiently strong to unite them to one another and to consolidate them into one nation. But as each of them had always had a separate existence and a government within its reach, separate interests and peculiar customs had sprung up which were opposed to such a compact and intimate union as would have absorbed the individual importance of each in the general importance of all. Hence arose two opposite tendencies, the one prompting the Anglo-Americans to unite, the other to divide, their strength.

As long as the war with the mother country lasted, the principle of union was kept alive by necessity; and although the laws that constituted it were defective, the common tie subsisted in spite of their imperfections.[1] But no sooner was

[1] See the Articles of the first Confederation, formed in 1778. This Constitution was not adopted by all the states until 1781. See also the analysis given of this Constitution in *The Federalist*,

peace concluded than the faults of this legislation became manifest, and the state seemed to be suddenly dissolved. Each colony became an independent republic, and assumed an absolute sovereignty. The Federal government, condemned to impotence by its Constitution and no longer sustained by the presence of a common danger, witnessed the outrages offered to its flag by the great nations of Europe, while it was scarcely able to maintain its ground against the Indian tribes, and to pay the interest of the debt which had been contracted during the War of Independence. It was already on the verge of destruction when it officially proclaimed its inability to conduct the government and appealed to the constituent authority.[2]

If America ever approached (for however brief a time) that lofty pinnacle of glory to which the proud imagination of its inhabitants is wont to point, it was at this solemn moment, when the national power abdicated, as it were, its authority. All ages have furnished the spectacle of a people struggling with energy to win its independence; and the efforts of the Americans in throwing off the English yoke have been considerably exaggerated. Separated from their enemies by three thousand miles of ocean, and backed by a powerful ally, the United States owed their victory much more to their geographical position than to the valor of their armies or the patriotism of their citizens. It would be ridiculous to compare the American war to the wars of the French Revolution, or the efforts of the Americans to those of the French when France, attacked by the whole of Europe, without money, without credit, without allies, threw forward a twentieth part of her population to meet her enemies and with one hand carried the torch of revolution beyond the frontiers, while she stifled with the other a flame that was devouring the country within. But it is new in the history of society to see a great people turn a calm and scrutinizing eye upon itself when apprised by the legislature that the wheels of its government are stopped, to see it carefully examine the extent of the evil, and patiently wait two whole years until a remedy is discovered, to which

---

from No. 15 to No. 22 inclusive, and Story's *Commentaries on the Constitution of the United States,* pp. 85–115.

[2] Congress made this declaration on February 21, 1787.

it voluntarily submitted without its costing a tear or a drop of blood from mankind.

When the inadequacy of the first Constitution was discovered, America had the double advantage of that calm which had succeeded the effervescence of the Revolution, and of the aid of those great men whom the Revolution had created. The assembly which accepted the task of composing the second Constitution was small;[3] but George Washington was its President, and it contained the finest minds and the noblest characters that had ever appeared in the New World. This national Convention, after long and mature deliberation, offered for the acceptance of the people the body of general laws which still rules the Union. All the states adopted it successively.[4] The new Federal government commenced its functions in 1789, after an interregnum of two years. The Revolution of America terminated precisely when that of France began.

SUMMARY OF THE FEDERAL CONSTITUTION. *Division of authority between the Federal government and the states— The government of the states is the rule, the Federal government the exception.*

THE FIRST question which awaited the Americans was so to divide the sovereignty that each of the different states which composed the Union should continue to govern itself in all that concerned its internal prosperity, while the entire nation, represented by the Union, should continue to form a compact body and to provide for all general exigencies. The problem was a complex and difficult one. It was as impossible to determine beforehand, with any degree of accuracy, the share of authority that each of the two governments was to enjoy as to foresee all the incidents in the life of a nation.

The obligations and the claims of the Federal government were simple and easily definable because the Union had been formed with the express purpose of meeting certain great general wants; but the claims and obligations of the

---

[3] It consisted of fifty-five members; Washington, Madison, Hamilton, and the two Morrises were among the number.

[4] It was not adopted by the legislatures, but representatives were elected by the people for this sole purpose; and the new Constitution was discussed at length in each of these assemblies.

individual states, on the other hand, were complicated and various because their government had penetrated into all the details of social life. The attributes of the Federal government were therefore carefully defined, and all that was not included among them was declared to remain to the governments of the several states. Thus the government of the states remained the rule, and that of the confederation was the exception.[5]

But as it was foreseen that, in practice, questions might arise as to the exact limits of this exceptional authority, and it would be dangerous to submit these questions to the decision of the ordinary courts of justice, established in the different states by the states themselves, a high Federal court was created,[6] one of whose duties was to maintain the balance of power between the two rival governments as it had been established by the Constitution.[7]

[5] See amendment to the Federal Constitution; *The Federalist*, No. 31; Story, p. 711; Kent's *Commentaries*, Vol. I, p. 364. It is to be observed that whenever the *exclusive* right of regulating certain matters is not reserved to Congress by the Constitution, the states may legislate concerning them till Congress sees fit to act. For instance, Congress has the right of making a general law on bankruptcy, which, however, it has not done. Each state is then at liberty to make such a law for itself. This point, however, has been established only after discussion in the law courts, and may be said to belong more properly to jurisprudence.

[6] The action of this court is indirect, as I shall hereafter show.

[7] It is thus that *The Federalist*, No. 45, explains this division of sovereignty between the Union and the states: "The powers delegated by the Constitution to the Federal government are few and defined. Those which are to remain in the State governments are numerous and indefinite. The former will be exercised principally on external objects, as war, peace, negotiation, and foreign commerce. The powers reserved to the several States will extend to all the objects which, in the ordinary course of affairs, concern the internal order and prosperity of the State."

I shall often have occasion to quote *The Federalist* in this work. When the bill which has since become the Constitution of the United States was before the people and the discussions were still pending, three men who had already acquired a portion of that celebrity which they have since enjoyed—John Jay, Hamilton, Madison—undertook together to explain to the nation the advantages of the measure that was proposed. With this view, they published in a journal a series of articles, which now form a complete treatise. They entitled their journal *The Federalist*, a name which has been retained in the work. *The Federalist* is an excellent book, which ought to be familiar to the statesmen of all countries, though it specially concerns America.

POWERS OF THE FEDERAL GOVERNMENT. *Power of declaring war, making peace, and levying general taxes vested in the Federal government—What part of the internal policy of the country it may direct—The government of the Union in some respects more centralized than the king's government in the old French monarchy.*

THE PEOPLE in themselves are only individuals; and the special reason why they need to be united under one government is that they may appear to advantage before foreigners. The exclusive right of making peace and war, of concluding treaties of commerce, raising armies, and equipping fleets, was therefore granted to the Union.[8] The necessity of a national government was less imperiously felt in the conduct of the internal affairs of society; but there are certain general interests that can only be attended to with advantage by a general authority. The Union was invested with the power of controlling the monetary system, carrying the mails, and opening the great roads that were to unite the different parts of the country.[9] The independence of the government of each state in its sphere was recognized; yet the Federal government was authorized to interfere in the internal affairs of the states[10] in a few predetermined cases in which an indiscreet use of their independence might compromise the safety of the whole Union. Thus, while the power of modifying and changing their legislation at pleasure was preserved to each of the confederate republics, they are forbidden to enact *ex post facto* laws or to grant any titles of nobility. Lastly, as it was necessary that the Federal government should be able to fulfill its engagements, it has an unlimited power of levying taxes.[11]

In examining the division of powers as established by

[8] See Constitution, Article I, Sections 8, 10, § I; *The Federalist*, Nos. 41 and 42; Kent's *Commentaries*, Vol. I, pp. 207 ff.; Story, pp. 338–82, 409–26.

[9] Several other powers of the same kind exist, such as that of legislating on bankruptcy and granting patents. The necessity of confiding such matters to the Federal government is obvious enough.

[10] Even in these cases its interference is indirect. The Union interferes by means of the tribunals, as will hereafter be shown.

[11] Constitution, Article I, Sections 8, 9, and 10; *The Federalist*, Nos. 30–36 inclusive; ibid., Nos. 41, 42, 43, 44; Kent's *Commentaries*, Vol. I, pp. 207, 381; Story, pp. 329, 514.

the Federal Constitution, remarking on the one hand the portion of sovereignty which has been reserved to the several states, and on the other the share of power which has been given to the Union, it is evident that the Federal legislators entertained very clear and accurate notions respecting the centralization of government. The United States form not only a republic but a confederation; yet the national authority is more centralized there than it was in several of the absolute monarchies of Europe. I will cite only two examples.

Thirteen supreme courts of justice existed in France, which, generally speaking, had the right of interpreting the law without appeal; and those provinces that were styled *pays d'État* were authorized to refuse their assent to an impost which had been levied by the sovereign, who represented the nation.

In the Union there is but one tribunal to interpret, as there is one legislature to make, the laws; and a tax voted by the representatives of the nation is binding upon all the citizens. In these two essential points, therefore, the Union is more centralized than the French monarchy, although the Union is only an assemblage of confederate republics.

In Spain certain provinces had the right of establishing a system of custom-house duties peculiar to themselves, although that privilege belongs, by its very nature, to the national sovereignty. In America Congress alone has the right of regulating the commercial relations of the states with each other. The government of the confederation is therefore more centralized in this respect than the Kingdom of Spain. It is true that the power of the crown in France or Spain was always able to obtain by force whatever the constitution of the country denied, and that the ultimate result was consequently the same; but I am here discussing the theory of the constitution.

After having settled the limits within which the Federal government was to act, the next point was to determine how it should be put in action.

LEGISLATIVE POWERS OF THE FEDERAL GOVERNMENT. *Division of the legislative body into two branches—Difference in the manner of forming the two houses—The principle of the independence of the states predominates in the formation of the Senate—That of the sovereignty of the nation in the composition of the House of Representatives—Singular effect of the fact that a constitution can be logical only when the nation is young.*

THE PLAN which had been laid down beforehand in the constitutions of the several states was followed, in many respects, in the organization of the powers of the Union. The Federal legislature of the Union was composed of a Senate and a House of Representatives. A spirit of compromise caused these two assemblies to be constituted on different principles. I have already shown that two interests were opposed to each other in the establishment of the Federal Constitution. These two interests had given rise to two opinions. It was the wish of one party to convert the Union into a league of independent states, or a sort of congress, at which the representatives of the several nations would meet to discuss certain points of common interest. The other party desired to unite the inhabitants of the American colonies into one and the same people and to establish a government that should act as the sole representative of the nation, although in a limited sphere. The practical consequences of these two theories were very different.

If the object was that a league should be established instead of a national government, then the majority of the states, instead of the majority of the inhabitants of the Union, would make the laws; for every state, great or small, would then remain in full independence and enter the Union upon a footing of perfect equality. If, however, the inhabitants of the United States were to be considered as belonging to one and the same nation, it would be natural that the majority of the citizens of the Union should make the law. Of course, the lesser states could not subscribe to the application of this doctrine without in fact abdicating their existence in respect to the sovereignty of the confederation, since they would cease to be a coequal and coauthoritative power and become an insignificant fraction of a great people. The former system would have invested them with excessive authority, the latter would have destroyed their influence altogether. Under these circumstances the result was that the rules of logic were broken, as is usually the case when interests are opposed to arguments. The legislators hit upon a middle course which brought together by force two systems theoretically irreconcilable.

The principle of the independence of the states triumphed in the formation of the Senate, and that of the sovereignty of the nation in the composition of the House of Representatives. Each state was to send two senators to Congress, and a number of representatives proportioned to its population.[12] It results from this arrangement that the state of New York has at the present day thirty-three representatives, and only two senators; the state of Delaware has two senators, and only one representative; the state of Delaware is therefore equal to the state of New York in the Senate, while the latter has thirty-three times the influence of the former in the House of Representatives. Thus the minority of the nation in the Senate may paralyze the decisions of the majority represented in the other house, which is contrary to the spirit of constitutional government.

These facts show how rare and difficult it is rationally and logically to combine all the several parts of legislation. The course of time always gives birth to different interests, and sanctions different principles, among the same people; and when a general constitution is to be established, these interests and principles are so many natural obstacles to the rigorous application of any political system with all its consequences. The early stages of national existence are the only periods at which it is possible to make legislation strictly logical; and when we perceive a nation in the enjoyment of this advantage, we should not hastily conclude that it is wise, but only remember that it is young. When the Federal Constitution was formed, the interest of independence for the separate states and the interest of union for

[12] Every ten years Congress fixes anew the number of representatives which each state is to furnish. The total number was 69 in 1789, and 240 in 1833. *American Almanac* (1834), p. 194.

The Constitution decided that there should not be more than one representative for every 30,000 persons; but no minimum was fixed on. Congress has not thought fit to augment the number of representatives in proportion to the increase of population. The first Act which was passed (April 14, 1792) on the subject (see Story: *Laws of the United States*, Vol. I, p. 235) decided that there should be one representative for every 33,000 inhabitants.

the whole people were the only two conflicting interests that existed among the Anglo-Americans, and a compromise was necessarily made between them.

It is just to acknowledge, however, that this part of the Constitution has not hitherto produced those evils which might have been feared. All the states are young and contiguous; their customs, their ideas, and their wants are not dissimilar; and the differences which result from their size are not enough to set their interests much at variance. The small states have consequently never leagued themselves together in the Senate to oppose the designs of the larger ones. Besides, there is so irresistible an authority in the legal expression of the will of a people that the Senate could offer but a feeble opposition to the vote of the majority expressed by the House of Representatives.

It must not be forgotten, moreover, that it was not in the power of the American legislators to reduce to a single nation the people for whom they were making laws. The object of the Federal Constitution was not to destroy the independence of the states, but to restrain it. By acknowledging the real power of these secondary communities (and it was impossible to deprive them of it) they disavowed beforehand the habitual use of compulsion in enforcing the decisions of the majority. This being laid down, the introduction of the influence of the states into the mechanism of the Federal government was by no means to be wondered at, since it only attested the existence of an acknowledged power, which was to be humored and not forcibly checked.

A FURTHER DIFFERENCE BETWEEN THE SENATE AND THE HOUSE OF REPRESENTATIVES. *The Senate named by the state legislatures; the Representatives by the people—Double election of the former; single election of the latter—Term of the different offices—Peculiar functions of each house.*

THE SENATE differs from the other house not only in the very principle of representation, but also in the mode of its election, in the term for which it is chosen, and in the nature of its functions. The House of Representatives is chosen by the people, the Senate by the legislatures of the states; the former is directly elected, the latter is elected by an elected body; the term for which the representatives are chosen is only two years, that of the senators is six. The functions of the House of Representatives are purely legislative, and the only share it takes in the judicial power is in the impeachment of public officers. The Senate co-operates in the work of legislation and tries those political offenses which the House of Representatives submits to its decision. It also acts as the great executive council of the nation; the treaties that are concluded by the President must be ratified by the Senate; and the appointments he may make, in order to be legally effective, must be approved by the same body.[13]

THE EXECUTIVE POWER.[14] *Dependence of the President—He is elective and responsible—Free in his own sphere, under the inspection, but not under the direction, of the Senate—His salary fixed at his entry into office—Suspensive veto.*

THE AMERICAN legislators undertook a difficult task in attempting to create an executive power dependent on the majority of the people and nevertheless sufficiently strong to act without restraint in its own sphere. It was indispensable to the maintenance of the republican form of government that the representative of the executive power should be subject to the will of the nation.

The President is an elective magistrate. His honor, his property, his liberty, and his life are the securities which the people have for the temperate use of his power. But in the exercise of his authority he is not perfectly independent; the Senate takes cognizance of his relations with foreign powers, and of his distribution of public appointments, so that he can neither corrupt nor be corrupted. The legislators of the Union acknowledge that the executive power could not fulfill its task with dignity and advantage unless it enjoyed more stability and strength than had been granted it in the separate states.

The President is chosen for four years, and he may be re-elected, so that the chances of a future administration may inspire him with hopeful undertakings for the public good and give him the means of carrying them into execu-

---

[13] See _The Federalist,_ Nos. 52–66 inclusive; Story, pp. 199–314; Constitution, Article I, Sections 2 and 3.

[14] _The Federalist,_ Nos. 66–77 inclusive; Constitution, Article II; Story, pp. 315, 518–780; Kent's _Commentaries,_ p. 255.

tion. The President was made the sole representative of the executive power of the Union; and care was taken not to render his decisions subordinate to the vote of a council, a dangerous measure which tends at the same time to clog the action of the government and to diminish its responsibility. The Senate has the right of annulling certain acts of the President; but it cannot compel him to take any steps, nor does it participate in the exercise of the executive power.

The action of the legislature on the executive power may be direct, and I have just shown that the Americans carefully obviated this influence; but it may, on the other hand, be indirect. Legislative assemblies which have the power of depriving an officer of state of his salary encroach upon his independence; and as they are free to make the laws, it is to be feared lest they should gradually appropriate to themselves a portion of that authority which the Constitution had vested in his hands. This dependence of the executive power is one of the defects inherent in republican constitutions. The Americans have not been able to counteract the tendency which legislative assemblies have to get possession of the government, but they have rendered this propensity less irresistible. The salary of the President is fixed, at the time of his entering upon office, for the whole period of his magistracy. The President, moreover, is armed with a suspensive veto, which allows him to oppose the passing of such laws as might destroy the portion of independence that the Constitution awards him. Yet the struggle between the President and the legislature must always be an unequal one, since the latter is certain of bearing down all resistance by persevering in its plans; but the suspensive veto forces it at least to reconsider the matter, and if the motion be persisted in, it must then be backed by a majority of two thirds of the whole house. The veto, moreover, is a sort of appeal to the people. The executive power, which without this security might have been secretly oppressed, adopts this means of pleading its cause and stating its motives. But if the legislature perseveres in its design, can it not always overpower all resistance? I reply that in the constitutions of all nations, of whatever kind they may be, a certain point exists at which the legislator must have recourse to the good sense and the virtue of his fellow citizens. This point is nearer and more prominent in republics, while it is more remote and

more carefully concealed in monarchies; but it always exists somewhere. There is no country in which everything can be provided for by the laws, or in which political institutions can prove a substitute for common sense and public morality.

IN WHAT THE POSITION OF A PRESIDENT OF THE UNITED STATES DIFFERS FROM THAT OF A CONSTITUTIONAL KING OF FRANCE. *Executive power in the United States as limited and exceptional as the sovereignty that it represents—Executive power in France, like the state's sovereignty, extends to everything—The King a branch of the legislature—The President the mere executor of the law —Other differences resulting from the duration of the two powers—The President checked in the exercise of executive authority—The King independent in its exercise—In spite of these differences, France is more akin to a republic than the Union to a monarchy—Comparison of the number of public officers depending upon the executive power in the two countries.*

THE EXECUTIVE power has so important an influence on the destinies of nations that I wish to dwell for an instant on this portion of my subject in order more clearly to explain the part it sustains in America. In order to form a clear and precise idea of the position of the President of the United States it may be well to compare it with that of one of the constitutional kings of France. In this comparison I shall pay but little attention to the external signs of power, which are more apt to deceive the eye of the observer than to guide his researches. When a monarchy is being gradually transformed into a republic, the executive power retains the titles, the honors, the etiquette, and even the funds of royalty long after its real authority has disappeared. The English, after having cut off the head of one king, and expelled another from his throne, were still wont to address the successors of those princes only upon their knees. On the other hand, when a republic falls under the sway of a single man, the demeanor of the sovereign remains as simple and unpretending as if his authority was not yet paramount. When the emperors exercised an unlimited control over the fortunes and the lives of their fellow citizens, it was customary to call them Cæsar in conversation; and they were in the habit of supping without formality at their friends' houses. It is therefore necessary to look below the surface.

The sovereignty of the United States is shared between the Union and the states, while in France it is undivided and compact; hence arises the first and most notable difference that exists between the President of the United States and the King of France. In the United States the executive power is as limited and exceptional as the sovereignty in whose name it acts; in France it is as universal as the authority of the state. The Americans have a Federal and the French a national government.

This cause of inferiority results from the nature of things, but it is not the only one; the second in importance is as follows. Sovereignty may be defined to be the right of making laws. In France, the King really exercises a portion of the sovereign power, since the laws have no weight if he refuses to sanction them; he is, moreover, the executor of all they ordain. The President is also the executor of the laws; but he does not really co-operate in making them, since the refusal of his assent does not prevent their passage. He is not, therefore, a part of the sovereign power, but only its agent. But not only does the King of France constitute a portion of the sovereign power; he also contributes to the nomination of the legislature, which is the other portion. He participates in it through appointing the members of one chamber and dissolving the other at his pleasure; whereas the President of the United States has no share in the formation of the legislative body and cannot dissolve it. The King has the same right of bringing forward measures as the chambers, a right which the President does not possess. The King is represented in each assembly by his ministers, who explain his intentions, support his opinions, and maintain the principles of the government. The President and his ministers are alike excluded from Congress, so that his influence and his opinions can only penetrate indirectly into that great body. The King of France is therefore on an equal footing with the legislature, which can no more act without him than he can without it. The President is placed beside the legislature like an inferior and dependent power.

Even in the exercise of the executive power, properly so called, the point upon which his position seems to be most analogous to that of the King of France, the President labors under several causes of inferiority. The authority of the King in France has, in the first place, the advantage of duration over that of the President; and durability is one of the chief elements of strength; nothing is either loved or feared but what is likely to endure. The President of the United States is a magistrate elected for four years. The King in France is a hereditary sovereign.

In the exercise of the executive power the President of the United States is constantly subject to a jealous supervision. He may prepare, but he cannot conclude, a treaty; he may nominate, but he cannot appoint, a public officer.[15] The King of France is absolute within the sphere of executive power.

The President of the United States is responsible for his actions; but the person of the King is declared inviolable by French law.

Nevertheless, public opinion as a directing power is no less above the head of the one than of the other. This power is less definite, less evident, and less sanctioned by the laws in France than in America; but it really exists there. In America it acts by elections and decrees; in France it proceeds by revolutions. Thus, notwithstanding the different constitutions of these two countries, public opinion is the predominant authority in both of them. The fundamental principle of legislation, a principle essentially republican, is the same in both countries, although its developments may be more or less free and its consequences different. Thus I am led to conclude that France with its King is nearer akin to a republic than the Union with its President is to a monarchy.

In all that precedes I have touched only upon the main points of distinction; if I could have entered into details, the contrast would have been still more striking.

I have remarked that the authority of the President in the United States is only exercised within the limits of a partial sovereignty, while that of the King in France is un-

---

[15] The Constitution has left it doubtful whether the President is obliged to consult the Senate in the removal as well as in the appointment of Federal officers. *The Federalist* (No. 77) seems to establish the affirmative; but in 1789 Congress formally decided that as the President was responsible for his actions, he ought not to be forced to employ agents who had forfeited his esteem. See Kent's *Commentaries,* Vol. I, p. 289.

divided. I might have gone on to show that the power of the King's government in France exceeds its natural limits, however extensive these may be, and penetrates in a thousand different ways into the administration of private interests. Among the examples of this influence may be quoted that which results from the great number of public functionaries, who all derive their appointments from the executive government. This number now exceeds all previous limits; it amounts to 138,000 [16] nominations, each of which may be considered as an element of power. The President of the United States has not the exclusive right of making any public appointments, and their whole number scarcely exceeds 12,000.[17]

ACCIDENTAL CAUSES WHICH MAY INCREASE THE INFLUENCE OF EXECUTIVE GOVERNMENT. *External security of the Union —Army of six thousand men—Few ships—The President has great prerogatives, but no opportunity of exercising them—In the prerogatives which he does exercise he is weak.*

IF THE executive government is feebler in America than in France, the cause is perhaps more attributable to the circumstances than to the laws of the country.

It is chiefly in its foreign relations that the executive power of a nation finds occasion to exert its skill and its strength. If the existence of the Union were perpetually threatened, if its chief interests were in daily connection with those of other powerful nations, the executive government would assume an increased importance in proportion to the measures expected of it and to those which it would execute. The President of the United States, it is true, is the commander-in-chief of the army, but the army is composed of only six thousand men; he commands the fleet, but the fleet reckons but few sail; he conducts the foreign relations

[16] The sums annually paid by the state to these officers amount to 200,000,000 francs.

[17] Each year an almanac called the *National Calendar* is published in the United States. It gives the names of all Federal office-holders. This number is extracted from the *National Calendar* for 1833.

It results from this comparison that the King of France has eleven times as many places at his disposal as the President, although the population of France is not much more than one and one-half times that of the Union.

of the Union, but the United States is a nation without neighbors. Separated from the rest of the world by the ocean, and too weak as yet to aim at the dominion of the seas, it has no enemies, and its interests rarely come into contact with those of any other nation of the globe. This proves that the practical operation of the government must not be judged by the theory of its constitution. The President of the United States possesses almost royal prerogatives, which he has no opportunity of exercising; and the privileges which he can at present use are very circumscribed. The laws allow him to be strong, but circumstances keep him weak.

On the other hand, the great strength of the loyal prerogative in France arises from circumstances far more than from the laws. There the executive government is constantly struggling against immense obstacles, and has immense resources in order to overcome them; so that it is enlarged by the extent of its achievements, and by the importance of the events it controls, without modifying its constitution. If the laws had made it as feeble and as circumscribed as that of the American Union, its influence would soon become still more preponderant.

WHY THE PRESIDENT OF THE UNITED STATES DOES NOT NEED A
MAJORITY IN THE TWO HOUSES IN ORDER TO CARRY ON
THE GOVERNMENT

IT IS an established axiom in Europe that a constitutional king cannot govern when opposed by the two branches of the legislature. But several Presidents of the United States have been known to lose the majority in the legislative body without being obliged to abandon the supreme power and without inflicting any serious evil upon society. I have heard this fact quoted to prove the independence and the power of the executive government in America; a moment's reflection will convince us, on the contrary, that it is a proof of its weakness.

A king in Europe requires the support of the legislature to enable him to perform the duties imposed upon him by the constitution, because those duties are enormous. A constitutional king in Europe is not merely the executor of the law, but the execution of its provisions devolves so completely upon him that he has the power of paralyzing its force if it opposes his designs. He requires the assistance of the legislative assemblies to make the law, but these assemblies need his aid to execute it. These two authorities cannot function without each other, and the mechanism of government is stopped as soon as they are at variance.

In America the President cannot prevent any law from being passed, nor can he evade the obligation of enforcing it. His sincere and zealous co-operation is no doubt useful in carrying on public affairs, but is not indispensable. In all his important acts he is directly or indirectly subject to the legislature, and of his own free authority he can do but little. It is therefore his weakness, and not his power, that enables him to remain in opposition to Congress. In Europe harmony must reign between the crown and the legislature, because a collision between them may prove serious; in America this harmony is not indispensable, because such a collision is impossible.

ELECTION OF THE PRESIDENT. *The dangers of the elective system increase in proportion to the extent of the prerogative—This system possible in America because no powerful executive authority is required—How circumstances favor the establishment of the elective system—Why the election of the President does not change the principles of the government—Influence of the election of the President on secondary functionaries.*

THE DANGERS of the system of election, applied to the chief of the executive government of a great people, have been sufficiently exemplified by experience and by history. I wish to speak of them in reference to America alone.

These dangers may be more or less formidable in proportion to the place that the executive power occupies and to the importance it possesses in the state; and they may vary according to the mode of election and the circumstances in which the electors are placed. The most weighty argument against the election of a chief magistrate is that it offers so splendid a lure to private ambition and is so apt to inflame men in the pursuit of power that when legitimate means are wanting, force may not infrequently seize what right denies. It is clear that the greater the prerogatives of executive authority are, the greater is the temptation; the more the ambition of the candidates is excited, the more warmly are their interests espoused by a throng of partisans who hope to share the power when their patron has won the prize. The dangers of the elective system increase, therefore, in the exact ratio of the influence exercised by the executive power in the affairs of the state. The revolutions of Poland are attributable not solely to the elective system in general, but to the fact that the elected monarch was the sovereign of a powerful kingdom.

Before we can discuss the absolute advantages of the elective system, we must make preliminary inquiries as to whether the geographical position, the laws, the habits, the customs, and the opinions of the people among whom it is to be introduced will permit the establishment of a weak and dependent executive government; for to attempt to render the representative of the state a powerful sovereign, and at the same time elective, is, in my opinion, to entertain two incompatible designs. To reduce hereditary royalty to the condition of an elective authority, the only means that I am acquainted with are to circumscribe its sphere of action beforehand, gradually to diminish its prerogatives, and to accustom the people by degrees to live without its protection. But this is what the republicans of Europe never think of doing; as many of them hate tyranny only because they are exposed to its severity, it is oppression and not the extent of the executive power that excites their hostility; and they attack the former without perceiving how nearly it is connected with the latter.

Hitherto no citizen has cared to expose his honor and his life in order to become the President of the United States, because the power of that office is temporary, limited, and subordinate. The prize of fortune must be great to encourage adventurers in so desperate a game. No candidate has as yet been able to arouse the dangerous enthusiasm or the passionate sympathies of the people in his favor, for the simple reason that when he is at the head of the government, he has but little power, little wealth, and little glory to share among his friends; and his influence in the state is too small for the success or the ruin of a faction to depend upon his elevation to power.

The great advantage of hereditary monarchies is that, as the private interest of a family is always intimately connected with the interests of the state, these state interests are never neglected for a moment; and if the affairs of a monarchy are not better conducted than those of a republic, at least there is always someone to conduct them, well or ill, according to his capacity. In elective states, on the contrary, the wheels of government cease to act, as it were, of their own accord at the approach of an election, and even for some time previous to that event. The laws may, indeed, accelerate the operation of the election, which may be conducted with such simplicity and rapidity that the seat of power will never be left vacant; but notwithstanding these precautions, a break necessarily occurs in the minds of the people.

At the approach of an election the head of the executive government thinks only of the struggle that is coming on; he no longer has anything to look forward to; he can undertake nothing new, and he will only prosecute with indifference those designs which another will perhaps terminate. "I am so near the time of my retirement from office," said President Jefferson, on January 21, 1809, six weeks before the election [*sic;* actually, six weeks before he left office], "that I feel no passion, I take no part, I express no sentiment. It appears to me just to leave to my successor the commencement of those measures which he will have to prosecute, and for which he will be responsible." On the other hand, the eyes of the nation are centered on a single point; all are watching the gradual birth of so important an event.

The wider the influence of the executive power extends, the greater and the more necessary is its constant action, the more fatal is the term of suspense; and a nation that is accustomed to the government or, still more, one used to the administration of a powerful executive authority would be infallibly convulsed by an election. In the United States the action of the government may be slackened with impunity, because it is always weak and circumscribed.

One of the principal vices of the elective system is that it always introduces a certain degree of instability into the internal and external policy of the state. But this disadvantage is less acutely felt if the share of power vested in the elected magistrate is small. In Rome the principles of the government underwent no variation although the consuls were changed every year, because the Senate, which was a hereditary assembly, possessed the directing authority. In most of the European monarchies, if the king were elective, the kingdom would be revolutionized at every new election. In America the President exercises a certain influence on state affairs, but he does not conduct them; the preponderating power is vested in the representatives of the whole nation. The political maxims of the country depend, therefore, on the mass of the people, not on the President alone; and consequently in America the elective system has no very prejudicial influence on the fixity of the government. But the want of fixed principles is an evil so inherent in the elective system that it is still very perceptible in the narrow sphere to which the authority of the President extends.

The Americans have admitted that the head of the executive power, in order to discharge his duty and bear the whole weight of responsibility, ought to be free to choose his own agents and to remove them at pleasure; the legislative bodies watch the conduct of the President more than they direct it. The consequence is that at every new election the fate of all the Federal public officers is in suspense. It is sometimes made a subject of complaint that in the constitutional monarchies of Europe the fate of the humbler servants of an administration often depends upon that of the ministers. But in elective governments this evil is far greater; and the reason therefor is very obvious. In a constitutional monarchy successive ministries are rapidly formed; but as the principal representative of the executive power is never changed, the spirit of innovation is kept within bounds; the changes that take place are in the details of the administrative system rather than in its principles; but to substitute one system for another, as is done in America every four years by law, is to cause a sort of revolution. As to the misfortunes which may fall upon individuals in consequence of this state of things, it must be allowed that the uncertain tenure of the public offices does not produce the evil consequences in America which might be expected from it elsewhere. It is so easy to acquire an independent position in the United States that the public officer who loses his place may be deprived of the comforts of life, but not of the means of subsistence.

I remarked at the beginning of this chapter that the dangers of the elective system, applied to the head of the state, are augmented or decreased by the peculiar circumstances of the people which adopts it. However the functions of the executive power may be restricted, it must always exercise a great influence upon the foreign policy of the country; for a negotiation cannot be opened or successfully carried on otherwise than by a single agent. The more precarious and the more perilous the position of a people becomes, the more absolute is the want of a fixed and consistent external policy, and the more dangerous does the system of electing the chief magistrate become. The policy of the Americans in relation to the whole world is exceedingly simple; and it may almost be said that nobody stands in need of them, nor do they stand in need of anybody. Their independence is never threatened. In their present condition, therefore, the functions of the executive power are no less limited by circumstances than by the laws; and the President may frequently change his policy without involving the state in difficulty or destruction.

Whatever the prerogatives of the executive power may be, the period which immediately precedes an election, and that during which the election is taking place, must always be considered as a national crisis, which is perilous in proportion to the internal embarrassments and the external dangers of the country. Few of the nations of Europe could escape the calamities of anarchy or of conquest every time they might have to elect a new sovereign. In America society is so constituted that it can stand without assistance upon its own basis; nothing is to be feared from the pressure of external dangers; and the election of the President is a cause of agitation, but not of ruin.

MODE OF ELECTION. *Skill of the American legislators shown in the mode of election adopted by them—Creation of a special electoral body—Separate votes of these electors—Case in which the House of Representatives is called upon to choose the President—Results of the twelve elections that have taken place since the Constitution was established.*

BESIDES the dangers that are inherent in the system, many others may arise from the mode of election; but these may be obviated by the precautions of the legislator. When a people met in arms on some public spot to choose its head, it was exposed to all the chances of civil war resulting from such a mode of proceeding, besides the dangers of the elective system in itself. The Polish laws, which subjected the election of the sovereign to the veto of a single individual, suggested the murder of that individual or prepared the way for anarchy.

In the examination of the institutions and the political as well as social condition of the United States we are struck by the admirable harmony of the gifts of fortune and the efforts of man. That nation possessed two of the main causes of internal peace; it was a new country, but it was inhabited by a people grown old in the exercise of freedom. Besides, America had no hostile neighbors to dread; and the American legislators, profiting by these favorable circumstances, created a weak and subordinate executive power, which could without danger be made elective.

It then remained for them only to choose the least dangerous of the various modes of election; and the rules that they laid down upon this point admirably correspond to the securities which the physical and political constitution of the country already afforded. Their object was to find the mode of election that would best express the choice of the people with the least possible excitement and suspense. It was admitted, in the first place, that the simple majority should decide the point; but the difficulty was to obtain this majority without an interval of delay, which it was most important to avoid. It rarely happens that an individual can receive at the first trial a majority of the suffrages of a great people; and this difficulty is enhanced in a republic of confederate states, where local influences are far more developed and more powerful. The means by which it was proposed to obviate this second obstacle was to delegate the electoral powers of the nation to a body that should represent it. This mode of election rendered a majority more probable; for the fewer the electors are, the greater is the chance of their coming to an agreement. It also offered an additional probability of a judicious choice. It then remained to be decided whether this right of election was to be entrusted to the legislature itself, the ordinary representative of the nation, or whether a special electoral college should be formed for the sole purpose of choosing a President. The Americans chose the latter alternative, from a belief that those who were chosen only to make the laws would represent but imperfectly the wishes of the nation in the election of its chief magistrate; and that, as they are chosen for more than a year, the constituency they represented might have changed its opinion in that time. It was thought that if the legislature was empowered to elect the head of the executive power, its members would, for some time before the election, be exposed to the maneuvers of corruption and the tricks of intrigue; whereas the special electors would, like a jury, remain mixed up with the crowd till the day of action, when they would appear for a moment only to give their votes.

It was therefore determined that every state should name a certain number of electors,[18] who in their turn should elect the President; and as it had been observed that the assemblies to which the choice of a chief magistrate had been entrusted in elective countries inevitably became the centers of passion and cabal; that they sometimes usurped powers which did not belong to them; and that their proceedings, or the uncertainty which resulted from them, were sometimes prolonged so much as to endanger the welfare of the state, it was determined that the electors should all vote on the same day, without being convoked to the same place.[19] This double election rendered a majority probable, though not certain; for it was possible that the electors might not, any more than their constituents, come to an agreement. In that case it would be necessary to have recourse to one of three measures: either to appoint new electors, or to consult a second time those already appointed, or to give the election to another authority. The first two of these alternatives, independently of the uncertainty of their results, were likely to delay the final decision and to perpetuate an agitation which must always be accompanied with danger. The third expedient was therefore adopted, and it was agreed that the votes should be transmitted, sealed, to the president of the Senate, and that they should be opened and counted on an appointed day, in the presence of the Senate and the House of Representatives. If none of the candidates has received a majority, the House of Representatives then proceeds im-

[18] As many as it sends members to Congress. The number of electors at the election of 1833 was 288 (the *National Calendar*).

[19] The electors of the same state assemble, but they transmit to the central government the list of their individual votes, and not the mere result of the vote of the majority.

mediately to elect the President; but with the condition that it must fix upon one of the three candidates who have the highest number of votes in the electoral college.[20]

Thus it is only in case of an event which cannot often happen, and which can never be foreseen, that the election is entrusted to the ordinary representatives of the nation; and even then, they are obliged to choose a citizen who has already been designated by a powerful minority of the special electors. It is by this happy expedient that the respect due to the popular voice is combined with the utmost celerity of execution, and with those precautions which the interests of the country demand. But the decision of the question by the House of Representatives does not necessarily offer an immediate solution of the difficulty; for the majority of that assembly may still be doubtful, and in that case the Constitution prescribes no remedy. Nevertheless, by restricting the number of candidates to three, and by referring the matter to the judgment of an enlightened public body, it has smoothed all the obstacles[21] that are not inherent in the elective system itself.

In the forty-four years that have elapsed since the promulgation of the Federal Constitution, the United States have twelve times chosen a President. Ten of these elections took place at once by the simultaneous votes of the special electors in the different states. The House of Representatives has only twice exercised its conditional privilege of deciding in cases of uncertainty: the first time was at the election of Mr. Jefferson in 1801; the second was in 1825, when Mr. J. Quincy Adams was named.

CRISIS OF THE ELECTION. *The election may be considered as a moment of national crisis—Why?—Passions of the people—Anxiety of the President—Calm which succeeds the agitation of the election.*

[20] In this case it is the majority of the states, and not the majority of the members, that decides the question; so that New York has no more influence in the debate than Rhode Island. Thus the citizens of the Union are first consulted as members of one and the same community; and if they cannot agree, recourse is had to the division of the states, each of which has a separate and independent vote. This is one of the singularities of the Federal Constitution, which can be explained only by the jar of conflicting interests.

[21] Jefferson, in 1801, was not elected until the thirty-sixth ballot.

I HAVE shown what the circumstances are that favored the adoption of the elective system in the United States and what precautions were taken by the legislators to obviate its dangers. The Americans are accustomed to all kinds of elections; and they knew by experience the utmost degree of excitement which is compatible with security. The vast extent of the country and the dissemination of the inhabitants render a collision between parties less probable and less dangerous there than elsewhere. The political circumstances under which the elections have been carried on have not as yet caused any real danger. Still, the epoch of the election of the President of the United States may be considered as a crisis in the affairs of the nation.

The influence which the President exercises on public business is no doubt feeble and indirect; but the choice of the President, though of small importance to each individual citizen, concerns the citizens collectively; and however trifling an interest may be, it assumes a great degree of importance as soon as it becomes general. In comparison with the kings of Europe, the President possesses but few means of creating partisans; but the places that are at his disposal are sufficiently numerous to interest, directly or indirectly, several thousand electors in his success. Moreover, political parties in the United States are led to rally round an individual in order to acquire a more tangible shape in the eyes of the crowd, and the name of the candidate for the Presidency is put forward as the symbol and personification of their theories. For these reasons parties are strongly interested in winning the election, not so much with a view to the triumph of their principles under the auspices of the President elect as to show by his election that the supporters of those principles now form the majority.

For a long while before the appointed time has come, the election becomes the important and, so to speak, the all-engrossing topic of discussion. Factional ardor is redoubled, and all the artificial passions which the imagination can create in a happy and peaceful land are agitated and brought to light. The President, moreover, is absorbed by the cares of self-defense. He no longer governs for the interest of the state, but for that of his re-election; he does homage to the majority, and instead of checking its passions, as his duty commands, he frequently courts its worst caprices. As the election draws near, the activity of intrigue and the agitation of the populace increase; the citizens are divided into hostile camps, each of which assumes the name of its favorite candidate; the whole nation glows with feverish excitement; the election is the daily theme of the press, the subject of private conversation, the end of every thought and every action, the sole interest of the present. It is true that as soon as the choice is determined, this ardor is dispelled, calm returns, and the river, which had nearly broken its banks, sinks to its usual level; but who can refrain from astonishment that such a storm should have arisen?

RE-ELECTION OF THE PRESIDENT. *When the head of the executive power is re-eligible, it is the state that is the source of intrigue and corruption—The desire to be re-elected is the chief aim of a President of the United States—Disadvantage of the re-election peculiar to America—The natural evil of democracy is that it gradually subordinates all authority to the slightest desires of the majority—The re-election of the President encourages this evil.*

WERE the legislators of the United States right or wrong in allowing the re-election of the President? At first sight it seems contrary to all reason to prevent the head of the executive power from being elected a second time. The influence that the talents and the character of a single individual may exercise upon the fate of a whole people, especially in critical circumstances or arduous times, is well known. A law preventing the re-election of the chief magistrate would deprive the citizens of their best means of ensuring the prosperity and the security of the commonwealth; and, by a singular inconsistency, a man would be excluded from the government at the very time when he had proved his ability to govern well.

But if these arguments are strong, perhaps still more powerful reasons may be advanced against them. Intrigue and corruption are the natural vices of elective government; but when the head of the state can be re-elected, these evils rise to a great height and compromise the very existence of the country. When a simple candidate seeks to rise by intrigue, his maneuvers must be limited to a very narrow sphere; but when the chief magistrate enters the lists, he borrows the strength of the government for his own purposes. In the former case the feeble resources of an individual are in action; in the latter the state itself, with its immense influence, is busied in the work of corruption and cabal. The private citizen who employs culpable practices to acquire power can act in a manner only indirectly prejudicial to the public prosperity. But if the representative of the executive descends into the combat, the cares of government dwindle for him into second-rate importance, and the success of his election is his first concern. All public negotiations, as well as all laws, are to him nothing more than electioneering schemes; places become the reward of services rendered, not to the nation, but to its chief; and the influence of the government, if not injurious to the country, is at least no longer beneficial to the community for which it was created.

It is impossible to consider the ordinary course of affairs in the United States without perceiving that the desire to be re-elected is the chief aim of the President; that the whole policy of his administration, and even his most indifferent measures, tend to this object; and that, especially as the crisis approaches, his personal interest takes the place of his interest in the public good. The principle of re-eligibility renders the corrupting influence of elective government still more extensive and pernicious. It tends to degrade the political morality of the people and to substitute management and intrigue for patriotism.

In America it injures still more directly the very sources of national existence. Every government seems to be afflicted by some evil inherent in its nature, and the genius of the legislator consists in having a clear view of this evil. A state may survive the influence of a host of bad laws, and the mischief they cause is frequently exaggerated; but a law that encourages the growth of the canker within must prove fatal in the end, although its bad consequences may not be immediately perceived.

The principle of destruction in absolute monarchies lies in the unlimited and unreasonable extension of the royal power, and a measure tending to remove the constitutional provisions that counterbalance this influence would be radically bad even if its immediate consequences were unattended with evil. By parity of reasoning, in countries governed by a democracy, where the people is perpetually drawing all authority to itself, the laws that increase or accelerate this action directly attack the very principle of the government.

The greatest merit of the American legislators is that they clearly discerned this truth and had the courage to act up to it. They conceived that a certain authority above the body of the people was necessary, which should enjoy a degree of independence in its sphere without being entirely beyond the popular control; an authority which would be forced to comply with the *permanent* determinations of the majority, but which would be able to resist its caprices and refuse its most dangerous demands. To this end they centered the whole executive power of the nation in a single aim; they granted extensive prerogatives to the President and armed him with the veto to resist the encroachments of the legislature.

But by introducing the principle of re-election they partly destroyed their work; they conferred on the President a great power, but made him little inclined to use it. If ineligible a second time, the President would not be independent of the people, for his responsibility would not cease; but the favor of the people would not be so necessary to him as to induce him to submit in every respect to its desires. If re-eligible (and this is especially true at the present day, when political morality is relaxed and when great men are rare), the President of the United States becomes an easy tool in the hands of the majority. He adopts its likings and its animosities, he anticipates its wishes, he forestalls its complaints, he yields to its idlest cravings, and instead of guiding it, as the legislature intended that he should do, he merely follows its bidding. Thus, in order not to deprive the state of the talents of an individual, those talents have been rendered almost useless; and to retain an expedient for extraordinary perils, the country has been exposed to continual dangers.

FEDERAL COURTS OF JUSTICE.[22] *Political importance of the judiciary in the United States—Difficulty of treating*

[22] See Chapter VI, entitled "Judicial Power in the United States." This chapter explains the general principles of the American judiciary. See also the Federal Constitution, Article

*this subject—Utility of judicial power in confederations
—What tribunals could be introduced into the Union
—Necessity of establishing Federal courts of justice—
Organization of the national judiciary—The Supreme
Court—In what it differs from all other known tri-
bunals.*

I HAVE examined the legislative and executive power of the
Union, and the judicial power now remains to be considered; but here I cannot conceal my fears from the reader.
Their judicial institutions exercise a great influence on the
condition of the Anglo-Americans, and they occupy a very
important place among political institutions, properly so
called: in this respect they are peculiarly deserving of our
attention. But I am at a loss how to explain the political
action of the American tribunals without entering into some
technical details respecting their constitution and their forms
of proceeding; and I cannot descend to these minutiæ without wearying the reader by the natural dryness of the subject. Yet how can I be clear and at the same time brief? I
can scarcely hope to escape these different evils. Ordinary
readers will complain that I am tedious, lawyers that I am
too concise. But these are the natural disadvantages of my
subject, and especially of the point that I am now to discuss.

The great difficulty was, not to know how to constitute
the Federal government, but to find out a method of enforcing its laws. Governments have generally but two means
of overcoming the opposition of the governed: namely, the
physical force that is at their own disposal, and the moral
force that they derive from the decisions of the courts of
justice.

A government which should have no other means of
exacting obedience than open war must be very near its ruin,
for one of two things would then probably happen to it. If
it was weak and temperate, it would resort to violence only
at the last extremity and would connive at many partial acts
of insubordination; then the state would gradually fall into

III; *The Federalist,* Nos. 78–83 inclusive; *Constitutional Law,
Being a View of the Practise and Jurisdiction of the Courts of
the United States,* by Thomas Sergeant; Story, pp. 134–62, 489–
511, 581, 668. See the organic law of September 24, 1789, in
the collection entitled *Laws of the United States,* by Story, Vol.
I, p. 53.

anarchy. If it was enterprising and powerful, it would every day have recourse to physical strength, and thus would soon fall into a military despotism. Thus its activity and its inertness would be equally prejudicial to the community.

The great end of justice is to substitute the notion of right for that of violence and to place a legal barrier between the government and the use of physical force. It is a strange thing, the authority that is accorded to the intervention of a court of justice by the general opinion of mankind! It clings even to the mere formalities of justice, and gives a bodily influence to the mere shadow of the law. The moral force which courts of justice possess renders the use of physical force very rare and is frequently substituted for it; but if force proves to be indispensable, its power is doubled by the association of the idea of law.

A federal government stands in greater need than any other of the support of judicial institutions, because it is naturally weak and exposed to formidable opposition.[23] If it were always obliged to resort to violence in the first instance, it could not fulfill its task. The Union, therefore, stood in special need of a judiciary to make its citizens obey the laws and to repel the attacks that might be directed against them. But what tribunals were to exercise these privileges? Were they to be entrusted to the courts of justice which were already organized in every state? Or was it necessary to create Federal courts? It may easily be proved that the Union could not adapt to its wants the judicial power of the states. The separation of the judiciary from the other powers of the state is necessary for the security of each and the liberty of all. But it is no less important to the existence of the nation that the several powers of the state should have the same origin, follow the same principles, and act in the same sphere; in a word, that they should be correlative and homogeneous. No one, I presume, ever thought of causing offenses committed in France to be tried by a foreign court of justice in order to ensure the im-

[23] Federal laws are those which most require courts of justice, and at the same time those which have most rarely established them. The reason is that confederations have usually been formed by independent states, which had no real intention of obeying the central government; and though they readily ceded the right of command to the central government, they carefully reserved the right of non-compliance to themselves.

partiality of the judges. The Americans form but one people people in relation to their Federal government; but in the bosom of this people divers political bodies have been allowed to exist, which are dependent on the national government in a few points and independent in all the rest, which have all a distinct origin, maxims peculiar to themselves, and special means of carrying on their affairs. To entrust the execution of the laws of the Union to tribunals instituted by these political bodies would be to allow foreign judges to preside over the nation. Nay, more; not only is each state foreign to the Union at large, but it is a perpetual adversary, since whatever authority the Union loses turns to the advantage of the states. Thus, to enforce the laws of the Union by means of the state tribunals would be to allow not only foreign, but partial judges to preside over the nation.

But the number, still more than the mere character, of the state tribunals made them unfit for the service of the nation. When the Federal Constitution was formed, there were already thirteen courts of justice in the United States which decided causes without appeal. That number has now increased to twenty-four. To suppose that a state can exist when its fundamental laws are subjected to four-and-twenty different interpretations at the same time is to advance a proposition contrary alike to reason and to experience.

The American legislators therefore agreed to create a Federal judicial power to apply the laws of the Union and to determine certain questions affecting general interests, which were carefully defined beforehand. The entire judicial power of the Union was centered in one tribunal, called the Supreme Court of the United States. But to facilitate the expedition of business, inferior courts were added to it, which were empowered to decide causes of small importance without appeal, and, with appeal, causes of more magnitude. The members of the Supreme Court are appointed neither by the people nor by the legislature, but by the President of the United States, acting with the advice of the Senate. In order to render them independent of the other authorities, their office was made inalienable; and it was determined that their salary, when once fixed, should not be diminished by the legislature.[24] It was easy to proclaim the

[24] The Union was divided into districts, in each of which a resident Federal judge was appointed, and the court in which

principle of a Federal judiciary, but difficulties multiplied
when the extent of its jurisdiction was to be determined.

MEANS OF DETERMINING THE JURISDICTION OF THE FEDERAL
COURTS. *Difficulty of determining the jurisdiction of
the different courts of justice in confederations—The
courts of the Union obtained the right of fixing their
own jurisdiction—In what respects this rule attacks the
portion of sovereignty reserved to the several states—
The sovereignty of these states restricted by the laws
and by the interpretation of the laws—Danger thus incurred by the several states more apparent than real.*

As the Constitution of the United States recognized two
distinct sovereignties, in presence of each other, represented
in a judicial point of view by two distinct classes of courts
of justice, the utmost care taken in defining their separate
jurisdictions would have been insufficient to prevent frequent collisions between those tribunals. The question then
arose to whom the right of deciding the competency of each
court was to be referred.

In nations that constitute a single body politic, when a
question of jurisdiction is debated between two courts, a
third tribunal is generally within reach to decide the difference; and this is effected without difficulty because in these
nations questions of judicial competence have no connection

---

he presided was termed a "District Court." Each of the judges
of the Supreme Court annually visits a certain portion of the
country, in order to try the most important causes on the spot;
the court presided over by this magistrate is styled a "Circuit
Court." Lastly, all the most serious cases of litigation are
brought, either directly or by appeal before the Supreme Court,
which holds a solemn session once a year, at which all the
judges of the circuit courts must attend. The jury was introduced
into the Federal courts in the same manner and for the same
cases as into the courts of the states.

It will be observed that no analogy exists between the Supreme
Court of the United States and our *Cour de Cassation.* The
Supreme Court has original, the *Cour de Cassation* only
appellate jurisdiction. The Supreme Court is in fact, as is the
Cour de Cassation, a unique tribunal responsible for establishing a uniform jurisprudence; but the Supreme Court
judges of the fact as well as the law and makes a final judgment
without recourse to another tribunal, two things which the
Cour de Cassation cannot do.

See the organic law of September 24, 1789, *Laws of the
United States,* by Story, Vol. I, p. 53.

with questions of national sovereignty. But it was impossible to create an arbiter between a superior court of the Union and the superior court of a separate state, which would not belong to one of these two classes. It was therefore necessary to allow one of these courts to judge its own cause and to take or to retain cognizance of the point that was contested. To grant this privilege to the different courts of the states would have been to destroy the sovereignty of the Union *de facto,* after having established it *de jure;* for the interpretation of the Constitution would soon have restored to the states that portion of independence of which the terms of the Constitution deprived them. The object of creating a Federal tribunal was to prevent the state courts from deciding, each after its own fashion, questions affecting the national interests, and so to form a uniform body of jurisprudence for the interpretation of the laws of the Union. This end would not have been attained if the courts of the several states, even while they abstained from deciding cases avowedly Federal in their nature, had been able to decide them by pretending that they were not Federal. The Supreme Court of the United States was therefore invested with the right of determining all questions of jurisdiction.[25]

This was a severe blow to the sovereignty of the states, which was thus restricted not only by the laws, but by the interpretation of them, by one limit which was known and by another which was unknown, by a rule which was certain and one which was arbitrary. It is true, the Constitution had laid down the precise limits of the Federal supremacy; but whenever this supremacy is contested by one of the states, a Federal tribunal decides the question. Nevertheless, the dangers with which the independence of the states is threatened by this mode of proceeding are less serious than they appear to be. We shall see hereafter that in America the real power is vested in the states far more than in the

---

[25] In order to diminish the number of these suits, however, it was decided that in a great many Federal causes the courts of the states should be empowered to decide conjointly with those of the Union, the losing party having then a right of appeal to the Supreme Court of the United States. The Supreme Court of Virginia contested the right of the Supreme Court of the United States to judge an appeal from its decisions, but unsuccessfully. See Kent's *Commentaries,* Vol. I, pp. 300, 370, et seq.; Story's *Commentaries,* p. 646; and the organic law of 1789, *Laws of the United States,* Vol. I, p. 53.

Federal government. The Federal judges are conscious of the relative weakness of the power in whose name they act; and they are more inclined to abandon the right of jurisdiction in cases where the law gives it to them than to assert a privilege to which they have no legal claim.

DIFFERENT CASES OF JURISDICTION. *The matter and the party are the first conditions of the Federal jurisdiction— Suits in which ambassadors are engaged—Or the Union —Or a separate state—By whom tried—Causes resulting from the laws of the Union—Why judged by the Federal tribunals—Causes relating to the non-performance of contracts tried by the Federal courts—Consequences of this arrangement.*

AFTER establishing the competence of the Federal courts the legislators of the Union defined the cases that should come within their jurisdiction. It was determined, on the one hand, that certain parties must always be brought before the Federal courts, without regard to the special nature of the suit; and, on the other, that certain causes must always be brought before the same courts, no matter who were the parties to them. The party and the cause were therefore admitted to be the two bases of Federal jurisdiction.

Ambassadors represent nations in amity with the Union, and whatever concerns these personages concerns in some degree the whole Union. When an ambassador, therefore, is a party in a suit, its issue affects the welfare of the nation, and a Federal tribunal is naturally called upon to decide it.

The Union itself may be involved in legal proceedings, and in this case it would be contrary to reason and to the customs of all nations to appeal to a tribunal representing any other sovereignty than its own; the Federal courts alone, therefore, take cognizance of these affairs.

When two parties belonging to two different states are engaged in a suit, the case cannot with propriety be brought before a court of either state. The surest expedient is to select a tribunal which can excite the suspicions of neither party, and this is naturally a Federal court.

When the two parties are not private individuals, but states, an important political motive is added to the same consideration of equity. The quality of the parties, in this case, gives a national importance to all their disputes; and the most trifling litigation between two states may be said to involve the peace of the whole Union.[26]

The nature of the cause frequently prescribes the rule of competency. Thus, all questions which concern maritime affairs evidently fall under the cognizance of the Federal tribunals.[27] Almost all these questions depend on the interpretation of the law of nations, and in this respect they essentially interest the Union in relation to foreign powers. Moreover, as the sea is not included within the limits of any one state jurisdiction rather than another, only the national courts can hear causes which originate in maritime affairs.

The Constitution comprises under one head almost all the cases which by their very nature come before the Federal courts. The rule that it lays down is simple, but pregnant with an entire system of ideas and with a multitude of facts. It declares that the judicial power of the Supreme Court shall extend to all cases in law and equity *arising under the laws of the United States.*

Two examples will put the intention of the legislator in the clearest light.

The Constitution prohibits the states from making laws on the value and circulation of money. If, notwithstanding this prohibition, a state passes a law of this kind, with which the interested parties refuse to comply because it is contrary to the Constitution, the case must come before a Federal court, because it arises under the laws of the United States. Again, if difficulties arise in the levying of import duties that have been voted by Congress, the Federal court must decide the case, because it arises under the interpretation of a law of the United States.

This rule is in perfect accordance with the fundamental

[26] The Constitution also says that the Federal courts shall decide "controversies between a State and the citizens of another State." And here a most important question arose, whether the jurisdiction given by the Constitution in cases in which a state is a party extended to suits brought *against* a state as well as *by* it, or was exclusively confined to the latter. The Supreme Court decided in the affirmative. The decision created general alarm among the states which feared that they would be subjected to Federal justice in spite of themselves. An amendment was proposed and ratified by which the power was entirely taken away so far as it regards suits brought *against* a state by the citizens of another. See Story's *Commentaries,* p. 624.

[27] As, for instance, all cases of piracy.

principles of the Federal Constitution. The Union, as it was established in 1789, possesses, it is true, a limited sovereignty; but it was intended that within its limits it should form one and the same people.[28] Within those limits the Union is sovereign. When this point is established and admitted, the inference is easy; for if it is acknowledged that the United States, within the bounds prescribed by their Constitution, constitute but one people, it is impossible to refuse them the rights which belong to other nations. But it has been allowed, from the origin of society, that every nation has the right of deciding by its own courts those questions which concern the execution of its own laws. To this it is answered that the Union is in such a singular position that in relation to some matters it constitutes but one people, and in relation to all the rest it is a nonentity. But the inference to be drawn is that in the laws relating to these matters the Union possesses all the rights of absolute sovereignty. The difficulty is to know what these matters are; and when once it is settled (and in speaking of the means of determining the jurisdiction of the Federal courts I have shown how it was settled), no further doubt can arise; for as soon as it is established that a suit is Federal—that is to say, that it belongs to the share of sovereignty reserved by the Constitution to the Union—the natural consequence is that it should come within the jurisdiction of a Federal court.

Whenever the laws of the United States are attacked, or whenever they are resorted to in self-defense, the Federal courts must be appealed to. Thus the jurisdiction of the tribunals of the Union extends and narrows its limits exactly in the same ratio as the sovereignty of the Union augments or decreases. I have shown that the principal aim of the legislators of 1789 was to divide the sovereign authority into two parts. In the one they placed the control of all the general interests of the Union, in the other the control of the special interests of its component states. Their chief concern was to arm the Federal government with sufficient power to enable it to resist, within its sphere, the encroachments of the several states. As for these communities, the general

---

[28] This principle was, in some measure, restricted by the introduction of the several states as independent powers into the Senate, and by allowing them to vote separately in the House of Representatives when the President is elected by that body. But these are exceptions, and the contrary principle is the rule.

principle of independence within certain limits of their own was adopted on their behalf; there the central government cannot control, nor even inspect, their conduct. In speaking of the division of authority, I observed that this latter principle had not always been respected, since the states are prevented from passing certain laws which apparently belong to their own particular sphere of interest. When a state of the Union passes a law of this kind, the citizens who are injured by its execution can appeal to the Federal courts.

Thus the jurisdiction of the Federal courts extends, not only to all the cases which arise under the laws of the Union, but also to those which arise under laws made by the several states in opposition to the Constitution. The states are prohibited from making *ex posto facto* laws in criminal cases; and any person condemned by virtue of a law of this kind can appeal to the judicial power of the Union. The states are likewise prohibited from making laws that may impair the obligation of contracts.[29] If a citizen thinks that an obligation of this kind is impaired by a law passed in his state, he may refuse to obey it and may appeal to the Federal courts.[30]

[29] It is perfectly clear, says Mr. Story (*Commentaries,* p. 503), that any law which enlarges, abridges, or in any manner changes the intention of the parties, resulting from the stipulations in the contract, necessarily impairs it. He gives in the same place a very careful definition of what is understood by a contract in Federal jurisprudence. The definition is very broad. A grant made by the state to a private individual and accepted by him is a contract, and cannot be revoked by any future law. A charter granted by the state to a company is a contract, and equally binding on the state as on the grantee. The clause of the Constitution here referred to ensures, therefore, the existence of a great part of *acquired rights,* but not of all. Property may legally be held, though it may not have passed into the possessor's hands by means of a contract; and its possession is an acquired right, not guaranteed by the Federal Constitution.

[30] A remarkable instance of this is given by Mr. Story (p. 508). Dartmouth College in New Hampshire had been founded by a charter granted to certain individuals before the American Revolution, and its trustees formed a *corporation* under this charter. The legislature of New Hampshire had, without the consent of this corporation, passed an act changing the terms of the original charter of the college, and transferring all the rights, privileges, and franchises derived from the old charter to new trustees appointed under the act. The constitutionality of the act was contested, and the cause was carried up to the Supreme (Federal) Court, where it was held, that since the original charter was an inviolable contract between the state

This provision appears to me to be the most serious attack upon the independence of the states. The rights accorded to the Federal government for purposes obviously national are definite and easily understood; but those with which this clause invests it are neither clearly appreciable nor accurately defined. For there are many political laws that affect the existence of contracts, which might thus furnish a pretext for the encroachments of the central authority.

PROCEDURE OF THE FEDERAL COURTS. *Natural weakness of the judicial power in confederations—Legislators ought, as much as possible, to bring private individuals, and not states, before the Federal courts—How the Americans have succeeded in this—Direct prosecution of private individuals in the Federal courts—Indirect prosecution of the states which violate the laws of the Union—The decrees of the Supreme Court enervate, but do not destroy, state laws.*

I HAVE shown what the rights of the Federal courts are, and it is no less important to show how they are exercised. The irresistible authority of justice in countries in which the sovereignty is undivided is derived from the fact that the tribunals of those countries represent the entire nation at issue with the individual against whom their decree is directed; and the idea of power is thus introduced to corroborate the idea of right. But it is not always so in countries in which the sovereignty is divided; in them the judicial power is more frequently opposed to a fraction of the nation than to an isolated individual, and its moral authority and physical strength are consequently diminished. In Federal states the power of the judge is naturally decreased and that of the justiciable parties is augmented. The aim of the legislator in confederate states ought therefore to be to render the position of the courts of justice analogous to that which they occupy in countries where the sovereignty is undivided; in other words, his efforts ought constantly to tend to maintain the judicial power of the confederation as the representative of the nation, and the justiciable party as the representative of an individual interest.

and the incorporators, the new law could not change the terms of this charter without violating acquired rights as in a contract, and that therefore it violated Article I, Section 10 of the Constitution of the United States.

Every government, whatever may be its constitution, requires the means of constraining its subjects to discharge their obligations and of protecting its privileges from their assaults. As far as the direct action of the government on the community is concerned, the Constitution of the United States contrived, by a master stroke of policy, that the Federal courts, acting in the name of the laws, should take cognizance only of parties in an individual capacity. For, as it had been declared that the Union consisted of one and the same people within the limits laid down by the Constitution, the inference was that the government created by this Constitution, and acting within these limits, was invested with all the privileges of a national government, of which one of the principal is the right of transmitting its injunctions directly to the private citizen. When, for instance, the Union votes an impost, it does not apply to the states for the levying of it, but to every American citizen, in proportion to his assessment. The Supreme Court, which is empowered to enforce the execution of this law of the Union, exerts its influence not upon a refractory state, but upon the private taxpayer; and, like the judicial power of other nations, it acts only upon the person of an individual. It is to be observed that the Union chose its own antagonist; and as that antagonist is feeble, he is naturally worsted.

But the difficulty increases when the proceedings are not brought forward *by*, but *against* the Union. The Constitution recognizes the legislative power of the states; and a law enacted by that power may violate the rights of the Union. In this case a collision is unavoidable between that body and the state which has passed the law, and it only remains to select the least dangerous remedy. The general principles that I have before established show what this remedy is.[31]

It may be conceived that in the case under consideration the Union might have sued the state before a Federal court, which would have annulled the act; this would have been the most natural proceeding. But the judicial power would thus have been placed in direct opposition to the state, and it was desirable to avoid this predicament as much as possible. The Americans hold that it is nearly impossible that a new law should not injure some private interests by its provisions. These private interests are assumed by the American

[31] See Chapter VI, on "The Judicial Power in America."

legislators as the means of assailing such measures as may be prejudicial to the Union, and it is to these interests that the protection of the Supreme Court is extended.

Suppose a state sells a portion of its public lands to a company, and that a year afterwards it passes a law by which the lands are otherwise disposed of and that clause of the Constitution which prohibits laws impairing the obligation of contracts is thereby violated. When the purchaser under the second act appears to take possession, the possessor under the first act brings his action before the tribunals of the Union and causes the title of the claimant to be pronounced null and void.[32] Thus, in point of fact, the judicial power of the Union is contesting the claims of the sovereignty of a state; but it acts only indirectly and upon an application of detail. It attacks the law in its consequences, not in its principle, and rather weakens than destroys it.

The last case to be provided for was that each state formed a corporation enjoying a separate existence and distinct civil rights, and that it could therefore sue or be sued before a tribunal. Thus a state could bring an action against another state. In this instance the Union was not called upon to contest a state law, but to try a suit in which a state was a party. This suit was perfectly similar to any other cause except that the quality of the parties was different; and here the danger pointed out at the beginning of this chapter still exists, with less chance of being avoided. It is inherent in the very essence of Federal constitutions that they should create parties in the bosom of the nation which present powerful obstacles to the free course of justice.

HIGH RANK OF THE SUPREME COURT AMONG THE GREAT POWERS OF STATE. *No nation ever constituted so great a judicial power as the Americans—Extent of its prerogatives—Its political influence—The tranquillity and the very existence of the Union depend on the discretion of the seven Federal judges.*

WHEN we have examined in detail the organization of the Supreme Court and the entire prerogatives which it exercises, we shall readily admit that a more imposing judicial power was never constituted by any people. The Supreme

[32] See Kent's *Commentaries,* Vol. I, p. 387.

Court is placed higher than any other known tribunal, both by the nature of its rights and the class of justiciable parties which it controls.

In all the civilized countries of Europe the government has always shown the greatest reluctance to allow the cases in which it was itself interested to be decided by the ordinary course of justice. This repugnance is naturally greater as the government is more absolute; and, on the other hand, the privileges of the courts of justice are extended with the increasing liberties of the people; but no European nation has yet held that all judicial controversies, without regard to their origin, can be left to the judges of common law.

In America this theory has been actually put in practice; and the Supreme Court of the United States is the sole tribunal of the nation. Its power extends to all cases arising under laws and treaties made by the national authorities, to all cases of admiralty and maritime jurisdiction, and, in general, to all points that affect the law of nations. It may even be affirmed that, although its constitution is essentially judicial, its prerogatives are almost entirely political. Its sole object is to enforce the execution of the laws of the Union; and the Union regulates only the relations of the government with the citizens, and of the nation with foreign powers; the relations of citizens among themselves are almost all regulated by the sovereignty of the states.

A second and still greater cause of the preponderance of this court may be adduced. In the nations of Europe the courts of justice are called upon to try only the controversies of private individuals; but the Supreme Court of the United States summons sovereign powers to its bar. When the clerk of the court advances on the steps of the tribunal and simply says: "The State of New York *versus* The State of Ohio," it is impossible not to feel that the court which he addresses is no ordinary body; and when it is recollected that one of these parties represents one million, and the other two millions of men, one is struck by the responsibility of the seven judges, whose decision is about to satisfy or to disappoint so large a number of their fellow citizens.

The peace, the prosperity, and the very existence of the Union are vested in the hands of the seven Federal judges. Without them the Constitution would be a dead letter: the executive appeals to them for assistance against the encroachments of the legislative power; the legislature demands their protection against the assaults of the executive; they defend the Union from the disobedience of the states, the states from the exaggerated claims of the Union, the public interest against private interests, and the conservative spirit of stability against the fickleness of the democracy. Their power is enormous, but it is the power of public opinion. They are all-powerful as long as the people respect the law; but they would be impotent against popular neglect or contempt of the law. The force of public opinion is the most intractable of agents, because its exact limits cannot be defined; and it is not less dangerous to exceed than to remain below the boundary prescribed.

Not only must the Federal judges be good citizens, and men of that information and integrity which are indispensable to all magistrates, but they must be statesmen, wise to discern the signs of the times, not afraid to brave the obstacles that can be subdued, nor slow to turn away from the current when it threatens to sweep them off, and the supremacy of the Union and the obedience due to the laws along with them.

The President, who exercises a limited power, may err without causing great mischief in the state. Congress may decide amiss without destroying the Union, because the electoral body in which the Congress originates may cause it to retract its decision by changing its members. But if the Supreme Court is ever composed of imprudent or bad men, the Union may be plunged into anarchy or civil war.

The original cause of this danger, however, does not lie in the constitution of the tribunal, but in the very nature of federal governments. We have seen that in confederate states it is especially necessary to strengthen the judicial power, because in no other nations do those independent persons who are able to contend with the social body exist in greater power, or in a better condition to resist the physical strength of the government. But the more a power requires to be strengthened, the more extensive and independent it must be made; and the dangers which its abuse may create are heightened by its independence and its strength. The source of the evil is not, therefore, in the constitution of the power, but in the constitution of the state which renders the existence of such a power necessary.

IN WHAT RESPECTS THE FEDERAL CONSTITUTION IS SUPERIOR TO
THAT OF THE STATES. *How the Constitution of the Union can be compared with that of the states—Superiority of the Constitution of the Union attributable
to the wisdom of the Federal legislators—Legislature of
the Union less dependent on the people than that of
the states—Executive power more independent in its
sphere—Judicial power less subjected to the will of the
majority—Practical consequence of these facts—The
dangers inherent in a democratic government diminished by the Federal legislators, and increased by the
legislators of the states.*

THE FEDERAL CONSTITUTION differs essentially from that of
the states in the ends which it is intended to accomplish; but
in the means by which these ends are attained a greater
analogy exists between them. The objects of the governments are different, but their forms are the same; and in this
special point of view there is some advantage in comparing
them with each other.

I am of opinion, for several reasons, that the Federal
Constitution is superior to any of the state constitutions.

The present Constitution of the Union was formed at a
later period than those of the majority of the states, and it
may have profited by this additional experience. But we shall
be convinced that this is only a secondary cause of its superiority, when we recollect that eleven new states have
since been added to the Union, and that these new republics
have almost always rather exaggerated than remedied the
defects that existed in the former constitutions.

The chief cause of the superiority of the Federal Constitution lay in the character of the legislators who composed
it. At the time when it was formed, the ruin of the Confederation seemed imminent, and its danger was universally
known. In this extremity the people chose the men who most
deserved the esteem rather than those who had gained the
affections of the country. I have already observed that, distinguished as almost all the legislators of the Union were
for their intelligence, they were still more so for their patriotism. They had all been nurtured at a time when the
spirit of liberty was braced by a continual struggle against a
powerful and dominant authority. When the contest was

terminated, while the excited passions of the populace persisted, as usual, in warring against dangers which had ceased to exist, these men stopped short; they cast a calmer and more penetrating look upon their country; they perceived that a definitive revolution had been accomplished, and that the only dangers which America had now to fear were those which might result from the abuse of freedom. They had the courage to say what they believed to be true, because they were animated by a warm and sincere love of liberty; and they ventured to propose restrictions, because they were resolutely opposed to destruction.[33]

Most of the state constitutions assign one year for the duration of the House of Representatives and two years for that of the Senate, so that members of the legislative body

---

[33] At this time the celebrated Alexander Hamilton, who was one of the principal founders of the Constitution, ventured to express the following sentiments in *The Federalist,* No. 71:
"There are some who would be inclined to regard the servile pliancy of the Executive to a prevailing current, either in the community or in the legislature, as its best recommendation. But such men entertain very crude notions, as well of the purposes for which government was instituted, as of the true means by which the public happiness may be promoted. The republican principle demands, that the deliberative sense of the community should govern the conduct of those to whom they entrust the management of their affairs; but it does not require an unqualified complaisance to every sudden breeze of passion, or to every transient impulse which the people may receive from the arts of men who flatter their prejudices to betray their interests. It is a just observation, that the people commonly *intend the public good.* This often applies to their very errors. But their good sense would despise the adulator who should pretend that they always *reason right* about the *means* of promoting it. They know from experience that they sometimes err; and the wonder is, that they so seldom err as they do, beset, as they continually are, by the wiles of parasites and sycophants; by the snares of the ambitious, the avaricious, the desperate; by the artifices of men who possess their confidence more than they deserve it, and of those who seek to possess rather than to deserve it. When occasions present themselves in which the interests of the people are at variance with their inclinations, it is the duty of the persons whom they have appointed to be the guardians of those interests to withstand the temporary delusion, in order to give them time and opportunity for more cool and sedate reflection. Instances might be cited, in which a conduct of this kind has saved the people from very fatal consequences of their own mistakes, and has procured lasting monuments of their gratitude to the men who had courage and magnanimity enough to serve them at the peril of their displeasure."

are constantly and narrowly tied down by the slightest desires of their constituents. The legislators of the Union were of opinion that this excessive dependence of the legislature altered the nature of the main consequences of the representative system, since it vested not only the source of authority, but the government, in the people. They increased the length of the term in order to give the representatives freer scope for the exercise of their own judgment.

The Federal Constitution, as well as the state constitutions, divided the legislative body into two branches. But in the states these two branches were composed of the same elements and elected in the same manner. The consequence was that the passions and inclinations of the populace were as rapidly and easily represented in one chamber as in the other, and that laws were made with violence and precipitation. By the Federal Constitution the two houses originate in like manner in the choice of the people; but the conditions of eligibility and the mode of election were changed in order that if, as is the case in certain nations, one branch of the legislature should not represent the same interests as the other, it might at least represent more wisdom. A mature age was necessary to become a Senator, and the Senate was chosen by an elected assembly of a limited number of members.

To concentrate the whole social force in the hands of the legislative body is the natural tendency of democracies; for as this is the power that emanates the most directly from the people, it has the greater share of the people's overwhelming power, and it is naturally led to monopolize every species of influence. This concentration of power is at once very prejudicial to a well-conducted administration and favorable to the despotism of the majority. The legislators of the states frequently yielded to these democratic propensities, which were invariably and courageously resisted by the founders of the Union.

In the states the executive power is vested in the hands of a magistrate who is apparently placed upon a level with the legislature, but who is in reality only the blind agent and the passive instrument of its will. He can derive no power from the duration of his office, which terminates in one year, or from the exercise of prerogatives, for he can scarcely be said to have any. The legislature can condemn him to in-action by entrusting the execution of its laws to special committees of its own members, and can annul his temporary dignity by cutting down his salary. The Federal Constitution vests all the privileges and all the responsibility of the executive power in a single individual. The duration of the Presidency is fixed at four years; the salary cannot be altered during this term; the President is protected by a body of official dependents and armed with a suspensive veto: in short, every effort was made to confer a strong and independent position upon the executive authority, within the limits that were prescribed to it.

In the state constitutions, the judicial power is that which is the most independent of the legislative authority; nevertheless, in all the states the legislature has reserved to itself the right of regulating the emoluments of the judges, a practice that necessarily subjects them to its immediate influence. In some states the judges are appointed only temporarily, which deprives them of a great portion of their power and their freedom. In others the legislative and judicial powers are entirely confounded. The Senate of New York, for instance, constitutes in certain cases the superior court of the state. The Federal Constitution, on the other hand, carefully separates the judicial power from all the others; and it provides for the independence of the judges, by declaring that their salary shall not be diminished, and that their functions shall be inalienable.

The practical consequences of these different systems may easily be perceived. An attentive observer will soon notice that the business of the Union is incomparably better conducted than that of any individual state. The conduct of the Federal government is more fair and temperate than that of the states; it has more prudence and discretion, its projects are more durable and more skillfully combined, its measures are executed with more vigor and consistency.

I recapitulate the substance of this chapter in a few words.

The existence of democracies is threatened by two principal dangers: namely, the complete subjection of the legislature to the will of the electoral body, and the concentration of all the other powers of the government in the legislative branch.

The development of these evils has been favored by the legislators of the states; but the legislators of the Union have done all they could to render them less formidable.

CHARACTERISTICS OF THE FEDERAL CONSTITUTION OF THE UNITED STATES OF AMERICA AS COMPARED WITH ALL OTHER FEDERAL CONSTITUTIONS. *The American Union appears to resemble all other confederations—Yet its effects are different—Reason for this—In what this Union differs from all other confederations—The American government not a Federal but an imperfect national government.*

THE UNITED STATES of America does not afford the first or the only instance of a confederation, several of which have existed in modern Europe, without referring to those of antiquity. Switzerland, the Germanic Empire, and the Republic of the Low Countries either have been or still are confederations. In studying the constitutions of these different countries one is surprised to see that the powers with which they invested the federal government are nearly the same as those awarded by the American Constitution to the government of the United States. They confer upon the central power the same rights of making peace and war, of raising money and troops, and of providing for the general exigencies and the common interests of the nation. Nevertheless, the federal government of these different states has always been as remarkable for its weakness and inefficiency as that of the American Union is for its vigor and capacity. Again, the first American Confederation perished through the excessive weakness of its government; and yet this weak government has as large rights and privileges as those of the Federal government of the present day, and in some respects even larger. But the present Constitution of the United States contains certain novel principles which exercise a most important influence, although they do not at once strike the observer.

This Constitution, which may at first sight be confused with the federal constitutions that have preceded it, rests in truth upon a wholly novel theory, which may be considered as a great discovery in modern political science. In all the confederations that preceded the American Constitution of 1789, the states allied for a common object agreed to obey

the injunctions of a federal government; but they reserved
to themselves the right of ordaining and enforcing the execution of the laws of the union. The American states which
combined in 1789 agreed that the Federal government should
not only dictate the laws, but execute its own enactments.
In both cases the right is the same, but the exercise of the
right is different; and this difference produced the most momentous consequences.

In all the confederations that preceded the American
Union the federal government, in order to provide for its
wants, had to apply to the separate governments; and if
what it prescribed was disagreeable to any one of them,
means were found to evade its claims. If it was powerful,
it then had recourse to arms; if it was weak, it connived at
the resistance which the law of the union, its sovereign, met
with, and did nothing, under the plea of inability. Under
these circumstances one of two results invariably followed:
either the strongest of the allied states assumed the privileges
of the federal authority and ruled all the others in its
name;[34] or the federal government was abandoned by its
natural supporters, anarchy arose between the confederates,
and the union lost all power of action.[35]

In America the subjects of the Union are not states, but
private citizens: the national government levies a tax, not
upon the state of Massachusetts, but upon each inhabitant
of Massachusetts. The old confederate governments presided
over communities, but that of the Union presides over individuals. Its force is not borrowed, but self-derived; and it is
served by its own civil and military officers, its own army,
and its own courts of justice. It cannot be doubted that the
national spirit, the passions of the multitude, and the provincial prejudices of each state still tend singularly to diminish the extent of the Federal authority thus constituted and
to facilitate resistance to its mandates; but the comparative

[34] This was the case in Greece when Philip undertook to
execute the decrees of the Amphictyons; in the Low Countries,
where the province of Holland always gave the law; and in
our own time in the Germanic Confederation, in which Austria
and Prussia make themselves the agents of the Diet and rule the
whole confederation in its name.
[35] Such has always been the situation of the Swiss Confederation, which would have perished ages ago but for the mutual
jealousies of its neighbors.

weakness of a restricted sovereignty is an evil inherent in the federal system. In America each state has fewer opportunities and temptations to resist; nor can such a design be put in execution (if indeed it be entertained) without an open violation of the laws of the Union, a direct interruption of the ordinary course of justice, and a bold declaration of revolt; in a word, without taking the decisive step that men always hesitate to adopt.

In all former confederations the privileges of the union furnished more elements of discord than of power, since they multiplied the claims of the nation without augmenting the means of enforcing them; and hence the real weakness of federal governments has almost always been in the exact ratio of their nominal power. Such is not the case in the American Union, in which, as in ordinary governments, the Federal power has the means of enforcing all it is empowered to demand.

The human understanding more easily invents new things than new words, and we are hence constrained to employ many improper and inadequate expressions. When several nations form a permanent league and establish a supreme authority, which, although it cannot act upon private individuals like a national government, still acts upon each of the confederate states in a body, this government, which is so essentially different from all others, is called Federal. Another form of society is afterwards discovered in which several states are fused into one with regard to certain common interests, although they remain distinct, or only confederate, with regard to all other concerns. In this case the central power acts directly upon the governed, whom it rules and judges in the same manner as a national government, but in a more limited circle. Evidently this is no longer a federal government, but an incomplete national government, which is neither exactly national nor exactly federal; but the new word which ought to express this novel thing does not yet exist.

Ignorance of this new species of confederation has been the cause that has brought all unions to civil war, to servitude, or to inertness; and the states which formed these leagues have been either too dull to discern, or too pusillanimous to apply, this great remedy. The first American Confederation perished by the same defects.

But in America the confederate states had been long accustomed to form a portion of one empire before they had won their independence; they had not contracted the habit of governing themselves completely; and their national prejudices had not taken deep root in their minds. Superior to the rest of the world in political knowledge, and sharing that knowledge equally among themselves, they were little agitated by the passions that generally oppose the extension of federal authority in a nation, and those passions were checked by the wisdom of their greatest men. The Americans applied the remedy with firmness as soon as they were conscious of the evil; they amended their laws and saved the country.

ADVANTAGES OF THE FEDERAL SYSTEM IN GENERAL, AND ITS SPECIAL UTILITY IN AMERICA. *Happiness and freedom of small nations—Power of great nations—Great empires favorable to the growth of civilization—Strength often the first element of national prosperity—Aim of the federal system to unite the twofold advantages resulting from a small and from a large territory—Advantages derived by the United States from this system—The law adapts itself to the exigencies of the population; population does not conform to the exigencies of the law—Activity, progress, the love and enjoyment of freedom, in American communities—Public spirit of the Union is only the aggregate of provincial patriotism—Principles and things circulate freely over the territory of the United States—The Union is happy and free as a little nation, and respected as a great one.*

IN small states, the watchfulness of society penetrates everywhere, and a desire for improvement pervades the smallest details; the ambition of the people being necessarily checked by its weakness, all the efforts and resources of the citizens are turned to the internal well-being of the community and are not likely to be wasted upon an empty pursuit of glory. The powers of every individual being generally limited, his desires are proportionally small. Mediocrity of fortune makes the various conditions of life nearly equal, and the manners of the inhabitants are orderly and simple. Thus, all things considered, and allowance being made for the various degrees of morality and enlightenment, we shall generally find more persons in easy circumstances, more contentment and tranquillity, in small nations than in large ones.

When tyranny is established in the bosom of a small state, it is more galling than elsewhere, because, acting in a narrower circle, everything in that circle is affected by it. It supplies the place of those great designs which it cannot entertain, by a violent or exasperating interference in a multitude of minute details; and it leaves the political world, to which it properly belongs, to meddle with the arrangements of private life. Tastes as well as actions are to be regulated; and the families of the citizens, as well as the state, are to be governed. This invasion of rights occurs but seldom, however, freedom being in truth the natural state of small communities. The temptations that the government offers to ambition are too weak and the resources of private individuals are too slender for the sovereign power easily to fall into the grasp of a single man; and should such an event occur, the subjects of the state can easily unite and overthrow the tyrant and the tyranny at once by a common effort.

Small nations have therefore always been the cradle of political liberty; and the fact that many of them have lost their liberty by becoming larger shows that their freedom was more a consequence of their small size than of the character of the people.

The history of the world affords no instance of a great nation retaining the form of republican government for a long series of years;[36] and this has led to the conclusion that such a thing is impracticable. For my own part, I think it imprudent for men who are every day deceived in relation to the actual and the present, and often taken by surprise in the circumstances with which they are most familiar, to attempt to limit what is possible and to judge the future. But it may be said with confidence, that a great republic will always be exposed to more perils than a small one.

All the passions that are most fatal to republican institutions increase with an increasing territory, while the virtues that favor them do not augment in the same proportion. The ambition of private citizens increases with the power of the state; the strength of parties with the importance of the ends they have in view; but the love of country, which ought to

[36] I do not speak of a confederation of small republics, but of a great consolidated republic.

check these destructive agencies, is not stronger in a large than in a small republic. It might, indeed, be easily proved that it is less powerful and less developed. Great wealth and extreme poverty, capital cities of large size, a lax morality, selfishness, and antagonism of interests are the dangers which almost invariably arise from the magnitude of states. Several of these evils scarcely injure a monarchy, and some of them even contribute to its strength and duration. In monarchical states the government has its peculiar strength; it may use, but it does not depend on, the community; and the more numerous the people, the stronger is the prince. But the only security that a republican government possesses against these evils lies in the support of the majority. This support is not, however, proportionably greater in a large republic than in a small one; and thus, while the means of attack perpetually increase, in both number and influence, the power of resistance remains the same; or it may rather be said to diminish, since the inclinations and interests of the people are more diversified by the increase of the population, and the difficulty of forming a compact majority is constantly augmented. It has been observed, moreover, that the intensity of human passions is heightened not only by the importance of the end which they propose to attain, but by the multitude of individuals who are animated by them at the same time. Everyone has had occasion to remark that his emotions in the midst of a sympathizing crowd are far greater than those which he would have felt in solitude. In great republics, political passions become irresistible, not only because they aim at gigantic objects, but because they are felt and shared by millions of men at the same time.

It may therefore be asserted as a general proposition that nothing is more opposed to the well-being and the freedom of men than vast empires. Nevertheless, it is important to acknowledge the peculiar advantages of great states. For the very reason that the desire for power is more intense in these communities than among ordinary men, the love of glory is also more developed in the hearts of certain citizens, who regard the applause of a great people as a reward worthy of their exertions and an elevating encouragement to man. If we would learn why great nations contribute more powerfully to the increase of knowledge and the advance of civilization than small states, we shall discover an adequate cause in the more rapid and energetic circulation of ideas and in those great cities which are the intellectual centers where all the rays of human genius are reflected and combined. To this it may be added that most important discoveries demand a use of national power which the government of a small state is unable to make: in great nations the government has more enlarged ideas, and is more completely disengaged from the routine of precedent and the selfishness of local feeling; its designs are conceived with more talent and executed with more boldness.

In time of peace the well-being of small nations is undoubtedly more general and complete; but they are apt to suffer more acutely from the calamities of war than those great empires whose distant frontiers may long avert the presence of the danger from the mass of the people, who are therefore more frequently afflicted than ruined by the contest.

But in this matter, as in many others, the decisive argument is the necessity of the case. If none but small nations existed, I do not doubt that mankind would be more happy and more free; but the existence of great nations is unavoidable.

Political strength thus becomes a condition of national prosperity. It profits a state but little to be affluent and free if it is perpetually exposed to be pillaged or subjugated; its manufactures and commerce are of small advantage if another nation has the empire of the seas and gives the law in all the markets of the globe. Small nations are often miserable, not because they are small, but because they are weak; and great empires prosper less because they are great than because they are strong. Physical strength is therefore one of the first conditions of the happiness and even of the existence of nations. Hence it occurs that, unless very peculiar circumstances intervene, small nations are always united to large empires in the end, either by force or by their own consent. I do not know a more deplorable condition than that of a people unable to defend itself or to provide for its own wants.

The federal system was created with the intention of combining the different advantages which result from the magnitude and the littleness of nations; and a glance at the

United States of America discovers the advantages which they have derived from its adoption.

In great centralized nations the legislator is obliged to give a character of uniformity to the laws, which does not always suit the diversity of customs and of districts; as he takes no cognizance of special cases, he can only proceed upon general principles; and the population are obliged to conform to the requirements of the laws, since legislation cannot adapt itself to the exigencies and the customs of the population, which is a great cause of trouble and misery. This disadvantage does not exist in confederations; Congress regulates the principal measures of the national government, and all the details of the administration are reserved to the provincial legislatures. One can hardly imagine how much this division of sovereignty contributes to the well-being of each of the states that compose the Union. In these small communities, which are never agitated by the desire of aggrandizement or the care of self-defense, all public authority and private energy are turned towards internal improvements. The central government of each state, which is in immediate relationship with the citizens, is daily apprised of the wants that arise in society; and new projects are proposed every year, which are discussed at town meetings or by the legislature, and which are transmitted by the press to stimulate the zeal and to excite the interest of the citizens. This spirit of improvement is constantly alive in the American republics, without compromising their tranquillity; the ambition of power yields to the less refined and less dangerous desire for well-being. It is generally believed in America that the existence and the permanence of the republican form of government in the New World depend upon the existence and the duration of the federal system; and it is not unusual to attribute a large share of the misfortunes that have befallen the new states of South America to the injudicious erection of great republics instead of a divided and confederate sovereignty.

It is incontestably true that the tastes and the habits of republican government in the United States were first created in the townships and the provincial assemblies. In a small state, like that of Connecticut, for instance, where cutting a canal or laying down a road is a great political question, where the state has no army to pay and no wars to carry on, and where much wealth or much honor cannot be given to the rulers, no form of government can be more natural or more appropriate than a republic. But it is this same republican spirit, it is these manners and customs of a free people, which have been created and nurtured in the different states, that must be afterwards applied to the country at large. The public spirit of the Union is, so to speak, nothing more than an aggregate or summary of the patriotic zeal of the separate provinces. Every citizen of the United States transfers, so to speak, his attachment to his little republic into the common store of American patriotism. In defending the Union he defends the increasing prosperity of his own state or county, the right of conducting its affairs, and the hope of causing measures of improvement to be adopted in it which may be favorable to his own interests; and these are motives that are wont to stir men more than the general interests of the country and the glory of the nation.

On the other hand, if the temper and the manners of the inhabitants especially fitted them to promote the welfare of a great republic, the federal system renders their task less difficult. The confederation of all the American states presents none of the ordinary inconveniences resulting from large associations of men. The Union is a great republic in extent, but the paucity of objects for which its government acts assimilates it to a small state. Its acts are important, but they are rare. As the sovereignty of the Union is limited and incomplete, its exercise is not dangerous to liberty; for it does not excite those insatiable desires for fame and power which have proved so fatal to great republics. As there is no common center to the country, great capital cities, colossal wealth, abject poverty, and sudden revolutions are alike unknown; and political passion, instead of spreading over the land like a fire on the prairies, spends its strength against the interests and the individual passions of every state.

Nevertheless, tangible objects and ideas circulate throughout the Union as freely as in a country inhabited by one people. Nothing checks the spirit of enterprise. The government invites the aid of all who have talents or knowledge to serve it. Inside of the frontiers of the Union profound peace prevails, as within the heart of some great empire; abroad it ranks with the most powerful nations of the earth: two thousand miles of coast are open to the commerce of the world; and as it holds the keys of a new world, its flag is respected in the most remote seas. The Union is happy and free as a small people, and glorious and strong as a great nation.

WHY THE FEDERAL SYSTEM IS NOT PRACTICABLE FOR ALL NATIONS, AND HOW THE ANGLO-AMERICANS WERE ENABLED TO ADOPT IT. *Every federal system has inherent faults that baffle the efforts of the legislator—The federal system is complex—It demands a daily exercise of the intelligence of the citizens—Practical knowledge of government common among the Americans—Relative weakness of the government of the Union another defect inherent in the federal system—The Americans have diminished without remedying it—The sovereignty of the separate states apparently weaker, but really stronger, than that of the Union—Why—Natural causes of Union, then, must exist between confederate nations besides the laws—What these causes are among the Anglo-Americans—Maine and Georgia, separated by a distance of a thousand miles, more naturally united than Normandy and Brittany—War the main peril of confederations—This proved even by the example of the United States—The Union has no great wars to fear—Why—Dangers which Europeans would incur if they adopted the federal system of the Americans.*

WHEN, after many efforts, a legislator succeeds in exercising an indirect influence upon the destiny of nations, his genius is lauded by mankind, while, in point of fact, the geographical position of the country, which he is unable to change, a social condition which arose without his co-operation, customs and opinions which he cannot trace to their source, and an origin with which he is unacquainted exercise so irresistible an influence over the courses of society that he is himself borne away by the current after an ineffectual resistance. Like the navigator, he may direct the vessel which bears him, but he can neither change its structure, nor raise the winds, nor lull the waters that swell beneath him.

I have shown the advantages that the Americans derive from their federal system; it remains for me to point out the circumstances that enabled them to adopt it, as its benefits cannot be enjoyed by all nations. The accidental defects of the federal system which originate in the laws may be corrected by the skill of the legislator, but there are evils inherent in the system which cannot be remedied by any effort. The people must therefore find in themselves the strength necessary to bear the natural imperfections of their government.

The most prominent evil of all federal systems is the complicated nature of the means they employ. Two sovereignties are necessarily in presence of each other. The legislator may simplify and equalize as far as possible the action of these two sovereignties, by limiting each of them to a sphere of authority accurately defined; but he cannot combine them into one or prevent them from coming into collision at certain points. The federal system, therefore, rests upon a theory which is complicated at the best, and which demands the daily exercise of a considerable share of discretion on the part of those it governs.

A proposition must be plain, to be adopted by the understanding of a people. A false notion which is clear and precise will always have more power in the world than a true principle which is obscure or involved. Thus it happens that parties, which are like small communities in the heart of the nation, invariably adopt some principle or name as a symbol, which very inadequately represents the end they have in view and the means that they employ, but without which they could neither act nor exist. The governments that are founded upon a single principle or a single feeling which is easily defined are perhaps not the best, but they are unquestionably the strongest and the most durable in the world.

In examining the Constitution of the United States, which is the most perfect federal constitution that ever existed, one is startled at the variety of information and the amount of discernment that it presupposes in the people whom it is meant to govern. The government of the Union depends almost entirely upon legal fictions; the Union is an ideal nation, which exists, so to speak, only in the mind, and whose limits and extent can only be discerned by the understanding.

After the general theory is comprehended, many difficulties remain to be solved in its application; for the sovereignty of the Union is so involved in that of the states that it is impossible to distinguish its boundaries at the first glance. The whole structure of the government is artificial and conventional, and it would be ill adapted to a people which has not been long accustomed to conduct its own affairs, or to one in which the science of politics has not descended to the humblest classes of society. I have never been more struck by the good sense and the practical judgment of the Americans than in the manner in which they elude the numberless difficulties resulting from their Federal Constitution. I scarcely ever met with a plain American citizen who could not distinguish with surprising facility the obligations created by the laws of Congress from those created by the laws of his own state, and who, after having discriminated between the matters which come under the cognizance of the Union and those which the local legislature is competent to regulate, could not point out the exact limit of the separate jurisdictions of the Federal courts and the tribunals of the state.

The Constitution of the United States resembles those fine creations of human industry which ensure wealth and renown to their inventors, but which are profitless in other hands. This truth is exemplified by the condition of Mexico at the present time. The Mexicans were desirous of establishing a federal system, and they took the Federal Constitution of their neighbors, the Anglo-Americans, as their model and copied it almost entirely.[37] But although they had borrowed the letter of the law, they could not carry over the spirit that gives it life. They were involved in ceaseless embarrassments by the mechanism of their dual government; the sovereignty of the states and that of the Union perpetually exceeded their respective privileges and came into collision; and to the present day Mexico is alternately the victim of anarchy and the slave of military despotism.

The second and most fatal of all defects, and that which I believe to be inherent in the federal system, is the relative weakness of the government of the Union. The principle upon which all confederations rest is that of a divided sovereignty. Legislators may render this partition less perceptible, they may even conceal it for a time from the public eye, but they cannot prevent it from existing; and a divided sovereignty must always be weaker than an entire one. The

[37] See the Mexican Constitution of 1824.

remarks made on the Constitution of the United States have shown with what skill the Americans, while restraining the power of the Union within the narrow limits of a federal government, have given it the semblance, and to a certain extent the force, of a national government. By this means the legislators of the Union have diminished the natural danger of confederations, but have not entirely obviated it.

The American government, it is said, does not address itself to the states, but transmits its injunctions directly to the citizens and compels them individually to comply with its demands. But if the Federal law were to clash with the interests and the prejudices of a state, it might be feared that all the citizens of that state would conceive themselves to be interested in the cause of a single individual who refused to obey. If all the citizens of the state were aggrieved at the same time and in the same manner by the authority of the Union, the Federal government would vainly attempt to subdue them individually; they would instinctively unite in a common defense and would find an organization already prepared for them in the sovereignty that their state is allowed to enjoy. Fiction would give way to reality, and an organized portion of the nation might then contest the central authority.

The same observation holds good with regard to the Federal jurisdiction. If the courts of the Union violated an important law of a state in a private case, the real though not the apparent contest would be between the aggrieved state represented by a citizen and the Union represented by its courts of justice.[38]

He would have but a partial knowledge of the world who should imagine that it is possible by the aid of legal fictions

[38] For instance, the Union possesses by the Constitution the right of selling unoccupied lands for its own profit. Suppose that the state of Ohio should claim the same right in behalf of certain tracts lying within its own boundaries, upon the plea that the Constitution refers only to those lands which do not belong to the jurisdiction of any particular state, and consequently should choose to dispose of them itself. The litigation would be carried on, it is true, in the names of the purchasers from the state of Ohio and the purchasers from the Union, and not in the names of Ohio and the Union. But what would become of this legal fiction if the Federal purchaser was confirmed in his right by the courts of the Union while the other competitor was ordered to retain possession by the tribunals of the state of Ohio?

to prevent men from finding out and employing those means of gratifying their passions which have been left open to them. The American legislators, though they have rendered a collision between the two sovereignties less probable, have not destroyed the causes of such a misfortune. It may even be affirmed that, in case of such a collision, they have not been able to ensure the victory of the Federal element. The Union is possessed of money and troops, but the states have kept the affections and the prejudices of the people. The sovereignty of the Union is an abstract being, which is connected with but few external objects; the sovereignty of the states is perceptible by the senses, easily understood, and constantly active. The former is of recent creation, the latter is coeval with the people itself. The sovereignty of the Union is factitious, that of the states is natural and self-existent, without effort, like the authority of a parent. The sovereignty of the nation affects a few of the chief interests of society; it represents an immense but remote country, a vague and ill-defined sentiment. The authority of the states controls every individual citizen at every hour and in all circumstances; it protects his property, his freedom, and his life; it affects at every moment his well-being or his misery. When we recollect the traditions, the customs, the prejudices of local and familiar attachment with which it is connected, we cannot doubt the superiority of a power that rests on the instinct of patriotism, so natural to the human heart.

Since legislators cannot prevent such dangerous collisions as occur between the two sovereignties which coexist in the Federal system, their first object must be, not only to dissuade the confederate states from warfare, but to encourage such dispositions as lead to peace. Hence it is that the Federal compact cannot be lasting unless there exists in the communities which are leagued together a certain number of inducements to union which render their common dependence agreeable and the task of the government light. The Federal system cannot succeed without the presence of favorable circumstances added to the influence of good laws. All the nations that have ever formed a confederation have been held together by some common interests, which served as the intellectual ties of association.

But men have sentiments and principles as well as material interests. A certain uniformity of civilization is not less necessary to the durability of a confederation than a uniformity of interests in the states that compose it. In Switzerland the difference between the civilization of the Canton of Uri and that of the Canton of Vaud is like the difference between the fifteenth and the nineteenth centuries; therefore, properly speaking, Switzerland has never had a federal government. The union between these two cantons exists only on the map; and this would soon be perceived if an attempt were made by a central authority to prescribe the same laws to the whole territory.

The circumstance which makes it easy to maintain a Federal government in America is not only that the states have similar interests, a common origin, and a common language, but that they have also arrived at the same stage of civilization, which almost always renders a union feasible. I do not know of any European nation, however small, that does not present less uniformity in its different provinces than the American people, which occupy a territory as extensive as one half of Europe. The distance from Maine to Georgia is about one thousand miles; but the difference between the civilization of Maine and that of Georgia is slighter than the difference between the habits of Normandy and those of Brittany. Maine and Georgia, which are placed at the opposite extremities of a great empire, have therefore more real inducements to form a confederation than Normandy and Brittany, which are separated only by a brook.

The geographical position of the country increased the facilities that the American legislators derived from the usages and customs of the inhabitants; and it is to this circumstance that the adoption and the maintenance of the Federal system are mainly attributable.

The most important occurrence in the life of a nation is the breaking out of a war. In war a people act as one man against foreign nations in defense of their very existence. The skill of the government, the good sense of the community, and the natural fondness that men almost always entertain for their country may be enough as long as the only object is to maintain peace in the interior of the state and to favor its internal prosperity; but that the nation may carry on a great war the people must make more numerous and painful sacrifices; and to suppose that a great number of men will of their own accord submit to these exigencies is to betray an ignorance of human nature. All the nations that have been obliged to sustain a long and serious warfare have consequently been led to augment the power of their government. Those who have not succeeded in this attempt have been subjugated. A long war almost always reduces nations to the wretched alternative of being abandoned to ruin by defeat or to despotism by success. War therefore renders the weakness of a government most apparent and most alarming; and I have shown that the inherent defect of federal governments is that of being weak.

The federal system not only has no centralized administration, and nothing that resembles one, but the central government itself is imperfectly organized, which is always a great cause of weakness when the nation is opposed to other countries which are themselves governed by a single authority. In the Federal Constitution of the United States, where the central government has more real force than in any other confederation, this evil is still extremely evident. A single example will illustrate the case.

The Constitution confers upon Congress the right of "calling forth the militia to execute the laws of the Union, suppress insurrections, and repel invasions"; and another article declares that the President of the United States is the commander-in-chief of the militia. In the war of 1812 the President ordered the militia of the Northern states to march to the frontiers; but Connecticut and Massachusetts, whose interests were impaired by the war, refused to obey the command. They argued that the Constitution authorizes the Federal government to call forth the militia in case of *insurrection* or *invasion;* but in the present instance there was neither invasion nor insurrection. They added that the same Constitution which conferred upon the Union the right of calling the militia into active service reserved to the states that of naming the officers; and consequently (as they understood the clause) no officer of the Union had any right to command the militia, even during war, except the President in person: and in this case they were ordered to join an army commanded by another individual. These absurd and pernicious doctrines received the sanction not only of the governors and the legislative bodies, but also of the courts of justice in both states; and the Federal government was forced to raise elsewhere the troops that it required.[39]

How does it happen, then, that the American Union, with all the relative perfection of its laws, is not dissolved by the occurrence of a great war? It is because it has no great wars to fear. Placed in the center of an immense continent, which offers a boundless field for human industry, the Union is almost as much insulated from the world as if all its frontiers were girt by the ocean. Canada contains only a million inhabitants, and its population is divided into two inimical nations. The rigor of the climate limits the extension of its territory, and shuts up its ports during the six months of winter. From Canada to the Gulf of Mexico a few savage tribes are to be met with, which retire, perishing in their retreat, before six thousand soldiers. To the south the Union has a point of contact with the empire of Mexico; and it is thence that serious hostilities may one day be expected to arise. But for a long while to come the uncivilized state of the Mexican people, the depravity of their morals, and their extreme poverty will prevent that country from ranking high among nations. As for the powers of Europe, they are too distant to be formidable.[40]

The great advantage of the United States does not, then, consist in a Federal Constitution which allows it to carry on great wars, but in a geographical position which renders such wars extremely improbable.

No one can be more inclined than I am to appreciate the advantages of the federal system, which I hold to be one of the combinations most favorable to the prosperity and freedom of man. I envy the lot of those nations which have been able to adopt it; but I cannot believe that any confederate people could maintain a long or an equal contest with a

[39] Kent's *Commentaries*, Vol. I, p. 244. I have selected an example that relates to a time long after the promulgation of the present Constitution. If I had gone back to the days of the Confederation, I might have given still more striking instances. The whole nation was at that time in a state of high enthusiasm; the Revolution was represented by a man who was the idol of the people; but at that very period, Congress, to say the truth, had no resources at all at its disposal. Troops and supplies were perpetually wanting. The best-devised projects failed in their execution, and the Union, constantly on the verge of destruction, was saved by the weakness of its enemies far more than by its own strength.

[40] See Appendix O.

nation of similar strength in which the government is centralized. A people which, in the presence of the great military monarchies of Europe, should divide its sovereignty into fractional parts would, in my opinion, by that very act abdicate its power, and perhaps its existence and its name. But such is the admirable position of the New World that man has no other enemy than himself, and that, in order to be happy and to be free, he has only to determine that he will be so.

Chapter IX

THUS FAR *I have examined the institutions of the United States; I have passed their legislation in review and have described the present forms of political society in that country. But above these institutions and beyond all these characteristic forms, there is a sovereign power, that of the people, which may destroy or modify them at its pleasure. It remains to be shown in what manner this power, superior to the laws, acts; what are its instincts and its passions, what the secret springs that retard, accelerate, or direct its irresistible course, what the effects of its unbounded authority, and what the destiny that is reserved for it.*

HOW IT CAN BE STRICTLY SAID THAT THE PEOPLE GOVERN IN THE UNITED STATES

IN AMERICA the people appoint the legislative and the executive power and furnish the jurors who punish all infractions of the laws. The institutions are democratic, not only in their principle, but in all their consequences; and the people elect their representatives *directly,* and for the most part *annually,* in order to ensure their dependence. The people are therefore the real directing power; and although the form of government is representative, it is evident that the opinions, the prejudices, the interests, and even the passions of the people are hindered by no permanent obstacles from exercising a perpetual influence on the daily conduct of affairs. In the United States the majority governs in the name of the people, as is the case in all countries in which the people are supreme. This majority is principally composed of peaceable citizens, who, either by inclination or by interest, sincerely wish the welfare of their country. But they are surrounded by the incessant agitation of parties, who attempt to gain their co-operation and support.

Chapter X

PARTIES IN THE UNITED STATES

GREAT DISTINCTION *to be made between parties—Parties that are to each other as rival nations—Parties properly so called—Difference between great and small parties —Epochs that produce them—Their characteristics— America has had great parties—They are extinct—Federalists—Republicans—Defeat of the Federalists—Difficulty of creating parties in the United States—What is done with this intention—Aristocratic or democratic character to be met with in all parties—Struggle of General Jackson against the Bank of the United States.*

A GREAT distinction must be made between parties. Some countries are so large that the different populations which inhabit them, although united under the same government, have contradictory interests, and they may consequently be in a perpetual state of opposition. In this case the different fractions of the people may more properly be considered as distinct nations than as mere parties; and if a civil war breaks out, the struggle is carried on by rival states rather than by factions in the same state.

But when the citizens entertain different opinions upon subjects which affect the whole country alike, such, for instance, as the principles upon which the government is to be conducted, then distinctions arise that may correctly be styled parties. Parties are a necessary evil in free governments; but they have not at all times the same character and the same propensities.

At certain periods a nation may be oppressed by such insupportable evils as to conceive the design of effecting a total change in its political constitution; at other times, the mischief lies still deeper and the existence of society itself is endangered. Such are the times of great revolutions and of great parties. But between these epochs of misery and confusion there are periods during which human society seems to rest and mankind to take breath. This pause is, indeed, only apparent, for time does not stop its course for nations any more than for men; they are all advancing every day towards a goal with which they are unacquainted. We imagine them to be stationary only when their progress escapes our observation, as men who are walking seem to be standing still to those who run.

But however this may be, there are certain epochs in which the changes that take place in the social and political constitution of nations are so slow and imperceptible that men imagine they have reached a final state; and the human mind, believing itself to be firmly based upon sure foundations, does not extend its researches beyond a certain horizon. These are the times of small parties and of intrigue.

The political parties that I style great are those which cling to principles rather than to their consequences; to general and not to special cases; to ideas and not to men. These parties are usually distinguished by nobler features, more generous passions, more genuine convictions, and a more bold and open conduct than the others. In them private interest, which always plays the chief part in political passions, is more studiously veiled under the pretext of the public good; and it may even be sometimes concealed from the eyes of the very persons whom it excites and impels.

Minor parties, on the other hand, are generally deficient in political good faith. As they are not sustained or dignified by lofty purposes, they ostensibly display the selfishness of their character in their actions. They glow with a factitious zeal; their language is vehement, but their conduct is timid and irresolute. The means which they employ are as wretched as the end at which they aim. Hence it happens that when a calm state succeeds a violent revolution, great men seem suddenly to disappear and the powers of the human mind to lie concealed. Society is convulsed by great parties, it is only agitated by minor ones; it is torn by the former, by the latter it is degraded; and if the first sometimes save it by a salutary perturbation, the last invariably disturb it to no good end.

America has had great parties, but has them no longer; and if her happiness is thereby considerably increased, her morality has suffered. When the War of Independence was

terminated and the foundations of the new government were
to be laid down, the nation was divided between two opinions—two opinions which are as old as the world and which
are perpetually to be met with, under different forms and
various names, in all free communities, the one tending to
limit, the other to extend indefinitely, the power of the people. The conflict between these two opinions never assumed
that degree of violence in America which it has frequently
displayed elsewhere. Both parties of the Americans were
agreed upon the most essential points; and neither of them
had to destroy an old constitution or to overthrow the structure of society in order to triumph. In neither of them, consequently, were a great number of private interests affected
by success or defeat: but moral principles of a high order,
such as the love of equality and of independence, were concerned in the struggle, and these sufficed to kindle violent
passions.

The party that desired to limit the power of the people,
endeavored to apply its doctrines more especially to the
Constitution of the Union, whence it derived its name of
Federal. The other party, which affected to be exclusively
attached to the cause of liberty, took that of *Republican*.
America is the land of democracy, and the Federalists,
therefore, were always in a minority; but they reckoned on
their side almost all the great men whom the War of Independence had produced, and their moral power was very
considerable. Their cause, moreover, was favored by circumstances. The ruin of the first Confederation had impressed the people with a dread of anarchy, and the Federalists profited by this transient disposition of the multitude.
For ten or twelve years, they were at the head of affairs, and
they were able to apply some, though not all, of their principles; for the hostile current was becoming from day to day
too violent to be checked. In 1801 the Republicans got
possession of the government: Thomas Jefferson was elected
President; and he increased the influence of their party by
the weight of his great name, the brilliance of his talents,
and his immense popularity.

The means by which the Federalists had maintained their
position were artificial, and their resources were temporary;
it was by the virtues or the talents of their leaders, as well as
by fortunate circumstances, that they had risen to power.

When the Republicans attained that station in their turn, their opponents were overwhelmed by utter defeat. An immense majority declared itself against the retiring party, and the Federalists found themselves in so small a minority that they at once despaired of future success. From that moment the Republican or Democratic Party has proceeded from conquest to conquest, until it has acquired absolute supremacy in the country. The Federalists, perceiving that they were vanquished, without resource, and isolated in the midst of the nation, fell into two divisions, of which one joined the victorious Republicans, and the other laid down their banners and changed their name. Many years have elapsed since they wholly ceased to exist as a party.

The accession of the Federalists to power was, in my opinion, one of the most fortunate incidents that accompanied the formation of the great American Union: they resisted the inevitable propensities of their country and their age. But whether their theories were good or bad, they had the fault of being inapplicable, as a whole, to the society which they wished to govern, and that which occurred under the auspices of Jefferson must therefore have taken place sooner or later. But their government at least gave the new republic time to acquire a certain stability, and afterwards to support without inconvenience the rapid growth of the very doctrines which they had combated. A considerable number of their principles, moreover, were embodied at last in the political creed of their opponents; and the Federal Constitution, which subsists at the present day, is a lasting monument of their patriotism and their wisdom.

Great political parties, then, are not to be met with in the United States at the present time. Parties, indeed, may be found which threaten the future of the Union; but there is none which seems to contest the present form of government or the present course of society. The parties by which the Union is menaced do not rest upon principles, but upon material interests. These interests constitute, in the different provinces of so vast an empire, rival nations rather than parties. Thus, upon a recent occasion the North contended for the system of commercial prohibition, and the South took up arms in favor of free trade, simply because the North is a manufacturing and the South an agricultural community; and the restrictive system that was profitable to the one was prejudicial to the other.

In the absence of great parties the United States swarms with lesser controversies, and public opinion is divided into a thousand minute shades of difference upon questions of detail. The pains that are taken to create parties are inconceivable, and at the present day it is no easy task. In the United States there is no religious animosity, because all religion is respected and no sect is predominant; there is no jealousy of rank, because the people are everything and none can contest their authority; lastly, there is no public misery to serve as a means of agitation, because the physical position of the country opens so wide a field to industry that man only needs to be let alone to be able to accomplish prodigies. Nevertheless, ambitious men will succeed in creating parties, since it is difficult to eject a person from authority upon the mere ground that this place is coveted by others. All the skill of the actors in the political world lies in the art of creating parties. A political aspirant in the United States begins by discerning his own interest, and discovering those other interests which may be collected around and amalgamated with it. He then contrives to find out some doctrine or principle that may suit the purposes of this new association, which he adopts in order to bring forward his party and secure its popularity: just as the imprimatur of the king was in former days printed upon the title page of a volume and was thus incorporated with a book to which it in no wise belonged. This being done, the new party is ushered into the political world.

To a stranger all the domestic controversies of the Americans at first appear to be incomprehensible or puerile, and he is at a loss whether to pity a people who take such arrant trifles in good earnest or to envy that happiness which enables a community to discuss them. But when he comes to study the secret propensities that govern the factions of America, he easily perceives that the greater part of them are more or less connected with one or the other of those two great divisions which have always existed in free communities. The deeper we penetrate into the inmost thought of these parties, the more we perceive that the object of the one is to limit and that of the other to extend the authority of the people. I do not assert that the ostensible purpose or even that the secret aim of American parties is to promote the rule of aristocracy or democracy in the country; but I affirm that aristocratic or democratic passions may easily be detected at the bottom of all parties, and that, although they escape a superficial observation, they are the main point and soul of every faction in the United States.

To quote a recent example, when President Jackson attacked the Bank of the United States, the country was excited, and parties were formed; the well-informed classes rallied round the bank, the common people round the President. But it must not be imagined that the people had formed a rational opinion upon a question which offers so many difficulties to the most experienced statesmen. By no means. The bank is a great establishment, which has an independent existence; and the people, accustomed to make and unmake whatsoever they please, are startled to meet with this obstacle to their authority. In the midst of the perpetual fluctuation of society, the community is irritated by so permanent an institution and is led to attack it, in order to see whether it can be shaken, like everything else.

REMAINS OF THE ARISTOCRATIC PARTY IN THE UNITED STATES.
*Secret opposition of wealthy individuals to democracy
—Their retirement—Their taste for exclusive pleasures
and for luxury at home—Their simplicity abroad—
Their affected condescension towards the people.*

IT sometimes happens in a people among whom various opinions prevail that the balance of parties is lost and one of them obtains an irresistible preponderance, overpowers all obstacles, annihilates its opponents, and appropriates all the resources of society to its own use. The vanquished despair of success, hide their heads, and are silent. The nation seems to be governed by a single principle, universal stillness prevails, and the prevailing party assumes the credit of having restored peace and unanimity to the country. But under this apparent unanimity still exist profound differences of opinion, and real opposition.

This is what occurred in America; when the democratic party got the upper hand, it took exclusive possession of the conduct of affairs, and from that time the laws and the customs of society have been adapted to its caprices. At the present day the more affluent classes of society have no influence in political affairs; and wealth, far from conferring a right, is rather a cause of unpopularity than a means of attaining power. The rich abandon the lists, through unwillingness to contend, and frequently to contend in vain, against the poorer classes of their fellow citizens. As they cannot occupy in public a position equivalent to what they hold in private life, they abandon the former and give themselves up to the latter; and they constitute a private society in the state which has its own tastes and pleasures. They submit to this state of things as an irremediable evil, but they are careful not to show that they are galled by its continuance; one often hears them laud the advantages of a republican government and democratic institutions when they are in public. Next to hating their enemies, men are most inclined to flatter them.

Mark, for instance, that opulent citizen, who is as anxious as a Jew of the Middle Ages to conceal his wealth. His dress is plain, his demeanor unassuming; but the interior of his dwelling glitters with luxury, and none but a few chosen guests, whom he haughtily styles his equals, are allowed to penetrate into this sanctuary. No European noble is more exclusive in his pleasures or more jealous of the smallest advantages that a privileged station confers. But the same individual crosses the city to reach a dark counting-house in the center of traffic, where everyone may accost him who pleases. If he meets his cobbler on the way, they stop and converse; the two citizens discuss the affairs of the state and shake hands before they part.

But beneath this artificial enthusiasm and these obsequious attentions to the preponderating power, it is easy to perceive that the rich have a hearty dislike of the democratic institutions of their country. The people form a power which they at once fear and despise. If the maladministration of the democracy ever brings about a revolutionary crisis and monarchical institutions ever become practicable in the United States, the truth of what I advance will become obvious.

The two chief weapons that parties use in order to obtain success are the newspapers and public associations.

Chapter XI

LIBERTY OF THE PRESS IN THE UNITED STATES

DIFFICULTY of restraining the liberty of the press—Particular reasons that some nations have for cherishing this liberty—The liberty of the press a necessary consequence of the sovereignty of the people as it is understood in America—Violent language of the periodical press in the United States—The periodical press has some peculiar instincts, proved by the example of the United States—Opinion of the Americans upon the judicial repression of the abuses of the press—Why the press is less powerful in America than in France.

THE INFLUENCE of the liberty of the press does not affect political opinions alone, but extends to all the opinions of men and modifies customs as well as laws. In another part of this work I shall attempt to determine the degree of influence that the liberty of the press has exercised upon civil society in the United States and to point out the direction which it has given to the ideas as well as the tone which it has imparted to the character and the feelings of the Anglo-Americans. At present I propose only to examine the effects produced by the liberty of the press in the political world.

I confess that I do not entertain that firm and complete attachment to the liberty of the press which is wont to be excited by things that are supremely good in their very nature. I approve of it from a consideration more of the evils it prevents than of the advantages it ensures.

If anyone could point out an intermediate and yet a tenable position between the complete independence and the entire servitude of opinion, I should perhaps be inclined to adopt it, but the difficulty is to discover this intermediate position. Intending to correct the licentiousness of the press and to restore the use of orderly language, you first try the offender by a jury; but if the jury acquits him, the opinion

which was that of a single individual becomes the opinion of
the whole country. Too much and too little has therefore
been done; go farther, then. You bring the delinquent before
permanent magistrates; but even here the cause must be
heard before it can be decided; and the very principles which
no book would have ventured to avow are blazoned forth in
the pleadings, and what was obscurely hinted at in a single
composition is thus repeated in a multitude of other publications. The language is only the expression and, if I may
so speak, the body of the thought, but it is not the thought
itself. Tribunals may condemn the body, but the sense, the
spirit of the work is too subtle for their authority. Too much
has still been done to recede, too little to attain your end;
you must go still farther. Establish a censorship of the press.
But the tongue of the public speaker will still make itself
heard, and your purpose is not yet accomplished; you have
only increased the mischief. Thought is not, like physical
strength, dependent upon the number of its agents; nor can
authors be counted like the troops that compose an army.
On the contrary, the authority of a principle is often increased by the small number of men by whom it is expressed. The words of one strong-minded man addressed to
the passions of a listening assembly have more power than
the vociferations of a thousand orators; and if it be allowed
to speak freely in any one public place, the consequence
is the same as if free speaking was allowed in every village.
The liberty of speech must therefore be destroyed as well as
the liberty of the press. And now you have succeeded, everybody is reduced to silence. But your object was to repress
the abuses of liberty, and you are brought to the feet of a
despot. You have been led from the extreme of independence to the extreme of servitude without finding a single
tenable position on the way at which you could stop.

There are certain nations which have peculiar reasons
for cherishing the liberty of the press, independently of the
general motives that I have just pointed out. For in certain
countries which profess to be free, every individual agent of
the government may violate the laws with impunity, since
the constitution does not give to those who are injured a
right of complaint before the courts of justice. In this case
the liberty of the press is not merely one of the guarantees,
but it is the only guarantee of their liberty and security that

the citizens possess. If the rulers of these nations proposed to abolish the independence of the press, the whole people might answer: Give us the right of prosecuting your offenses before the ordinary tribunals, and perhaps we may then waive our right of appeal to the tribunal of public opinion.

In countries where the doctrine of the sovereignty of the people ostensibly prevails, the censorship of the press is not only dangerous, but absurd. When the right of every citizen to a share in the government of society is acknowledged, everyone must be presumed to be able to choose between the various opinions of his contemporaries and to appreciate the different facts from which inferences may be drawn. The sovereignty of the people and the liberty of the press may therefore be regarded as correlative, just as the censorship of the press and universal suffrage are two things which are irreconcilably opposed and which cannot long be retained among the institutions of the same people. Not a single individual of the millions who inhabit the United States has as yet dared to propose any restrictions on the liberty of the press. The first newspaper over which I cast my eyes, upon my arrival in America, contained the following article:

> In all this affair, the language of Jackson [the President] has been that of a heartless despot, solely occupied with the preservation of his own authority. Ambition is his crime, and it will be his punishment, too: intrigue is his native element, and intrigue will confound his tricks, and deprive him of his power. He governs by means of corruption, and his immoral practices will redound to his shame and confusion. His conduct in the political arena has been that of a shameless and lawless gamester. He succeeded at the time; but the hour of retribution approaches, and he will be obliged to disgorge his winnings, to throw aside his false dice, and to end his days in some retirement, where he may curse his madness at his leisure; for repentance is a virtue with which his heart is likely to remain forever unacquainted. (*Vincennes Gazette.*)

Many persons in France think that the violence of the press originates in the instability of the social state, in our political passions and the general feeling of uneasiness that consequently prevails; and it is therefore supposed that as soon as society has resumed a certain degree of composure, the press will abandon its present vehemence. For my own part, I would willingly attribute to these causes the extraordinary ascendancy which the press has acquired over the nation; but I do not think that they exercise much influence on its language. The periodical press appears to me to have passions and instincts of its own, independent of the circumstances in which it is placed; and the present condition of America corroborates this opinion.

America is perhaps, at this moment, the country of the whole world that contains the fewest germs of revolution; but the press is not less destructive in its principles there than in France, and it displays the same violence without the same reasons for indignation. In America as in France it constitutes a singular power, so strangely composed of mingled good and evil that liberty could not live without it, and public order can hardly be maintained against it. Its power is certainly much greater in France than in the United States, though nothing is more rare in the latter country than to hear of a prosecution being instituted against it. The reason for this is perfectly simple: the Americans, having once admitted the doctrine of the sovereignty of the people, apply it with perfect sincerity. It was never their intention out of elements which are changing every day to create institutions that should last forever; and there is consequently nothing criminal in an attack upon the existing laws, provided a violent infraction of them is not intended. They are also of the opinion that courts of justice are powerless to check the abuses of the press, and that, as the subtlety of human language perpetually eludes judicial analysis, offenses of this nature somehow escape the hand which attempts to seize them. They hold that to act with efficacy upon the press it would be necessary to find a tribunal not only devoted to the existing order of things, but capable of surmounting the influence of public opinion; a tribunal which should conduct its proceedings without publicity, which should pronounce its decrees without assigning its motives, and punish the intentions even more than the language of a writer. Whoever should be able to create and maintain a tribunal of this kind would waste his time in prosecuting the liberty of the press; for he would be the absolute master of the whole community and would be as free to rid himself of the authors as of their writings. In this question, therefore, there is no medium between servitude and license; in order to enjoy the inestimable benefits that the liberty of the press ensures, it is necessary to submit to the inevitable evils that it creates. To expect to acquire the former and to escape the latter is to cherish one of those illusions which commonly mislead nations in their times of sickness when, tired with faction and exhausted by effort, they attempt to make hostile opinions and contrary principles coexist upon the same soil.

The small influence of the American journals is attributable to several reasons, among which are the following:

The liberty of writing, like all other liberty, is most formidable when it is a novelty, for a people who have never been accustomed to hear state affairs discussed before them place implicit confidence in the first tribune who presents himself. The Anglo-Americans have enjoyed this liberty ever since the foundation of the colonies; moreover, the press cannot create human passions, however skillfully it may kindle them where they exist. In America political life is active, varied, even agitated, but is rarely affected by those deep passions which are excited only when material interests are impaired; and in the United States these interests are prosperous. A glance at a French and an American newspaper is sufficient to show the difference that exists in this respect between the two nations. In France the space allotted to commercial advertisements is very limited, and the news intelligence is not considerable, but the essential part of the journal is the discussion of the politics of the day. In America three quarters of the enormous sheet are filled with advertisements, and the remainder is frequently occupied by political intelligence or trivial anecdotes; it is only from time to time that one finds a corner devoted to passionate discussions like those which the journalists of France every day give to their readers.

It has been demonstrated by observation, and discovered by the sure instinct even of the pettiest despots, that the influence of a power is increased in proportion as its direction is centralized. In France the press combines a twofold centralization; almost all its power is centered in the same spot and, so to speak, in the same hands, for its organs are far from numerous. The influence upon a skeptical nation of a public press thus constituted must be almost unbounded. It is an enemy with whom a government may sign an occasional truce, but which it is difficult to resist for any length of time.

Neither of these kinds of centralization exists in America. The United States has no metropolis; the intelligence and the power of the people are disseminated through all the parts of this vast country, and instead of radiating from a common point they cross each other in every direction; the Americans have nowhere established any central direction of opinion, any more than of the conduct of affairs. This difference arises from local circumstances and not from human power; but it is owing to the laws of the Union that there are no licenses to be granted to printers, no securities demanded from editors, as in France, and no stamp duty, as in France and England. The consequence is that nothing is easier than to set up a newspaper, as a small number of subscribers suffices to defray the expenses.

Hence the number of periodical and semi-periodical publications in the United States is almost incredibly large. The most enlightened Americans attribute the little influence of the press to this excessive dissemination of its power; and it is an axiom of political science in that country that the only way to neutralize the effect of the public journals is to multiply their number. I cannot see how a truth which is so self-evident should not already have been more generally admitted in Europe. I can see why the persons who hope to bring about revolutions by means of the press should be desirous of confining it to a few powerful organs, but it is inconceivable that the official partisans of the existing state of things and the natural supporters of the laws should attempt to diminish the influence of the press by concentrating its power. The governments of Europe seem to treat the press with the courtesy which the knights of old showed to their opponents; having found from their own experience that centralization is a powerful weapon, they have furnished their enemies with it in order doubtless to have more glory for overcoming them.

In America there is scarcely a hamlet that has not its

newspaper. It may readily be imagined that neither discipline nor unity of action can be established among so many combatants, and each one consequently fights under his own standard. All the political journals of the United States are, indeed, arrayed on the side of the administration or against it; but they attack and defend it in a thousand different ways. They cannot form those great currents of opinion which sweep away the strongest dikes. This division of the influence of the press produces other consequences scarcely less remarkable. The facility with which newspapers can be established produces a multitude of them; but as the competition prevents any considerable profit, persons of much capacity are rarely led to engage in these undertakings. Such is the number of the public prints that even if they were a source of wealth, writers of ability could not be found to direct them all. The journalists of the United States are generally in a very humble position, with a scanty education and a vulgar turn of mind. The will of the majority is the most general of laws, and it establishes certain habits to which everyone must then conform; the aggregate of these common habits is what is called the class spirit (*esprit de corps*) of each profession; thus there is the class spirit of the bar, of the court, etc. The class spirit of the French journalists consists in a violent but frequently an eloquent and lofty manner of discussing the great interests of the state, and the exceptions to this mode of writing are only occasional. The characteristics of the American journalist consist in an open and coarse appeal to the passions of his readers; he abandons principles to assail the characters of individuals, to track them into private life and disclose all their weaknesses and vices.

Nothing can be more deplorable than this abuse of the powers of thought. I shall have occasion to point out hereafter the influence of the newspapers upon the taste and the morality of the American people, but my present subject exclusively concerns the political world. It cannot be denied that the political effects of this extreme license of the press tend indirectly to the maintenance of public order. Individuals who already stand high in the esteem of their fellow citizens are afraid to write in the newspapers, and they are thus deprived of the most powerful instrument that they can use to excite the passions of the multitude to their own advantage.[1]

The personal opinions of the editors have no weight in the eyes of the public. What they seek in a newspaper is a knowledge of facts, and it is only by altering or distorting those facts that a journalist can contribute to the support of his own views.

But although the press is limited to these resources, its influence in America is immense. It causes political life to circulate through all the parts of that vast territory. Its eye is constantly open to detect the secret springs of political designs and to summon the leaders of all parties in turn to the bar of public opinion. It rallies the interests of the community round certain principles and draws up the creed of every party; for it affords a means of intercourse between those who hear and address each other without ever coming into immediate contact. When many organs of the press adopt the same line of conduct, their influence in the long run becomes irresistible, and public opinion, perpetually assailed from the same side, eventually yields to the attack. In the United States each separate journal exercises but little authority; but the power of the periodical press is second only to that of the people.[2]

THE OPINIONS *established in the United States under the influence of the liberty of the press are frequently more firmly rooted than those which are formed elsewhere under the sanction of a censor.*

IN the United States democracy perpetually brings new men to the conduct of public affairs, and the administration consequently seldom preserves consistency or order in its measures. But the general principles of the government are more stable and the chief opinions which regulate society are more durable there than in many other countries. When once the Americans have taken up an idea, whether it be well or ill founded, nothing is more difficult than to eradicate it from their minds. The same tenacity of opinion has been

[1] They write in the papers only when they choose to address the people in their own name; as, for instance, when they are called upon to repel calumnious imputations or to correct a misstatement of facts.

[2] See Appendix P.

observed in England, where for the last century greater freedom of thought and more invincible prejudices have existed than in any other country of Europe. I attribute this to a cause that may at first sight appear to have an opposite tendency: namely, to the liberty of the press. The nations among whom this liberty exists cling to their opinions as much from pride as from conviction. They cherish them because they hold them to be just and because they chose them of their own free will; and they adhere to them, not only because they are true, but because they are their own. Several other reasons conduce to the same end.

It was remarked by a man of genius that "ignorance lies at the two ends of knowledge." Perhaps it would have been more correct to say that strong convictions are found only at the two ends, and that doubt lies in the middle. The human intellect, in truth, may be considered in three distinct states, which frequently succeed one another.

A man believes firmly because he adopts a proposition without inquiry. He doubts as soon as objections present themselves. But he frequently succeeds in satisfying these doubts, and then he begins again to believe. This time he has not a dim and casual glimpse of the truth, but sees it clearly before him and advances by the light it gives.[3]

When the liberty of the press acts upon men who are in the first of these three states, it does not immediately disturb their habit of believing implicitly without investigation, but it changes every day the objects of their unreflecting convictions. The human mind continues to discern but one point at a time upon the whole intellectual horizon, and that point is constantly changing. This is the period of sudden revolutions. Woe to the generations which first abruptly adopt the freedom of the press.

The circle of novel ideas, however, is soon traveled over. Experience comes to undeceive men and plunges them into doubt and general mistrust. We may rest assured that the majority of mankind will always remain in one of these two states, will either believe they know not wherefore, or will not know what to believe. Few are those who can ever attain to that other state of rational and independent con-

---

[3] It may be doubted, however, whether this rational and self-guiding conviction arouses as much fervor or enthusiastic devotion in men as does their first dogmatical belief.

viction which true knowledge can produce out of the midst of doubt.

It has been remarked that in times of great religious fervor men sometimes change their religious opinions; whereas in times of general skepticism everyone clings to his old persuasion. The same thing takes place in politics under the liberty of the press. In countries where all the theories of social science have been contested in their turn, men who have adopted one of them stick to it, not so much because they are sure of its truth as because they are not sure that there is any better to be had. In the present age men are not very ready to die for their opinions, but they are rarely inclined to change them; there are few martyrs as well as few apostates.

Another still more valid reason may be adduced: when no opinions are looked upon as certain, men cling to the mere instincts and material interests of their position, which are naturally more tangible, definite, and permanent than any opinions in the world.

It is a very difficult question to decide whether an aristocracy or a democracy governs the best. But it is certain that democracy annoys one part of the community and that aristocracy oppresses another. It is a truth which is self-established, and one which it is needless to discuss, that "you are rich and I am poor."

Chapter XII

POLITICAL ASSOCIATIONS
IN THE UNITED STATES

*DAILY USE which the Anglo-Americans make of the right
of association—Three kinds of political associations—
How the Americans apply the representative system
to associations—Dangers resulting to the state—Great
Convention of 1831 relative to the tariff—Legislative
character of this Convention—Why the unlimited exercise of the right of association is less dangerous in the
United States than elsewhere—Why it may be looked
upon as necessary—Utility of associations among a democratic people.*

IN NO country in the world has the principle of association been more successfully used or applied to a greater
multitude of objects than in America. Besides the permanent associations which are established by law under the
names of townships, cities, and counties, a vast number of
others are formed and maintained by the agency of private
individuals.

The citizen of the United States is taught from infancy
to rely upon his own exertions in order to resist the evils
and the difficulties of life; he looks upon the social authority with an eye of mistrust and anxiety, and he claims its
assistance only when he is unable to do without it. This habit
may be traced even in the schools, where the children in
their games are wont to submit to rules which they have
themselves established, and to punish misdemeanors which
they have themselves defined. The same spirit pervades
every act of social life. If a stoppage occurs in a thorough-
fare and the circulation of vehicles is hindered, the neighbors immediately form themselves into a deliberative body;
and this extemporaneous assembly gives rise to an executive power which remedies the inconvenience before anybody has thought of recurring to a pre-existing authority
superior to that of the persons immediately concerned. If

some public pleasure is concerned, an association is formed to give more splendor and regularity to the entertainment. Societies are formed to resist evils that are exclusively of a moral nature, as to diminish the vice if intemperance. In the United States associations are established to promote the public safety, commerce, industry, morality, and religion. There is no end which the human will despairs of attaining through the combined power of individuals united into a society.

I shall have occasion hereafter to show the effects of association in civil life; I confine myself for the present to the political world. When once the right of association is recognized, the citizens may use it in different ways.

An association consists simply in the public assent which a number of individuals give to certain doctrines and in the engagement which they contract to promote in a certain manner the spread of those doctrines. The right of associating in this fashion almost merges with freedom of the press, but societies thus formed possess more authority than the press. When an opinion is represented by a society, it necessarily assumes a more exact and explicit form. It numbers its partisans and engages them in its cause; they, on the other hand, become acquainted with one another, and their zeal is increased by their number. An association unites into one channel the efforts of divergent minds and urges them vigorously towards the one end which it clearly points out.

The second degree in the exercise of the right of association is the power of meeting. When an association is allowed to establish centers of action at certain important points in the country, its activity is increased and its influence extended. Men have the opportunity of seeing one another; means of execution are combined; and opinions are maintained with a warmth and energy that written language can never attain.

Lastly, in the exercise of the right of political association there is a third degree: the partisans of an opinion may unite in electoral bodies and choose delegates to represent them in a central assembly. This is, properly speaking, the application of the representative system to a party.

Thus, in the first instance, a society is formed between individuals professing the same opinion, and the tie that keeps it together is of a purely intellectual nature. In the second case, small assemblies are formed, which represent only a fraction of the party. Lastly, in the third case, they constitute, as it were, a separate nation in the midst of the nation, a government within the government. Their delegates, like the real delegates of the majority, represent the whole collective force of their party, and like them, also, have an appearance of nationality and all the moral power that results from it. It is true that they have not the right, like the others, of making the laws; but they have the power of attacking those which are in force and of drawing up beforehand those which ought to be enacted.

If, among a people who are imperfectly accustomed to the exercise of freedom, or are exposed to violent political passions, by the side of the majority which makes the laws is placed a minority which only deliberates and gets laws ready for adoption, I cannot but believe that public tranquillity would there incur very great risks. There is doubtless a wide difference between proving that one law is in itself better than another and proving that the former ought to be substituted for the latter. But the imagination of the multitude is very apt to overlook this difference, which is so apparent to the minds of thinking men. It sometimes happens that a nation is divided into two nearly equal parties, each of which affects to represent the majority. If, near the directing power, another power is established which exercises almost as much moral authority as the former, we are not to believe that it will long be content to speak without acting; or that it will always be restrained by the abstract consideration that associations are meant to direct opinions, but not to enforce them, to suggest but not to make the laws.

The more I consider the independence of the press in its principal consequences, the more am I convinced that in the modern world it is the chief and, so to speak, the constitutive element of liberty. A nation that is determined to remain free is therefore right in demanding, at any price, the exercise of this independence. But the *unlimited* liberty of political association cannot be entirely assimilated to the liberty of the press. The one is at the same time less necessary and more dangerous than the other. A nation may confine it within certain limits without forfeiting any part of its self-directing power; and it may sometimes be obliged to do so in order to maintain its own authority.

In America the liberty of association for political purposes is unlimited. An example will show in the clearest light to what an extent this privilege is tolerated.

The question of a tariff or free trade has much agitated the minds of Americans. The tariff was not only a subject of debate as a matter of opinion, but it affected some great material interests of the states. The North attributed a portion of its prosperity, and the South nearly all its sufferings, to this system. For a long time the tariff was the sole source of the political animosities that agitated the Union.

In 1831, when the dispute was raging with the greatest violence, a private citizen of Massachusetts proposed, by means of the newspapers, to all the enemies of the tariff to send delegates to Philadelphia in order to consult together upon the best means of restoring freedom of trade. This proposal circulated in a few days, by the power of the press, from Maine to New Orleans. The opponents of the tariff adopted it with enthusiasm; meetings were held in all quarters, and delegates were appointed. The majority of these delegates were well known, and some of them had earned a considerable degree of celebrity. South Carolina alone, which afterwards took up arms in the same cause, sent sixty-three delegates. On the 1st of October 1831 this assembly, which, according to the American custom, had taken the name of a Convention, met at Philadelphia; it consisted of more than two hundred members. Its debates were public, and they at once assumed a legislative character; the extent of the powers of Congress, the theories of free trade, and the different provisions of the tariff were discussed. At the end of ten days the Convention broke up, having drawn up an address to the American people in which it declared: (1) that Congress had not the right of making a tariff, and that the existing tariff was unconstitutional; (2) that the prohibition of free trade was prejudicial to the interests of any nation, and to those of the American people especially.

It must be acknowledged that the unrestrained liberty of political association has not hitherto produced in the United States the fatal results that might perhaps be expected from it elsewhere. The right of association was imported from England, and it has always existed in America; the exercise of this privilege is now incorporated with the manners and customs of the people. At the present time the liberty of association has become a necessary guarantee against the tyranny of the majority. In the United States, as soon as a party has become dominant, all public authority passes into its hands; its private supporters occupy all the offices and have all the force of the administration at their disposal. As the most distinguished members of the opposite party cannot surmount the barrier that excludes them from power, they must establish themselves outside of it and oppose the whole moral authority of the minority to the physical power that domineers over it. Thus a dangerous expedient is used to obviate a still more formidable danger.

The omnipotence of the majority appears to me to be so full of peril to the American republics that the dangerous means used to bridle it seem to be more advantageous than prejudicial. And here I will express an opinion that may remind the reader of what I said when speaking of the freedom of townships. There are no countries in which associations are more needed to prevent the despotism of faction or the arbitrary power of a prince than those which are democratically constituted. In aristocratic nations the body of the nobles and the wealthy are in themselves natural associations which check the abuses of power. In countries where such associations do not exist, if private individuals cannot create an artificial and temporary substitute for them I can see no permanent protection against the most galling tyranny; and a great people may be oppressed with impunity by a small faction or by a single individual.

The meeting of a great political convention (for there are conventions of all kinds), which may frequently become a necessary measure, is always a serious occurrence, even in America, and one that judicious patriots cannot regard without alarm. This was very perceptible in the Convention of 1831, at which all the most distinguished members strove to moderate its language and to restrain its objects within certain limits. It is probable that this Convention exercised a great influence on the minds of the malcontents and prepared them for the open revolt against the commercial laws of the Union that took place in 1832.

It cannot be denied that the unrestrained liberty of association for political purposes is the privilege which a people is longest in learning how to exercise. If it does not throw the nation into anarchy, it perpetually augments the chances of that calamity. On one point, however, this perilous liberty offers a security against dangers of another kind; in countries where associations are free, secret societies are unknown. In America there are factions, but no conspiracies.

DIFFERENT WAYS *in which the right of association is understood in Europe and in the United States—Different use which is made of it.*

THE MOST natural privilege of man, next to the right of acting for himself, is that of combining his exertions with those of his fellow creatures and of acting in common with them. The right of association therefore appears to me almost as inalienable in its nature as the right of personal liberty. No legislator can attack it without impairing the foundations of society. Nevertheless, if the liberty of association is only a source of advantage and prosperity to some nations, it may be perverted or carried to excess by others, and from an element of life may be changed into a cause of destruction. A comparison of the different methods that associations pursue in those countries in which liberty is well understood and in those where liberty degenerates into license may be useful both to governments and to parties.

Most Europeans look upon association as a weapon which is to be hastily fashioned and immediately tried in the conflict. A society is formed for discussion, but the idea of impending action prevails in the minds of all those who constitute it. It is, in fact, an army; and the time given to speech serves to reckon up the strength and to animate the courage of the host, after which they march against the enemy. To the persons who compose it, resources which lie within the bounds of law may suggest themselves as means of success, but never as the only means.

Such, however, is not the manner in which the right of association is understood in the United States. In America the citizens who form the minority associate in order, first, to show their numerical strength and so to diminish the moral power of the majority; and, secondly, to stimulate competition and thus to discover those arguments that are most fitted to act upon the majority; for they always entertain hopes of drawing over the majority to their own side, and then controlling the supreme power in its name. Political associations in the United States are therefore peaceable in their intentions and strictly legal in the means which they employ; and they assert with perfect truth that they aim at success only by lawful expedients.

The difference that exists in this respect between Americans and Europeans depends on several causes. In Europe there are parties which differ so much from the majority that they can never hope to acquire its support, and yet they think they are strong enough in themselves to contend against it. When a party of this kind forms an association, its object is not to convince, but to fight. In America the individuals who hold opinions much opposed to those of the majority can do nothing against it, and all other parties hope to win it over to their own principles. The exercise of the right of association becomes dangerous, then, in proportion as great parties find themselves wholly unable to acquire the majority. In a country like the United States, in which the differences of opinion are mere differences of hue, the right of association may remain unrestrained without evil consequences. Our inexperience of liberty leads us to regard the liberty of association only as a right of attacking the government. The first notion that presents itself to a party, as well as to an individual, when it has acquired a consciousness of its own strength is that of violence; the notion of persuasion arises at a later period, and is derived from experience. The English, who are divided into parties which differ essentially from each other, rarely abuse the right of association because they have long been accustomed to exercise it. In France, the passion for war is so intense that there is no undertaking so mad, or so injurious to the welfare of the state, that a man does not consider himself honored in defending it at the risk of his life.

But perhaps the most powerful of the causes that tend to mitigate the violence of political associations in the United States is universal suffrage. In countries in which universal suffrage exists, the majority is never doubtful, because neither party can reasonably pretend to represent that portion of the community which has not voted. The associations know as well as the nation at large that they do not represent the majority. This results, indeed, from the very fact of their existence; for if they did represent the preponderating power, they would change the law instead of soliciting its reform. The consequence of this is that the moral influence of the government which they attack is much increased, and their own power is much enfeebled.

In Europe there are few associations which do not affect to represent the majority, or which do not believe that they represent it. This conviction or this pretension tends to augment their force amazingly and contributes no less to legalize their measures. Violence may seem to be excusable in defense of the cause of oppressed right. Thus it is, in the vast complication of human laws, that extreme liberty sometimes corrects the abuses of liberty, and that extreme democracy obviates the dangers of democracy. In Europe associations consider themselves, in some degree, as the legislative and executive council of the people, who are unable to speak for themselves; moved by this belief, they act and they command. In America, where they represent in the eyes of all only a minority of the nation, they argue and petition.

The means that associations in Europe employ are in accordance with the end which they propose to obtain. As the principal aim of these bodies is to act and not to debate, to fight rather than to convince, they are naturally led to adopt an organization which is not civic and peaceable, but partakes of the habits and maxims of military life. They also centralize the direction of their forces as much as possible and entrust the power of the whole party to a small number of leaders.

The members of these associations respond to a watchword, like soldiers on duty; they profess the doctrine of passive obedience; say, rather, that in uniting together they at once abjure the exercise of their own judgment and free will; and the tyrannical control that these societies exercise is often far more insupportable than the authority possessed over society by the government which they attack. Their moral force is much diminished by these proceedings, and they lose the sacred character which always attaches to a struggle of the oppressed against their oppressors. He who in given cases consents to obey his fellows with servility and who submits his will and even his thoughts to their control, how can he pretend that he wishes to be free?

The Americans have also established a government in their associations, but it is invariably borrowed from the forms of the civil administration. The independence of each individual is recognized; as in society, all the members advance at the same time towards the same end, but they are not all obliged to follow the same track. No one abjures the exercise of his reason and free will, but everyone exerts that reason and will to promote a common undertaking.

Chapter XIII

GOVERNMENT OF THE DEMOCRACY IN AMERICA

I AM well aware of the difficulties that attend this part of my subject; but although every expression which I am about to use may clash, upon some points, with the feelings of the different parties which divide my country, I shall still speak my whole thought.

In Europe we are at a loss how to judge the true character and the permanent instincts of democracy, because in Europe two conflicting principles exist and we do not know what to attribute to the principles themselves and what to the passions that the contest produces. Such is not the case in America, however; there the people reign without impediment, and they have no perils to dread and no injuries to avenge. In America democracy is given up to its own propensities; its course is natural and its activity is unrestrained; there, consequently, its real character must be judged. And to no people can this inquiry be more vitally interesting than to the French nation, who are blindly driven onwards, by a daily and irresistible impulse, towards a state of things which may prove either despotic or republican, but which will assuredly be democratic.

UNIVERSAL SUFFRAGE

I HAVE already observed that universal suffrage has been adopted in all the states of the Union; it consequently exists in communities that occupy very different positions in the social scale. I have had opportunities of observing its effects in different localities and among races of men who are nearly strangers to each other in their language, their religion, and their modes of life; in Louisiana as well as in New England, in Georgia as in Canada. I have remarked that universal suffrage is far from producing in America either all the good or all the evil consequences which may be expected from it in Europe, and that its effects generally differ very much from those which are attributed to it.

THE CHOICE OF THE PEOPLE, AND THE INSTINCTIVE PREFERENCES OF THE AMERICAN DEMOCRACY. *In the United States the ablest men are rarely placed at the head of affairs— Reason for this peculiarity—The envy which prevails in the lower orders of France against the higher classes is not a French but a purely democratic feeling—Why the most distinguished men in America frequently seclude themselves from public affairs.*

MANY people in Europe are apt to believe without saying it, or to say without believing it, that one of the great advantages of universal suffrage is that it entrusts the direction of affairs to men who are worthy of the public confidence. They admit that the people are unable to govern of themselves, but they aver that the people always wish the welfare of the state and instinctively designate those who are animated by the same good will and who are the most fit to wield the supreme authority. I confess that the observations I made in America by no means coincide with these opinions. On my arrival in the United States I was surprised to find so much distinguished talent among the citizens and so little among the heads of the government. It is a constant fact that at the present day the ablest men in the United States are rarely placed at the head of affairs; and it must be acknowledged that such has been the result in proportion as democracy has exceeded all its former limits. The race of American statesmen has evidently dwindled most remarkably in the course of the last fifty years.

Several causes may be assigned for this phenomenon. It is impossible, after the most strenuous exertions, to raise the intelligence of the people above a certain level. Whatever may be the facilities of acquiring information, whatever may be the profusion of easy methods and cheap science, the human mind can never be instructed and developed without devoting considerable time to these objects.

The greater or lesser ease with which people can live without working is a sure index of intellectual progress. This boundary is more remote in some countries and more restricted in others, but it must exist somewhere as long as the people are forced to work in order to procure the means of subsistence; that is to say, as long as they continue to be the people. It is therefore quite as difficult to imagine a state in which all the citizens are very well informed as a state in which they are all wealthy; these two difficulties are correlative. I readily admit that the mass of the citizens sincerely wish to promote the welfare of the country; nay, more, I even grant that the lower classes mix fewer considerations of personal interest with their patriotism than the higher orders; but it is always more or less difficult for them to discern the best means of attaining the end which they sincerely desire. Long and patient observation and much acquired knowledge are requisite to form a just estimate of the character of a single individual. Men of the greatest genius often fail to do it, and can it be supposed that the common people will always succeed? The people have neither the time nor the means for an investigation of this kind. Their conclusions are hastily formed from a superficial inspection of the more prominent features of a question. Hence it often happens that mountebanks of all sorts are able to please the people, while their truest friends frequently fail to gain their confidence.

Moreover, democracy not only lacks that soundness of judgment which is necessary to select men really deserving of their confidence, but often have not the desire or the inclination to find them out. It cannot be denied that democratic institutions strongly tend to promote the feeling of envy in the human heart; not so much because they afford to everyone the means of rising to the same level with others as because those means perpetually disappoint the persons who employ them. Democratic institutions awaken and foster a passion for equality which they can never entirely satisfy. This complete equality eludes the grasp of the people at the very moment when they think they have grasped it, and "flies," as Pascal says, "with an eternal flight"; the people are excited in the pursuit of an advantage, which is more precious because it is not sufficiently remote to be unknown or sufficiently near to be enjoyed. The lower orders are agitated by the chance of success, they are irritated by its uncertainty; and they pass from the enthusiasm of pursuit to the exhaustion of ill success, and lastly to the acrimony of disappointment. Whatever transcends their own limitations appears to be an obstacle to their desires, and there is no superiority, however legitimate it may be, which is not irksome in their sight.

It has been supposed that the secret instinct which leads the lower orders to remove their superiors as much as possible from the direction of public affairs is peculiar to France. This is an error, however; the instinct to which I allude is not French, it is democratic; it may have been heightened by peculiar political circumstances, but it owes its origin to a higher cause.

In the United States the people do not hate the higher classes of society, but are not favorably inclined towards them and carefully exclude them from the exercise of authority. They do not fear distinguished talents, but are rarely fond of them. In general, everyone who rises without their aid seldom obtains their favor.

While the natural instincts of democracy induce the people to reject distinguished citizens as their rulers, an instinct not less strong induces able men to retire from the political arena, in which it is so difficult to retain their independence, or to advance without becoming servile. This opinion has been candidly expressed by Chancellor Kent, who says, in speaking with high praise of that part of the Constitution which empowers the executive to nominate the judges: "It is indeed probable that the men who are best fitted to discharge the duties of this high office would have too much reserve in their manners, and too much austerity in their principles, for them to be returned by the majority at an election where universal suffrage is adopted." [1] Such were the opinions which were printed without contradiction in America in the year 1830!

I hold it to be sufficiently demonstrated that universal suffrage is by no means a guarantee of the wisdom of the popular choice. Whatever its advantages may be, this is not one of them.

CAUSES WHICH MAY PARTLY CORRECT THESE TENDENCIES OF THE DEMOCRACY. *Contrary effects produced on nations as on individuals by great dangers—Why so many distinguished men stood at the head of affairs in America fifty years ago—Influence which intelligence and morality exercise upon the popular choice—Example of New England—States of the Southwest—How certain laws influence the choice of the people—Election by*

[1] Kent's *Commentaries*, Vol. I, p. 272.

an elected body—*Its effects upon the composition of
the Senate.*

WHEN serious dangers threaten the state, the people frequently succeed in selecting the citizens who are the most
able to save it. It has been observed that man rarely retains
his customary level in very critical circumstances; he rises
above or sinks below his usual condition, and the same thing
is true of nations. Extreme perils sometimes quench the
energy of a people instead of stimulating it; they excite
without directing its passions; and instead of clearing they
confuse its powers of perception. The Jews fought and
killed one another amid the smoking ruins of their temple.
But it is more common, with both nations and individuals,
to find extraordinary virtues developed from the very im-
minence of the danger. Great characters are then brought
into relief as the edifices which are usually concealed by the
gloom of night are illuminated by the glare of a conflagra-
tion. At those dangerous times genius no longer hesitates to
come forward; and the people, alarmed by the perils of their
situation, for a time forget their envious passions. Great
names may then be drawn from the ballot box.

I have already observed that the American statesmen of
the present day are very inferior to those who stood at the
head of affairs fifty years ago. This is as much a consequence
of the circumstances as of the laws of the country. When
America was struggling in the high cause of independence
to throw off the yoke of another country, and when it was
about to usher a new nation into the world, the spirits of its
inhabitants were roused to the height which their great objects required. In this general excitement distinguished men
were ready to anticipate the call of the community, and
the people clung to them for support and placed them at
their head. But such events are rare, and it is from the
ordinary course of affairs that our judgment must be
formed.

If passing occurrences sometimes check the passions of
democracy, the intelligence and the morals of the community exercise an influence on them which is not less powerful
and far more permanent. This is very perceptible in the
United States.

In New England, where education and liberty are the daughters of morality and religion, where society has acquired age and stability enough to enable it to form principles and hold fixed habits, the common people are accustomed to respect intellectual and moral superiority and to submit to it without complaint, although they set at naught all those privileges which wealth and birth have introduced among mankind. In New England, consequently, the democracy makes a more judicious choice than it does elsewhere.

But as we descend towards the South, to those states in which the constitution of society is more recent and less strong, where instruction is less general and the principles of morality, religion, and liberty are less happily combined, we perceive that talents and virtues become more rare among those who are in authority.

Lastly, when we arrive at the new Southwestern states, in which the constitution of society dates but from yesterday and presents only an agglomeration of adventurers and speculators, we are amazed at the persons who are invested with public authority, and we are led to ask by what force, independent of legislation and of the men who direct it, the state can be protected and society be made to flourish.

There are certain laws of a democratic nature which contribute, nevertheless, to correct in some measure these dangerous tendencies of democracy. On entering the House of Representatives at Washington, one is struck by the vulgar demeanor of that great assembly. Often there is not a distinguished man in the whole number. Its members are almost all obscure individuals, whose names bring no associations to mind. They are mostly village lawyers, men in trade, or even persons belonging to the lower classes of society. In a country in which education is very general, it is said that the representatives of the people do not always know how to write correctly.

At a few yards' distance is the door of the Senate, which contains within a small space a large proportion of the celebrated men of America. Scarcely an individual is to be seen in it who has not had an active and illustrious career: the Senate is composed of eloquent advocates, distinguished generals, wise magistrates, and statesmen of note, whose arguments would do honor to the most remarkable parliamentary debates of Europe.

How comes this strange contrast, and why are the ablest citizens found in one assembly rather than in the other? Why is the former body remarkable for its vulgar elements, while the latter seems to enjoy a monopoly of intelligence and talent? Both of these assemblies emanate from the people; both are chosen by universal suffrage; and no voice has hitherto been heard to assert in America that the Senate is hostile to the interests of the people. From what cause, then, does so startling a difference arise? The only reason which appears to me adequately to account for it is that the House of Representatives is elected by the people directly, while the Senate is elected by elected bodies. The whole body of the citizens name the legislature of each state, and the Federal Constitution converts these legislatures into so many electoral bodies, which return the members of the Senate. The Senators are elected by an indirect application of the popular vote; for the legislatures which appoint them are not aristocratic or privileged bodies, that elect in their own right, but they are chosen by the totality of the citizens; they are generally elected every year, and enough new members may be chosen every year to determine the senatorial appointments. But this transmission of the popular authority through an assembly of chosen men operates an important change in it by refining its discretion and improving its choice. Men who are chosen in this manner accurately represent the majority of the nation which governs them; but they represent only the elevated thoughts that are current in the community and the generous propensities that prompt its nobler actions rather than the petty passions that disturb or the vices that disgrace it.

The time must come when the American republics will be obliged more frequently to introduce the plan of election by an elected body into their system of representation or run the risk of perishing miserably among the shoals of democracy.

I do not hesitate to avow that I look upon this peculiar system of election as the only means of bringing the exercise of political power to the level of all classes of the people. Those who hope to convert this institution into the exclusive weapon of a party, and those who fear to use it, seem to me to be equally in error.

INFLUENCE WHICH THE AMERICAN DEMOCRACY HAS EXERCISED
ON THE LAWS RELATING TO ELECTIONS. *When elections
are rare, they expose the state to a violent crisis—When
they are frequent, they keep up a feverish excitement
—The Americans have preferred the second of these
two evils—Mutability of the laws—Opinions of Hamilton, Madison, and Jefferson on this subject.*

WHEN elections recur only at long intervals, the state is exposed to violent agitation every time they take place. Parties then exert themselves to the utmost in order to gain a prize which is so rarely within their reach; and as the evil is almost irremediable for the candidates who fail, everything is to be feared from their disappointed ambition. If, on the other hand, the legal struggle is soon to be repeated, the defeated parties take patience.

When elections occur frequently, their recurrence keeps society in a feverish excitement and gives a continual instability to public affairs. Thus, on the one hand, the state is exposed to the perils of a revolution, on the other to perpetual mutability; the former system threatens the very existence of the government, the latter prevents any steady and consistent policy. The Americans have preferred the second of these evils to the first; but they were led to this conclusion by instinct more than by reason, for a taste for variety is one of the characteristic passions of democracy. Hence their legislation is strangely mutable.

Many Americans consider the instability of their laws as a necessary consequence of a system whose general results are beneficial. But no one in the United States affects to deny the fact of this instability or contends that it is not a great evil.

Hamilton, after having demonstrated the utility of a power that might prevent or at least impede the promulgation of bad laws, adds: "It may perhaps be said, that the power of preventing bad laws includes that of preventing good ones, and may be used to the one purpose as well as to the other. But this objection will have little weight with those who can properly estimate the mischiefs of that in-

constancy and mutability in the laws which form the greatest
blemish in the character and genius of our governments."
(*Federalist*, No. 73.)

And again, in No. 62 of the same work, he observes: "The
facility and excess of law-making seem to be the diseases to
which our governments are most liable."

Jefferson himself, the greatest democrat whom the democracy of America has as yet produced, pointed out the
same dangers.

"The instability of our laws," said he, "is really a very
serious inconvenience. I think that we ought to have obviated it by deciding that a whole year should always be
allowed to elapse between the bringing in of a bill and the
final passing of it. It should afterwards be discussed and
put to the vote without the possibility of making any alteration in it; and if the circumstances of the case required a
more speedy decision, the question should not be decided
by a simple majority, but by a majority of at least two
thirds of each house." [2]

PUBLIC OFFICERS UNDER THE CONTROL OF THE AMERICAN
DEMOCRACY. *Simple exterior of American public officers
—No official costume—All public officers are remunerated—Political consequences of this system—No
public career exists in America—Results of this fact.*

PUBLIC officers in the United States are not separate from
the mass of citizens; they have neither palaces nor guards
nor ceremonial costumes. This simple exterior of persons in
authority is connected not only with the peculiarities of the
American character, but with the fundamental principles of
society. In the estimation of the democracy a government is
not a benefit, but a necessary evil. A certain degree of power
must be granted to public officers, for they would be of no
use without it. But the ostensible semblance of authority is
by no means indispensable to the conduct of affairs, and it is
needlessly offensive to the susceptibility of the public. The
public officers themselves are well aware that the superiority
over their fellow citizens which they derive from their authority they enjoy only on condition of putting themselves
on a level with the whole community by their manners. A

[2] *Letter to Madison*, December 20, 1787, translation of M.
Conseil.

public officer in the United States is uniformly simple in his manners, accessible to all the world, attentive to all requests, and obliging in his replies. I was pleased by these characteristics of a democratic government; I admired the manly independence that respects the office more than the officer and thinks less of the emblems of authority than of the man who bears them.

I believe that the influence which costumes really exercise in an age like that in which we live has been a good deal exaggerated. I never perceived that a public officer in America, while in the discharge of his duties, was the less respected because his own merit was set off by no adventitious signs. On the other hand, it is very doubtful whether a peculiar dress induces public men to respect themselves when they are not otherwise inclined to do so. When a magistrate snubs the parties before him, or indulges his wit at their expense, or shrugs his shoulders at their pleas of defense, or smiles complacently as the charges are enumerated (and in France such instances are not rare), I should like to deprive him of his robes of office, to see whether, when he is reduced to the garb of a private citizen, he would not recall some portion of the natural dignity of mankind.

No public officer in the United States has an official costume, but every one of them receives a salary. And this, also, still more naturally than what precedes, results from democratic principles. A democracy may allow some magisterial pomp and clothe its officers in silks and gold without seriously compromising its principles. Privileges of this kind are transitory; they belong to the place and not to the man. But if public officers are unpaid, a class of rich and independent public functionaries will be created who will constitute the basis of an aristocracy; and if the people still retain their right of election, the choice can be made only from a certain class of citizens.

When a democratic republic requires salaried officials to serve without pay, it may safely be inferred that the state is advancing towards monarchy. And when a monarchy begins to remunerate such officers as had hitherto been unpaid, it is a sure sign that it is approaching a despotic or a republican form of government. The substitution of paid for unpaid functionaries is of itself, in my opinion, sufficient to constitute a real revolution.

I look upon the entire absence of unpaid offices in America as one of the most prominent signs of the absolute dominion which democracy exercises in that country. All public services, of whatever nature they may be, are paid; so that everyone has not merely a right, but also the means of performing them. Although in democratic states all the citizens are qualified to hold offices, all are not tempted to try for them. The number and the capacities of the candidates more than the conditions of the candidateship restrict the choice of the electors.

In nations where the principle of election extends to everything, no political career can, properly speaking, be said to exist. Men arrive as if by chance at the post which they hold, and they are by no means sure of retaining it. This is especially true when the elections are held annually. The consequence is that in tranquil times public functions offer but few lures to ambition. In the United States those who engage in the perplexities of political life are persons of very moderate pretensions. The pursuit of wealth generally diverts men of great talents and strong passions from the pursuit of power; and it frequently happens that a man does not undertake to direct the fortunes of the state until he has shown himself incompetent to conduct his own. The vast number of very ordinary men who occupy public stations is quite as attributable to these causes as to the bad choice of democracy. In the United States I am not sure that the people would choose men of superior abilities even if they wished to be elected; but it is certain that candidates of this description do not come forward.

ARBITRARY POWER OF MAGISTRATES[3] UNDER THE RULE OF AMERICAN DEMOCRACY. *For what reason the arbitrary power of magistrates is greater in absolute monarchies and in democratic republics than it is in limited monarchies—Arbitrary power of the magistrates in New England.*

IN two kinds of government the magistrates exercise considerable arbitrary power: namely, under the absolute government of an individual, and under that of a democracy. This identical result proceeds from very similar causes.

[3] I here use the word *magistrates* in its widest sense; I apply it to all officers to whom the execution of the laws is entrusted.

In despotic states the fortune of no one is secure; public officers are not more safe than private persons. The sovereign, who has under his control the lives, the property, and sometimes the honor of the men whom he employs, thinks he has nothing to fear from them and allows them great latitude of action because he is convinced that they will not use it against him. In despotic states the sovereign is so much attached to his power that he dislikes the constraint even of his own regulations, and likes to see his agents acting irregularly and, as it were, by chance in order to be sure that their actions will never counteract his desires.

In democracies, as the majority has every year the right of taking away the power of the officers whom it had appointed, it has no reason to fear any abuse of their authority. As the people are always able to signify their will to those who conduct the government, they prefer leaving them to their own free action instead of prescribing an invariable rule of conduct, which would at once fetter their activity and the popular authority.

It may even be observed, on attentive consideration, that, under the rule of a democracy the arbitrary action of the magistrate must be still greater than in despotic states. In the latter the sovereign can immediately punish all the faults with which he becomes acquainted, but he cannot hope to become acquainted with all those which are committed. In democracies, on the contrary, the sovereign power is not only supreme, but universally present. The American functionaries are, in fact, much more free in the sphere of action which the law traces out for them than any public officer in Europe. Very frequently the object which they are to accomplish is simply pointed out to them, and the choice of the means is left to their own discretion.

In New England, for instance, the selectmen of each township are bound to draw up the list of persons who are to serve on the jury; the only rule which is laid down to guide them in their choice is that they are to select citizens possessing the elective franchise and enjoying a fair reputation.[4] In France the lives and liberties of the subjects would be thought to be in danger if a public officer of any kind

---

[4] See the law of February 27, 1813, *General Collection of the Laws of Massachusetts*, Vol. II, p. 331. It should be added, that the jurors are afterwards drawn from these lists by lot.

was entrusted with so formidable a right. In New England the same magistrates are empowered to post the names of habitual drunkards in public houses and to prohibit the inhabitants of a town from supplying them with liquor.[5] Such a censorial power would be revolting to the population of the most absolute monarchies; here, however, it is submitted to without difficulty.

Nowhere has so much been left by the law to the arbitrary determination of the magistrate as in democratic republics, because they have nothing to fear from arbitrary power. It may even be asserted that the freedom of the magistrate increases as the elective franchise is extended and as the duration of the term of office is shortened. Hence arises the great difficulty of converting a democratic republic into a monarchy. The magistrate ceases to be elective, but he retains the rights and the habits of an elected officer, which lead directly to despotism.

It is only in limited monarchies that the law which prescribes the sphere in which public officers are to act regulates all their measures. The cause of this may be easily detected. In limited monarchies the power is divided between the king and the people, both of whom are interested in the stability of the magistrate. The king does not venture to place the public officers under the control of the people, lest they should be tempted to betray his interests; on the other hand, the people fear lest the magistrates should serve to oppress the liberties of the country if they were entirely dependent upon the crown; they cannot, therefore, be said to depend on either the one or the other. The same cause that induces the king and the people to render public officers independent suggests the necessity of such securities as may prevent their independence from encroaching upon the authority of the former or upon the liberties of the latter. They consequently agree as to the necessity of restricting the func-

[5] Law of February 28, 1787. See *General Collection of the Laws of Massachusetts*, Vol. I, p. 302. The text is as follows: "The select-men of each township shall post in the shops of tavern-keepers, inn-keepers, and tradesmen a list of persons known to be drunkards, gamblers, and who are accustomed to spend their time and their money in such places; and the proprietor of the aforesaid establishments who, after posting such notice, shall allow the aforesaid persons to drink or gamble on his premises, or sell them spiritous liquors, shall be subject to a fine."

tionary to a line of conduct laid down beforehand and find it to their interest to impose upon him certain regulations that he cannot evade.

INSTABILITY OF THE ADMINISTRATION IN THE UNITED STATES. *In America the public acts of a community frequently leave fewer traces than the actions within a family— Newspapers the only historical remains—Instability of the administration prejudicial to the art of government.*

THE AUTHORITY which public men possess in America is so brief and they are so soon commingled with the ever changing population of the country that the acts of a community frequently leave fewer traces than events in a private family. The public administration is, so to speak, oral and traditional. But little is committed to writing, and that little is soon wafted away forever, like the leaves of the Sibyl, by the smallest breeze.

The only historical remains in the United States are the newspapers; if a number be wanting, the chain of time is broken and the present is severed from the past. I am convinced that in fifty years it will be more difficult to collect authentic documents concerning the social condition of the Americans at the present day than it is to find remains of the administration of France during the Middle Ages; and if the United States were ever invaded by barbarians, it would be necessary to have recourse to the history of other nations in order to learn anything of the people who now inhabit them.

The instability of administration has penetrated into the habits of the people; it even appears to suit the general taste, and no one cares for what occurred before his time: no methodical system is pursued, no archives are formed, and no documents are brought together when it would be very easy to do so. Where they exist, little store is set upon them. I have among my papers several original public documents which were given to me in the public offices in answer to some of my inquiries. In America society seems to live from hand to mouth, like an army in the field. Nevertheless, the art of administration is undoubtedly a science, and no sciences can be improved if the discoveries and observations of successive generations are not connected together in the order in which they occur. One man in the short space of his life remarks a fact, another conceives an idea; the former invents a means of execution, the latter reduces a truth to a formula; and mankind gathers the fruits of individual experience on its way and gradually forms the sciences. But the persons who conduct the administration in America can seldom afford any instruction to one another; and when they assume the direction of society, they simply possess those attainments which are widely disseminated in the community, and no knowledge peculiar to themselves. Democracy, pushed to its furthest limits, is therefore prejudicial to the art of government; and for this reason it is better adapted to a people already versed in the conduct of administration than to a nation that is uninitiated in public affairs.

This remark, indeed, is not exclusively applicable to the science of administration. Although a democratic government is founded upon a very simple and natural principle, it always presupposes the existence of a high degree of culture and enlightenment in society.[6] At first it might be supposed to belong to the earliest ages of the world, but maturer observation will convince us that it could come only last in the succession of human history.

CHARGES LEVIED BY THE STATE UNDER THE RULE OF THE AMERICAN DEMOCRACY. *In all communities citizens are divisible into certain classes—Habits of each of the classes in the direction of public finances—Why public expenditure must tend to increase when the people govern—What renders the extravagance of a democracy less to be feared in America—Public expenditure under a democracy.*

BEFORE we can tell whether a democratic government is economical or not we must establish a standard of comparison. The question would be of easy solution if we were to draw a parallel between a democratic republic and an absolute monarchy. The public expenditure in the former would be found to be more considerable than in the latter; such is the case with all free states compared with those which are not so. It is certain that despotism ruins individuals by preventing them from producing wealth much more than by depriv-

[6] It is unnecessary to observe that I speak here of the democratic form of government as applied to a people and not merely to a tribe.

ing them of what they have already produced; it dries up the source of riches, while it usually respects acquired property. Freedom, on the contrary, produces far more goods than it destroys; and the nations which are favored by free institutions invariably find that their resources increase even more rapidly than their taxes.

My present object is to compare free nations with one another and to point out the influence of democracy upon the finances of a state.

Communities as well as organic bodies are subject in their formation to certain fixed rules from which they cannot depart. They are composed of certain elements that are common to them at all times and under all circumstances. The people may always be mentally divided into three classes. The first of these classes consists of the wealthy; the second, of those who are in easy circumstances; and the third is composed of those who have little or no property and who subsist by the work that they perform for the two superior orders. The proportion of the individuals in these several divisions may vary according to the condition of society, but the divisions themselves can never be obliterated.

It is evident that each of these classes will exercise an influence peculiar to its own instincts upon the administration of the finances of the state. If the first of the three exclusively possesses the legislative power, it is probable that it will not be sparing of the public funds, because the taxes which are levied on a large fortune only diminish the sum of superfluities and are, in fact, but little felt. If the second class has the power of making the laws, it will certainly not be lavish of taxes, because nothing is so onerous as a large impost levied upon a small income. The government of the middle classes appears to me the most economical, I will not say the most enlightened, and certainly not the most generous, of free governments.

Let us now suppose that the legislative authority is vested in the lowest order: there are two striking reasons which show that the tendency of the expenditures will be to increase, not to diminish.

As the great majority of those who create the laws have no taxable property, all the money that is spent for the community appears to be spent to their advantage, at no cost of their own; and those who have some little property readily find means of so regulating the taxes that they weigh upon the wealthy and profit the poor, although the rich cannot take the same advantage when they are in possession of the government.

In countries in which the poor[7] have the exclusive power of making the laws, no great economy of public expenditure ought to be expected; that expenditure will always be considerable, either because the taxes cannot weigh upon those who levy them, or because they are levied in such a manner as not to reach these poorer classes. In other words, the government of the democracy is the only one under which the power that votes the taxes escapes the payment of them.

In vain will it be objected that the true interest of the people is to spare the fortunes of the rich, since they must suffer in the long run from the general impoverishment which will ensue. Is it not the true interest of kings also, to render their subjects happy, and of nobles to admit recruits into their order on suitable grounds? If remote advantages had power to prevail over the passions and the exigencies of the moment, no such thing as a tyrannical sovereign or an exclusive aristocracy could ever exist.

Again, it may be objected that the poor never have the sole power of making the laws; but I reply that wherever universal suffrage has been established, the majority unquestionably exercises the legislative authority; and if it be proved that the poor always constitute the majority, may it not be added with perfect truth that in the countries in which they possess the elective franchise they possess the sole power of making the laws? It is certain that in all the nations of the world the greater number has always consisted of those persons who hold no property, or of those whose property is insufficient to exempt them from the necessity of working in order to procure a comfortable subsistence. Universal suffrage, therefore, in point of fact does invest the poor with the government of society.

The disastrous influence that popular authority may sometimes exercise upon the finances of a state was clearly seen in some of the democratic republics of antiquity, in which

[7] The word *poor* is used here and throughout the remainder of this chapter in a relative, not in an absolute sense. Poor men in America would often appear rich in comparison with the poor of Europe; but they may with propriety be styled poor in comparison with their more affluent countrymen.

the public treasure was exhausted in order to relieve indigent citizens or to supply games and theatrical amusements for the populace. It is true that the representative system was then almost unknown, and that at the present time the influence of popular passions is less felt in the conduct of public affairs; but it may well be believed that in the end the delegate will conform to the principles of his constituents and favor their propensities as much as their interests.

The extravagance of democracy is less to be dreaded, however, in proportion as the people acquire a share of property, because, on the one hand, the contributions of the rich are then less needed, and, on the other, it is more difficult to impose taxes that will not reach the imposers. On this account universal suffrage would be less dangerous in France than in England, where nearly all the taxable property is vested in the hands of a few. America, where the great majority of the citizens possess some fortune, is in a still more favorable position than France.

There are further causes that may increase the amount of public expenditure in democratic countries. When an aristocracy governs, those who conduct the affairs of state are exempted, by their very station in society, from any want: content with their lot, power and renown are the only objects for which they strive; placed far above the obscure crowd, they do not always clearly perceive how the well-being of the mass of the people will redound to their own grandeur. They are not, indeed, callous to the sufferings of the poor; but they cannot feel those miseries as acutely as if they were themselves partakers of them. Provided that the people appear to submit to their lot, the rulers are satisfied and demand nothing further from the government. An aristocracy is more intent upon the means of maintaining than of improving its condition.

When, on the contrary, the people are invested with the supreme authority, they are perpetually seeking for something better, because they feel the hardship of their lot. The thirst for improvement extends to a thousand different objects; it descends to the most trivial details, and especially to those changes which are accompanied with considerable expense, since the object is to improve the condition of the poor, who cannot pay for the improvement. Moreover, all democratic communities are agitated by an ill-defined excitement and a kind of feverish impatience that creates a multitude of innovations, almost all of which are expensive.

In monarchies and aristocracies those who are ambitious flatter the natural taste which the rulers have for power and renown and thus often incite them to very costly undertakings. In democracies, where the rulers are poor and in want, they can be courted only by such means as will improve their well-being, and these improvements cannot take place without money. When a people begin to reflect on their situation, they discover a multitude of wants that they had not before been conscious of, and to satisfy these exigencies recourse must be had to the coffers of the state. Hence it happens that the public charges increase in proportion to the civilization of the country, and taxes are augmented as knowledge becomes more diffused.

The last cause which renders a democratic government dearer than any other is that a democracy does not always lessen its expenditures even when it wishes to do so, because it does not understand the art of being economical. As it frequently changes its purposes, and still more frequently its agents, its undertakings are often ill-conducted or left unfinished; in the former case the state spends sums out of all proportion to the end that it proposes to accomplish; in the latter the expense brings no return.

TENDENCIES OF THE AMERICAN DEMOCRACY AS REGARDS THE SALARIES OF PUBLIC OFFICERS. *In democracies those who establish high salaries have no chance of profiting by them—Tendency of the American democracy to increase the salaries of subordinate officers and to lower those of the more important functionaries—Reason for this—Comparative statement of the salaries of public officers in the United States and in France.*

THERE is a powerful reason that usually induces democracies to economize upon the salaries of public officers. Those who fix the amount of the salaries, being very numerous, have but little chance of obtaining office so as to be in receipt of those salaries. In aristocratic countries, on the contrary, the individuals who appoint high salaries have almost always a vague hope of profiting by them. These appointments may be looked upon as a capital which they create for their own use, or at least as a resource for their children.

It must be allowed, moreover, that a democratic state is most parsimonious towards its principal agents. In America the secondary officers are much better paid and the higher functionaries much worse than elsewhere.

These opposite effects result from the same cause: the people fix the salaries of the public officers in both cases, and the scale of remuneration is determined by a comparison with their own wants. It is held to be fair that the servants of the public should be placed in the same easy circumstances as the public themselves;[8] but when the question turns upon the salaries of the great officers of state, this rule fails, and chance alone guides the popular decision. The poor have no adequate conception of the wants which the higher classes of society feel. The sum which is scanty to the rich appears enormous to him whose wants do not extend beyond the necessities of life; and in his estimation, the governor of a state, with his twelve hundred or two thousand dollars a year, is a fortunate and enviable being.[9] If you try to convince him that the representative of a great people ought to appear with some splendor in the eyes of foreign nations, he will at first assent to your assertion; but when he reflects on his own humble dwelling and the small earnings of his hard toil, he remembers all that he could do with a salary which you judge to be insufficient, and he is startled and almost frightened at the view of so much wealth. Besides, the secondary public officer is almost on a level with the people, while the others are raised above them. The former may therefore excite his sympathy, but the latter begin to arouse his envy.

This is clearly seen in the United States, where the salaries seem, if I may so speak, to decrease as the authority of those who receive them is augmented.[10]

---

[8] The easy circumstances in which lower officials are placed in the United States result also from another cause, which is independent of the general tendencies of democracy: every kind of private business is very lucrative, and the state would not be served at all if it did not pay its servants well. The country is in the position of a commercial house, which is obliged to meet heavy competition, notwithstanding its inclination to be economical.

[9] Ohio, which has a million inhabitants, gives its governor a salary of $1,200 or 6,504 francs.

[10] To render this assertion perfectly evident, it will suffice to examine the scale of salaries of the agents of the Federal

Under the rule of an aristocracy, on the contrary, the high officers receive munificent salaries, while the inferior ones often have not more than enough to procure the necessaries of life. The reason for this fact is easily discoverable from causes very analogous to those that I have just pointed out. As a democracy is unable to conceive the pleasures of the rich or to witness them without envy, so an aristocracy is slow to understand the privations of the poor, or rather is unacquainted with them. The poor man is not, properly speaking, of the same kind as the rich one, but a being of another species. An aristocracy therefore cares but little for the condition of its subordinate agents; and their salaries are raised only when they refuse to serve for too scanty a remuneration.

It is the parsimonious conduct of democracy towards its principal officers that has caused more economical propensities to be attributed to it than it really possesses. It is true that it scarcely allows the means of decent maintenance to those who conduct its affairs; but it lavishes enormous sums to succor wants or facilitate the enjoyments of the people.[11]

---

government. I have added the salaries of the corresponding officers in France to complete the comparison.

UNITED STATES		FRANCE	
Treasury Department		*Ministère de Finances*	
Messenger	$ 700	Messenger	1,500 fr.
Clerk with lowest salary	1,000	Clerk with lowest salary	1,000 to 1,800 fr.
Clerk with highest salary	1,600	Clerk with highest salary	3,200 to 3,600 fr.
Chief Clerk	2,000	Secretary-General	20,000 fr.
Secretary of State	6,000	The Minister	80,000 fr.
The President	25,000	The King	12,000,000 fr.

I have perhaps done wrong in selecting France as my standard of comparison. In France, as the democratic tendencies of the nation exercise an ever increasing influence on the government, the Chambers show a disposition to raise the low salaries and to lower the principal ones. Thus the Minister of Finance, who received 160,000 fr. under the Empire, receives 80,000 fr. in 1835; the Directors-General of Finance, who then received 50,000 fr., now receive only 20,000 fr.

[11] See the American budgets for the support of paupers and for public instruction. In 1831 over $250,000 or 1,290,000 francs were spent in the state of New York for the maintenance of the poor; and at least $1,000,000 or 5,240,000 francs were devoted to public instruction. (Williams's *New York Annual Register*, 1832, pp. 205 and 243.) The state of New York contained only 1,900,000 inhabitants in the year 1830, which is

The money raised by taxation may be better employed, but it is not economically used. In general, democracy gives largely to the people and very sparingly to those who govern them. The reverse is the case in aristocratic countries, where the money of the state profits the persons who are at the head of affairs.

DIFFICULTY OF DISTINGUISHING THE CAUSES THAT INCLINE THE AMERICAN GOVERNMENT TO ECONOMY

WE ARE liable to frequent errors in seeking among facts for the real influence that laws exercise upon the fate of mankind, since nothing is more difficult to appreciate than a fact. One nation is naturally fickle and enthusiastic; another is sober and calculating; and these characteristics originate in their physical constitution or in remote causes with which we are unacquainted.

There are nations which are fond of parade, bustle, and festivity, and which do not regret millions spent upon the gayeties of an hour. Others, on the contrary, are attached to more quiet enjoyments and seem almost ashamed of appearing to be pleased. In some countries high value is set upon the beauty of public edifices; in others the productions of art are treated with indifference, and everything that is unproductive is regarded with contempt. In some, renown, in others, money, is the ruling passion.

Independently of the laws, all these causes exercise a powerful influence upon the conduct of the finances of the state. If the Americans never spend the money of the people in public festivities, it is not merely because the taxes are under the control of the people, but because the people take no delight in festivities. If they repudiate all ornament from their architecture and set no store on any but practical and homely advantages, it is not because they live under democratic institutions, but because they are a commercial nation. The habits of private life are continued in public; and we ought carefully to distinguish that economy which depends upon their institutions from that which is the natural result of their habits and customs.

WHETHER THE EXPENDITURE OF THE UNITED STATES CAN BE COMPARED WITH THAT OF FRANCE. *Two points to be es-*

not more than double the amount of population in the Département du Nord in France.

tablished in order to estimate the extent of the public charges: viz., the national wealth and the rate of taxation —The wealth and the charges of France not accurately known—Why the wealth and charges of the Union cannot be accurately known—Researches of the author to discover the amount of taxation of Pennsylvania— General symptoms that may serve to indicate the amount of the public charges in a given nation—Result of this investigation for the Union.

MANY attempts have recently been made in France to compare the public expenditure of that country with the expenditure of the United States. All these attempts have been fruitless, however, and a few words will suffice to show that they could not have a satisfactory result.

In order to estimate the amount of the public charges of a people, two preliminaries are indispensable: it is necessary, in the first place, to know the wealth of that people; and, in the second, to learn what portion of that wealth is devoted to the expenditure of the state. To show the amount of taxation without showing the resources which are destined to meet it would be a futile task; for it is not the expenditure, but the relation of the expenditure to the revenue that it is desirable to know. The same rate of taxation which may easily be supported by a wealthy contributor will reduce a poor one to extreme misery.

The wealth of nations is composed of several elements; real property is the first of these, and personal property the second. It is difficult to know precisely the amount of cultivable land in a country and its natural or acquired value; and it is still more difficult to estimate the whole personal property which is at the disposal of a nation, and which eludes the strictest analysis because the diversity and the number of shapes under which it may occur. And, indeed, we find that the nations of Europe which have been the longest civilized, including even those in which the administration is most centralized, have not succeeded as yet in determining the exact amount of their wealth.

In America the attempt has never been made; for how would such an investigation be possible in a new country, where society has not yet settled into fixed and tranquil habits, where the national government is not assisted by a multitude of agents whose exertions it can command and direct to one end, and where statistics are not studied because no one is able to collect the necessary documents or find time to peruse them? Thus the primary elements of the calculations that have been made in France cannot be obtained in the Union; the relative wealth of the two countries is unknown: the property of the former is not yet accurately determined, and no means exist of computing that of the latter.

I consent therefore, for the moment, to abandon this necessary term of the comparison, and I confine myself to a computation of the actual amount of taxation, without investigating the ratio of the taxation to the revenue. But the reader will perceive that my task has not been facilitated by thus narrowing the circle of my researches.

It cannot be doubted that the central administration of France, assisted by all the public officers who are at its disposal, might determine precisely the amount of the direct and indirect taxes levied upon the citizens. But this investigation, which no private individual can undertake, has not hitherto been completed by the French government, or at least its results have not been made public. We are acquainted with the sum total of the charges of the state; we know the amount of the departmental expenditure; but the expenses of the communes have not been computed, and the total of the public expenses of France is consequently unknown.

If we now turn to America, we perceive that the difficulties are multiplied and enhanced. The Union publishes an exact return of the amount of its expenditure; the budgets of the four-and-twenty states publish similar returns; but the expenses of the counties and the townships are unknown.[12]

[12] The Americans, as we have seen, have four separate budgets: the Union, the states, the counties, and the townships having each its own. During my stay in America, I made every endeavor to discover the amount of the public expenditure in the townships and counties of the principal states of the Union; and I readily obtained the budget of the larger townships, but found it quite impossible to procure that of the smaller ones. Hence for these latter I have no exact figures. I possess, however, some documents relating to county expenses which, although incomplete, may still interest the reader. I have to thank Mr. Richards, former Mayor of Philadelphia, for the budgets of

The Federal authority cannot oblige the state governments to throw any light upon this point; and even if these governments were inclined to give their simultaneous aid, it may be doubted whether they are able to furnish a satisfactory answer. Independently of the natural difficulties of the task, the political organization of the country would hinder the success of their efforts. The country and town magistrates are not appointed by the authorities of the state and are not subjected to their control. It is therefore allowable to suppose that even if the state was desirous of obtaining the returns which we require, its design would be counteracted by the neglect of those subordinate officers whom it would be obliged to employ.[13] It is in fact useless to in-

---

thirteen of the counties of Pennsylvania: viz., Lebanon, Centre, Franklin, Fayette, Montgomery, Luzerne, Dauphin, Butler, Allegheny, Columbia, Northampton, Northumberland, and Philadelphia, for the year 1830. Their population at the time consisted of 495,207 inhabitants. On looking at the map of Pennsylvania it will be seen that these thirteen counties are scattered in every direction, and so generally affected by the causes which usually influence the condition of a country that they may fairly be supposed to furnish a correct average of the financial state of the counties of Pennsylvania in general. The expenses of these counties amounted in the year 1830 to about 1,800,221, or nearly 3 fr. 64 cent. for each inhabitant; and, calculating that each of them contributed in the same year about 12 fr. 70 cent. towards the Union, and about 3 fr. 80 cent. to the state of Pennsylvania, it appears that they each contributed, as their share of all the public expenses (except those of the townships), the sum of 20 fr. 14 cent. This calculation is doubly incomplete, as it applies only to a single year and to one part of the public expenditure; but it has at least the merit of being exact.

[13] Those who have attempted to demonstrate a similarity between the expenses of France and America have at once perceived that no such comparison could be drawn between the total expenditures of the two countries; but they have endeavored to compare detached portions of this expenditure. It may readily be shown that this second system is not at all less defective than the first.

If I attempt to compare the French budget with the budget of the Union, it must be remembered that the latter embraces far fewer objects than the centralized government of the former country, and that the American expenditure must consequently be much smaller. If I contrast the budgets of our departments with those of the states that constitute the Union, it must be observed that as the states have the supervision of more numerous and important interests than the departments, their expenditure is naturally more considerable. As for the budgets of the counties, nothing of the kind occurs in the French system of finances, and it is doubtful whether the corresponding expenses in France

quire what the Americans might do to forward this inquiry, since it is certain that they have hitherto done nothing. There does not exist a single individual at the present day, in America or in Europe, who can inform us what each citizen of the Union annually contributes to the public charges of the nation.[14]

should be referred to the budget of the state or to those of the municipal divisions.

Municipal expenses exist in both countries, but they are not always analogous. In America the townships discharge a variety of offices which are reserved in France to the departments or to the state. Moreover, it may be asked what is to be understood by the municipal expenses of America. The organization of the municipal bodies or townships differs in the several states. Are we to be guided by what occurs in New England or in Georgia, in Pennsylvania or in Illinois?

A kind of analogy may very readily be perceived between certain budgets in the two countries; but as the elements of which they are composed always differ more or less, no fair comparison can be drawn between them.

[14] Even if we knew the exact pecuniary contributions of every French and American citizen to the coffers of the state, we should only arrive at a portion of the truth. Governments not only demand supplies of money, but call for personal services, which may be looked upon as equivalent to a given sum. When a state raises an army, besides the pay of the troops, which is furnished by the entire nation, each soldier must give up his time, the value of which depends on the use he might make of it if he were not in the service. The same remark applies to the militia; the citizen who is in the militia devotes a certain portion of valuable time to the maintenance of the public security, and in reality surrenders to the state those earnings that he is prevented from gaining. Many other instances might be cited. The governments of France and America both levy taxes of this kind, which weigh upon the citizens; but who can estimate with accuracy their relative amount in the two countries?

This, however, is not the last of the difficulties which prevent us from comparing the expenditure of the Union with that of France. The French government contracts certain obligations which are not assumed by the state in America, and vice versa. The French government pays the clergy; in America the voluntary principle prevails. In America the state provides for the poor; in France they are abandoned to the charity of the public. All French public officers are paid a fixed salary; in America they are allowed certain perquisites. In France contributions in labor take place on very few roads, in America upon almost all the thoroughfares: in the former country both roads are free to all travelers; in the latter toll roads abound. All these differences in the manner in which taxes are levied in the two countries enhance the difficulty of comparing their expenditure; for there are certain expenses which the citizens would not be subject to, or which would at any rate be less considerable, if the state did not undertake to act in their name.

Hence we must conclude that it is no less difficult to compare the social expenditure than it is to estimate the relative wealth of France and America. I will even add that it would be dangerous to attempt this comparison; for when statistics are not based upon computations that are strictly accurate, they mislead instead of guiding aright. The mind is easily imposed upon by the affectation of exactitude which marks even the misstatements of statistics; and it adopts with confidence the errors which are appareled in the forms of mathematical truth.

We abandon, therefore, the numerical investigation, with the hope of meeting with data of another kind. In the absence of positive documents, we may form an opinion as to the proportion that the taxation of a people bears to its real wealth, by observing whether its external appearance is flourishing; whether, after having paid the dues of the state, the poor man retains the means of subsistence, and the rich the means of enjoyment; and whether both classes seem contented with their position, seeking, however, to ameliorate it by perpetual exertions, so that industry is never in want of capital, nor capital unemployed by industry. The observer who draws his inferences from these signs will undoubtedly be led to the conclusion that the American of the United States contributes a much smaller portion of his income to the state than the citizen of France. Nor, indeed, can the result be otherwise.

A portion of the French debt is the consequence of two invasions; and the Union has no similar calamity to fear. The position of France obliges it to maintain a large standing army; the isolation of the Union enables it to have only six thousand soldiers. The French have a fleet of three hundred sail; the Americans have only fifty-two vessels.[15] How, then, can the inhabitant of the Union be taxed as heavily as the inhabitant of France? No parallel can be drawn between the finances of two countries so differently situated.

It is by examining what actually takes place in the Union, and not by comparing the Union with France, that we can judge whether the American government is really economical. On casting my eyes over the different republics which

[15] See the budget of the Ministry of Marine for France and, for America, the *National Calendar* (1833), p. 228.

form the confederation, I perceive that their governments often lack perseverance in their undertakings, and that they exercise no steady control over the men whom they employ. I naturally infer that they must often spend the money of the people to no purpose, or consume more of it than is really necessary for their enterprises. Faithful to its popular origin, the government makes great efforts to satisfy the wants of the lower classes, to open to them the road to power, and to diffuse knowledge and comfort among them. The poor are maintained, immense sums are annually devoted to public instruction, all services remunerated, and the humblest agents are liberally paid. This kind of government appears to be useful and rational, but I am bound to admit that it is expensive.

Wherever the poor direct public affairs and dispose of the national resources, it appears certain that, as they profit by the expenditure of the state, they will often augment that expenditure.

I conclude, therefore, without having recourse to inaccurate statistics, and without hazarding a comparison which might prove incorrect, that the democratic government of the Americans is not a cheap government, as is sometimes asserted; and I do not fear to predict that, if the United States is ever involved in serious difficulties, taxation will speedily be raised as high there as in most of the aristocracies or the monarchies of Europe.

CORRUPTION AND THE VICES OF THE RULERS IN A DEMOCRACY, AND CONSEQUENT EFFECTS UPON PUBLIC MORALITY. *In aristocracies, rulers sometimes endeavor to corrupt the people—In democracies, rulers frequently show themselves to be corrupt—In the former, their vices are directly prejudicial to the morality of the people—In the latter, their indirect influence is still more pernicious.*

A DISTINCTION must be made when aristocracies and democracies accuse each other of facilitating corruption. In aristocratic governments, those who are placed at the head of affairs are rich men, who are desirous only of power. In democracies, statesmen are poor and have their fortunes to make. The consequence is that in aristocratic states the rulers are rarely accessible to corruption and have little craving for money, while the reverse is the case in democratic nations.

But in aristocracies, as those who wish to attain the head of affairs possess considerable wealth, and as the number of persons by whose assistance they may rise is comparatively small, the government is, if I may so speak, put up at auction. In democracies, on the contrary, those who are covetous of power are seldom wealthy, and the number of those who confer power is extremely great. Perhaps in democracies the number of men who might be bought is not smaller, but buyers are rarely to be found; and, besides, it would be necessary to buy so many persons at once that the attempt would be useless.

Many of the men who have governed France during the last forty years have been accused of making their fortunes at the expense of the state or its allies, a reproach which was rarely addressed to the public men of the old monarchy. But in France the practice of bribing electors is almost unknown, while it is notoriously and publicly carried on in England. In the United States I never heard anyone accused of spending his wealth in buying votes, but I have often heard the probity of public officers questioned; still more frequently have I heard their success attributed to low intrigues and immoral practices.

If, then, the men who conduct an aristocracy sometimes endeavor to corrupt the people, the heads of a democracy are themselves corrupt. In the former case the morality of the people is directly assailed; in the latter an indirect influence is exercised which is still more to be dreaded.

As the rulers of democratic nations are almost always suspected of dishonorable conduct, they in some measure lend the authority of the government to the base practices of which they are accused. They thus afford dangerous examples, which discourage the struggles of virtuous independence and cloak with authority the secret designs of wickedness. If it be asserted that evil passions are found in all ranks of society, that they ascend the throne by hereditary right, and that we may find despicable characters at the head of aristocratic nations as well as in the bosom of a democracy, the plea has but little weight in my estimation. The corruption of men who have casually risen to power has a coarse and vulgar infection in it that renders it dangerous to the multitude. On the contrary, there is a kind of aristocratic refinement and an air of grandeur in the depravity of the great, which frequently prevent it from spreading abroad.

The people can never penetrate into the dark labyrinth of court intrigue, and will always have difficulty in detecting the turpitude that lurks under elegant manners, refined tastes, and graceful language. But to pillage the public purse and to sell the favors of the state are arts that the meanest villain can understand and hope to practice in his turn.

Besides, what is to be feared is not so much the immorality of the great as the fact that immorality may lead to greatness. In a democracy private citizens see a man of their own rank in life who rises from that obscure position in a few years to riches and power; the spectacle excites their surprise and their envy, and they are led to inquire how the person who was yesterday their equal is today their ruler. To attribute his rise to his talents or his virtues is unpleasant, for it is tacitly to acknowledge that they are themselves less virtuous or less talented than he was. They are therefore led, and often rightly, to impute his success mainly to some of his vices; and an odious connection is thus formed between the ideas of turpitude and power, unworthiness and success, utility and dishonor.

EFFORTS OF WHICH A DEMOCRACY IS CAPABLE. *The Union has only had one struggle hitherto for its existence—Enthusiasm at the commencement of the war—Indifference towards its close—Difficulty of establishing military conscription or impressment of seamen in America —Why a democratic people is less capable than any other of sustained effort.*

I WARN the reader that I here speak of a government that follows the real will of the people, and not of a government that simply commands in their name. Nothing is so irresistible as a tyrannical power commanding in the name of the people, because, while wielding the moral power which belongs to the will of the greater number, it acts at the same time with the quickness and persistence of a single man.

It is difficult to say what degree of effort a democratic government may be capable of making on the occurrence of a national crisis. No great democratic republic has hitherto existed in the world. To style the oligarchy which ruled over France in 1793 by that name would be an insult to the republican form of government. The United States affords the first example of the kind.

The American Union has now subsisted for half a century, and its existence has only once been attacked; namely, during the War of Independence. At the commencement of that long war, extraordinary efforts were made with enthusiasm for the service of the country.[16] But as the contest was prolonged, private selfishness began to reappear. No money was brought into the public treasury; few recruits could be raised for the army; the people still wished to acquire independence, but would not employ the only means by which it could be obtained. "Tax laws," says Hamilton, in *The Federalist* (No. 12), "have in vain been multiplied; new methods to enforce the collection have in vain been tried; the public expectation has been uniformly disappointed; and the treasuries of the States have remained empty. The popular system of administration inherent in the nature of popular government, coinciding with the real scarcity of money incident to a languid and mutilated state of trade, has hitherto defeated every experiment for extensive collections, and has at length taught the different legislatures the folly of attempting them."

Since that period the United States has not had a single serious war to carry on. In order, therefore, to know what sacrifices democratic nations may impose upon themselves, we must wait until the American people are obliged to put half their entire income at the disposal of the government, as was done by the English; or to send forth a twentieth part of its population to the field of battle, as was done by France.

In America conscription is unknown and men are induced to enlist by bounties. The notions and habits of the people of the United States are so opposed to compulsory recruiting that I do not think it can ever be sanctioned by the laws. What is termed conscription in France is assuredly the heaviest tax upon the people; yet how could a great Con-

---

[16] One of the most singular, in my opinion, was the resolution that the Americans took of temporarily abandoning the use of tea. Those who know that men usually cling more to their habits than to their life will doubtless admire this great though obscure sacrifice, which was made by a whole people.

tinental war be carried on without it? The Americans have not adopted the British practice of impressing seamen, and they have nothing that corresponds to the French system of maritime conscription; the navy as well as the merchant service is supplied by volunteers. But it is not easy to conceive how a people can sustain a great maritime war without having recourse to one or the other of these two systems. Indeed, the Union, which has already fought with honor upon the seas, has never had a numerous fleet, and the equipment of its few vessels has always been very expensive.

I have heard American statesmen confess that the Union will with difficulty maintain its power on the seas without adopting the system of impressment or maritime conscription; but the difficulty is to induce the people, who exercise the supreme authority, to submit to such measures.

It is incontestable that, in times of danger, a free people display far more energy than any other. But I incline to believe that this is especially true of those free nations in which the aristocratic element preponderates. Democracy appears to me better adapted for the conduct of society in times of peace, or for a sudden effort of remarkable vigor, than for the prolonged endurance of the great storms that beset the political existence of nations. The reason is very evident; enthusiasm prompts men to expose themselves to dangers and privations; but without reflection they will not support them long. There is more calculation even in the impulses of bravery than is generally supposed; and although the first efforts are made by passion alone, perseverance is maintained only by a distinct view of what one is fighting for. A portion of what is dear to us is hazarded in order to save the remainder.

But it is this clear perception of the future, founded upon judgment and experience, that is frequently wanting in democracies. The people are more apt to feel than to reason; and if their present sufferings are great, it is to be feared that the still greater sufferings attendant upon defeat will be forgotten.

Another cause tends to render the efforts of a democratic government less persevering than those of an aristocracy. Not only are the lower less awake than the higher orders to the good or evil chances of the future, but they suffer more acutely from present privations. The noble exposes his life, indeed, but the chance of glory is equal to the chance of harm. If he sacrifices a large portion of his income to the state, he deprives himself for a time of some of the pleasures of affluence; but to the poor man death has no glory, and the imposts that are merely irksome to the rich often deprive him of the necessaries of life.

This relative weakness of democratic republics in critical times is perhaps the greatest obstacle to the foundation of such a republic in Europe. In order that one such state should exist in the European world, it would be necessary that similar institutions should be simultaneously introduced into all the other nations.

I am of opinion that a democratic government tends, in the long run, to increase the real strength of society; but it can never combine, upon a single point and at a given time, so much power as an aristocracy or an absolute monarchy. If a democratic country remained during a whole century subject to a republican government, it would probably at the end of that period be richer, more populous, and more prosperous than the neighboring despotic states. But during that century it would often have incurred the risk of being conquered by them.

SELF-CONTROL OF THE AMERICAN DEMOCRACY. *The American people acquiesce slowly, and sometimes do not acquiesce, in what is beneficial to their interests—The faults of the American democracy are, for the most part, reparable.*

THE DIFFICULTY that a democracy finds in conquering the passions and subduing the desires of the moment with a view to the future is observable in the United States in the most trivial things. The people, surrounded by flatterers, find great difficulty in surmounting their inclinations; whenever they are required to undergo a privation or any inconvenience, even to attain an end sanctioned by their own rational conviction, they almost always refuse at first to comply. The deference of the Americans to the laws has been justly applauded; but it must be added that in America legislation is made by the people and for the people. Consequently, in the United States the law favors those classes that elsewhere are most interested in evading it. It may therefore be supposed that an offensive law of which the majority should not see the immediate utility would either not be enacted or not be obeyed.

In America there is no law against fraudulent bankruptcies, not because they are few, but because they are many. The dread of being prosecuted as a bankrupt is greater in the minds of the majority than the fear of being ruined by the bankruptcy of others; and a sort of guilty tolerance is extended by the public conscience to an offense which everyone condemns in his individual capacity. In the new states of the Southwest the citizens generally take justice into their own hands, and murders are of frequent occurrence. This arises from the rude manners and the ignorance of the inhabitants of those deserts, who do not perceive the utility of strengthening the law, and who prefer duels to prosecutions.

Someone observed to me one day in Philadelphia that almost all crimes in America are caused by the abuse of intoxicating liquors, which the lower classes can procure in great abundance because of their cheapness. "How comes it," said I, "that you do not put a duty upon brandy?" "Our legislators," rejoined my informant, "have frequently thought of this expedient; but the task is difficult: a revolt might be anticipated; and the members who should vote for such a law would be sure of losing their seats." "Whence I am to infer," replied I, "that drunkards are the majority in your country, and that temperance is unpopular."

When these things are pointed out to the American statesmen, they answer: "Leave it to time, and experience of the evil will teach the people their true interests." This is frequently true: though a democracy is more liable to error than a monarch or a body of nobles, the chances of its regaining the right path when once it has acknowledged its mistake are greater also; because it is rarely embarrassed by interests that conflict with those of the majority and resist the authority of reason. But a democracy can obtain truth only as the result of experience; and many nations may perish while they are awaiting the consequences of their errors. The great privilege of the Americans does not consist in being more enlightened than other nations, but in being able to repair the faults they may commit.

It must be added that a democracy cannot profit by past experience unless it has arrived at a certain pitch of knowledge and civilization. There are nations whose first education has been so vicious and whose character presents so strange a mixture of passion, ignorance, and erroneous notions upon all subjects that they are unable to discern the causes of their own wretchedness, and they fall a sacrifice to ills of which they are ignorant.

I have crossed vast tracts of country formerly inhabited by powerful Indian nations who are now extinct; I have passed some time among remnants of tribes, which witness the daily decline of their numbers and of the glory of their independence; and I have heard these Indians themselves anticipate the impending doom of their race. Every European can perceive means that would rescue these unfortunate beings from the destruction otherwise inevitable. They alone are insensible to the remedy; they feel the woes which year after year heaps upon their heads, but they will perish to a man without accepting the cure. Force would have to be employed to compel them to live.

The incessant revolutions that have convulsed the South American states for the last quarter of a century are regarded with astonishment, and we are constantly hoping that before long they will return to what is called their *natural state*. But who can affirm that revolutions are not, at the present time, the most natural state of the South American Spaniards? In that country society is struggling in the depths of an abyss whence its own efforts are insufficient to rescue it. The inhabitants of that fair portion of the Western hemisphere seem obstinately bent on the work of destroying one another. If they fall into momentary quiet, from exhaustion, that repose soon prepares them for a new frenzy. When I consider their condition, alternating between misery and crime, I am tempted to believe that despotism itself would be a blessing to them, if it were possible that the words "despotism" and "blessing" could ever be united in my mind.

CONDUCT OF FOREIGN AFFAIRS BY THE AMERICAN DEMOCRACY. *Direction given to the foreign policy of the United States by Washington and Jefferson—Almost all the defects inherent in democratic institutions are brought to light in the conduct of foreign affairs; their advantages are less perceptible.*

WE have seen that the Federal Constitution entrusts the permanent direction of the external interests of the nation to the President and the Senate,[17] which tends in some degree to detach the general foreign policy of the Union from the direct control of the people. It cannot, therefore, be asserted with truth that the foreign affairs of the state are conducted by the democracy.

There are two men who have imparted to American foreign policy a tendency that is still being followed today; the first is Washington and the second Jefferson. Washington said, in the admirable Farewell Address which he made to his fellow citizens, and which may be regarded as his political testament:

"The great rule of conduct for us in regard to foreign nations is, in extending our commercial relations, to have with them as little *political* connection as possible. So far as we have already formed engagements, let them be fulfilled with perfect good faith. Here let us stop.

"Europe has a set of primary interests, which to us have none, or a very remote relation. Hence she must be engaged in frequent controversies, the causes of which are essentially foreign to our concerns. Hence, therefore, it must be unwise in us to implicate ourselves, by artificial ties, in the ordinary vicissitudes of her politics, or the ordinary combinations and collisions of her friendships or enmities.

"Our detached and distant situation invites and enables us to pursue a different course. If we remain one people, under an efficient government, the period is not far off when we may defy material injury from external annoyance; when we may take such an attitude as will cause the neutrality we may at any time resolve upon to be scrupulously respected; when belligerent nations, under the impossibility of making acquisitions upon us, will not lightly hazard the giving us provocation; when we may choose peace or war, as our interest, guided by justice, shall counsel.

"Why forego the advantages of so peculiar a situation?

---

[17] "The President," says the Constitution, Article II, Section 2, § 2, "shall have power, by and with the advice and consent of the Senate, to make treaties, provided two thirds of the Senators present concur." The reader is reminded that the Senators are returned for a term of six years, and that they are chosen by the legislature of each state.

Why quit our own to stand upon foreign ground? Why, by interweaving our destiny with that of any part of Europe, entangle our peace and prosperity in the toils of European ambition, rivalship, interest, humor, or caprice?

"It is our true policy to steer clear of permanent alliances with any portion of the foreign world, so far, I mean, as we are now at liberty to do it; for let me not be understood as capable of patronizing infidelity to existing engagements. I hold the maxim no less applicable to public than to private affairs, that honesty is always the best policy. I repeat it, therefore, let those engagements be observed in their genuine sense; but in my opinion it is unnecessary, and would be unwise, to extend them.

"Taking care always to keep ourselves, by suitable establishments, in a respectable defensive posture, we may safely trust to temporary alliances for extraordinary emergencies."

In a previous part of the same address Washington makes this admirable and just remark: "The nation which indulges towards another an habitual hatred, or an habitual fondness, is in some degree a slave. It is a slave to its animosity or to its affection, either of which is sufficient to lead it astray from its duty and its interest."

The political conduct of Washington was always guided by these maxims. He succeeded in maintaining his country in a state of peace while all the other nations of the globe were at war; and he laid it down as a fundamental doctrine that the true interest of the Americans consisted in a perfect neutrality with regard to the internal dissensions of the European powers.

Jefferson went still further and introduced this other maxim into the policy of the Union, that "the Americans ought never to solicit any privileges from foreign nations, in order not to be obliged to grant similar privileges themselves."

These two principles, so plain and just as to be easily understood by the people, have greatly simplified the foreign policy of the United States. As the Union takes no part in the affairs of Europe, it has, properly speaking, no foreign interests to discuss, since it has, as yet, no powerful neighbors on the American continent. The country is as much removed from the passions of the Old World by its position as by its wishes, and it is called upon neither to repudiate nor to espouse them; while the dissensions of the New World are still concealed within the bosom of the future.

The Union is free from all pre-existing obligations; it can profit by the experience of the old nations of Europe, without being obliged, as they are, to make the best of the past and to adapt it to their present circumstances. It is not, like them, compelled to accept an immense inheritance bequeathed by their forefathers, an inheritance of glory mingled with calamities, and of alliances conflicting with national antipathies. The foreign policy of the United States is eminently expectant; it consists more in abstaining than in acting.

It is therefore very difficult to ascertain, at present, what degree of sagacity the American democracy will display in the conduct of the foreign policy of the country; upon this point its adversaries as well as its friends must suspend their judgment. As for myself, I do not hesitate to say that it is especially in the conduct of their foreign relations that democracies appear to me decidedly inferior to other governments. Experience, instruction, and habit almost always succeed in creating in a democracy a homely species of practical wisdom and that science of the petty occurrences of life which is called good sense. Good sense may suffice to direct the ordinary course of society; and among a people whose education is completed, the advantages of democratic liberty in the internal affairs of the country may more than compensate for the evils inherent in a democratic government. But it is not always so in the relations with foreign nations.

Foreign politics demand scarcely any of those qualities which are peculiar to a democracy; they require, on the contrary, the perfect use of almost all those in which it is deficient. Democracy is favorable to the increase of the internal resources of a state; it diffuses wealth and comfort, promotes public spirit, and fortifies the respect for law in all classes of society: all these are advantages which have only an indirect influence over the relations which one people bears to another. But a democracy can only with great difficulty regulate the details of an important undertaking, persevere in a fixed design, and work out its execution in spite of serious obstacles. It cannot combine its measures with secrecy or await their consequences with patience.

These are qualities which more especially belong to an individual or an aristocracy; and they are precisely the qualities by which a nation, like an individual, attains a dominant position.

If, on the contrary, we observe the natural defects of aristocracy, we shall find that, comparatively speaking, they do not injure the direction of the external affairs of the state. The capital fault of which aristocracies may be accused is that they work for themselves and not for the people. In foreign politics it is rare for the interest of the aristocracy to be distinct from that of the people.

The propensity that induces democracies to obey impulse rather than prudence, and to abandon a mature design for the gratification of a momentary passion, was clearly seen in America on the breaking out of the French Revolution. It was then as evident to the simplest capacity as it is at the present time that the interest of the Americans forbade them to take any part in the contest which was about to deluge Europe with blood, but which could not injure their own country. But the sympathies of the people declared themselves with so much violence in favor of France that nothing but the inflexible character of Washington and the immense popularity which he enjoyed could have prevented the Americans from declaring war against England. And even then the exertions which the austere reason of that great man made to repress the generous but imprudent passions of his fellow citizens nearly deprived him of the sole recompense which he ever claimed, that of his country's love. The majority reprobated his policy, but it was afterwards approved by the whole nation.[18]

[18] See the fifth volume of Marshall's *Life of Washington.* "In a government constituted like that of the United States," he says, at p. 314, "it is impossible for the chief magistrate, however firm he may be, to oppose for any length of time the torrent of popular opinion; and the prevalent opinion of that day seemed to incline to war. In fact, in the session of Congress held at the time, it was frequently seen that Washington had lost the majority in the House of Representatives." The violence of the language used against him in public was extreme, and, in a political meeting, they did not scruple to compare him indirectly with the traitor Arnold (p. 265). "By the opposition," says Marshall (p. 355), "the friends of the administration were declared to be an aristocratic and corrupt faction, who, from a desire to introduce monarchy, were hostile to France, and under the influence of Britain; that they were a paper nobility, whose

If the Constitution and the favor of the public had not entrusted the direction of the foreign affairs of the country to Washington, it is certain that the American nation would at that time have adopted the very measures which it now condemns.

Almost all the nations that have exercised a powerful influence upon the destinies of the world, by conceiving, following out, and executing vast designs, from the Romans to the English, have been governed by aristocratic institutions. Nor will this be a subject of wonder when we recollect that nothing in the world is so conservative in its views as an aristocracy. The mass of the people may be led astray by ignorance or passion; the mind of a king may be biased and made to vacillate in his designs, and, besides, a king is not immortal. But an aristocratic body is too numerous to be led astray by intrigue, and yet not numerous enough to yield readily to the intoxication of unreflecting passion. An aristocracy is a firm and enlightened body that never dies.

---

extreme sensibility at every measure which threatened the funds induced a tame submission to injuries and insults which the interests and honor of the nation required them to resist."

Chapter XIV

WHAT ARE THE REAL ADVANTAGES WHICH AMERICAN SOCIETY DERIVES FROM A DEMOCRATIC GOVERNMENT

Before entering upon the present chapter I must remind the reader of what I have more than once observed in this book. The political Constitution of the United States appears to me to be one of the forms of government that a democracy may adopt; but I do not regard the American Constitution as the best, or as the only one, that a democratic people may establish. In showing the advantages which the Americans derive from the government of democracy, I am therefore very far from affirming, or believing, that similar advantages can be obtained only from the same laws.

GENERAL TENDENCY OF THE LAWS UNDER AMERICAN DEMOCRACY, AND INSTINCTS OF THOSE WHO APPLY THEM. *Defects of a democratic government easy to be discovered—Its advantages discerned only by long observation—Democracy in America often inexpert, but the general tendency of the laws is advantageous—In the American democracy public officers have no permanent interests distinct from those of the majority—Results of this state of things.*

THE DEFECTS and weaknesses of a democratic government may readily be discovered; they can be proved by obvious facts, whereas their healthy influence becomes evident in ways which are not obvious and are, so to speak, hidden. A glance suffices to detect its faults, but its good qualities can be discerned only by long observation. The laws of the American democracy are frequently defective or incomplete: they sometimes attack vested rights, or sanction others which are dangerous to the community; and even if they were good, their frequency would still be a great evil. How comes it, then, that the American republics prosper and continue?

In the consideration of laws a distinction must be carefully observed between the end at which they aim and the means by which they pursue that end; between their absolute and their relative excellence. If it be the intention of the legislator to favor the interests of the minority at the expense of the majority, and if the measures he takes are so combined as to accomplish the object he has in view with the least possible expense of time and exertion, the law may be well drawn up although its purpose is bad; and the more efficacious it is, the more dangerous it will be.

Democratic laws generally tend to promote the welfare of the greatest possible number; for they emanate from the majority of the citizens, who are subject to error, but who cannot have an interest opposed to their own advantage. The laws of an aristocracy tend, on the contrary, to concentrate wealth and power in the hands of the minority; because an aristocracy, by its very nature, constitutes a minority. It may therefore be asserted, as a general proposition, that the purpose of a democracy in its legislation is more useful to humanity than that of an aristocracy. This, however, is the sum total of its advantages.

Aristocracies are infinitely more expert in the science of legislation than democracies ever can be. They are possessed of a self-control that protects them from the errors of temporary excitement; and they form far-reaching designs, which they know how to mature till a favorable opportunity arrives. Aristocratic government proceeds with the dexterity of art; it understands how to make the collective force of all its laws converge at the same time to a given point. Such is not the case with democracies, whose laws are almost always ineffective or inopportune. The means of democracy are therefore more imperfect than those of aristocracy, and the measures that it unwittingly adopts are frequently opposed to its own cause; but the object it has in view is more useful.

Let us now imagine a community so organized by nature or by its constitution that it can support the transitory action of bad laws, and that it can await, without destruction, the general tendency of its legislation: we shall then conceive how a democratic government, notwithstanding its faults, may be best fitted to produce the prosperity of this community. This is precisely what has occurred in the United States; and I repeat, what I have before remarked, that the

Democracy in America

248

to commit faults which they may afterwards repair.

An analogous observation may be made respecting public
officers. It is easy to perceive that American democracy frequently errs in the choice of the individuals to whom it entrusts the power of the administration; but it is more difficult
to say why the state prospers under their rule. In the first
place, it is to be remarked that if, in a democratic state, the
governors have less honesty and less capacity than elsewhere, the governed are more enlightened and more attentive to their interests. As the people in democracies are more
constantly vigilant in their affairs and more jealous of their
rights, they prevent their representatives from abandoning
that general line of conduct which their own interest prescribes. In the second place, it must be remembered that if
the democratic magistrate is more apt to misuse his power,
he possesses it for a shorter time. But there is yet another
reason which is still more general and conclusive. It is no
doubt of importance to the welfare of nations that they
should be governed by men of talents and virtue; but it is
perhaps still more important for them that the interests of
those men should not differ from the interests of the community at large; for if such were the case, their virtues might
become almost useless and their talents might be turned to
a bad account. I have said that it is important that the interests of the persons in authority should not differ from or
oppose the interests of the community at large; but I do not
insist upon their having the same interests as the *whole* population, because I am not aware that such a state of things
ever existed in any country.

No political form has hitherto been discovered that is
equally favorable to the prosperity and the development of
all the classes into which society is divided. These classes
continue to form, as it were, so many distinct communities
in the same nation; and experience has shown that it is no
less dangerous to place the fate of these classes exclusively
in the hands of any one of them than it is to make one people the arbiter of the destiny of another. When the rich alone
govern, the interest of the poor is always endangered; and
when the poor make the laws, that of the rich incurs very
serious risks. The advantage of democracy does not consist,
therefore, as has sometimes been asserted, in favoring the

prosperity of all, but simply in contributing to the well-being of the greatest number.

The men who are entrusted with the direction of public affairs in the United States are frequently inferior, in both capacity and morality, to those whom an aristocracy would raise to power. But their interest is identified and mingled with that of the majority of their fellow citizens. They may frequently be faithless and frequently mistaken, but they will never systematically adopt a line of conduct hostile to the majority; and they cannot give a dangerous or exclusive tendency to the government.

The maladministration of a democratic magistrate, more-over, is an isolated fact, which has influence only during the short period for which he is elected. Corruption and inca-pacity do not act as common interests which may connect men permanently with one another. A corrupt or incapable magistrate will not combine his measures with another mag-istrate simply because the latter is as corrupt and incapable as himself; and these two men will never unite their en-deavors to promote the corruption and inaptitude of their remote posterity. The ambition and the maneuvers of the one will serve, on the contrary, to unmask the other. The vices of a magistrate in democratic states are usually wholly personal.

But under aristocratic governments public men are swayed by the interest of their order, which, if it is some-times confused with the interests of the majority, is very fre-quently distinct from them. This interest is the common and lasting bond that unites them; it induces them to coalesce and combine their efforts to attain an end which is not al-ways the happiness of the greatest number; and it serves not only to connect the persons in authority with one another, but to unite them with a considerable portion of the commu-nity, since a numerous body of citizens belong to the aristoc-racy without being invested with official functions. The aris-tocratic magistrate is therefore constantly supported by a portion of the community as well as by the government of which he is a member.

The common purpose which in aristocracies connects the interest of the magistrates with that of a portion of their contemporaries identifies it also with that of future genera-tions; they labor for the future as well as for the present. The aristocratic magistrate is urged at the same time towards the same point by the passions of the community, by his own, and, I may almost add, by those of his posterity. Is it, then, wonderful that he does not resist such repeated impulses? And, indeed, aristocracies are often carried away by their class spirit without being corrupted by it; and they unconsciously fashion society to their own ends and prepare it for their own descendants.

The English aristocracy is perhaps the most liberal that has ever existed, and no body of men has ever, uninterruptedly, furnished so many honorable and enlightened individuals to the government of a country. It cannot escape observation, however, that in the legislation of England the interests of the poor have often been sacrificed to the advantages of the rich, and the rights of the majority to the privileges of a few. The result is that England at the present day combines the extremes of good and evil fortune in the bosom of her society; and the miseries and privations of her poor almost equal her power and renown.

In the United States, where public officers have no class interests to promote, the general and constant influence of the government is beneficial, although the individuals who conduct it are frequently unskillful and sometimes contemptible. There is, indeed, a secret tendency in democratic institutions that makes the exertions of the citizens subservient to the prosperity of the community in spite of their vices and mistakes; while in aristocratic institutions there is a secret bias which, notwithstanding the talents and virtues of those who conduct the government, leads them to contribute to the evils that oppress their fellow creatures. In aristocratic governments public men may frequently do harm without intending it; and in democratic states they bring about good results of which they have never thought.

PUBLIC SPIRIT IN THE UNITED STATES. *Instinctive patriotism— Patriotism of reflection—Their different characteristics —Nations ought to strive to acquire the second when the first has disappeared—Efforts of the Americans to acquire it—Interest of the individual intimately connected with that of the country.*

THERE is one sort of patriotic attachment which principally arises from that instinctive, disinterested, and undefinable feeling which connects the affections of man with his birth-place. This natural fondness is united with a taste for ancient customs and a reverence for traditions of the past; those who cherish it love their country as they love the mansion of their fathers. They love the tranquillity that it affords them; they cling to the peaceful habits that they have contracted within its bosom; they are attached to the reminiscences that it awakens; and they are even pleased by living there in a state of obedience. This patriotism is sometimes stimulated by religious enthusiasm, and then it is capable of making prodigious efforts. It is in itself a kind of religion: it does not reason, but it acts from the impulse of faith and sentiment. In some nations the monarch is regarded as a personification of the country; and, the fervor of patriotism being converted into the fervor of loyalty, they take a sympathetic pride in his conquests, and glory in his power. There was a time under the ancient monarchy when the French felt a sort of satisfaction in the sense of their dependence upon the arbitrary will of their king; and they were wont to say with pride: "We live under the most powerful king in the world."

But, like all instinctive passions, this kind of patriotism incites great transient exertions, but no continuity of effort. It may save the state in critical circumstances, but often allows it to decline in times of peace. While the manners of a people are simple and its faith unshaken, while society is steadily based upon traditional institutions whose legitimacy has never been contested, this instinctive patriotism is wont to endure.

But there is another species of attachment to country which is more rational than the one I have been describing. It is perhaps less generous and less ardent, but it is more fruitful and more lasting: it springs from knowledge; it is nurtured by the laws; it grows by the exercise of civil rights; and, in the end, it is confounded with the personal interests of the citizen. A man comprehends the influence which the well-being of his country has upon his own; he is aware that the laws permit him to contribute to that prosperity, and he labors to promote it, first because it benefits him, and secondly because it is in part his own work.

But epochs sometimes occur in the life of a nation when the old customs of a people are changed, public morality is destroyed, religious belief shaken, and the spell of tradition broken, while the diffusion of knowledge is yet imperfect and the civil rights of the community are ill secured or confined within narrow limits. The country then assumes a dim and dubious shape in the eyes of the citizens; they no longer behold it in the soil which they inhabit, for that soil is to them an inanimate clod; nor in the usages of their fore-fathers, which they have learned to regard as a debasing yoke; nor in religion, for of that they doubt; nor in the laws, which do not originate in their own authority; nor in the legislator, whom they fear and despise. The country is lost to their senses; they can discover it neither under its own nor under borrowed features, and they retire into a narrow and unenlightened selfishness. They are emancipated from preju-dice without having acknowledged the empire of reason; they have neither the instinctive patriotism of a monarchy nor the reflecting patriotism of a republic; but they have stopped between the two in the midst of confusion and dis-tress.

In this predicament to retreat is impossible, for a people cannot recover the sentiments of their youth any more than a man can return to the innocent tastes of childhood; such things may be regretted, but they cannot be renewed. They must go forward and accelerate the union of private with public interests, since the period of disinterested patriotism is gone by forever.

I am certainly far from affirming that in order to obtain this result the exercise of political rights should be immedi-ately granted to all men. But I maintain that the most pow-erful and perhaps the only means that we still possess of interesting men in the welfare of their country is to make them partakers in the government. At the present time civic zeal seems to me to be inseparable from the exercise of political rights; and I think that the number of citizens will be found to augment or decrease in Europe in proportion as those rights are extended.

How does it happen that in the United States, where the inhabitants have only recently immigrated to the land which they now occupy, and brought neither customs nor tradi-tions with them there; where they met one another for the first time with no previous acquaintance; where, in short, the instinctive love of country can scarcely exist; how does it happen that everyone takes as zealous an interest in the affairs of his township, his county, and the whole state as if they were his own? It is because everyone, in his sphere, takes an active part in the government of society.

The lower orders in the United States understand the influence exercised by the general prosperity upon their own welfare; simple as this observation is, it is too rarely made by the people. Besides, they are accustomed to regard this prosperity as the fruit of their own exertions. The citizen looks upon the fortune of the public as his own, and he labors for the good of the state, not merely from a sense of pride or duty, but from what I venture to term cupidity.

It is unnecessary to study the institutions and the history of the Americans in order to know the truth of this remark, for their manners render it sufficiently evident. As the American participates in all that is done in his country, he thinks himself obliged to defend whatever may be censured in it; for it is not only his country that is then attacked, it is himself. The consequence is that his national pride resorts to a thousand artifices and descends to all the petty tricks of personal vanity.

Nothing is more embarrassing in the ordinary intercourse of life than this irritable patriotism of the Americans. A stranger may be well inclined to praise many of the institutions of their country, but he begs permission to blame some things in it, a permission that is inexorably refused. America is therefore a free country in which, lest anybody should be hurt by your remarks, you are not allowed to speak freely of private individuals or of the state, of the citizens or of the authorities, of public or of private undertakings, or, in short, of anything at all except, perhaps, the climate and the soil; and even then Americans will be found ready to defend both as if they had co-operated in producing them.

In our times we must choose between the patriotism of all and the government of a few; for the social force and activity which the first confers are irreconcilable with the pledges of tranquillity which are given by the second.

THE IDEA OF RIGHTS IN THE UNITED STATES. *No great people without an idea of right—How the idea of right can be given to a people—Respect for right in the United States—Whence it arises.*

AFTER the general idea of virtue, I know no higher principle than that of right; or rather these two ideas are united in one. The idea of right is simply that of virtue introduced into the political world. It was the idea of right that enabled men to define anarchy and tyranny, and that taught them how to be independent without arrogance and to obey without servility. The man who submits to violence is debased by his compliance; but when he submits to that right of authority which he acknowledges in a fellow creature, he rises in some measure above the person who gives the command. There are no great men without virtue; and there are no great nations—it may almost be added, there would be no society—without respect for right; for what is a union of rational and intelligent beings who are held together only by the bond of force?

I am persuaded that the only means which we possess at the present time of inculcating the idea of right and of rendering it, as it were, palpable to the senses is to endow all with the peaceful exercise of certain rights; this is very clearly seen in children, who are men without the strength and the experience of manhood. When a child begins to move in the midst of the objects that surround him, he is instinctively led to appropriate to himself everything that he can lay his hands upon; he has no notion of the property of others; but as he gradually learns the value of things and begins to perceive that he may in his turn be despoiled, he becomes more circumspect, and he ends by respecting those rights in others which he wishes to have respected in himself. The principle which the child derives from the possession of his toys is taught to the man by the objects which he may call his own. In America, the most democratic of nations, those complaints against property in general, which are so frequent in Europe, are never heard, because in America there are no paupers. As everyone has property of his own to defend, everyone recognizes the principle upon which he holds it.

The same thing occurs in the political world. In America, the lowest classes have conceived a very high notion of political rights, because they exercise those rights; and they refrain from attacking the rights of others in order that their own may not be violated. While in Europe the same classes sometimes resist even the supreme power, the American submits without a murmur to the authority of the pettiest magistrate.

This truth appears even in the trivial details of national life. In France few pleasures are exclusively reserved for the higher classes; the poor are generally admitted wherever the rich are received; and they consequently behave with propriety, and respect whatever promotes the enjoyments that they themselves share. In England, where wealth has a monopoly of amusement as well as of power, complaints are made that whenever the poor happen to enter the places reserved for the pleasures of the rich, they do wanton mischief: can this be wondered at, since care has been taken that they should have nothing to lose?

The government of a democracy brings the notion of political rights to the level of the humblest citizens, just as the dissemination of wealth brings the notion of property within the reach of all men; to my mind, this is one of its greatest advantages. I do not say it is easy to teach men how to exercise political rights, but I maintain that, when it is possible, the effects which result from it are highly important; and I add that, if there ever was a time at which such an attempt ought to be made, that time is now. Do you not see that religious belief is shaken and the divine notion of right is declining, that morality is debased and the notion of moral right is therefore fading away? Argument is substituted for faith, and calculation for the impulses of sentiment. If, in the midst of this general disruption, you do not succeed in connecting the notion of right with that of private interest, which is the only immutable point in the human heart, what means will you have of governing the world except by fear? When I am told that the laws are weak and the people are turbulent, that passions are excited and the authority of virtue is paralyzed, and therefore no measures must be taken to increase the rights of the democracy, I reply that for these very reasons some measures of the kind ought to be taken; and I believe that governments are still more interested in taking them than society at large, for governments may perish, but society cannot die.

But I do not wish to exaggerate the example that America furnishes. There the people were invested with political rights at a time when they could not be abused, for the inhabitants were few in number and simple in their manners.

As they have increased, the Americans have not augmented the power of the democracy; they have rather extended its domain.

It cannot be doubted that the moment at which political rights are granted to a people that had before been without them is a very critical one, that the measure, though often necessary, is always dangerous. A child may kill before he is aware of the value of life; and he may deprive another person of his property before he is aware that his own may be taken from him. The lower orders, when they are first invested with political rights, stand in relation to those rights in the same position as the child does to the whole of nature; and the celebrated adage may then be applied to them: *Homo puer robustus*. This truth may be perceived even in America. The states in which the citizens have enjoyed their rights longest are those in which they make the best use of them.

It cannot be repeated too often that nothing is more fertile in prodigies than the art of being free; but there is nothing more arduous than the apprenticeship of liberty. It is not so with despotism: despotism often promises to make amends for a thousand previous ills; it supports the right, it protects the oppressed, and it maintains public order. The nation is lulled by the temporary prosperity that it produces, until it is roused to a sense of its misery. Liberty, on the contrary, is generally established with difficulty in the midst of storms; it is perfected by civil discord; and its benefits cannot be appreciated until it is already old.

RESPECT FOR LAW IN THE UNITED STATES. *Respect of the Americans for law—Parental affection which they entertain for it—Personal interest of everyone to increase the power of law.*

IT is not always feasible to consult the whole people, either directly or indirectly, in the formation of law; but it cannot be denied that, when this is possible, the authority of law is much augmented. This popular origin, which impairs the excellence and the wisdom of legislation, contributes much to increase its power. There is an amazing strength in the expression of the will of a whole people; and when it declares itself, even the imagination of those who would wish to contest it is overawed. The truth of this fact is well known by parties, and they consequently strive to make out a majority whenever they can. If they have not the greater number of voters on their side, they assert that the true majority abstained from voting; and if they are foiled even there, they have recourse to those persons who had no right to vote.

In the United States, except slaves, servants, and paupers supported by the townships, there is no class of persons who do not exercise the elective franchise and who do not indirectly contribute to make the laws. Those who wish to attack the laws must consequently either change the opinion of the nation or trample upon its decision.

A second reason, which is still more direct and weighty, may be adduced: in the United States everyone is personally interested in enforcing the obedience of the whole community to the law; for as the minority may shortly rally the majority to its principles, it is interested in professing that respect for the decrees of the legislator which it may soon have occasion to claim for its own. However irksome an enactment may be, the citizen of the United States complies with it, not only because it is the work of the majority, but because it is his own, and he regards it as a contract to which he is himself a party.

In the United States, then, that numerous and turbulent multitude does not exist who, regarding the law as their natural enemy, look upon it with fear and distrust. It is impossible, on the contrary, not to perceive that all classes display the utmost reliance upon the legislation of their country and are attached to it by a kind of parental affection.

I am wrong, however, in saying all classes; for as in America the European scale of authority is inverted, there the wealthy are placed in a position analogous to that of the poor in the Old World, and it is the opulent classes who frequently look upon law with suspicion. I have already observed that the advantage of democracy is not, as has been sometimes asserted, that it protects the interests of all, but simply that it protects those of the majority. In the United States, where the poor rule, the rich have always something to fear from the abuse of their power. This natural anxiety of the rich may produce a secret dissatisfaction; but society is not disturbed by it, for the same reason that withholds the confidence of the rich from the legislative authority makes them obey its mandates: their wealth, which prevents them from making the law, prevents them from withstanding it. Among civilized nations, only those who have nothing to lose ever revolt; and if the laws of a democracy are not always worthy of respect, they are always respected; for those who usually infringe the laws cannot fail to obey those which they have themselves made and by which they are benefited; while the citizens who might be interested in their infraction are induced, by their character and station, to submit to the decisions of the legislature, whatever they may be. Besides, the people in America obey the law, not only because it is their own work, but because it may be changed if it is harmful; a law is observed because, first, it is a self-imposed evil, and, secondly, it is an evil of transient duration.

ACTIVITY THAT PERVADES ALL PARTS OF THE BODY POLITIC IN THE UNITED STATES; INFLUENCE THAT IT EXERCISES UPON SOCIETY. *More difficult to conceive the political activity that pervades the United States than the freedom and equality that reign there—The great activity that perpetually agitates the legislative bodies is only an episode, a prolongation of the general activity—Difficult for an American to confine himself to his own business —Political agitation extends to all social intercourse— Commercial activity of the Americans partly attributable to this cause—Indirect advantages which society derives from a democratic government.*

ON passing from a free country into one which is not free the traveler is struck by the change; in the former all is bustle and activity; in the latter everything seems calm and motionless. In the one, amelioration and progress are the topics of inquiry; in the other, it seems as if the community wished only to repose in the enjoyment of advantages already acquired. Nevertheless, the country which exerts itself so strenuously to become happy is generally more wealthy and prosperous than that which appears so contented with its lot; and when we compare them, we can scarcely conceive how so many new wants are daily felt in the former, while so few seems to exist in the latter.

If this remark is applicable to those free countries which have preserved monarchical forms and aristocratic institutions. It is still more so to democratic republics. In these states it is not a portion only of the people who endeavor to improve the state of society, but the whole community is engaged in the task; and it is not the exigencies and convenience of a single class for which provision is to be made, but the exigencies and convenience of all classes at once.

It is not impossible to conceive the surprising liberty that the Americans enjoy; some idea may likewise be formed of their extreme equality; but the political activity that pervades the United States must be seen in order to be understood. No sooner do you set foot upon American ground than you are stunned by a kind of tumult; a confused clamor is heard on every side, and a thousand simultaneous voices demand the satisfaction of their social wants. Everything is in motion around you; here the people of one quarter of a town are met to decide upon the building of a church; there the election of a representative is going on; a little farther, the delegates of a district are hastening to the town in order to consult upon some local improvements; in another place, the laborers of a village quit their plows to deliberate upon the project of a road or a public school. Meetings are called for the sole purpose of declaring their disapprobation of the conduct of the government; while in other assemblies citizens salute the authorities of the day as the fathers of their country. Societies are formed which regard drunkenness as the principal cause of the evils of the state, and solemnly bind themselves to give an example of temperance.[1]

The great political agitation of American legislative bodies, which is the only one that attracts the attention of foreigners, is a mere episode, or a sort of continuation, of that universal movement which originates in the lowest classes of the people and extends successively to all the ranks of society. It is impossible to spend more effort in the pursuit of happiness.

It is difficult to say what place is taken up in the life of an inhabitant of the United States by his concern for politics.

[1] At the time of my stay in the United States the temperance societies already consisted of more than 270,000 members; and their effect had been to diminish the consumption of strong liquors by 500,000 gallons per annum in Pennsylvania alone. Temperance societies are organizations the members of which undertake to abstain from strong liquors.

To take a hand in the regulation of society and to discuss it is his biggest concern and, so to speak, the only pleasure an American knows. This feeling pervades the most trifling habits of life; even the women frequently attend public meetings and listen to political harangues as a recreation from their household labors. Debating clubs are, to a certain extent, a substitute for theatrical entertainments: an American cannot converse, but he can discuss, and his talk falls into a dissertation. He speaks to you as if he was addressing a meeting; and if he should chance to become warm in the discussion, he will say "Gentlemen" to the person with whom he is conversing.

In some countries the inhabitants seem unwilling to avail themselves of the political privileges which the law gives them; it would seem that they set too high a value upon their time to spend it on the interests of the community; and they shut themselves up in a narrow selfishness, marked out by four sunk fences and a quickset hedge. But if an American were condemned to confine his activity to his own affairs, he would be robbed of one half of his existence; he would feel an immense void in the life which he is accustomed to lead, and his wretchedness would be unbearable.[2] I am persuaded that if ever a despotism should be established in America, it will be more difficult to overcome the habits that freedom has formed than to conquer the love of freedom itself.

This ceaseless agitation which democratic government has introduced into the political world influences all social intercourse. I am not sure that, on the whole, this is not the greatest advantage of democracy; and I am less inclined to applaud it for what it does than for what it causes to be done.

It is incontestable that the people frequently conduct public business very badly; but it is impossible that the lower orders should take a part in public business without extending the circle of their ideas and quitting the ordinary routine of their thoughts. The humblest individual who cooperates in the government of society acquires a certain degree of self-respect; and as he possesses authority, he can

[2] The same remark was made at Rome under the first Cæsars. Montesquieu somewhere alludes to the excessive despondency of certain Roman citizens who, after the excitement of political life, were all at once flung back into the stagnation of private life.

command the services of minds more enlightened than his own. He is canvassed by a multitude of applicants, and in seeking to deceive him in a thousand ways, they really enlighten him. He takes a part in political undertakings which he did not originate, but which give him a taste for undertakings of the kind. New improvements are daily pointed out to him in the common property, and this gives him the desire of improving that property which is his own. He is perhaps neither happier nor better than those who came before him, but he is better informed and more active. I have no doubt that the democratic institutions of the United States, joined to the physical constitution of the country, are the cause (not the direct, as is so often asserted, but the indirect cause) of the prodigious commercial activity of the inhabitants. It is not created by the laws, but the people learn how to promote it by the experience derived from legislation.

When the opponents of democracy assert that a single man performs what he undertakes better than the government of all, it appears to me that they are right. The government of an individual, supposing an equality of knowledge on either side, is more consistent, more persevering, more uniform, and more accurate in details than that of a multitude, and it selects with more discrimination the men whom it employs. If any deny this, they have never seen a democratic government, or have judged upon partial evidence. It is true that, even when local circumstances and the dispositions of the people allow democratic institutions to exist, they do not display a regular and methodical system of government. Democratic liberty is far from accomplishing all its projects with the skill of an adroit despotism. It frequently abandons them before they have borne their fruits, or risks them when the consequences may be dangerous; but in the end it produces more than any absolute government; if it does fewer things well, it does a greater number of things. Under its sway the grandeur is not in what the public administration does, but in what is done without it or outside of it. Democracy does not give the people the most skillful government, but it produces what the ablest governments are frequently unable to create: namely, an all-pervading and restless activity, a superabundant force, and an energy which is inseparable from it and which may, however unfavorable circumstances may be, produce wonders. These are the true advantages of democracy.

In the present age, when the destinies of Christendom seem to be in suspense, some hasten to assail democracy as a hostile power while it is yet growing; and others already adore this new deity which is springing forth from chaos. But both parties are imperfectly acquainted with the object of their hatred or their worship; they strike in the dark and distribute their blows at random.

We must first understand what is wanted of society and its government. Do you wish to give a certain elevation to the human mind and teach it to regard the things of this world with generous feelings, to inspire men with a scorn of mere temporal advantages, to form and nourish strong convictions and keep alive the spirit of honorable devotedness? Is it your object to refine the habits, embellish the manners, and cultivate the arts, to promote the love of poetry, beauty, and glory? Would you constitute a people fitted to act powerfully upon all other nations, and prepared for those high enterprises which, whatever be their results, will leave a name forever famous in history? If you believe such to be the principal object of society, avoid the government of the democracy, for it would not lead you with certainty to the goal.

But if you hold it expedient to divert the moral and intellectual activity of man to the production of comfort and the promotion of general well-being; if a clear understanding be more profitable to man than genius; if your object is not to stimulate the virtues of heroism, but the habits of peace; if you had rather witness vices than crimes, and are content to meet with fewer noble deeds, provided offenses be diminished in the same proportion; if, instead of living in the midst of a brilliant society, you are contented to have prosperity around you; if, in short, you are of the opinion that the principal object of a government is not to confer the greatest possible power and glory upon the body of the nation, but to ensure the greatest enjoyment and to avoid the most misery to each of the individuals who compose it—if such be your desire, then equalize the conditions of men and establish democratic institutions.

But if the time is past at which such a choice was possible, and if some power superior to that of man already hurries us, without consulting our wishes, towards one or the other of these two governments, let us endeavor to make the best of that which is allotted to us and, by finding out both its good and its evil tendencies, be able to foster the former and repress the latter to the utmost.

Chapter XV

UNLIMITED POWER OF THE MAJORITY IN THE UNITED STATES, AND ITS CONSEQUENCES

NATURAL STRENGTH of the majority in democracies—Most of the American constitutions have increased this strength by artificial means—How this has been done—Pledged delegates—Moral power of the majority—Opinion as to its infallibility—Respect for its rights, how augmented in the United States.

THE VERY essence of democratic government consists in the absolute sovereignty of the majority; for there is nothing in democratic states that is capable of resisting it. Most of the American constitutions have sought to increase this natural strength of the majority by artificial means.[1]

Of all political institutions, the legislature is the one that is most easily swayed by the will of the majority. The Americans determined that the members of the legislature should be elected by the people *directly,* and for a *very brief term,* in order to subject them, not only to the general convictions, but even to the daily passions, of their constituents. The members of both houses are taken from the same classes in society and nominated in the same manner; so that the movements of the legislative bodies are almost as rapid, and quite as irresistible, as those of a single assembly. It is to a legislature thus constituted that almost all the authority of the government has been entrusted.

At the same time that the law increased the strength of

[1] We have seen, in examining the Federal Constitution, that the efforts of the legislators of the Union were directed against this absolute power. The consequence has been that the Federal government is more independent in its sphere than that of the states. But the Federal government scarcely ever interferes in any but foreign affairs; and the governments of the states in reality direct society in America.

those authorities which of themselves were strong, it enfeebled more and more those which were naturally weak. It deprived the representatives of the executive power of all stability and independence; and by subjecting them completely to the caprices of the legislature, it robbed them of the slender influence that the nature of a democratic government might have allowed them to exercise. In several states the judicial power was also submitted to the election of the majority; and in all of them its existence was made to depend on the pleasure of the legislative authority, since the representatives were empowered annually to regulate the stipend of the judges.

Custom has done even more than law. A proceeding is becoming more and more general in the United States which will, in the end, do away with the guarantees of representative government: it frequently happens that the voters, in electing a delegate, point out a certain line of conduct to him and impose upon him certain positive obligations that he is pledged to fulfill. With the exception of the tumult, this comes to the same thing as if the majority itself held its deliberations in the market-place.

Several particular circumstances combine to render the power of the majority in America not only preponderant, but irresistible. The moral authority of the majority is partly based upon the notion that there is more intelligence and wisdom in a number of men united than in a single individual, and that the number of the legislators is more important than their quality. The theory of equality is thus applied to the intellects of men; and human pride is thus assailed in its last retreat by a doctrine which the minority hesitate to admit, and to which they will but slowly assent. Like all other powers, and perhaps more than any other, the authority of the many requires the sanction of time in order to appear legitimate. At first it enforces obedience by constraint; and its laws are not *respected* until they have been long maintained.

The right of governing society, which the majority supposes itself to derive from its superior intelligence, was introduced into the United States by the first settlers; and this idea, which of itself would be sufficient to create a free nation, has now been amalgamated with the customs of the people and the minor incidents of social life.

The French under the old monarchy held it for a maxim that the king could do no wrong; and if he did do wrong, the blame was imputed to his advisers. This notion made obedience very easy; it enabled the subject to complain of the law without ceasing to love and honor the lawgiver. The Americans entertain the same opinion with respect to the majority.

The moral power of the majority is founded upon yet another principle, which is that the interests of the many are to be preferred to those of the few. It will readily be perceived that the respect here professed for the rights of the greater number must naturally increase or diminish according to the state of parties. When a nation is divided into several great irreconcilable interests, the privilege of the majority is often overlooked, because it is intolerable to comply with its demands.

If there existed in America a class of citizens whom the legislating majority sought to deprive of exclusive privileges which they had possessed for ages and to bring down from an elevated station to the level of the multitude, it is probable that the minority would be less ready to submit to its laws. But as the United States was colonized by men holding equal rank, there is as yet no natural or permanent disagreement between the interests of its different inhabitants.

There are communities in which the members of the minority can never hope to draw the majority over to their side, because they must then give up the very point that is at issue between them. Thus an aristocracy can never become a majority while it retains its exclusive privileges, and it cannot cede its privileges without ceasing to be an aristocracy.

In the United States, political questions cannot be taken up in so general and absolute a manner; and all parties are willing to recognize the rights of the majority, because they all hope at some time to be able to exercise them to their own advantage. The majority in that country, therefore, exercise a prodigious actual authority, and a power of opinion which is nearly as great; no obstacles exist which can impede or even retard its progress, so as to make it heed the complaints of those whom it crushes upon its path. This state of things is harmful in itself and dangerous for the future.

How the omnipotence of the majority increases, in America, the instability of legislation and administration inherent in democracy. *The Americans increase the mutability of law that is inherent in a democracy by changing the legislature every year, and investing it with almost unbounded authority—The same effect is produced upon the administration—In America the pressure for social improvements is vastly greater, but less continuous, than in Europe.*

I have already spoken of the natural defects of democratic institutions; each one of them increases in the same ratio as the power of the majority. To begin with the most evident of them all, the mutability of the laws is an evil inherent in a democratic government, because it is natural to democracies to raise new men to power. But this evil is more or less perceptible in proportion to the authority and the means of action which the legislature possesses.

In America the authority exercised by the legislatures is supreme; nothing prevents them from accomplishing their wishes with celerity and with irresistible power, and they are supplied with new representatives every year. That is to say, the circumstances which contribute most powerfully to democratic instability, and which admit of the free application of caprice to the most important objects, are here in full operation. Hence America is, at the present day, the country beyond all others where laws last the shortest time. Almost all the American constitutions have been amended within thirty years; there is therefore not one American state which has not modified the principles of its legislation in that time. As for the laws themselves, a single glance at the archives of the different states of the Union suffices to convince one that in America the activity of the legislator never slackens. Not that the American democracy is naturally less stable than any other, but it is allowed to follow, in the formation of the laws, the natural instability of its desires.[2]

[2] The legislative acts promulgated by the state of Massachusetts alone from the year 1780 to the present time already fill three stout volumes; and it must not be forgotten that the collection to which I allude was revised in 1823, when many old laws which had fallen into disuse were omitted. The state of Massachusetts, which is not more populous than a department of

The omnipotence of the majority and the rapid as well as absolute manner in which its decisions are executed in the United States not only render the law unstable, but exercise the same influence upon the execution of the law and the conduct of the administration. As the majority is the only power that it is important to court, all its projects are taken up with the greatest ardor; but no sooner is its attention distracted than all this ardor ceases; while in the free states of Europe, where the administration is at once independent and secure, the projects of the legislature continue to be executed even when its attention is directed to other objects.

In America certain improvements are prosecuted with much more zeal and activity than elsewhere; in Europe the same ends are promoted by much less social effort more continuously applied.

Some years ago several pious individuals undertook to ameliorate the condition of the prisons. The public were moved by their statements, and the reform of criminals became a popular undertaking. New prisons were built; and for the first time the idea of reforming as well as punishing the delinquent formed a part of prison discipline.

But this happy change, in which the public had taken so hearty an interest and which the simultaneous exertions of the citizens rendered irresistible, could not be completed in a moment. While the new penitentiaries were being erected and the will of the majority was hastening the work, the old prisons still existed and contained a great number of offenders. These jails became more unwholesome and corrupt in proportion as the new establishments were reformed and improved, forming a contrast that may readily be understood. The majority was so eagerly employed in founding the new prisons that those which already existed were forgotten; and as the general attention was diverted to a novel object, the care which had hitherto been bestowed upon the others ceased. The salutary regulations of discipline were first relaxed and afterwards broken; so that in the immediate neighborhood of a prison that bore witness to the mild and enlightened spirit of our times, dungeons existed that reminded one of the barbarism of the Middle Ages.

France, may be considered as the most stable, the most consistent, and the most sagacious in its undertakings of the whole Union.

TYRANNY OF THE MAJORITY. *How the principle of the sovereignty of the people is to be understood—Impossibility of conceiving a mixed government—The sovereign power must exist somewhere—Precautions to be taken to control its action—These precautions have not been taken in the United States—Consequences.*

I HOLD it to be an impious and detestable maxim that, politically speaking, the people have a right to do anything; and yet I have asserted that all authority originates in the will of the majority. Am I, then, in contradiction with myself?

A general law, which bears the name of justice, has been made and sanctioned, not only by a majority of this or that people, but by a majority of mankind. The rights of every people are therefore confined within the limits of what is just. A nation may be considered as a jury which is empowered to represent society at large and to apply justice, which is its law. Ought such a jury, which represents society, to have more power than the society itself whose laws it executes?

When I refuse to obey an unjust law, I do not contest the right of the majority to command, but I simply appeal from the sovereignty of the people to the sovereignty of mankind. Some have not feared to assert that a people can never outstep the boundaries of justice and reason in those affairs which are peculiarly its own; and that consequently full power may be given to the majority by which it is represented. But this is the language of a slave.

A majority taken collectively is only an individual, whose opinions, and frequently whose interests, are opposed to those of another individual, who is styled a minority. If it be admitted that a man possessing absolute power may misuse that power by wronging his adversaries, why should not a majority be liable to the same reproach? Men do not change their characters by uniting with one another; nor does their patience in the presence of obstacles increase with their strength.[3] For my own part, I cannot believe it; the power to

[3] No one will assert that a people cannot forcibly wrong another people; but parties may be looked upon as lesser nations within a great one, and they are aliens to each other. If, therefore, one admits that a nation can act tyrannically towards another nation, can it be denied that a party may do the same towards another party?

do everything, which I should refuse to one of my equals, I will never grant to any number of them.

I do not think that, for the sake of preserving liberty, it is possible to combine several principles in the same government so as really to oppose them to one another. The form of government that is usually termed *mixed* has always appeared to me a mere chimera. Accurately speaking, there is no such thing as a *mixed government,* in the sense usually given to that word, because in all communities some one principle of action may be discovered which preponderates over the others. England in the last century, which has been especially cited as an example of this sort of government, was essentially an aristocratic state, although it comprised some great elements of democracy; for the laws and customs of the country were such that the aristocracy could not but preponderate in the long run and direct public affairs according to its own will. The error arose from seeing the interests of the nobles perpetually contending with those of the people, without considering the issue of the contest, which was really the important point. When a community actually has a mixed government—that is to say, when it is equally divided between adverse principles—it must either experience a revolution or fall into anarchy.

I am therefore of the opinion that social power superior to all others must always be placed somewhere; but I think that liberty is endangered when this power finds no obstacle which can retard its course and give it time to moderate its own vehemence.

Unlimited power is in itself a bad and dangerous thing. Human beings are not competent to exercise it with discretion. God alone can be omnipotent, because his wisdom and his justice are always equal to his power. There is no power on earth so worthy of honor in itself or clothed with rights so sacred that I would admit its uncontrolled and all-predominant authority. When I see that the right and the means of absolute command are conferred on any power whatever, be it called a people or a king, an aristocracy or a democracy, a monarchy or a republic, I say there is the germ of tyranny, and I seek to live elsewhere, under other laws.

In my opinion, the main evil of the present democratic institutions of the United States does not arise, as is often asserted in Europe, from their weakness, but from their irresistible strength. I am not so much alarmed at the excessive liberty which reigns in that country as at the inadequate securities which one finds there against tyranny.

When an individual or a party is wronged in the United States, to whom can he apply for redress? If to public opinion, public opinion constitutes the majority; if to the legislature, it represents the majority and implicitly obeys it; if to the executive power, it is appointed by the majority and serves as a passive tool in its hands. The public force consists of the majority under arms; the jury is the majority invested with the right of hearing judicial cases; and in certain states even the judges are elected by the majority. However iniquitous or absurd the measure of which you complain, you must submit to it as well as you can.[4]

---

[4] A striking instance of the excesses that may be occasioned by the despotism of the majority occurred at Baltimore during the War of 1812. At that time the war was very popular in Baltimore. A newspaper that had taken the other side excited, by its opposition, the indignation of the inhabitants. The mob assembled, broke the printing-presses, and attacked the house of the editors. The militia was called out, but did not obey the call; and the only means of saving the wretches who were threatened by the frenzy of the mob was to throw them into prison as common malefactors. But even this precaution was ineffectual; the mob collected again during the night; the magistrates again made a vain attempt to call out the militia; the prison was forced, one of the newspaper editors was killed upon the spot, and the others were left for dead. The guilty parties, when they were brought to trial, were acquitted by the jury.

I said one day to an inhabitant of Pennsylvania: "Be so good as to explain to me how it happens that in a state founded by Quakers, and celebrated for its toleration, free blacks are not allowed to exercise civil rights. They pay taxes; is it not fair that they should vote?"

"You insult us," replied my informant, "if you imagine that our legislators could have committed so gross an act of injustice and intolerance."

"Then the blacks possess the right of voting in this country?"

"Without doubt."

"How comes it, then, that at the polling-booth this morning I did not perceive a single Negro?"

"That is not the fault of the law. The Negroes have an undisputed right of voting, but they voluntarily abstain from making their appearance."

"A very pretty piece of modesty on their part!" rejoined I.

"Why, the truth is that they are not disinclined to vote, but they are afraid of being maltreated; in this country the law is sometimes unable to maintain its authority without the support of the majority. But in this case the majority entertains very strong prejudices against the blacks, and the magistrates are

If, on the other hand, a legislative power could be so constituted as to represent the majority without necessarily being the slave of its passions, an executive so as to retain a proper share of authority, and a judiciary so as to remain independent of the other two powers, a government would be formed which would still be democratic while incurring scarcely any risk of tyranny.

I do not say that there is a frequent use of tyranny in America at the present day; but I maintain that there is no sure barrier against it, and that the causes which mitigate the government there are to be found in the circumstances and the manners of the country more than in its laws.

EFFECTS OF THE OMNIPOTENCE OF THE MAJORITY UPON THE ARBITRARY AUTHORITY OF AMERICAN PUBLIC OFFICERS. *Liberty left by the American laws to public officers within a certain sphere—Their power.*

A DISTINCTION must be drawn between tyranny and arbitrary power. Tyranny may be exercised by means of the law itself, and in that case it is not arbitrary; arbitrary power may be exercised for the public good, in which case it is not tyrannical. Tyranny usually employs arbitrary means, but if necessary it can do without them.

In the United States the omnipotence of the majority, which is favorable to the legal despotism of the legislature, likewise favors the arbitrary authority of the magistrate. The majority has absolute power both to make the laws and to watch over their execution; and as it has equal authority over those who are in power and the community at large, it considers public officers as its passive agents and readily confides to them the task of carrying out its designs. The details of their office and the privileges that they are to enjoy are rarely defined beforehand. It treats them as a master does his servants, since they are always at work in his sight and he can direct or reprimand them at any instant.

In general, the American functionaries are far more independent within the sphere that is prescribed to them than the French civil officers. Sometimes, even, they are allowed by the popular authority to exceed those bounds; and as

unable to protect them in the exercise of their legal rights."
"Then the majority claims the right not only of making the laws. but of breaking the laws it has made?"

they are protected by the opinion and backed by the power of the majority, they dare do things that even a European, accustomed as he is to arbitrary power, is astonished at. By this means habits are formed in the heart of a free country which may some day prove fatal to its liberties.

POWER EXERCISED BY THE MAJORITY IN AMERICA UPON OPIN-ION. *In America, when the majority has once irrevocably decided a question, all discussion ceases—Reason for this—Moral power exercised by the majority upon opinion—Democratic republics have applied despotism to the minds of men.*

IT is in the examination of the exercise of thought in the United States that we clearly perceive how far the power of the majority surpasses all the powers with which we are acquainted in Europe. Thought is an invisible and subtle power that mocks all the efforts of tyranny. At the present time the most absolute monarchs in Europe cannot prevent certain opinions hostile to their authority from circulating in secret through their dominions and even in their courts. It is not so in America; as long as the majority is still undecided, discussion is carried on; but as soon as its decision is irrevocably pronounced, everyone is silent, and the friends as well as the opponents of the measure unite in assenting to its propriety. The reason for this is perfectly clear: no monarch is so absolute as to combine all the powers of society in his own hands and to conquer all opposition, as a majority is able to do, which has the right both of making and of executing the laws.

The authority of a king is physical and controls the actions of men without subduing their will. But the majority possesses a power that is physical and moral at the same time, which acts upon the will as much as upon the actions and represses not only all contest, but all controversy.

I know of no country in which there is so little independence of mind and real freedom of discussion as in America. In any constitutional state in Europe every sort of religious and political theory may be freely preached and disseminated; for there is no country in Europe so subdued by any single authority as not to protect the man who raises his voice in the cause of truth from the consequences of his hardihood. If he is unfortunate enough to live under an absolute government, the people are often on his side; if he inhabits a free country, he can, if necessary, find a shelter behind the throne. The aristocratic part of society supports him in some countries, and the democracy in others. But in a nation where democratic institutions exist, organized like those of the United States, there is but one authority, one element of strength and success, with nothing beyond it.

In America the majority raises formidable barriers around the liberty of opinion; within these barriers an author may write what he pleases, but woe to him if he goes beyond them. Not that he is in danger of an auto-da-fé, but he is exposed to continued obloquy and persecution. His political career is closed forever, since he has offended the only authority that is able to open it. Every sort of compensation, even that of celebrity, is refused to him. Before making public his opinions he thought he had sympathizers; now it seems to him that he has none any more since he has revealed himself to everyone; then those who blame him criticize loudly and those who think as he does keep quiet and move away without courage. He yields at length, overcome by the daily effort which he has to make, and subsides into silence, as if he felt remorse for having spoken the truth.

Fetters and headsmen were the coarse instruments that tyranny formerly employed; but the civilization of our age has perfected despotism itself, though it seemed to have nothing to learn. Monarchs had, so to speak, materialized oppression; the democratic republics of the present day have rendered it as entirely an affair of the mind as the will which it is intended to coerce. Under the absolute sway of one man the body was attacked in order to subdue the soul; but the soul escaped the blows which were directed against it and rose proudly superior. Such is not the course adopted by tyranny in democratic republics; there the body is left free, and the soul is enslaved. The master no longer says: "You shall think as I do or you shall die"; but he says: "You are free to think differently from me and to retain your life, your property, and all that you possess; but you are henceforth a stranger among your people. You may retain your civil rights, but they will be useless to you, for you will never be chosen by your fellow citizens if you solicit their votes; and they will affect to scorn you if you ask for their esteem. You will remain among men, but you will be deprived of the rights of mankind. Your fellow creatures will shun you like an impure being; and even those who believe in your innocence will abandon you, lest they should be shunned in their turn. Go in peace! I have given you your life, but it is an existence worse than death."

Absolute monarchies had dishonored despotism; let us beware lest democratic republics should reinstate it and render it less odious and degrading in the eyes of the many by making it still more onerous to the few.

Works have been published in the proudest nations of the Old World expressly intended to censure the vices and the follies of the times: Labruyère inhabited the palace of Louis XIV when he composed his chapter upon the Great, and Molière criticized the courtiers in the plays that were acted before the court. But the ruling power in the United States is not to be made game of. The smallest reproach irritates its sensibility, and the slightest joke that has any foundation in truth renders it indignant; from the forms of its language up to the solid virtues of its character, everything must be made the subject of encomium. No writer, whatever be his eminence, can escape paying this tribute of adulation to his fellow citizens. The majority lives in the perpetual utterance of self-applause, and there are certain truths which the Americans can learn only from strangers or from experience.

If America has not as yet had any great writers, the reason is given in these facts; there can be no literary genius without freedom of opinion, and freedom of opinion does not exist in America. The Inquisition has never been able to prevent a vast number of anti-religious books from circulating in Spain. The empire of the majority succeeds much better in the United States, since it actually removes any wish to publish them. Unbelievers are to be met with in America, but there is no public organ of infidelity. Attempts have been made by some governments to protect morality by prohibiting licentious books. In the United States no one is punished for this sort of books, but no one is induced to write them; not because all the citizens are immaculate in conduct, but because the majority of the community is decent and orderly.

In this case the use of power is unquestionably good; and I am discussing the nature of the power itself. This irresistible authority is a constant fact, and its judicious exercise is only an accident.

EFFECTS OF THE TYRANNY OF THE MAJORITY UPON THE NA-TIONAL CHARACTER OF THE AMERICANS—THE COURTIER SPIRIT IN THE UNITED STATES. *Effects of the tyranny of the majority more sensibly felt hitherto on the manners than on the conduct of society—They check the development of great characters—Democratic republics, organized like the United States, infuse the courtier spirit into the mass of the people—Proofs of this spirit in the United States—Why there is more patriotism in the people than in those who govern in their name.*

THE TENDENCIES that I have just mentioned are as yet but slightly perceptible in political society, but they already exercise an unfavorable influence upon the national character of the Americans. I attribute the small number of distinguished men in political life to the ever increasing despotism of the majority in the United States.

When the American Revolution broke out, they arose in great numbers; for public opinion then served, not to tyrannize over, but to direct the exertions of individuals. Those celebrated men, sharing the agitation of mind common at that period, had a grandeur peculiar to themselves, which was reflected back upon the nation, but was by no means borrowed from it.

In absolute governments the great nobles who are nearest to the throne flatter the passions of the sovereign and voluntarily truckle to his caprices. But the mass of the nation does not degrade itself by servitude; it often submits from weakness, from habit, or from ignorance, and sometimes from loyalty. Some nations have been known to sacrifice their own desires to those of the sovereign with pleasure and pride, thus exhibiting a sort of independence of mind in the very act of submission. These nations are miserable, but they are not degraded. There is a great difference between doing what one does not approve, and feigning to approve what one does; the one is the weakness of a feeble person, the other befits the temper of a lackey.

In free countries, where everyone is more or less called upon to give his opinion on affairs of state, in democratic republics, where public life is incessantly mingled with domestic affairs, where the sovereign authority is accessible on every side, and where its attention can always be attracted by vociferation, more persons are to be met with who speculate upon its weaknesses and live upon ministering to its passions than in absolute monarchies. Not because men are naturally worse in these states than elsewhere, but the temptation is stronger and at the same time of easier access. The result is a more extensive debasement of character.

Democratic republics extend the practice of currying favor with the many and introduce it into all classes at once; this is the most serious reproach that can be addressed to them. This is especially true in democratic states organized like the American republics, where the power of the majority is so absolute and irresistible that one must give up one's rights as a citizen and almost abjure one's qualities as a man if one intends to stray from the track which it prescribes.

In that immense crowd which throngs the avenues to power in the United States, I found very few men who displayed that manly candor and masculine independence of opinion which frequently distinguished the Americans in former times, and which constitutes the leading feature in distinguished characters wherever they may be found. It seems at first sight as if all the minds of the Americans were formed upon one model, so accurately do they follow the same route. A stranger does, indeed, sometimes meet with Americans who dissent from the rigor of these formulas. with men who deplore the defects of the laws, the mutability and the ignorance of democracy, who even go so far as to observe the evil tendencies that impair the national character, and to point out such remedies as it might be possible to apply; but no one is there to hear them except yourself, and you, to whom these secret reflections are confided, are a stranger and a bird of passage. They are very ready to communicate truths which are useless to you, but they hold a different language in public.

If these lines are ever read in America, I am well assured of two things: in the first place, that all who peruse them will raise their voices to condemn me; and, in the second place, that many of them will acquit me at the bottom of their conscience.

I have heard of patriotism in the United States, and I have found true patriotism among the people, but never among the leaders of the people. This may be explained by analogy: despotism debases the oppressed much more than the oppressor: in absolute monarchies the king often has great virtues, but the courtiers are invariably servile. It is true that American courtiers do not say "Sire," or "Your Majesty," a distinction without a difference. They are forever talking of the natural intelligence of the people whom they serve; they do not debate the question which of the virtues of their master is pre-eminently worthy of admiration, for they assure him that he possesses all the virtues without having acquired them, or without caring to acquire them; they do not give him their daughters and their wives to be raised at his pleasure to the rank of his concubines; but by sacrificing their opinions they prostitute themselves. Moralists and philosophers in America are not obliged to conceal their opinions under the veil of allegory; but before they venture upon a harsh truth, they say: "We are aware that the people whom we are addressing are too superior to the weaknesses of human nature to lose the command of their temper for an instant. We should not hold this language if we were not speaking to men whom their virtues and their intelligence render more worthy of freedom than all the rest of the world." The sycophants of Louis XIV could not flatter more dexterously.

For my part, I am persuaded that in all governments, whatever their nature may be, servility will cower to force, and adulation will follow power. The only means of preventing men from degrading themselves is to invest no one with that unlimited authority which is the sure method of debasing them.

THE GREATEST DANGERS OF THE AMERICAN REPUBLICS PROCEED FROM THE OMNIPOTENCE OF THE MAJORITY. *Democratic republics liable to perish from a misuse of their power, and not from impotence—The governments of the American republics are more centralized and more energetic than those of the monarchies of Europe—Dan-*

gers resulting from this—Opinions of Madison and Jefferson upon this point.

GOVERNMENTS usually perish from impotence or from tyranny. In the former case, their power escapes from them; it is wrested from their grasp in the latter. Many observers who have witnessed the anarchy of democratic states have imagined that the government of those states was naturally weak and impotent. The truth is that when war is once begun between parties, the government loses its control over society. But I do not think that a democratic power is naturally without force or resources; say, rather, that it is almost always by the abuse of its force and the misemployment of its resources that it becomes a failure. Anarchy is almost always produced by its tyranny or its mistakes, but not by its want of strength.

It is important not to confuse stability with force, or the greatness of a thing with its duration. In democratic republics the power that directs[5] society is not stable, for it often changes hands and assumes a new direction. But whichever way it turns, its force is almost irresistible. The governments of the American republics appear to me to be as much centralized as those of the absolute monarchies of Europe, and more energetic than they are. I do not, therefore, imagine that they will perish from weakness.[6]

If ever the free institutions of America are destroyed, that event may be attributed to the omnipotence of the majority, which may at some future time urge the minorities to desperation and oblige them to have recourse to physical force. Anarchy will then be the result, but it will have been brought about by despotism.

Mr. Madison expresses the same opinion in *The Federalist*, No. 51. "It is of great importance in a republic, not only to guard the society against the oppression of its rulers, but to guard one part of the society against the injustice of

[5] This power may be centralized in an assembly, in which case it will be strong without being stable; or it may be centralized in an individual, in which case it will be less strong, but more stable.

[6] I presume that it is scarcely necessary to remind the reader here, as well as throughout this chapter, that I am speaking, not of the Federal government, but of the governments of the individual states, which the majority controls at its pleasure.

the other part. Justice is the end of government. It is the end of civil society. It ever has been, and ever will be, pursued until it be obtained, or until liberty be lost in the pursuit. In a society, under the forms of which the stronger faction can readily unite and oppress the weaker, anarchy may as truly be said to reign as in a state of nature, where the weaker individual is not secured against the violence of the stronger: and as, in the latter state, even the stronger individuals are prompted by the uncertainty of their condition to submit to a government which may protect the weak as well as themselves, so, in the former state, will the more powerful factions be gradually induced by a like motive to wish for a government which will protect all parties, the weaker as well as the more powerful. It can be little doubted, that, if the State of Rhode Island was separated from the Confederacy and left to itself, the insecurity of right under the popular form of government within such narrow limits would be displayed by such reiterated oppressions of the factious majorities, that some power altogether independent of the people would soon be called for by the voice of the very factions whose misrule had proved the necessity of it."

Jefferson also said: "The executive power in our government is not the only, perhaps not even the principal, object of my solicitude. The tyranny of the legislature is really the danger most to be feared, and will continue to be so for many years to come. The tyranny of the executive power will come in its turn, but at a more distant period." [7]

I am glad to cite the opinion of Jefferson upon this subject rather than that of any other, because I consider him the most powerful advocate democracy has ever had.

[7] *Letter from Jefferson to Madison,* March 15, 1789.

Chapter XVI

CAUSES WHICH MITIGATE THE TYRANNY OF THE MAJORITY IN THE UNITED STATES

ABSENCE OF CENTRALIZED ADMINISTRATION. *The national majority does not pretend to do everything—Is obliged to employ the town and county magistrates to execute its sovereign will.*

I HAVE already pointed out the distinction between a centralized government and a centralized administration. The former exists in America, but the latter is nearly unknown there. If the directing power of the American communities had both these instruments of government at its disposal and united the habit of executing its commands to the right of commanding; if, after having established the general principles of government, it descended to the details of their application; and if, having regulated the great interests of the country, it could descend to the circle of individual interests, freedom would soon be banished from the New World.

But in the United States the majority, which so frequently displays the tastes and the propensities of a despot, is still destitute of the most perfect instruments of tyranny.

In the American republics the central government has never as yet busied itself except with a small number of objects, sufficiently prominent to attract its attention. The secondary affairs of society have never been regulated by its authority; and nothing has hitherto betrayed its desire of even interfering in them. The majority has become more and more absolute, but has not increased the prerogatives of the central government; those great prerogatives have been confined to a certain sphere; and although the despotism of the majority may be galling upon one point, it cannot be said to extend to all. However the predominant party in the nation may be carried away by its passions, however ardent it may be in the pursuit of its projects, it cannot oblige all the citizens to comply with its desires in the same manner and at the same time throughout the country. When the central government which represents that majority has issued a decree, it must entrust the execution of its will to agents over whom it frequently has no control and whom it cannot perpetually direct. The townships, municipal bodies, and counties form so many concealed breakwaters, which check or part the tide of popular determination. If an oppressive law were passed, liberty would still be protected by the mode of executing that law; the majority cannot descend to the details and what may be called the puerilities of administrative tyranny. It does not even imagine that it can do so, for it has not a full consciousness of its authority. It knows only the extent of its natural powers, but is unacquainted with the art of increasing them.

This point deserves attention; for if a democratic republic, similar to that of the United States, were ever founded in a country where the power of one man had previously established a centralized administration and had sunk it deep into the habits and the laws of the people, I do not hesitate to assert that in such a republic a more insufferable despotism would prevail than in any of the absolute monarchies of Europe; or, indeed, than any that could be found on this side of Asia.

THE TEMPER OF THE LEGAL PROFESSION IN THE UNITED STATES, AND HOW IT SERVES AS A COUNTERPOISE TO DEMOCRACY. *Utility of ascertaining what are the natural instincts of the legal profession—These men are to act a prominent part in future society—How the peculiar pursuits of lawyers give an aristocratic turn to their ideas—Accidental causes that may check this tendency—Ease with which the aristocracy coalesces with legal men—Use of lawyers to a despot—The profession of the law constitutes the only aristocratic element with which the natural elements of democracy will combine—Peculiar causes which tend to give an aristocratic turn of mind to English and American lawyers—The aristocracy of America is on the bench and at the bar—Influence of lawyers upon American society—Their peculiar magisterial spirit affects the legislature, the administration, and even the people.*

the analogy of their studies and the uniformity of their

IN VISITING the Americans and studying their laws, we perceive that the authority they have entrusted to members of the legal profession, and the influence that these individuals exercise in the government, are the most powerful existing security against the excesses of democracy. This effect seems to me to result from a general cause, which it is useful to investigate, as it may be reproduced elsewhere.

The members of the legal profession have taken a part in all the movements of political society in Europe for the last five hundred years. At one time they have been the instruments of the political authorities, and at another they have succeeded in converting the political authorities into their instruments. In the Middle Ages they afforded a powerful support to the crown; and since that period they have exerted themselves effectively to limit the royal prerogative. In England they have contracted a close alliance with the aristocracy; in France they have shown themselves its most dangerous enemies. Under all these circumstances have the members of the legal profession been swayed by sudden and fleeting impulses, or have they been more or less impelled by instincts which are natural to them and which will always recur in history? I am incited to this investigation, for perhaps this particular class of men will play a prominent part in the political society that is soon to be created.

Men who have made a special study of the laws derive from occupation certain habits of order, a taste for formalities, and a kind of instinctive regard for the regular connection of ideas, which naturally render them very hostile to the revolutionary spirit and the unreflecting passions of the multitude.

The special information that lawyers derive from their studies ensures them a separate rank in society, and they constitute a sort of privileged body in the scale of intellect. This notion of their superiority perpetually recurs to them in the practice of their profession: they are the masters of a science which is necessary, but which is not very generally known; they serve as arbiters between the citizens; and the habit of directing to their purpose the blind passions of parties in litigation inspires them with a certain contempt for the judgment of the multitude. Add to this that they naturally constitute *a body;* not by any previous understanding, or by an agreement that directs them to a common end; but the analogy of their studies and the uniformity of their methods connect their minds as a common interest might unite their endeavors.

Some of the tastes and the habits of the aristocracy may consequently be discovered in the characters of lawyers. They participate in the same instinctive love of order and formalities; and they entertain the same repugnance to the actions of the multitude, and the same secret contempt of the government of the people. I do not mean to say that the natural propensities of lawyers are sufficiently strong to sway them irresistibly; for they, like most other men, are governed by their private interests, and especially by the interests of the moment.

In a state of society in which the members of the legal profession cannot hold that rank in the political world which they enjoy in private life, we may rest assured that they will be the foremost agents of revolution. But it must then be asked whether the cause that then induces them to innovate and destroy results from a permanent disposition or from an accident. It is true that lawyers mainly contributed to the overthrow of the French monarchy in 1789; but it remains to be seen whether they acted thus because they had studied the laws or because they were prohibited from making them.

Five hundred years ago the English nobles headed the people and spoke in their name; at the present time the aristocracy supports the throne and defends the royal prerogative. But notwithstanding this, aristocracy has its peculiar instincts and propensities. We must be careful not to confound isolated members of a body with the body itself. In all free governments, of whatever form they may be, members of the legal profession will be found in the front ranks of all parties. The same remark is also applicable to the aristocracy; almost all the democratic movements that have agitated the world have been directed by nobles. A privileged body can never satisfy the ambition of all its members: it has always more talents and more passions than it can find places to employ, so that a considerable number of individuals are usually to be met with who are inclined to attack those very privileges which they cannot soon enough turn to their own account.

I do not, then, assert that *all* the members of the legal profession are at *all* times the friends of order and the opponents of innovation, but merely that most of them are usually so. In a community in which lawyers are allowed to occupy without opposition that high station which naturally belongs to them, their general spirit will be eminently conservative and anti-democratic. When an aristocracy excludes the leaders of that profession from its ranks, it excites enemies who are the more formidable as they are independent of the nobility by their labors and feel themselves to be their equals in intelligence though inferior in opulence and power. But whenever an aristocracy consents to impart some of its privileges to these same individuals, the two classes coalesce very readily and assume, as it were, family interests.

I am in like manner inclined to believe that a monarch will always be able to convert legal practitioners into the most serviceable instruments of his authority. There is a far greater affinity between this class of persons and the executive power than there is between them and the people, though they have often aided to overturn the former; just as there is a greater natural affinity between the nobles and the monarch than between the nobles and the people, although the higher orders of society have often, in concert with the lower classes, resisted the prerogative of the crown.

Lawyers are attached to public order beyond every other consideration, and the best security of public order is authority. It must not be forgotten, also, that if they prize freedom much, they generally value legality still more: they are less afraid of tyranny than of arbitrary power; and, provided the legislature undertakes of itself to deprive men of their independence, they are not dissatisfied.

I am therefore convinced that the prince who, in presence of an encroaching democracy, should endeavor to impair the judicial authority in his dominions, and to diminish the political influence of lawyers, would commit a great mistake: he would let slip the substance of authority to grasp the shadow. He would act more wisely in introducing lawyers into the government; and if he entrusted despotism to them under the form of violence, perhaps he would find it again in their hands under the external features of justice and law.

The government of democracy is favorable to the political power of lawyers; for when the wealthy, the noble, and the prince are excluded from the government, the lawyers take possession of it, in their own right, as it were, since they are the only men of information and sagacity, beyond the sphere of the people, who can be the object of the popular choice. If, then, they are led by their tastes towards the aristocracy and the prince, they are brought in contact with the people by their interests. They like the government of democracy without participating in its propensities and without imitating its weaknesses; whence they derive a twofold authority from it and over it. The people in democratic states do not mistrust the members of the legal profession, because it is known that they are interested to serve the popular cause; and the people listen to them without irritation, because they do not attribute to them any sinister designs. The lawyers do not, indeed, wish to overthrow the institutions of democracy, but they constantly endeavor to turn it away from its real direction by means that are foreign to its nature. Lawyers belong to the people by birth and interest, and to the aristocracy by habit and taste; they may be looked upon as the connecting link between the two great classes of society.

The profession of the law is the only aristocratic element that can be amalgamated without violence with the natural elements of democracy and be advantageously and permanently combined with them. I am not ignorant of the defects inherent in the character of this body of men; but without this admixture of lawyer-like sobriety with the democratic principle, I question whether democratic institutions could long be maintained; and I cannot believe that a republic could hope to exist at the present time if the influence of lawyers in public business did not increase in proportion to the power of the people.

This aristocratic character, which I hold to be common to the legal profession, is much more distinctly marked in the United States and in England than in any other country. This proceeds not only from the legal studies of the English and American lawyers, but from the nature of the law and the position which these interpreters of it occupy in the two countries. The English and the Americans have retained the law of precedents; that is to say, they continue to found their legal opinions and the decisions of their courts upon the opinions and decisions of their predecessors. In the mind of an English or American lawyer a taste and a reverence for what is old is almost always united with a love of regular and lawful proceedings.

This predisposition has another effect upon the character of the legal profession and upon the general course of society. The English and American lawyers investigate what has been done; the French advocate inquires what should have been done; the former produce precedents, the latter reasons. A French observer is surprised to hear how often an English or an American lawyer quotes the opinions of others and how little he alludes to his own, while the reverse occurs in France. There the most trifling litigation is never conducted without the introduction of an entire system of ideas peculiar to the counsel employed; and the fundamental principles of law are discussed in order to obtain a rod of land by the decision of the court. This abnegation of his own opinion and this implicit deference to the opinion of his forefathers, which are common to the English and American lawyer, this servitude of thought which he is obliged to profess, necessarily gives him more timid habits and more conservative inclinations in England and America than in France.

The French codes are often difficult to comprehend, but they can be read by everyone; nothing, on the other hand, can be more obscure and strange to the uninitiated than a legislation founded upon precedents. The absolute need of legal aid that is felt in England and the United States, and the high opinion that is entertained of the ability of the legal profession, tend to separate it more and more from the people and to erect it into a distinct class. The French lawyer is simply a man extensively acquainted with the statutes of his country; but the English or American lawyer resembles the hierophants of Egypt, for like them he is the sole interpreter of an occult science.

The position that lawyers occupy in England and America exercises no less influence upon their habits and opinions. The English aristocracy, which has taken care to attract to its sphere whatever is at all analogous to itself, has conferred a high degree of importance and authority upon the members of the legal profession. In English society, lawyers do not occupy the first rank, but they are contented with the station assigned to them: they constitute, as it were, the younger branch of the English aristocracy; and they are attached to their elder brothers, although they do not enjoy all their privileges. The English lawyers consequently mingle the aristocratic tastes and ideas of the circles in which they move with the aristocratic interests of their profession.

And, indeed, the lawyer-like character that I am endeavoring to depict is most distinctly to be met with in England: there laws are esteemed not so much because they are good as because they are old; and if it is necessary to modify them in any respect, to adapt them to the changes that time operates in society, recourse is had to the most inconceivable subtleties in order to uphold the traditionary fabric and to maintain that nothing has been done which does not square with the intentions and complete the labors of former generations. The very individuals who conduct these changes disclaim any desire for innovation and had rather resort to absurd expedients than plead guilty to so great a crime. This spirit appertains more especially to the English lawyers; they appear indifferent to the real meaning of what they treat, and they direct all their attention to the letter, seeming inclined to abandon reason and humanity rather than to swerve one tittle from the law. English legislation may be compared to the stock of an old tree upon which lawyers have engrafted the most dissimilar shoots in the hope that, although their fruits may differ, their foliage at least will be confused with the venerable trunk that supports them all.

In America there are no nobles or literary men, and the people are apt to mistrust the wealthy; lawyers consequently form the highest political class and the most cultivated portion of society. They have therefore nothing to gain by innovation, which adds a conservative interest to their natural taste for public order. If I were asked where I place the American aristocracy, I should reply without hesitation that it is not among the rich, who are united by no common tie, but that it occupies the judicial bench and the bar.

The more we reflect upon all that occurs in the United States, the more we shall be persuaded that the lawyers, as a body, form the most powerful, if not the only, counterpoise to the democratic element. In that country we easily perceive how the legal profession is qualified by its attributes, and even by its faults, to neutralize the vices inherent in popular government. When the American people are intoxicated by passion or carried away by the impetuosity of their ideas, they are checked and stopped by the almost invisible influence of their legal counselors. These secretly oppose their aristocratic propensities to the nation's democratic instincts, their superstitious attachment to what is old to its love of novelty, their narrow views to its immense designs, and their habitual procrastination to its ardent impatience.

The courts of justice are the visible organs by which the legal profession is enabled to control the democracy. The judge is a lawyer who, independently of the taste for regularity and order that he has contracted in the study of law, derives an additional love of stability from the inalienability of his own functions. His legal attainments have already raised him to a distinguished rank among his fellows; his political power completes the distinction of his station and gives him the instincts of the privileged classes.

Armed with the power of declaring the laws to be unconstitutional,[1] the American magistrate perpetually interferes in political affairs. He cannot force the people to make laws, but at least he can oblige them not to disobey their own enactments and not to be inconsistent with themselves. I am aware that a secret tendency to diminish the judicial power exists in the United States; and by most of the constitutions of the several states the government can, upon the demand of the two houses of the legislature, remove judges from their station. Some other state constitutions make the members of the judiciary elective, and they are even subjected to frequent re-elections. I venture to predict that these innovations will sooner or later be attended with fatal consequences; and that it will be found out at some future period that by thus lessening the independence of the judiciary they have attacked not only the judicial power, but the democratic republic itself.

It must not be supposed, moreover, that the legal spirit is confined in the United States to the courts of justice; it extends far beyond them. As the lawyers form the only enlightened class whom the people do not mistrust, they are naturally called upon to occupy most of the public stations. They fill the legislative assemblies and are at the head of

[1] See Chapter VI, on "The Judicial Power in the United States."

the administration; they consequently exercise a powerful influence upon the formation of the law and upon its execution. The lawyers are obliged, however, to yield to the current public opinion, which is too strong for them to resist; but it is easy to find indications of what they would do if they were free to act. The Americans, who have made so many innovations in their political laws, have introduced very sparing alterations in their civil laws, and that with great difficulty, although many of these laws are repugnant to their social condition. The reason for this is that in matters of civil law the majority are obliged to defer to the authority of the legal profession, and the American lawyers are disinclined to innovate when they are left to their own choice.

It is curious for a Frenchman to hear the complaints that are made in the United States against the stationary spirit of legal men and their prejudices in favor of existing institutions.

The influence of legal habits extends beyond the precise limits I have pointed out. Scarcely any political question arises in the United States that is not resolved, sooner or later, into a judicial question. Hence all parties are obliged to borrow, in their daily controversies, the ideas, and even the language, peculiar to judicial proceedings. As most public men are or have been legal practitioners, they introduce the customs and technicalities of their profession into the management of public affairs. The jury extends this habit to all classes. The language of the law thus becomes, in some measure, a vulgar tongue; the spirit of the law, which is produced in the schools and courts of justice, gradually penetrates beyond their walls into the bosom of society, where it descends to the lowest classes, so that at last the whole people contract the habits and the tastes of the judicial magistrate. The lawyers of the United States form a party which is but little feared and scarcely perceived, which has no badge peculiar to itself, which adapts itself with great flexibility to the exigencies of the time and accommodates itself without resistance to all the movements of the social body. But this party extends over the whole community and penetrates into all the classes which compose it; it acts upon the country imperceptibly, but finally fashions it to suit its own purposes.

TRIAL BY JURY IN THE UNITED STATES CONSIDERED AS A POLITI-
CAL INSTITUTION. *Trial by jury, which is one of the
forms of the sovereignty of the people, ought to be
compared with the other laws which establish that sovereignty—Composition of the jury in the United States
—Effect of trial by jury upon the national character—
It educates the people—How it tends to establish the
influence of the magistrates and to extend the legal
spirit among the people.*

SINCE my subject has led me to speak of the administration
of justice in the United States, I will not pass over it without referring to the institution of the jury. Trial by jury may
be considered in two separte points of view: as a judicial,
and as a political institution. If it was my purpose to inquire how far trial by jury, especially in civil cases, ensures
a good administration of justice, I admit that its utility
might be contested. As the jury was first established when
society was in its infancy and when courts of justice merely
decided simple questions of fact, it is not an easy task to
adapt it to the wants of a highly civilized community when
the mutual relations of men are multiplied to a surprising
extent and have assumed an enlightened and intellectual
character.[2]

My present purpose is to consider the jury as a political
institution; any other course would divert me from my
subject. Of trial by jury considered as a judicial institution
I shall here say but little. When the English adopted trial

[2] The consideration of trial by jury as a judicial institution, and
the appraisal of its effects in the United States, together with an
inquiry into the manner in which the Americans have used it,
would suffice to form a book, and a book very interesting to
France. One might trace therein, for example, what parts of
the American system pertaining to the jury might be introduced
among us, and by what steps. The state of Louisiana would
throw the most light upon the subject, as it has a mingled
population of French and English. The two systems of law, as
well as the two nations, are there found side by side and are
gradually combining with each other. The most useful books
to consult would be the *Digeste des Lois de la Louisiane;* and
the *Traité sur les Règles des Actions civiles,* printed in French
and English at New Orleans, in 1830, by Buisson. This book has
a special advantage; it presents, for Frenchmen, an exact and an
authentic glossary of English legal terms. The language of law
is everywhere different from that of the people, a fact particularly true of the English.

by jury, they were a semi-barbarous people; they have since become one of the most enlightened nations of the earth, and their attachment to this institution seems to have increased with their increasing cultivation. They have emigrated and colonized every part of the habitable globe; some have formed colonies, others independent states; the mother country has maintained its monarchical constitution; many of its offspring have founded powerful republics; but everywhere they have boasted of the privilege of trial by jury.[3] They have established it, or hastened to re-establish it, in all their settlements. A judicial institution which thus obtains the suffrages of a great people for so long a series of ages, which is zealously reproduced at every stage of civilization, in all the climates of the earth, and under every form of human government, cannot be contrary to the spirit of justice.[4]

[3] All the English and American jurists are unanimous on this point. Mr. Story, Justice of the Supreme Court of the United States, speaks, in his *Commentaries on the Constitution*, of the advantages of trial by jury in civil cases: "The inestimable privilege of a trial by jury in civil cases," says he, "a privilege scarcely inferior to that in criminal cases, which is counted by all persons to be essential to political and civil liberty." (Story, Book III, Ch. 38.)

[4] If it were our object to establish the utility of the jury as a judicial institution, many arguments might be brought forward, and among others the following:

In proportion as you introduce the jury into the business of the courts, you are enabled to diminish the number of judges, which is a great advantage. When judges are very numerous, death is perpetually thinning the ranks of the judicial functionaries and leaving places vacant for new-comers. The ambition of the magistrates is therefore continually excited, and they are naturally made dependent upon the majority or the person who nominates to vacant offices; the officers of the courts then advance as do the officers of an army. This state of things is entirely contrary to the sound administration of justice and to the intentions of the legislator. The office of a judge is made inalienable in order that he may remain independent; but of what advantage is it that his independence should be protected if he be tempted to sacrifice it of his own accord? When judges are very numerous, many of them must necessarily be incapable; for a great magistrate is a man of no common powers: I do not know if a half-enlightened tribunal is not the worst of all combinations for attaining those ends which underlie the establishment of courts of justice. For my own part, I had rather submit the decision of a case to ignorant jurors directed by a skillful judge than to judges a majority of whom are imperfectly acquainted with jurisprudence and with the laws.

But to leave this part of the subject. It would be a very narrow view to look upon the jury as a mere judicial institution; for however great its influence may be upon the decisions of the courts, it is still greater on the destinies of society at large. The jury is, above all, a political institution, and it must be regarded in this light in order to be duly appreciated.

By the jury I mean a certain number of citizens chosen by lot and invested with a temporary right of judging. Trial by jury, as applied to the repression of crime, appears to me an eminently republican element in the government, for the following reasons.

The institution of the jury may be aristocratic or democratic, according to the class from which the jurors are taken; but it always preserves its republican character, in that it places the real direction of society in the hands of the governed, or of a portion of the governed, and not in that of the government. Force is never more than a transient element of success, and after force comes the notion of right. A government able to reach its enemies only upon a field of battle would soon be destroyed. The true sanction of political laws is to be found in penal legislation; and if that sanction is wanting, the law will sooner or later lose its cogency. He who punishes the criminal is therefore the real master of society. Now, the institution of the jury raises the people itself, or at least a class of citizens, to the bench of judges. The institution of the jury consequently invests the people, or that class of citizens, with the direction of society.[5]

In England the jury is selected from the aristocratic portion of the nation; the aristocracy makes the laws, applies the laws, and punishes infractions of the laws;[6] everything is established upon a consistent footing, and England may

---

[5] An important remark must, however, be made. Trial by jury does unquestionably invest the people with a general control over the actions of the citizens, but it does not furnish means of exercising this control in all cases or with an absolute authority. When an absolute monarch has the right of trying offenses by his representatives, the fate of the prisoner is, as it were, decided beforehand. But even if the people were predisposed to convict, the composition and the non-responsibility of the jury would still afford some chances favorable to the protection of innocence.

[6] See Appendix Q.

with truth be said to constitute an aristocratic republic. In the United States the same system is applied to the whole people. Every American citizen is both an eligible and a legally qualified voter.[7] The jury system as it is understood in America appears to me to be as direct and as extreme a consequence of the sovereignty of the people as universal suffrage. They are two instruments of equal power, which contribute to the supremacy of the majority. All the sovereigns who have chosen to govern by their own authority, and to direct society instead of obeying its directions, have destroyed or enfeebled the institution of the jury. The Tudor monarchs sent to prison jurors who refused to convict, and Napoleon caused them to be selected by his agents.

However clear most of these truths may seem to be, they do not command universal assent; and in France, at least, trial by jury is still but imperfectly understood. If the question arises as to the proper qualification of jurors, it is confined to a discussion of the intelligence and knowledge of the citizens who may be returned, as if the jury was merely a judicial institution. This appears to me the least important part of the subject. The jury is pre-eminently a political institution; it should be regarded as one form of the sovereignty of the people: when that sovereignty is repudiated, it must be rejected, or it must be adapted to the laws by which that sovereignty is established. The jury is that portion of the nation to which the execution of the laws is entrusted, as the legislature is that part of the nation which makes the laws; and in order that society may be governed in a fixed and uniform manner, the list of citizens qualified to serve on juries must increase and diminish with the list of electors. This I hold to be the point of view most worthy of the attention of the legislator; all that remains is merely accessory.

I am so entirely convinced that the jury is pre-eminently a political institution that I still consider it in this light when it is applied in civil causes. Laws are always unstable unless they are founded upon the customs of a nation: customs are the only durable and resisting power in a people. When the jury is reserved for criminal offenses, the people witness only its occasional action in particular cases; they become accustomed to do without it in the ordinary course

[7] See Appendix R

of life, and it is considered as an instrument, but not as the only instrument, of obtaining justice.[8]

When, on the contrary, the jury acts also on civil causes, its application is constantly visible; it affects all the interests of the community; everyone co-operates in its work: it thus penetrates into all the usages of life, it fashions the human mind to its peculiar forms, and is gradually associated with the idea of justice itself.

The institution of the jury, if confined to criminal causes, is always in danger; but when once it is introduced into civil proceedings, it defies the aggressions of time and man. If it had been as easy to remove the jury from the customs as from the laws of England, it would have perished under the Tudors; and the civil jury did in reality at that period save the liberties of England. In whatever manner the jury be applied, it cannot fail to exercise a powerful influence upon the national character; but this influence is prodigiously increased when it is introduced into civil causes. The jury, and more especially the civil jury, serves to communicate the spirit of the judges to the minds of all the citizens; and this spirit, with the habits which attend it, is the soundest preparation for free institutions. It imbues all classes with a respect for the thing judged and with the notion of right. If these two elements be removed, the love of independence becomes a mere destructive passion. It teaches men to practice equity; every man learns to judge his neighbor as he would himself be judged. And this is especially true of the jury in civil causes; for while the number of persons who have reason to apprehend a criminal prosecution is small, everyone is liable to have a lawsuit. The jury teaches every man not to recoil before the responsibility of his own actions and impresses him with that manly confidence without which no political virtue can exist. It invests each citizen with a kind of magistracy; it makes them all feel the duties which they are bound to discharge towards society and the part which they take in its government. By obliging men to turn their attention to other affairs than their own, it rubs off that private selfishness which is the rust of society.

The jury contributes powerfully to form the judgment and to increase the natural intelligence of a people; and

---

[8] This is unequivocally true since the jury is employed only in certain criminal cases.

See Appendix K

this, in my opinion, is its greatest advantage. It may be regarded as a gratuitous public school, ever open, in which every juror learns his rights, enters into daily communication with the most learned and enlightened members of the upper classes, and becomes practically acquainted with the laws, which are brought within the reach of his capacity by the efforts of the bar, the advice of the judge, and even the passions of the parties. I think that the practical intelligence and political good sense of the Americans are mainly attributable to the long use that they have made of the jury in civil causes.

I do not know whether the jury is useful to those who have lawsuits, but I am certain it is highly beneficial to those who judge them; and I look upon it as one of the most efficacious means for the education of the people which society can employ.

What I have said applies to all nations, but the remark I am about to make is peculiar to the Americans and to democratic communities. I have already observed that in democracies the members of the legal profession and the judicial magistrates constitute the only aristocratic body which can moderate the movements of the people. This aristocracy is invested with no physical power; it exercises its conservative influence upon the minds of men; and the most abundant source of its authority is the institution of the civil jury. In criminal causes, when society is contending against a single man, the jury is apt to look upon the judge as the passive instrument of social power and to mistrust his advice. Moreover, criminal causes turn entirely upon simple facts, which common sense can readily appreciate; upon this ground the judge and the jury are equal. Such is not the case, however, in civil causes; then the judge appears as a disinterested arbiter between the conflicting passions of the parties. The jurors look up to him with confidence and listen to him with respect, for in this instance, his intellect entirely governs theirs. It is the judge who sums up the various arguments which have wearied their memory, and who guides them through the devious course of the proceedings; he points their attention to the exact question of fact that they are called upon to decide and tells them how to answer the question of law. His influence over them is almost unlimited.

If I am called upon to explain why I am but little

moved by the arguments derived from the ignorance of jurors in civil causes, I reply that in these proceedings, whenever the question to be solved is not a mere question of fact, the jury has only the semblance of a judicial body. The jury only sanctions the decision of the judge; they sanction this decision by the authority of society which they represent, and he by that of reason and of law.[9]

In England and in America the judges exercise an influence upon criminal trials that the French judges have never possessed. The reason for this difference may easily be discovered; the English and American magistrates have established their authority in civil causes and only transfer it afterwards to tribunals of another kind, where it was not first acquired. In some cases, and they are frequently the most important ones, the American judges have the right of deciding causes alone.[10] On these occasions they are accidentally placed in the position that the French judges habitually occupy, but their moral power is much greater; they are still surrounded by the recollection of the jury, and their judgment has almost as much authority as the voice of the community represented by that institution. Their influence extends far beyond the limits of the courts; in the recreations of private life, as well as in the turmoil of public business, in public, and in the legislative assemblies, the American judge is constantly surrounded by men who are accustomed to regard his intelligence as superior to their own; and after having exercised his power in the decision of causes, he continues to influence the habits of thought, and even the characters, of those who acted with him in his official capacity.

The jury, then, which seems to restrict the rights of the judiciary, does in reality consolidate its power; and in no country are the judges so powerful as where the people share their privileges. It is especially by means of the jury in civil causes that the American magistrates imbue even the lower classes of society with the spirit of their profession. Thus the jury, which is the most energetic means of making the people rule, is also the most efficacious means of teaching it how to rule well.

[9] See Appendix S.
[10] The Federal judges decide almost always only such questions as touch directly the government of the country.

Chapter XVII

PRINCIPAL CAUSES WHICH TEND TO MAINTAIN THE DEMOCRATIC REPUBLIC IN THE UNITED STATES

A DEMOCRATIC republic exists in the United States; and the principal object of this book has been to explain the causes of its existence. Several of these causes have been involuntarily passed by, or only hinted at, as I was borne along by my subject. Others I have been unable to discuss at all; and those on which I have dwelt most are, as it were, buried in the details of this work.

I think, therefore, that before I proceed to speak of the future, I ought to collect within a small compass the reasons that explain the present. In this retrospective chapter I shall be brief, for I shall take care to remind the reader only very summarily of what he already knows and shall select only the most prominent of those facts that I have not yet pointed out.

All the causes which contribute to the maintenance of the democratic republic in the United States are reducible to three heads:

I. The peculiar and accidental situation in which Providence has placed the Americans.

II. The laws.

III. The manners and customs of the people.

ACCIDENTAL OR PROVIDENTIAL CAUSES WHICH CONTRIBUTE TO MAINTAIN THE DEMOCRATIC REPUBLIC IN THE UNITED STATES. *The Union has no neighbors—No metropolis—The Americans have had the chance of birth in their favor—America an empty country—How this circumstance contributes powerfully to maintain the democratic republic in America—How the American wilds are peopled—Avidity of the Anglo-Americans in taking possession of the solitudes of the New World—Influence of physical prosperity upon the political opinions of the Americans.*

A THOUSAND circumstances independent of the will of man facilitate the maintenance of a democratic republic in the United States. Some of these are known, the others may easily be pointed out; but I shall confine myself to the principal ones.

The Americans have no neighbors and consequently they have no great wars, or financial crises, or inroads, or conquest, to dread; they require neither great taxes, nor large armies, nor great generals; and they have nothing to fear from a scourge which is more formidable to republics than all these evils combined: namely, military glory. It is impossible to deny the inconceivable influence that military glory exercises upon the spirit of a nation. General Jackson, whom the Americans have twice elected to be the head of their government, is a man of violent temper and very moderate talents; nothing in his whole career ever proved him qualified to govern a free people; and, indeed, the majority of the enlightened classes of the Union has always opposed him. But he was raised to the Presidency, and has been maintained there, solely by the recollection of a victory which he gained, twenty years ago, under the walls of New Orleans; a victory which was, however, a very ordinary achievement and which could only be remembered in a country where battles are rare. Now the people who are thus carried away by the illusions of glory are unquestionably the most cold and calculating, the most unmilitary, if I may so speak, and the most prosaic of all the nations of the earth.

America has no great capital[1] city, whose direct or in-

---

[1] The United States has no metropolis, but it already contains several very large cities. Philadelphia reckoned 161,000 inhabitants, and New York 202,000, in the year 1830. The lower ranks which inhabit these cities constitute a rabble even more formidable than the populace of European towns. They consist of freed blacks, in the first place, who are condemned by the laws and by public opinion to a hereditary state of misery and degradation. They also contain a multitude of Europeans who have been driven to the shores of the New World by their misfortunes or their misconduct; and they bring to the United States all our greatest vices, without any of those interests which counteract their baneful influence. As inhabitants of a country where they have no civil rights, they are ready to turn all the passions which agitate the community to their own advantage; thus, within the last few months, serious riots have broken out in Philadelphia and New York. Disturbances of this kind are unknown in the rest of the country, which is not alarmed by

direct influence is felt over the whole extent of the country; this I hold to be one of the first causes of the maintenance of republican institutions in the United States. In cities men cannot be prevented from concerting together and awakening a mutual excitement that prompts sudden and passionate resolutions. Cities may be looked upon as large assemblies, of which all the inhabitants are members; their populace exercise a prodigious influence upon the magistrates, and frequently execute their own wishes without the intervention of public officers.

To subject the provinces to the metropolis is therefore to place the destiny of the empire not only in the hands of a portion of the community, which is unjust, but in the hands of a populace carrying out its own impulses, which is very dangerous. The preponderance of capital cities is therefore a serious injury to the representative system; and it exposes modern republics to the same defect as the republics of antiquity, which all perished from not having known this system.

It would be easy for me to enumerate many secondary causes that have contributed to establish, and now concur to maintain, the democratic republic of the United States. But among these favorable circumstances I discern two principal ones, which I hasten to point out. I have already observed that the origin of the Americans, or what I have called their point of departure, may be looked upon as the first and most efficacious cause to which the present prosperity of the United States may be attributed. The Americans had the chances of birth in their favor; and their forefathers imported that equality of condition and of intellect into the country whence the democratic republic has very naturally taken its rise. Nor was this all; for besides this republican condition of society, the early settlers bequeathed

them, because the population of the cities has hitherto exercised neither power nor influence over the rural districts.

Nevertheless, I look upon the size of certain American cities, and especially on the nature of their population, as a real danger which threatens the future security of the democratic republics of the New World; and I venture to predict that they will perish from this circumstance, unless the government succeeds in creating an armed force which, while it remains under the control of the majority of the nation, will be independent of the town population and able to repress its excesses.

to their descendants the customs, manners, and opinions that contribute most to the success of a republic. When I reflect upon the consequences of this primary fact, I think I see the destiny of America embodied in the first Puritan who landed on those shores, just as the whole human race was represented by the first man.

The chief circumstance which has favored the establishment and the maintenance of a democratic republic in the United States is the nature of the territory that the Americans inhabit. Their ancestors gave them the love of equality and of freedom; but God himself gave them the means of remaining equal and free, by placing them upon a boundless continent. General prosperity is favorable to the stability of all governments, but more particularly of a democratic one, which depends upon the will of the majority, and especially upon the will of that portion of the community which is most exposed to want. When the people rule, they must be rendered happy or they will overturn the state; and misery stimulates them to those excesses to which ambition rouses kings. The physical causes, independent of the laws, which promote general prosperity are more numerous in America than they ever have been in any other country in the world, at any other period of history. In the United States not only is legislation democratic, but Nature herself favors the cause of the people.

In what part of human history can be found anything similar to what is passing before our eyes in North America? The celebrated communities of antiquity were all founded in the midst of hostile nations, which they were obliged to subjugate before they could flourish in their place. Even the moderns have found, in some parts of South America, vast regions inhabited by a people of inferior civilization, who nevertheless had already occupied and cultivated the soil. To found their new states it was necessary to extirpate or subdue a numerous population, and they made civilization blush for its own success. But North America was inhabited only by wandering tribes, who had no thought of profiting by the natural riches of the soil; that vast country was still, properly speaking, an empty continent, a desert land awaiting its inhabitants.

Everything is extraordinary in America, the social condition of the inhabitants as well as the laws; but the soil upon which these institutions are founded is more extraordinary than all the rest. When the earth was given to men by the Creator, the earth was inexhaustible; but men were weak and ignorant, and when they had learned to take advantage of the treasures which it contained, they already covered its surface and were soon obliged to earn by the sword an asylum for repose and freedom. Just then North America was discovered, as if it had been kept in reserve by the Deity and had just risen from beneath the waters of the Deluge.

That continent still presents, as it did in the primeval time, rivers that rise from never failing sources, green and moist solitudes, and limitless fields which the plowshare of the husbandman has never turned. In this state it is offered to man, not barbarous, ignorant, and isolated, as he was in the early ages, but already in possession of the most important secrets of nature, united to his fellow men, and instructed by the experience of fifty centuries. At this very time thirteen millions of civilized Europeans are peaceably spreading over those fertile plains, with whose resources and extent they are not yet themselves accurately acquainted. Three or four thousand soldiers drive before them the wandering races of the aborigines; these are followed by the pioneers, who pierce the woods, scare off the beasts of prey, explore the courses of the inland streams, and make ready the triumphal march of civilization across the desert.

Often, in the course of this work, I have alluded to the favorable influence of the material prosperity of America upon the institutions of that country. This reason had already been given by many others before me, and is the only one which, being palpable to the senses, as it were, is familiar to Europeans. I shall not, then, enlarge upon a subject so often handled and so well understood, beyond the addition of a few facts. An erroneous notion is generally entertained that the deserts of America are peopled by European emigrants who annually disembark upon the coasts of the New World, while the American population increase and multiply upon the soil which their forefatners tilled. The European settler usually arrives in the United States without friends and often without resources; in order to subsist, he is obliged to work for hire, and he rarely proceeds beyond that belt of industrious population which adjoins the ocean. The desert cannot be explored without capital or credit; and the body must be accustomed to the rigors of a new climate before it can be exposed in the midst of the forest. It is the Americans themselves who daily quit the spots which gave them birth, to acquire extensive domains in a remote region. Thus the European leaves his cottage for the transatlantic shores, and the American, who is born on that very coast, plunges in his turn into the wilds of central America. This double emigration is incessant; it begins in the middle of Europe, it crosses the Atlantic Ocean, and it advances over the solitudes of the New World. Millions of men are marching at once towards the same horizon; their language, their religion, their manners differ; their object is the same. Fortune has been promised to them somewhere in the West, and to the West they go to find it.

No event can be compared with this continuous removal of the human race, except perhaps those irruptions which caused the fall of the Roman Empire. Then, as well as now, crowds of men were impelled in the same direction, to meet and struggle on the same spot; but the designs of Providence were not the same. Then every new-comer brought with him destruction and death; now each one brings the elements of prosperity and life. The future still conceals from us the remote consequences of this migration of the Americans towards the West; but we can readily apprehend its immediate results. As a portion of the inhabitants annually leave the states in which they were born, the population of these states increases very slowly, although they have long been established. Thus in Connecticut, which yet contains only fifty-nine inhabitants to the square mile, the population has not been increased by more than one quarter in forty years, while that of England has been augmented by one third in the same period. The European emigrant always lands, therefore, in a country that is but half full, and where hands are in demand; he becomes a workman in easy circumstances, his son goes to seek his fortune in unpeopled regions and becomes a rich landowner. The former amasses the capital which the latter invests; and the stranger as well as the native is unacquainted with want.

The laws of the United States are extremely favorable to

the division of property; but a cause more powerful than the laws prevents property from being divided to excess.[2] This is very perceptible in the states which are at last beginning to be thickly peopled. Massachusetts is the most populous part of the Union, but it contains only eighty inhabitants to the square mile, which is much less than in France, where one hundred and sixty-two are reckoned to the same extent of country. But in Massachusetts estates are very rarely divided; the eldest son generally takes the land, and the others go to seek their fortune in the wilderness. The law has abolished the right of primogeniture, but circumstances have concurred to re-establish it under a form of which none can complain and by which no just rights are impaired.

A single fact will suffice to show the prodigious number of individuals who thus leave New England to settle in the wilds. We were assured in 1830 that thirty-six of the members of Congress were born in the little state of Connecticut. The population of Connecticut, which constitutes only one forty-third part of that of the United States, thus furnished one eighth of the whole body of representatives. The state of Connecticut of itself, however, sends only five delegates to Congress; and the thirty-one others sit for the new Western states. If these thirty-one individuals had remained in Connecticut, it is probable that, instead of becoming rich landowners, they would have remained humble laborers, that they would have lived in obscurity without being able to rise into public life, and that, far from becoming useful legislators, they might have been unruly citizens.

These reflections do not escape the observation of the Americans any more than of ourselves. "It cannot be doubted," says Chancellor Kent, in his *Treatise on American Law* (Vol. IV, p. 580), "that the division of landed estates must produce great evils, when it is carried to such excess as that each parcel of land is insufficient to support a family; but these disadvantages have never been felt in the United States, and many generations must elapse before they can be felt. The extent of our inhabited territory, the abundance of adjacent land, and the continual stream of emigration flowing from the shores of the Atlantic towards

[2] In New England estates are very small, but they are rarely divided further.

the interior of the country, suffice as yet, and will long suffice, to prevent the parcelling out of estates."

It would be difficult to describe the avidity with which the American rushes forward to secure this immense booty that fortune offers. In the pursuit he fearlessly braves the arrow of the Indian and the diseases of the forest; he is unimpressed by the silence of the woods; the approach of beasts of prey does not disturb him, for he is goaded onwards by a passion stronger than the love of life. Before him lies a boundless continent, and he urges onward as if time pressed and he was afraid of finding no room for his exertions. I have spoken of the emigration from the older states, but how shall I describe that which takes place from the more recent ones? Fifty years have scarcely elapsed since Ohio was founded; the greater part of its inhabitants were not born within its confines; its capital has been built only thirty years, and its territory is still covered by an immense extent of uncultivated fields; yet already the population of Ohio is proceeding westward, and most of the settlers who descend to the fertile prairies of Illinois are citizens of Ohio. These men left their first country to improve their condition; they quit their second to ameliorate it still more; fortune awaits them everywhere, but not happiness. The desire of prosperity has become an ardent and restless passion in their minds, which grows by what it feeds on. They early broke the ties that bound them to their natal earth, and they have contracted no fresh ones on their way. Emigration was at first necessary to them; and it soon becomes a sor of game of chance, which they pursue for the emotions it excites as much as for the gain it procures.

Sometimes the progress of man is so rapid that the desert reappears behind him. The woods stoop to give him a passage, and spring up again when he is past. It is not uncommon, in crossing the new states of the West, to meet with deserted dwellings in the midst of the wilds; the traveler frequently discovers the vestiges of a log house in the most solitary retreat, which bear witness to the power, and no less to the inconstancy, of man. In these abandoned fields and over these ruins of a day the primeval forest soon scatters a fresh vegetation; the beasts resume the haunts which were once their own; and Nature comes smiling to cover the traces of man with green branches and flowers, which obliterate his ephemeral track.

I remember that in crossing one of the woodland districts which still cover the state of New York, I reached the shores of a lake which was embosomed in forests coeval with the world. A small island, covered with woods whose thick foliage concealed its banks, rose from the center of the waters. Upon the shores of the lake no object attested the presence of man except a column of smoke which might be seen on the horizon rising from the tops of the trees to the clouds and seeming to hang from heaven rather than to be mounting to it. An Indian canoe was hauled up on the sand, which tempted me to visit the islet that had first attracted my attention, and in a few minutes I set foot upon its banks. The whole island formed one of those delightful solitudes of the New World, which almost led civilized man to regret the haunts of the savage. A luxuriant vegetation bore witness to the incomparable fruitfulness of the soil. The deep silence, which is common to the wilds of North America, was broken only by the monotonous cooing of the wood-pigeons and the tapping of the woodpecker on the bark of trees. I was far from supposing that this spot had ever been inhabited, so completely did Nature seem to be left to herself; but when I reached the center of the isle, I thought that I discovered some traces of man. I then proceeded to examine the surrounding objects with care, and I soon perceived that a European had undoubtedly been led to seek a refuge in this place. Yet what changes had taken place in the scene of his labors! The logs which he had hastily hewn to build himself a shed had sprouted afresh; the very props were intertwined with living verdure, and his cabin was transformed into a bower. In the midst of these shrubs a few stones were to be seen, blackened with fire and sprinkled with thin ashes; here the hearth had no doubt been, and the chimney in falling had covered it with rubbish. I stood for some time in silent admiration of the resources of Nature and the littleness of man; and when I was obliged to leave that enchanting solitude, I exclaimed with sadness: "Are ruins, then, already here?"

In Europe we are wont to look upon a restless disposition, an unbounded desire of riches, and an excessive love of independence as propensities very dangerous to society. Yet these are the very elements that ensure a long and peaceful future to the republics of America. Without these unquiet passions the population would collect in certain spots and would soon experience wants like those of the Old World, which it is difficult to satisfy; for such is the present good fortune of the New World that the vices of its inhabitants are scarcely less favorable to society than their virtues. These circumstances exercise a great influence on the estimation in which human actions are held in the two hemispheres. What we should call cupidity, the Americans frequently term a laudable industry; and they blame as faint-heartedness what we consider to be the virtue of moderate desires.

In France simple tastes, orderly manners, domestic affections, and the attachment that men feel to the place of their birth are looked upon as great guarantees of the tranquillity and happiness of the state. But in America nothing seems to be more prejudicial to society than such virtues. The French Canadians, who have faithfully preserved the traditions of their ancient customs, are already embarrassed for room in their small territory; and this little community, which has so recently begun to exist, will shortly be a prey to the calamities incident to old nations. In Canada the most enlightened, patriotic, and humane inhabitants make extraordinary efforts to render the people dissatisfied with those simple enjoyments which still content them. There the seductions of wealth are vaunted with as much zeal as the charms of a moderate competency in the Old World; and more exertions are made to excite the passions of the citizens there than to calm them elsewhere. If we listen to their accounts, we shall hear that nothing is more praiseworthy than to exchange the pure and tranquil pleasures which even the poor man tastes in his own country for the sterile delights of prosperity under a foreign sky; to leave the patrimonial hearth and the turf beneath which one's forefathers sleep—in short, to abandon the living and the dead, in quest of fortune.

At the present time America presents a field for human effort far more extensive than any sum of labor that can be applied to work it. In America too much knowledge cannot be diffused; for all knowledge, while it may serve him who possesses it, turns also to the advantage of those who are without it. New wants are not to be feared there, since they can be satisfied without difficulty; the growth of human passions need not be dreaded, since all passions may find an easy and a legitimate object; nor can men there be made too free, since they are scarcely ever tempted to misuse their liberties.

The American republics of the present day are like companies of adventurers, formed to explore in common the wastelands of the New World and busied in a flourishing trade. The passions that agitate the Americans most deeply are not their political, but their commercial passions; or, rather, they introduce the habits of business into their political life. They love order, without which affairs do not prosper; and they set an especial value upon regular conduct, which is the foundation of a solid business. They prefer the good sense which amasses large fortunes to that enterprising genius which frequently dissipates them; general ideas alarm their minds, which are accustomed to positive calculations; and they hold practice in more honor than theory.

It is in America that one learns to understand the influence which physical prosperity exercises over political actions, and even over opinions which ought to acknowledge no sway but that of reason; and it is more especially among strangers that this truth is perceptible. Most of the European emigrants to the New World carry with them that wild love of independence and change which our calamities are so apt to produce. I sometimes met with Europeans in the United States who had been obliged to leave their country on account of their political opinions. They all astonished me by the language they held, but one of them surprised me more than all the rest. As I was crossing one of the most remote districts of Pennsylvania, I was benighted and obliged to beg for hospitality at the gate of a wealthy planter, who was a Frenchman by birth. He bade me sit down beside his fire, and we began to talk with that freedom which befits persons who meet in the backwoods, two thousand leagues from their native country. I was aware that my host had been a great leveler and an ardent demagogue forty years ago, and that his name was in history. I was therefore not a little surprised to hear him discuss the rights of property as an economist or a landowner might have done: he spoke of the necessary gradations that fortune establishes among men, of obedience to established laws, of the influence of good morals in commonwealths, and of the support that religious opinions give to order and to freedom; he even went so far as to quote the authority of our Saviour in support of one of his political opinions.

I listened, and marveled at the feebleness of human reason. How can we discover whether a proposition is true or false in the midst of the uncertainties of science and the conflicting lessons of experience? A new fact disperses all my doubts. I was poor, I have become rich; and I am not to expect that prosperity will act upon my conduct and leave my judgment free. In truth, my opinions change with my fortune; and the happy circumstances which I turn to my advantage furnish me with that decisive argument which before was wanting.

The influence of prosperity acts still more freely upon Americans than upon strangers. The American has always seen public order and public prosperity intimately united and proceeding side by side before his eyes; he cannot even imagine that one can exist without the other; he has therefore nothing to forget, nor has he, like so many Europeans, to unlearn the lessons of his early education.

INFLUENCE OF THE LAWS UPON THE MAINTENANCE OF THE DEMOCRATIC REPUBLIC IN THE UNITED STATES. *Three principal causes of the maintenance of the democratic republic—Federal union—Township institutions—Judicial power.*

THE PRINCIPAL aim of this book has been to make known the laws of the United States; if this purpose has been accomplished, the reader is already enabled to judge for himself which are the laws that really tend to maintain the democratic republic, and which endanger its existence. If I have not succeeded in explaining this in the whole course of my work, I cannot hope to do so in a single chapter. It is not my intention to retrace the path I have already pursued, and a few lines will suffice to recapitulate what I have said.

Three circumstances seem to me to contribute more than all others to the maintenance of the democratic republic in the United States.

The first is that federal form of government which the Americans have adopted, and which enables the Union to combine the power of a great republic with the security of a small one.

The second consists in those township institutions which limit the despotism of the majority and at the same time impart to the people a taste for freedom and the art of being free.

The third is to be found in the constitution of the judicial power. I have shown how the courts of justice serve to repress the excesses of democracy, and how they check and direct the impulses of the majority without stopping its activity.

INFLUENCE OF CUSTOMS UPON THE MAINTENANCE OF A DEMOCRATIC REPUBLIC IN THE UNITED STATES

I HAVE previously remarked that the manners of the people may be considered as one of the great general causes to which the maintenance of a democratic republic in the United States is attributable. I here use the word *customs* with the meaning which the ancients attached to the word *mores;* for I apply it not only to manners properly so called —that is, to what might be termed *the habits of the heart* —but to the various notions and opinions current among men and to the mass of those ideas which constitute their character of mind. I comprise under this term, therefore, the whole moral and intellectual condition of a people. My intention is not to draw a picture of American customs, but simply to point out such features of them as are favorable to the maintenance of their political institutions.

RELIGION CONSIDERED AS A POLITICAL INSTITUTION WHICH POWERFULLY CONTRIBUTES TO THE MAINTENANCE OF A DEMOCRATIC REPUBLIC AMONG THE AMERICANS. *North America peopled by men who professed a democratic and republican Christianity—Arrival of the Catholics—Why the Catholics now form the most democratic and most republican class.*

BY THE side of every religion is to be found a political opinion, which is connected with it by affinity. If the human mind be left to follow its own bent, it will regulate the temporal and spiritual institutions of society in a uniform manner, and man will endeavor, if I may so speak, to *harmonize* earth with heaven.

The greatest part of British America was peopled by men who, after having shaken off the authority of the Pope, acknowledged no other religious supremacy: they brought with them into the New World a form of Christianity which I cannot better describe than by styling it a democratic and republican religion. This contributed powerfully to the establishment of a republic and a democracy in public affairs; and from the beginning, politics and religion contracted an alliance which has never been dissolved.

About fifty years ago Ireland began to pour a Catholic population into the United States; and on their part, the Catholics of America made proselytes, so that, at the present moment more than a million Christians professing the truths of the Church of Rome are to be found in the Union. These Catholics are faithful to the observances of their religion; they are fervent and zealous in the belief of their doctrines. Yet they constitute the most republican and the most democratic class in the United States. This fact may surprise the observer at first, but the causes of it may easily be discovered upon reflection.

I think that the Catholic religion has erroneously been regarded as the natural enemy of democracy. Among the various sects of Christians, Catholicism seems to me, on the contrary, to be one of the most favorable to equality of condition among men. In the Catholic Church the religious community is composed of only two elements: the priest and the people. The priest alone rises above the rank of his flock, and all below him are equal.

On doctrinal points the Catholic faith places all human capacities upon the same level; it subjects the wise and ignorant, the man of genius and the vulgar crowd, to the details of the same creed; it imposes the same observances upon the rich and the needy, it inflicts the same austerities upon the strong and the weak; it listens to no compromise with mortal man, but, reducing all the human race to the same standard, it confounds all the distinctions of society at the foot of the same altar, even as they are confounded in the sight of God. If Catholicism predisposes the faithful to obedience, it certainly does not prepare them for inequality; but the contrary may be said of Protestantism, which generally tends to make men independent more than to render them equal. Catholicism is like an absolute monarchy; if the sovereign be removed, all the other classes of society are more equal than in republics.

It has not infrequently occurred that the Catholic priest has left the service of the altar to mix with the governing powers of society and to take his place among the civil ranks of men. This religious influence has sometimes been used to secure the duration of that political state of things to which he belonged. Thus we have seen Catholics taking the side of aristocracy from a religious motive. But no sooner is the priesthood entirely separated from the government, as is the case in the United States, than it is found that no class of men is more naturally disposed than the Catholics to transfer the doctrine of the equality of condition into the political world.

If, then, the Catholic citizens of the United States are not forcibly led by the nature of their tenets to adopt democratic and republican principles, at least they are not necessarily opposed to them; and their social position, as well as their limited number, obliges them to adopt these opinions. Most of the Catholics are poor, and they have no chance of taking a part in the government unless it is open to all the citizens. They constitute a minority, and all rights must be respected in order to ensure to them the free exercise of their own privileges. These two causes induce them, even unconsciously, to adopt political doctrines which they would perhaps support with less zeal if they were rich and preponderant.

The Catholic clergy of the United States have never attempted to oppose this political tendency; but they seek rather to justify it. The Catholic priests in America have divided the intellectual world into two parts: in the one they place the doctrines of revealed religion, which they assent to without discussion; in the other they leave those political truths which they believe the Deity has left open to free inquiry. Thus the Catholics of the United States are at the same time the most submissive believers and the most independent citizens.

It may be asserted, then, that in the United States no religious doctrine displays the slightest hostility to democratic and republican institutions. The clergy of all the different sects there hold the same language; their opinions are in agreement with the laws, and the human mind flows onwards, so to speak, in one undivided current.

I happened to be staying in one of the largest cities in the Union when I was invited to attend a public meeting in favor of the Poles and of sending them supplies of arms and money. I found two or three thousand persons collected in a vast hall which had been prepared to receive them. In a short time a priest in his ecclesiastical robes advanced to the front of the platform. The spectators rose and stood uncovered in silence while he spoke in the following terms:

"Almighty God! the God of armies! Thou who didst strengthen the hearts and guide the arms of our fathers when they were fighting for the sacred rights of their national independence! Thou who didst make them triumph over a hateful oppression, and hast granted to our people the benefits of liberty and peace! turn, O Lord, a favorable eye upon the other hemisphere; pitifully look down upon an heroic nation which is even now struggling as we did in the former time, and for the same rights. Thou, who didst create man in the same image, let not tyranny mar thy work and establish inequality upon the earth. Almighty God! do thou watch over the destiny of the Poles, and make them worthy to be free. May thy wisdom direct their councils, may thy strength sustain their arms! Shed forth thy terror over their enemies; scatter the powers which take counsel against them; and permit not the injustice which the world has witnessed for fifty years to be consummated in our time. O Lord, who holdest alike the hearts of nations and of men in thy powerful hand, raise up allies to the sacred cause of right; arouse the French nation from the apathy in which its rulers retain it, that it may go forth again to fight for the liberties of the world.

"Lord, turn not thou thy face from us, and grant that we may always be the most religious, as well as the freest, people of the earth. Almighty God, hear our supplications this day. Save the Poles, we beseech thee, in the name of thy well-beloved Son, our Lord Jesus Christ, who died upon the cross for the salvation of all men. Amen."

The whole meeting responded: "Amen!" with devotion.

INDIRECT INFLUENCE OF RELIGIOUS OPINIONS UPON POLITICAL SOCIETY IN THE UNITED STATES. *Christian morality com-*

I HAVE just shown what the direct influence of religion upon politics is in the United States; but its indirect influence appears to me to be still more considerable, and it never instructs the Americans more fully in the art of being free than when it says nothing of freedom.

The sects that exist in the United States are innumerable. They all differ in respect to the worship which is due to the Creator; but they all agree in respect to the duties which are due from man to man. Each sect adores the Deity in its own peculiar manner, but all sects preach the same moral law in the name of God. If it be of the highest importance to man, as an individual, that his religion should be true, it is not so to society. Society has no future life to hope for or to fear; and provided the citizens profess a religion, the peculiar tenets of that religion are of little importance to its interests. Moreover, all the sects of the United States are comprised within the great unity of Christianity, and Christian morality is everywhere the same.

It may fairly be believed that a certain number of Americans pursue a peculiar form of worship from habit more than from conviction. In the United States the sovereign authority is religious, and consequently hypocrisy must be common; but there is no country in the world where the Christian religion retains a greater influence over the souls of men than in America; and there can be no greater proof of its utility and of its conformity to human nature than that its influence is powerfully felt over the most enlightened and free nation of the earth.

I have remarked that the American clergy in general, without even excepting those who do not admit religious liberty, are all in favor of civil freedom; but they do not support any particular political system. They keep aloof from parties and from public affairs. In the United States religion exercises but little influence upon the laws and upon the details of public opinion; but it directs the customs of the community, and, by regulating domestic life, it regulates the state.

I do not question that the great austerity of manners that is observable in the United States arises, in the first instance, from religious faith. Religion is often unable to restrain man from the numberless temptations which chance offers; nor can it check that passion for gain which everything contributes to arouse; but its influence over the mind of woman is supreme, and women are the protectors of morals. There is certainly no country in the world where the tie of marriage is more respected than in America or where conjugal happiness is more highly or worthily appreciated. In Europe almost all the disturbances of society arise from the irregularities of domestic life. To despise the natural bonds and legitimate pleasures of home is to contract a taste for excesses, a restlessness of heart, and fluctuating desires. Agitated by the tumultuous passions that frequently disturb his dwelling, the European is galled by the obedience which the legislative powers of the state exact. But when the American retires from the turmoil of public life to the bosom of his family, he finds in it the image of order and of peace. There his pleasures are simple and natural, his joys are innocent and calm; and as he finds that an orderly life is the surest path to happiness, he accustoms himself easily to moderate his opinions as well as his tastes. While the European endeavors to forget his domestic troubles by agitating society, the American derives from his own home that love of order which he afterwards carries with him into public affairs.

In the United States the influence of religion is not confined to the manners, but it extends to the intelligence of the people. Among the Anglo-Americans some profess the doctrines of Christianity from a sincere belief in them, and others do the same because they fear to be suspected of unbelief. Christianity, therefore, reigns without obstacle, by universal consent; the consequence is, as I have before observed, that every principle of the moral world is fixed and determinate, although the political world is abandoned to the debates and the experiments of men. Thus the human mind is never left to wander over a boundless field; and whatever may be its pretensions, it is checked from time to time by barriers that it cannot surmount. Before it can innovate, certain primary principles are laid down, and the boldest conceptions are subjected to certain forms which retard and stop their completion.

The imagination of the Americans, even in its greatest flights, is circumspect and undecided; its impulses are checked and its works unfinished. These habits of restraint recur in political society and are singularly favorable both to the tranquillity of the people and to the durability of the institutions they have established. Nature and circumstances have made the inhabitants of the United States bold, as is sufficiently attested by the enterprising spirit with which they seek for fortune. If the mind of the Americans were free from all hindrances, they would shortly become the most daring innovators and the most persistent disputants in the world. But the revolutionists of America are obliged to profess an ostensible respect for Christian morality and equity, which does not permit them to violate wantonly the laws that oppose their designs; nor would they find it easy to surmount the scruples of their partisans even if they were able to get over their own. Hitherto no one in the United States has dared to advance the maxim that everything is permissible for the interests of society, an impious adage which seems to have been invented in an age of freedom to shelter all future tyrants. Thus, while the law permits the Americans to do what they please, religion prevents them from conceiving, and forbids them to commit, what is rash or unjust.

Religion in America takes no direct part in the government of society, but it must be regarded as the first of their political institutions; for if it does not impart a taste for freedom, it facilitates the use of it. Indeed, it is in this same point of view that the inhabitants of the United States themselves look upon religious belief. I do not know whether all Americans have a sincere faith in their religion—for who can search the human heart?—but I am certain that they hold it to be indispensable to the maintenance of republican institutions. This opinion is not peculiar to a class of citizens or to a party, but it belongs to the whole nation and to every rank of society.

In the United States, if a politician attacks a sect, this may not prevent the partisans of that very sect from sup-

porting him; but if he attacks all the sects together, everyone abandons him, and he remains alone.

While I was in America, a witness who happened to be
called at the Sessions of the county of Chester (state of
New York) declared that he did not believe in the existence
of God or in the immortality of the soul. The judge refused
to admit his evidence, on the ground that the witness had
destroyed beforehand all the confidence of the court in what
he was about to say.[3] The newspapers related the fact without any further comment.

The Americans combine the notions of Christianity and
of liberty so intimately in their minds that it is impossible
to make them conceive the one without the other; and with
them this conviction does not spring from that barren, traditionary faith which seems to vegetate rather than to live in
the soul.

I have known of societies formed by Americans to send
out ministers of the Gospel into the new Western states, to
found schools and churches there, lest religion should be
allowed to die away in those remote settlements, and the
rising states be less fitted to enjoy free institutions than the
people from whom they came. I met with wealthy New
Englanders who abandoned the country in which they were
born in order to lay the foundations of Christianity and of
freedom on the banks of the Missouri or in the prairies of
Illinois. Thus religious zeal is perpetually warmed in the
United States by the fires of patriotism. These men do not
act exclusively from a consideration of a future life; eternity
is only one motive of their devotion to the cause. If you
converse with these missionaries of Christian civilization,
you will be surprised to hear them speak so often of the
goods of this world, and to meet a politician where you
expected to find a priest. They will tell you that "all the

---

[3] The New York *Spectator* of August 23, 1831 relates the
fact in the following terms: "The Court of Common Pleas of
Chester County (New York) a few days since rejected a
witness who declared his disbelief in the existence of God. The
presiding judge remarked, that he had not before been aware
that there was a man living who did not believe in the
existence of God; that this belief constituted the sanction of all
testimony in a court of justice; and that he knew of no cause
in a Christian country where a witness had been permitted to
testify without such belief."

American republics are collectively involved with each other; if the republics of the West were to fall into anarchy, or to be mastered by a despot, the republican institutions which now flourish upon the shores of the Atlantic Ocean would be in great peril. It is therefore our interest that the new states should be religious, in order that they may permit us to remain free."

Such are the opinions of the Americans; and if any hold that the religious spirit which I admire is the very thing most amiss in America, and that the only element wanting to the freedom and happiness of the human race on the other side of the ocean is to believe with Spinoza in the eternity of the world, or with Cabanis that thought is secreted by the brain, I can only reply that those who hold this language have never been in America and that they have never seen a religious or a free nation. When they return from a visit to that country, we shall hear what they have to say.

There are persons in France who look upon republican institutions only as a means of obtaining grandeur; they measure the immense space that separates their vices and misery from power and riches, and they aim to fill up this gulf with ruins, that they may pass over it. These men are the *condottieri* of liberty, and fight for their own advantage, whatever the colors they wear. The republic will stand long enough, they think, to draw them up out of their present degradation. It is not to these that I address myself. But there are others who look forward to a republican form of government as a tranquil and lasting state, towards which modern society is daily impelled by the ideas and manners of the time, and who sincerely desire to prepare men to be free. When these men attack religious opinions, they obey the dictates of their passions and not of their interests. Despotism may govern without faith, but liberty cannot. Religion is much more necessary in the republic which they set forth in glowing colors than in the monarchy which they attack; it is more needed in democratic republics than in any others. How is it possible that society should escape destruction if the moral tie is not strengthened in proportion as the political tie is relaxed? And what can be done with a people who are their own masters if they are not submissive to the Deity?

PRINCIPAL CAUSES WHICH RENDER RELIGION POWERFUL IN AMERICA. *Care taken by the Americans to separate the church from the state—The laws, public opinion, and even the exertions of the clergy concur to promote this end—Influence of religion upon the mind in the United States attributable to this cause—Reason for this—What is the natural state of men with regard to religion at the present time—What are the peculiar and incidental causes which prevent men, in certain countries, from arriving at this state.*

THE PHILOSOPHERS of the eighteenth century explained in a very simple manner the gradual decay of religious faith. Religious zeal, said they, must necessarily fail the more generally liberty is established and knowledge diffused. Unfortunately, the facts by no means accord with their theory. There are certain populations in Europe whose unbelief is only equaled by their ignorance and debasement; while in America, one of the freest and most enlightened nations in the world, the people fulfill with fervor all the outward duties of religion.

On my arrival in the United States the religious aspect of the country was the first thing that struck my attention; and the longer I stayed there, the more I perceived the great political consequences resulting from this new state of things. In France I had almost always seen the spirit of religion and the spirit of freedom marching in opposite directions. But in America I found they were intimately united and that they reigned in common over the same country. My desire to discover the causes of this phenomenon increased from day to day. In order to satisfy it I questioned the members of all the different sects; I sought especially the society of the clergy, who are the depositaries of the different creeds and are especially interested in their duration. As a member of the Roman Catholic Church, I was more particularly brought into contact with several of its priests, with whom I became intimately acquainted. To each of these men I expressed my astonishment and explained my doubts. I found that they differed upon matters of detail alone, and that they all attributed the peaceful dominion of religion in their country mainly to the separation of church and state. I do not hesitate to affirm that during my stay in America I did not meet a single individual, of the clergy or the laity, who was not of the same opinion on this point.

This led me to examine more attentively than I had hitherto done the station which the American clergy occupy in political society. I learned with surprise that they filled no public appointments;[4] I did not see one of them in the administration, and they are not even represented in the legislative assemblies. In several states[5] the law excludes them from political life; public opinion excludes them in all. And when I came to inquire into the prevailing spirit of the clergy, I found that most of its members seemed to retire of their own accord from the exercise of power, and that they made it the pride of their profession to abstain from politics.

I heard them inveigh against ambition and deceit, under whatever political opinions these vices might chance to lurk; but I learned from their discourses that men are not guilty in the eye of God for any opinions concerning political government which they may profess with sincerity, any more than they are for their mistakes in building a house or in driving a furrow. I perceived that these ministers of the Gospel eschewed all parties, with the anxiety attendant upon personal interest. These facts convinced me that what I had been told was true; and it then became my object to investigate their causes and to inquire how it happened that the real authority of religion was increased by a state of things which diminished its apparent force. These causes did not long escape my researches.

The short space of threescore years can never content the imagination of man; nor can the imperfect joys of this world

---

[4] Unless this term is applied to the functions which many of them fill in the schools. Almost all education is entrusted to the clergy.

[5] See the Constitution of New York, Art. VII, § 4:

"And whereas the ministers of the Gospel are, by their profession, dedicated to the service of God and the care of souls, and ought not to be diverted from the great duties of their functions; therefore no minister of the Gospel, or priest of any denomination whatsoever, shall at any time hereafter, under any pretence or description whatever, be eligible to, or capable of holding, any civil or military office or place within this State."

See also the Constitutions of North Carolina, Art. XXXI; Virginia; South Carolina, Art. I, § 23; Kentucky, Art. II, § 26; Tennessee, Art. VIII, § 1; Louisiana, Art. II, § 22.

satisfy his heart. Man alone, of all created beings, displays a natural contempt of existence, and yet a boundless desire to exist; he scorns life, but he dreads annihilation. These different feelings incessantly urge his soul to the contemplation of a future state, and religion directs his musings thither. Religion, then, is simply another form of hope, and it is no less natural to the human heart than hope itself. Men cannot abandon their religious faith without a kind of aberration of intellect and a sort of violent distortion of their true nature; they are invincibly brought back to more pious sentiments. Unbelief is an accident, and faith is the only permanent state of mankind. If we consider religious institutions merely in a human point of view, they may be said to derive an inexhaustible element of strength from man himself, since they belong to one of the constituent principles of human nature.

I am aware that at certain times religion may strengthen this influence, which originates in itself, by the artificial power of the laws and by the support of those temporal institutions that direct society. Religions intimately united with the governments of the earth have been known to exercise sovereign power founded on terror and faith; but when a religion contracts an alliance of this nature, I do not hesitate to affirm that it commits the same error as a man who should sacrifice his future to his present welfare; and in obtaining a power to which it has no claim, it risks that authority which is rightfully its own. When a religion founds its empire only upon the desire of immortality that lives in every human heart, it may aspire to universal dominion; but when it connects itself with a government, it must adopt maxims which are applicable only to certain nations. Thus, in forming an alliance with a political power, religion augments its authority over a few and forfeits the hope of reigning over all.

As long as a religion rests only upon those sentiments which are the consolation of all affliction, it may attract the affections of all mankind. But if it be mixed up with the bitter passions of the world, it may be constrained to defend allies whom its interests, and not the principle of love, have given to it; or to repel as antagonists men who are still attached to it, however opposed they may be to the powers with which it is allied. The church cannot share the tempo-

ral power of the state without being the object of a portion
of that animosity which the latter excites.

The political powers which seem to be most firmly established have frequently no better guarantee for their duration
than the opinions of a generation, the interests of the time,
or the life of an individual. A law may modify the social
condition which seems to be most fixed and determinate;
and with the social condition everything else must change.
The powers of society are more or less fugitive, like the
years that we spend upon earth; they succeed each other
with rapidity, like the fleeting cares of life; and no government has ever yet been founded upon an invariable disposition of the human heart or upon an imperishable interest.

As long as a religion is sustained by those feelings, propensities, and passions which are found to occur under the
same forms at all periods of history, it may defy the efforts
of time; or at least it can be destroyed only by another religion. But when religion clings to the interests of the world,
it becomes almost as fragile a thing as the powers of earth.
It is the only one of them all which can hope for immortality; but if it be connected with their ephemeral power, it
shares their fortunes and may fall with those transient passions which alone supported them. The alliance which religion contracts with political powers must needs be onerous
to itself, since it does not require their assistance to live,
and by giving them its assistance it may be exposed to decay.

The danger which I have just pointed out always exists,
but it is not always equally visible. In some ages governments seem to be imperishable; in others the existence of
society appears to be more precarious than the life of man.
Some constitutions plunge the citizens into a lethargic som-
nolence, and others rouse them to feverish excitement.
When governments seem so strong and laws so stable, men
do not perceive the dangers that may accrue from a union
of church and state. When governments appear weak and
laws inconstant, the danger is self-evident, but it is no longer
possible to avoid it. We must therefore learn how to perceive it from afar.

In proportion as a nation assumes a democratic condition
of society and as communities display democratic propensities, it becomes more and more dangerous to connect religion with political institutions; for the time is coming when

authority will be bandied from hand to hand, when political theories will succeed one another, and when men, laws, and constitutions will disappear or be modified from day to day, and this not for a season only, but unceasingly. Agitation and mutability are inherent in the nature of democratic republics, just as stagnation and sleepiness are the law of absolute monarchies.

If the Americans, who change the head of the government once in four years, who elect new legislators every two years, and renew the state officers every twelve months; if the Americans, who have given up the political world to the attempts of innovators, had not placed religion beyond their reach, where could it take firm hold in the ebb and flow of human opinions? Where would be that respect which belongs to it, amid the struggles of faction? And what would become of its immortality, in the midst of universal decay? The American clergy were the first to perceive this truth and to act in conformity with it. They saw that they must renounce their religious influence if they were to strive for political power, and they chose to give up the support of the state rather than to share its vicissitudes.

In America religion is perhaps less powerful than it has been at certain periods and among certain nations; but its influence is more lasting. It restricts itself to its own resources, but of these none can deprive it; its circle is limited, but it pervades it and holds it under undisputed control.

On every side in Europe we hear voices complaining of the absence of religious faith and inquiring the means of restoring to religion some remnant of its former authority. It seems to me that we must first attentively consider what ought to be *the natural state* of men with regard to religion at the present time; and when we know what we have to hope and to fear, we may discern the end to which our efforts ought to be directed.

The two great dangers which threaten the existence of religion are schism and indifference. In ages of fervent devotion men sometimes abandon their religion, but they only shake one off in order to adopt another. Their faith changes its objects, but suffers no decline. The old religion then excites enthusiastic attachment or bitter enmity in either party; some leave it with anger, others cling to it with increased devotedness, and although persuasions differ, irreligion is unknown. Such, however, is not the case when a religious belief is secretly undermined by doctrines which may be termed negative, since they deny the truth of one religion without affirming that of any other. Prodigious revolutions then take place in the human mind, without the apparent co-operation of the passions of man, and almost without his knowledge. Men lose the objects of their fondest hopes as if through forgetfulness. They are carried away by an imperceptible current, which they have not the courage to stem, but which they follow with regret, since it bears them away from a faith they love to a skepticism that plunges them into despair.

In ages which answer to this description men desert their religious opinions from lukewarmness rather than from dislike; they are not rejected, but they fall away. But if the unbeliever does not admit religion to be true, he still considers it useful. Regarding religious institutions in a human point of view, he acknowledges their influence upon manners and legislation. He admits that they may serve to make men live in peace and prepare them gently for the hour of death. He regrets the faith that he has lost; and as he is deprived of a treasure of which he knows the value, he fears to take it away from those who still possess it.

On the other hand, those who continue to believe are not afraid openly to avow their faith. They look upon those who do not share their persuasion as more worthy of pity than of opposition; and they are aware that to acquire the esteem of the unbelieving, they are not obliged to follow their example. They are not hostile, then, to anyone in the world; and as they do not consider the society in which they live as an arena in which religion is bound to face its thousand deadly foes, they love their contemporaries while they condemn their weaknesses and lament their errors.

As those who do not believe conceal their incredulity, and as those who believe display their faith, public opinion pronounces itself in favor of religion: love, support, and honor are bestowed upon it, and it is only by searching the human soul that we can detect the wounds which it has received. The mass of mankind, who are never without the feeling of religion, do not perceive anything at variance with the established faith. The instinctive desire of a future life brings the crowd about the altar and opens the hearts of men to the precepts and consolations of religion.

But this picture is not applicable to us, for there are men among us who have ceased to believe in Christianity, without adopting any other religion; others are in the perplexities of doubt and already affect not to believe; and others, again, are afraid to avow that Christian faith which they still cherish in secret.

Amid these lukewarm partisans and ardent antagonists a small number of believers exists who are ready to brave all obstacles and to scorn all dangers in defense of their faith. They have done violence to human weakness in order to rise superior to public opinion. Excited by the effort they have made, they scarcely know where to stop; and as they know that the first use which the French made of independence was to attack religion, they look upon their contemporaries with dread, and recoil in alarm from the liberty which their fellow citizens are seeking to obtain. As unbelief appears to them to be a novelty, they comprise all that is new in one indiscriminate animosity. They are at war with their age and country, and they look upon every opinion that is put forth there as the necessary enemy of faith.

Such is not the natural state of men with regard to religion at the present day, and some extraordinary or incidental cause must be at work in France to prevent the human mind from following its natural inclination and to drive it beyond the limits at which it ought naturally to stop.

I am fully convinced that this extraordinary and incidental cause is the close connection of politics and religion. The unbelievers of Europe attack the Christians as their political opponents rather than as their religious adversaries; they hate the Christian religion as the opinion of a party much more than as an error of belief; and they reject the clergy less because they are the representatives of the Deity than because they are the allies of government.

In Europe, Christianity has been intimately united to the powers of the earth. Those powers are now in decay, and it is, as it were, buried under their ruins. The living body of religion has been bound down to the dead corpse of superannuated polity; cut but the bonds that restrain it, and it will rise once more. I do not know what could restore the Christian church of Europe to the energy of its earlier days; that power belongs to God alone; but it may be for human policy to leave to faith the full exercise of the strength which it still retains.

How THE EDUCATION, THE HABITS, AND THE PRACTICAL EXPERI-
ENCE OF THE AMERICANS PROMOTE THE SUCCESS OF THEIR
DEMOCRATIC INSTITUTIONS. *What is to be understood by
the education of the American people—The human
mind more superficially instructed in the United States
than in Europe—No one completely uninstructed—
Reason for this—Rapidity with which opinions are
diffused even in the half-cultivated states of the West
—Practical experience more serviceable to the Americans than book-learning.*

I HAVE but little to add to what I have already said concerning the influence that the instruction and the habits of the Americans exercise upon the maintenance of their political institutions.

America has hitherto produced very few writers of distinction; it possesses no great historians and not a single eminent poet. The inhabitants of that country look upon literature properly so called with a kind of disapprobation; and there are towns of second-rate importance in Europe in which more literary works are annually published than in the twenty-four states of the Union put together. The spirit of the Americans is averse to general ideas; it does not seek theoretical discoveries. Neither politics nor manufactures direct them to such speculations; and although new laws are perpetually enacted in the United States, no great writers there have hitherto inquired into the general principles of legislation. The Americans have lawyers and commentators, but no jurists; and they furnish examples rather than lessons to the world. The same observation applies to the mechanical arts. In America the inventions of Europe are adopted with sagacity; they are perfected, and adapted with admirable skill to the wants of the country. Manufactures exist, but the science of manufacture is not cultivated; and they have good workmen, but very few inventors. Fulton was obliged to proffer his services to foreign nations for a long time before he was able to devote them to his own country.

The observer who is desirous of forming an opinion on

the state of instruction among the Anglo-Americans must consider the same object from two different points of view. If he singles out only the learned, he will be astonished to find how few they are; but if he counts the ignorant, the American people will appear to be the most enlightened in the world. The whole population, as I observed in another place, is situated between these two extremes.

In New England every citizen receives the elementary notions of human knowledge; he is taught, moreover, the doctrines and the evidences of his religion, the history of his country, and the leading features of its Constitution. In the states of Connecticut and Massachusetts, it is extremely rare to find a man imperfectly acquainted with all these things, and a person wholly ignorant of them is a sort of phenomenon.

When I compare the Greek and Roman republics with these American states; the manuscript libraries of the former, and their rude population, with the innumerable journals and the enlightened people of the latter; when I remember all the attempts that are made to judge the modern republics by the aid of those of antiquity, and to infer what will happen in our time from what took place two thousand years ago, I am tempted to burn my books in order to apply none but novel ideas to so novel a condition of society.

What I have said of New England must not, however, be applied to the whole Union without distinction; as we advance towards the West or the South, the instruction of the people diminishes. In the states that border on the Gulf of Mexico a certain number of individuals may be found, as in France, who are devoid even of the rudiments of instruction. But there is not a single district in the United States sunk in complete ignorance, and for a very simple reason. The nations of Europe started from the darkness of a barbarous condition, to advance towards the light of civilization; their progress has been unequal; some of them have improved rapidly, while others have loitered in their course, and some have stopped and are still sleeping upon the way.

Such has not been the case in the United States. The Anglo-Americans, already civilized, settled upon that territory which their descendants occupy; they did not have to begin to learn, and it was sufficient for them not to forget. Now the children of these same Americans are the persons who, year by year, transport their dwellings into the wilds, and, with their dwellings, their acquired information and their esteem for knowledge. Education has taught them the utility of instruction and has enabled them to transmit that instruction to their posterity. In the United States society has no infancy, but it is born in man's estate.

The Americans never use the word *peasant*, because they have no idea of the class which that term denotes; the ignorance of more remote ages, the simplicity of rural life, and the rusticity of the villager have not been preserved among them; and they are alike unacquainted with the virtues, the vices, the coarse habits, and the simple graces of an early stage of civilization. At the extreme borders of the confederated states, upon the confines of society and the wilderness, a population of bold adventurers have taken up their abode, who pierce the solitudes of the American woods and seek a country there in order to escape the poverty that awaited them in their native home. As soon as the pioneer reaches the place which is to serve him for a retreat, he fells a few trees and builds a log house. Nothing can offer a more miserable aspect than these isolated dwellings. The traveler who approaches one of them towards nightfall sees the flicker of the hearth flame through the chinks in the walls; and at night, if the wind rises, he hears the roof of boughs shake to and fro in the midst of the great forest trees. Who would not suppose that this poor hut is the asylum of rudeness and ignorance? Yet no sort of comparison can be drawn between the pioneer and the dwelling that shelters him. Everything about him is primitive and wild, but he is himself the result of the labor and experience of eighteen centuries. He wears the dress and speaks the language of cities; he is acquainted with the past, curious about the future, and ready for argument about the present; he is, in short, a highly civilized being, who consents for a time to inhabit the backwoods, and who penetrates into the wilds of the New World with the Bible, an axe, and some newspapers. It is difficult to imagine the incredible rapidity with which thought circulates in the midst of these deserts.[6] I do

[6] I traveled along a portion of the frontier of the United States in a sort of cart, which was termed the mail. Day and night we passed with great rapidity along the roads, which were scarcely marked out through immense forests. When the gloom of the woods became impenetrable, the driver lighted branches

not think that so much intellectual activity exists in the most enlightened and populous districts of France.[7]

It cannot be doubted that in the United States the instruction of the people powerfully contributes to the support of the democratic republic; and such must always be the case, I believe, where the instruction which enlightens the understanding is not separated from the moral education which amends the heart. But I would not exaggerate this advantage, and I am still further from thinking, as so many people do think in Europe, that men can be instantaneously made citizens by teaching them to read and write. True information is mainly derived from experience; and if the Americans had not been gradually accustomed to govern themselves, their book-learning would not help them much at the present day.

I have lived much with the people in the United States, and I cannot express how much I admire their experience and their good sense. An American should never be led to speak of Europe, for he will then probably display much presumption and very foolish pride. He will take up with those crude and vague notions which are so useful to the ignorant all over the world. But if you question him respecting his own country, the cloud that dimmed his intelligence will immediately disperse; his language will become as clear and precise as his thoughts. He will inform you what his rights are and by what means he exercises them; he will be

---

of pine, and we journeyed along by the light they cast. From time to time we came to a hut in the midst of the forest; this was a post-office. The mail dropped an enormous bundle of letters at the door of this isolated dwelling, and we pursued our way at full gallop, leaving the inhabitants of the neighboring log houses to send for their share of the treasure.

[7] In 1832 each inhabitant of Michigan paid 1 fr. 22 cent. to the post-office revenue; and each inhabitant of the Floridas paid 1 fr. 5 cent. (See *National Calendar* [1833], p. 244.) In the same year each inhabitant of the Département du Nord paid not quite 1 fr. 4 cent. to the revenue of the French post-office. (See the *Compte général de l'Administration des Finances* [1833], p. 623.) Now, the state of Michigan contained at that time only 7 inhabitants per square league, and Florida only 5. Instruction was less universal, and the commercial activity of these districts inferior to those of most of the states in the Union; while the Département du Nord, which contains 3,400 inhabitants per square league, is one of the most enlightened and most industrial parts of France.

able to point out the customs which obtain in the political world. You will find that he is well acquainted with the rules of the administration, and that he is familiar with the mechanism of the laws. The citizen of the United States does not acquire his practical science and his positive notions from books; the instruction he has acquired may have prepared him for receiving those ideas, but it did not furnish them. The American learns to know the laws by participating in the act of legislation; and he takes a lesson in the forms of government from governing. The great work of society is ever going on before his eyes and, as it were, under his hands.

In the United States politics are the end and aim of education; in Europe its principal object is to fit men for private life. The interference of the citizens in public affairs is too rare an occurrence to be provided for beforehand. Upon casting a glance over society in the two hemispheres, these differences are indicated even by their external aspect.

In Europe we frequently introduce the ideas and habits of private life into public affairs; and as we pass at once from the domestic circle to the government of the state, we may frequently be heard to discuss the great interests of society in the same manner in which we converse with our friends. The Americans, on the other hand, transport the habits of public life into their manners in private; in their country the jury is introduced into the games of schoolboys, and parliamentary forms are observed in the order of a feast.

THE LAWS CONTRIBUTE MORE TO THE MAINTENANCE OF THE DEMOCRATIC REPUBLIC IN THE UNITED STATES THAN THE PHYSICAL CIRCUMSTANCES OF THE COUNTRY, AND THE CUSTOMS MORE THAN THE LAWS. *All the nations of America have a democratic state of society—Yet democratic institutions are supported only among the Anglo-Americans—The Spaniards of South America, as much favored by physical causes as the Anglo-Americans, unable to maintain a democratic republic—Mexico, which has adopted the Constitution of the United States, in the same predicament—The Anglo-Americans of the West less able to maintain it than those of the East—Reason for these differences.*

I HAVE remarked that the maintenance of democratic institutions in the United States is attributable to the circumstances, the laws, and the customs of that country.[8] Most Europeans are acquainted with only the first of these three causes, and they are apt to give it a preponderant importance that it does not really possess.

It is true that the Anglo-Americans settled in the New World in a state of social equality; the low-born and the noble were not to be found among them; and professional prejudices were always as unknown as the prejudices of birth. Thus, as the condition of society was democratic, the rule of democracy was established without difficulty. But this circumstance is not peculiar to the United States; almost all the American colonies were founded by men equal among themselves, or who became so by inhabiting them. In no one part of the New World have Europeans been able to create an aristocracy. Nevertheless, democratic institutions prosper nowhere but in the United States.

The American Union has no enemies to contend with; it stands in the wilds like an island in the ocean. But the Spaniards of South America were no less isolated by nature; yet their position has not relieved them from the charge of standing armies. They make war upon one another when they have no foreign enemies to oppose; and the Anglo-American democracy is the only one that has hitherto been able to maintain itself in peace.

The territory of the Union presents a boundless field to human activity, and inexhaustible materials for labor. The passion for wealth takes the place of ambition, and the heat of faction is mitigated by a consciousness of prosperity. But in what portion of the globe shall we find more fertile plains, mightier rivers, or more unexplored and inexhaustible riches than in South America? Yet South America has been unable to maintain democratic institutions. If the welfare of nations depended on their being placed in a remote position, with an unbounded space of habitable territory before them, the Spaniards of South America would have no reason to complain of their fate. And although they might enjoy less pros-

---

[8] I remind the reader of the general signification which I give to the word *customs:* namely, the moral and intellectual characteristics of men in society.

perity than the inhabitants of the United States, their lot might still be such as to excite the envy of some nations in Europe. There are no nations upon the face of the earth, however, more miserable than those of South America.

Thus not only are physical causes inadequate to produce results analogous to those which occur in North America, but they cannot raise the population of South America above the level of European states, where they act in a contrary direction. Physical causes do not therefore affect the destiny of nations so much as has been supposed.

I have met with men in New England who were on the point of leaving a country where they might have remained in easy circumstances, to seek their fortune in the wilds. Not far from that region I found a French population in Canada, closely crowded on a narrow territory, although the same wilds were at hand; and while the emigrant from the United States purchased an extensive estate with the earnings of a short term of labor, the Canadian paid as much for land as he would have done in France. Thus Nature offers the solitudes of the New World to Europeans also; but they do not always know how to make use of her gifts. Other inhabitants of America have the same physical conditions of prosperity as the Anglo-Americans, but without their laws and their customs; and these people are miserable. The laws and customs of the Anglo-Americans are therefore that special and predominant cause of their greatness which is the object of my inquiry.

I am far from supposing that the American laws are preeminently good in themselves: I do not hold them to be applicable to all democratic nations; and several of them seem to me to be dangerous, even in the United States. But it cannot be denied that American legislation, taken as a whole, is extremely well adapted to the genius of the people and the nature of the country which it is intended to govern. American laws are therefore good, and to them must be attributed a large portion of the success that attends the government of democracy in America; but I do not believe them to be the principal cause of that success; and if they seem to me to have more influence than the nature of the country upon the social happiness of the Americans, there is still reason to believe that their effect is inferior to that produced by the customs of the people.

The Federal laws undoubtedly constitute the most important part of the legislation of the United States. Mexico, which is not less fortunately situated than the Anglo-American Union, has adopted these same laws, but is unable to accustom itself to the government of democracy. Some other cause is therefore at work, independently of physical circumstances and peculiar laws, which enables the democracy to rule in the United States.

Another still more striking proof may be adduced. Almost all the inhabitants of the territory of the Union are the descendants of a common stock; they speak the same language, they worship God in the same manner, they are affected by the same physical causes, and they obey the same laws. Whence, then, do their characteristic differences arise? Why, in the Eastern states of the Union, does the republican government display vigor and regularity and proceed with mature deliberation? Whence does it derive the wisdom and the durability which mark its acts, while in the Western states, on the contrary, society seems to be ruled by chance? There public business is conducted with an irregularity and a passionate, almost feverish excitement which do not announce a long or sure duration.

I am no longer comparing the Anglo-Americans with foreign nations; I am contrasting them with each other and endeavoring to discover why they are so unlike. The arguments that are derived from the nature of the country and the difference of legislation are here all set aside. Recourse must be had to some other cause; and what other cause can there be, except the customs of the people?

It is in the Eastern states that the Anglo-Americans have been longest accustomed to the government of democracy and have adopted the habits and conceived the opinions most favorable to its maintenance. Democracy has gradually penetrated into their customs, their opinions, and their forms of social intercourse; it is to be found in all the details of daily life as well as in the laws. In the Eastern states the book instruction and practical education of the people have been most perfected and religion has been most thoroughly amalgamated with liberty. What are these habits, opinions, usages, and beliefs if not what I have called customs?

In the Western states, on the contrary, a portion of the

same advantages is still wanting. Many of the Americans of the West were born in the woods, and they mix the ideas and customs of savage life with the civilization of their fathers. Their passions are more intense, their religious morality less authoritative, and their convictions less firm. The inhabitants exercise no sort of control over their fellows, for they are scarcely acquainted with one another. The nations of the West display, to a certain extent, the inexperience and the rude habits of a people in their infancy; for although they are composed of old elements, their assemblage is of recent date.

The customs of the Americans of the United States are, then, the peculiar cause which renders that people the only one of the American nations that is able to support a democratic government; and it is the influence of customs that produces the different degrees of order and prosperity which may be distinguished in the several Anglo-American democracies. Thus the effect which the geographical position of a country may have upon the duration of democratic institutions is exaggerated in Europe. Too much importance is attributed to legislation, too little to customs. These three great causes serve, no doubt, to regulate and direct American democracy; but if they were to be classed in their proper order, I should say that physical circumstances are less efficient than the laws, and the laws infinitely less so than the customs of the people. I am convinced that the most advantageous situation and the best possible laws cannot maintain a constitution in spite of the customs of a country; while the latter may turn to some advantage the most unfavorable positions and the worst laws. The importance of customs is a common truth to which study and experience incessantly direct our attention. It may be regarded as a central point in the range of observation, and the common termination of all my inquiries So seriously do I insist upon this head that, if I have hitherto failed in making the reader feel the important influence of the practical experience, the habits, the opinions, in short, of the customs of the Americans upon the maintenance of their institutions, I have failed in the principal object of my work.

WHETHER LAWS AND CUSTOMS ARE SUFFICIENT TO MAINTAIN DEMOCRATIC INSTITUTIONS IN OTHER COUNTRIES BESIDES AMERICA. *The Anglo-Americans, if transported into*

Europe, would be obliged to modify their laws—Distinction to be made between democratic institutions and American institutions—Democratic laws may be conceived better than, or at least different from, those which the American democracy has adopted—The example of America only proves that it is possible, by the aid of customs and legislation, to regulate democracy.

I HAVE asserted that the success of democratic institutions in the United States is more attributable to the laws themselves and the customs of the people than to the nature of the country. But does it follow that the same causes would of themselves produce the same results if they were put in operation elsewhere; and if the country is no adequate substitute for laws and customs, can laws and manners in their turn take the place of a country? It will readily be understood that the elements of a reply to this question are wanting: other inhabitants are to be found in the New World besides the Anglo-Americans, and, as these are affected by the same physical circumstances as the latter, they may fairly be compared with them. But there are no nations out of America which have adopted the same laws and customs, though destitute of the physical advantages peculiar to the Anglo-Americans. No standard of comparison therefore exists, and we can only hazard an opinion.

It appears to me, in the first place, that a careful distinction must be made between the institutions of the United States and democratic institutions in general. When I reflect upon the state of Europe, its mighty nations, its populous cities, its formidable armies, and the complex nature of its politics, I cannot suppose that even the Anglo-Americans, if they were transported to our hemisphere, with their ideas, their religion, and their customs, could exist without considerably altering their laws. But a democratic nation may be imagined organized differently from the American people. Is it, then, impossible to conceive a government really established upon the will of the majority, but in which the majority, rep

where the people would exercise a less direct and less irresistible influence upon public affairs, and yet every citizen, invested with certain rights, would participate, within his sphere, in the conduct of the government? What I have seen among the Anglo-Americans induces me to believe that democratic institutions of this kind, prudently introduced into society so as gradually to mix with the habits and to be interfused with the opinions of the people, might exist in other countries besides America. If the laws of the United States were the only imaginable democratic laws or the most perfect which it is possible to conceive, I should admit that their success in America affords no proof of the success of democratic institutions in general in a country less favored by nature. But as the laws of America appear to me to be defective in several respects, and as I can readily imagine others, the peculiar advantages of that country do not prove to me that democratic institutions cannot succeed in a nation less favored by circumstances if ruled by better laws.

If human nature were different in America from what it is elsewhere, or if the social condition of the Americans created habits and opinions among them different from those which originate in the same social condition in the Old World, the American democracies would afford no means of predicting what may occur in other democracies. If the Americans displayed the same propensities as all other democratic nations, and if their legislators had relied upon the nature of the country and the favor of circumstances to restrain those propensities within due limits, the prosperity of the United States, being attributable to purely physical causes, would afford no encouragement to a people inclined to imitate their example without sharing their natural advantages. But neither of these suppositions is borne out by facts.

In America the same passions are to be met with as in Europe, some originating in human nature, others in the democratic condition of society. Thus, in the United States I found that restlessness of heart which is natural to men when all ranks ... the same ... are the sam... envy expres... that the peo... affairs a mi...

should consent, with a view ... of the state, to invest a fam... attributes of executive pow... ciety be imagined in which ... be more centralized than ...

ferred that in America men are liable to the same failings and exposed to the same evils as among ourselves. But upon examining the state of society more attentively, I speedily discovered that the Americans had made great and successful efforts to counteract these imperfections of human nature and to correct the natural defects of democracy. Their divers municipal laws appeared to me so many means of restraining the restless ambition of the citizens within a narrow sphere and of turning those same passions which might have worked havoc in the state to the good of the township or the parish. The American legislators seem to have succeeded to some extent in opposing the idea of right to the feelings of envy; the permanence of religious morality to the continual shifting of politics; the experience of the people to their theoretical ignorance; and their practical knowledge of business to the impatience of their desires.

The Americans, then, have not relied upon the nature of their country to counterpoise those dangers which originate in their Constitution and their political laws. To evils that are common to all democratic nations they have applied remedies that none but themselves had ever thought of; and, although they were the first to make the experiment, they have succeeded in it. The manners and laws of the Americans are not the only ones which may suit a democratic people, but the Americans have shown that it would be wrong to despair of regulating democracy by the aid of customs and laws. If other nations should borrow this general and pregnant idea from the Americans, without, however, intending to imitate them in the peculiar application which they have made of it; if they should attempt to fit themselves for that social condition which it seems to be the will of Providence to impose upon the generations of this age, and so to escape from the despotism or the anarchy which threatens them, what reason is there to suppose that their efforts would not be crowned with success? The organization and the establishment of democracy in Christendom is the great political problem of our times. The Americans, unquestionably, have not resolved this problem, but they furnish useful data to those who undertake to resolve it.

IMPORTANCE OF WHAT PRECEDES WITH RESPECT TO THE STATE OF EUROPE

IT MAY readily be discovered with what intention I undertook the foregoing inquiries. The question here discussed is interesting not only to the United States, but to the whole world; it concerns, not a nation only, but all mankind. If those nations whose social condition is democratic could remain free only while they inhabit uncultivated regions, we must despair of the future destiny of the human race; for democracy is rapidly acquiring a more extended sway, and the wilds are gradually peopled with men. If it were true that laws and customs are insufficient to maintain democratic institutions, what refuge would remain open to the nations, except the despotism of one man? I am aware that there are many worthy persons at the present time who are not alarmed at this alternative and who are so tired of liberty as to be glad of repose far from its storms. But these persons are ill acquainted with the haven towards which they are bound. Preoccupied by their remembrances, they judge of absolute power by what it has been and not by what it might become in our times.

If absolute power were re-established among the democratic nations of Europe, I am persuaded that it would assume a new form and appear under features unknown to our fathers. There was a time in Europe when the laws and the consent of the people had invested princes with almost unlimited authority, but they scarcely ever availed themselves of it. I do not speak of the prerogatives of the nobility, of the authority of high courts of justice, of corporations and their chartered rights, or of provincial privileges, which served to break the blows of sovereign authority and to keep up a spirit of resistance in the nation. Independently of these political institutions, which, however opposed they might be to personal liberty, served to keep alive the love of freedom in the mind and which may be esteemed useful in this respect, the manners and opinions of the nation confined the royal authority within barriers that were not less powerful because less conspicuous. Religion, the affections of the people, the benevolence of the prince, the sense of honor, family pride, provincial prejudices, custom, and public opinion limited the power of kings and restrained their authority within an invisible circle. The constitution of nations was despotic at that time, but their customs were free. Princes had the right, but they had neither the means nor the desire of doing whatever they pleased.

But what now remains of those barriers which formerly arrested tyranny? Since religion has lost its empire over the souls of men, the most prominent boundary that divided good from evil is overthrown; everything seems doubtful and indeterminate in the moral world; kings and nations are guided by chance, and none can say where are the natural limits of despotism and the bounds of license. Long revolutions have forever destroyed the respect which surrounded the rulers of the state; and since they have been relieved from the burden of public esteem, princes may henceforward surrender themselves without fear to the intoxication of arbitrary power.

When kings find that the hearts of their subjects are turned towards them, they are lenient, because they are conscious of their strength; and they are careful of the affection of their people because the affection of their people is the bulwark of the throne. A mutual interchange of goodwill then takes place between the prince and the people, which resembles the gracious intercourse of domestic life. The subjects may murmur at the sovereign's decree, but they are grieved to displease him; and the sovereign chastises his subjects with the light hand of parental affection.

But when once the spell of royalty is broken in the tumult of revolution, when successive monarchs have crossed the throne, so as alternately to display to the people the weakness of their right and the harshness of their power, the sovereign is no longer regarded by any as the father of the state, and he is feared by all as its master. If he is weak, he is despised; if he is strong, he is detested. He is himself full of animosity and alarm; he finds that he is a stranger in his own country, and he treats his subjects like conquered enemies.

When the provinces and the towns formed so many different nations in the midst of their common country, each of them had a will of its own, which was opposed to the general spirit of subjection; but now that all the parts of the same empire, after having lost their immunities, their customs, their prejudices, their traditions, and even their names, have become accustomed to obey the same laws, it is not more difficult to oppress them all together than it was formerly to oppress one of them separately.

While the nobles enjoyed their power, and indeed long after that power was lost, the honor of aristocracy conferred an extraordinary degree of force upon their personal opposition. Men could then be found who, notwithstanding their weakness, still entertained a high opinion of their personal value, and dared to cope single-handed with the public authority. But at the present day, when all ranks are more and more undifferentiated, when the individual disappears in the throng and is easily lost in the midst of a common obscurity, when the honor of monarchy has almost lost its power, without being succeeded by virtue, and when nothing can enable man to rise above himself, who shall say at what point the exigencies of power and the servility of weakness will stop?

As long as family feeling was kept alive, the opponent of oppression was never alone; he looked about him and found his clients, his hereditary friends, and his kinsfolk. If this support was wanting, he felt himself sustained by his ancestors and animated by his posterity. But when patrimonial estates are divided, and when a few years suffice to confound the distinctions of race, where can family feeling be found? What force can there be in the customs of a country which has changed, and is still perpetually changing, its aspect, in which every act of tyranny already has a precedent and every crime an example, in which there is nothing so old that its antiquity can save it from destruction, and nothing so unparalleled that its novelty can prevent it from being done? What resistance can be offered by customs of so pliant a make that they have already often yielded? What strength can even public opinion have retained when no twenty persons are connected by a common tie, when not a man, nor a family, nor chartered corporation, nor class, nor free institution, has the power of representing or exerting that opinion, and when every citizen, being equally weak, equally poor, and equally isolated, has only his personal impotence to oppose to the organized force of the government?

The annals of France furnish nothing analogous to the condition in which that country might then be thrown. But it may more aptly be assimilated to the times of old, and to those hideous eras of Roman oppression when the manners of the people were corrupted, their traditions obliterated, their habits destroyed, their opinions shaken, and freedom, expelled from the laws, could find no refuge in the land; when nothing protected the citizens, and the citizens no longer protected themselves; when human nature was the sport of man, and princes wearied out the clemency of Heaven before they exhausted the patience of their subjects. Those who hope to revive the monarchy of Henry IV or of Louis XIV appear to me to be afflicted with mental blindness; and when I consider the present condition of several European nations, a condition to which all the others tend, I am led to believe that they will soon be left with no other alternative than democratic liberty or the tyranny of the Cæsars.

Is not this deserving of consideration? If men must really come to this point, that they are to be entirely emancipated or entirely enslaved, all their rights to be made equal or all to be taken away from them; if the rulers of society were compelled either gradually to raise the crowd to their own level or to allow all the citizens to fall below that of humanity, would not the doubts of many be resolved, the consciences of many be confirmed, and the community prepared to make great sacrifices with little difficulty? In that case the gradual growth of democratic manners and institutions should be regarded, not as the best, but as the only means of preserving freedom; and, without caring for the democratic form of government, it might be adopted as the most applicable, and the fairest remedy for the present ills of society.

It is difficult to make the people participate in the government, but it is still more difficult to supply them with experience and to inspire them with the feelings which they need in order to govern well. I grant that the wishes of the democracy are capricious, its instruments rude, its laws imperfect. But if it were true that soon no just medium would exist between the rule of democracy and the dominion of a single man, should we not rather incline towards the former than submit voluntarily to the latter? And if complete equality be our fate, is it not better to be leveled by free institutions than by a despot?

Those who, after having read this book, should imagine that my intention in writing it was to propose the laws and customs of the Anglo-Americans for the imitation of all democratic communities would make a great mistake; they must have paid more attention to the form than to the substance of my thought. My aim has been to show, by the example of America, that laws, and especially customs, may allow a democratic people to remain free. But I am very far from thinking that we ought to follow the example of the American democracy and copy the means that it has employed to attain this end; for I am well aware of the influence which the nature of a country and its political antecedents exercise upon its political constitution; and I should regard it as a great misfortune for mankind if liberty were to exist all over the world under the same features.

But I am of the opinion that if we do not succeed in gradually introducing democratic institutions into France, if we despair of imparting to all the citizens those ideas and sentiments which first prepare them for freedom and afterwards allow them to enjoy it, there will be no independence at all, either for the middle classes or for the nobility, for the poor or for the rich, but an equal tyranny over all; and I foresee that if the peaceable dominion of the majority is not founded among us in time, we shall sooner or later fall under the unlimited authority of a single man.

Chapter XVIII

THE PRESENT AND PROBABLE FUTURE CONDITION OF THE THREE RACES THAT INHABIT THE TERRITORY OF THE UNITED STATES

THE PRINCIPAL task that I had imposed upon myself is now performed: I have shown, as far as I was able, the laws and the customs of the American democracy. Here I might stop; but the reader would perhaps feel that I had not satisfied his expectations.

An absolute and immense democracy is not all that we find in America; the inhabitants of the New World may be considered from more than one point of view. In the course of this work my subject often led me to speak of the Indians and the Negroes, but I have never had time to stop in order to show what place these two races occupy in the midst of the democratic people whom I was engaged in describing. I have shown in what spirit and according to what laws the Anglo-American Union was formed; but I could give only a hurried and imperfect glance at the dangers which menace that confederation and could not furnish a detailed account of its chances of survival independently of its laws and manners. When speaking of the united republics, I hazarded no conjectures upon the permanence of republican forms in the New World; and when making frequent allusions to the commercial activity that reigns in the Union, I was unable to inquire into the future of the Americans as a commercial people.

These topics are collaterally connected with my subject without forming a part of it; they are American without being democratic, and to portray democracy has been my principal aim. It was therefore necessary to postpone these questions, which I now take up as the proper termination of my work.

* * *

The territory now occupied or claimed by the American Union spreads from the shores of the Atlantic to those of the Pacific Ocean. On the east and west its limits are those of the continent itself. On the south it advances nearly to the tropics, and it extends upward to the icy regions of the north.

The human beings who are scattered over this space do not form, as in Europe, so many branches of the same stock. Three races, naturally distinct, and, I might almost say, hostile to each other, are discoverable among them at the first glance. Almost insurmountable barriers had been raised between them by education and law, as well as by their origin and outward characteristics; but fortune has brought them together on the same soil, where, although they are mixed, they do not amalgamate, and each race fulfills its destiny apart.

Among these widely differing families of men, the first that attracts attention, the superior in intelligence, in power, and in enjoyment, is the white, or European, the MAN preeminently so called; below him appear the Negro and the Indian. These two unhappy races have nothing in common, neither birth, nor features, nor language, nor habits. Their only resemblance lies in their misfortunes. Both of them occupy an equally inferior position in the country they inhabit; both suffer from tyranny; and if their wrongs are not the same, they originate from the same authors.

If we reason from what passes in the world, we should almost say that the European is to the other races of mankind what man himself is to the lower animals: he makes them subservient to his use, and when he cannot subdue he destroys them. Oppression has, at one stroke, deprived the descendants of the Africans of almost all the privileges of humanity. The Negro of the United States has lost even the remembrance of his country; the language which his forefathers spoke is never heard around him; he abjured their religion and forgot their customs when he ceased to belong to Africa, without acquiring any claim to European privileges. But he remains half-way between the two communities, isolated between two races; sold by the one, repulsed by the other; finding not a spot in the universe to call by the name of country, except the faint image of a home which the shelter of his master's roof affords.

The Negro has no family: woman is merely the temporary companion of his pleasures, and his children are on an equality with himself from the moment of their birth. Am I to call it a proof of God's mercy, or a visitation of his wrath, that man, in certain states, appears to be insensible to his extreme wretchedness and almost obtains a depraved taste for the cause of his misfortunes? The Negro, plunged in this abyss of evils, scarcely feels his own calamitous situation. Violence made him a slave, and the habit of servitude gives him the thoughts and desires of a slave; he admires his tyrants more than he hates them, and finds his joy and his pride in the servile imitation of those who oppress him. His understanding is degraded to the level of his soul.

The Negro enters upon slavery as soon as he is born; nay, he may have been purchased in the womb, and have begun his slavery before he began his existence. Equally devoid of wants and of enjoyment, and useless to himself, he learns, with his first notions of existence, that he is the property of another, who has an interest in preserving his life, and that the care of it does not devolve upon himself; even the power of thought appears to him a useless gift of Providence, and he quietly enjoys all the privileges of his debasement.

If he becomes free, independence is often felt by him to be a heavier burden than slavery; for, having learned in the course of his life to submit to everything except reason, he is too unacquainted with her dictates to obey them. A thousand new desires beset him, and he has not the knowledge and energy necessary to resist them: these are masters which it is necessary to contend with, and he has learned only to submit and obey. In short, he is sunk to such a depth of wretchedness that while servitude brutalizes, liberty destroys him.

Oppression has been no less fatal to the Indian than to the Negro race, but its effects are different. Before the arrival of white men in the New World, the inhabitants of North America lived quietly in their woods, enduring the vicissitudes and practicing the virtues and vices common to savage nations. The Europeans, having dispersed the Indian tribes and driven them into the deserts, condemned them to a wandering life, full of inexpressible sufferings.

Savage nations are only controlled by opinion and cus-

tom. When the North American Indians had lost the sentiment of attachment to their country; when their families
were dispersed, their traditions obscured, and the chain of
their recollections broken; when all their habits were
changed, and their wants increased beyond measure, European tyranny rendered them more disorderly and less civilized than they were before. The moral and physical
condition of these tribes continually grew worse, and they
became more barbarous as they became more wretched.
Nevertheless, the Europeans have not been able to change
the character of the Indians; and though they have had
power to destroy, they have never been able to subdue and
civilize them.

The lot of the Negro is placed on the extreme limit of
servitude, while that of the Indian lies on the uttermost
verge of liberty; and slavery does not produce more fatal
effects upon the first than independence upon the second.
The Negro has lost all property in his own person, and he
cannot dispose of his existence without committing a sort
of fraud. But the savage is his own master as soon as he is
able to act; parental authority is scarcely known to him;
he has never bent his will to that of any of his kind, nor
learned the difference between voluntary obedience and a
shameful subjection; and the very name of law is unknown
to him. To be free, with him, signifies to escape from all the
shackles of society. As he delights in this barbarous independence and would rather perish than sacrifice the least
part of it, civilization has little hold over him.

The Negro makes a thousand fruitless efforts to insinuate
himself among men who repulse him; he conforms to the
tastes of his oppressors, adopts their opinions, and hopes by
imitating them to form a part of their community. Having
been told from infancy that his race is naturally inferior to
that of the whites, he assents to the proposition and is
ashamed of his own nature. In each of his features he discovers a trace of slavery, and if it were in his power, he
would willingly rid himself of everything that makes him
what he is.

The Indian, on the contrary, has his imagination inflated
with the pretended nobility of his origin, and lives and dies
in the midst of these dreams of pride. Far from desiring to
conform his habits to ours, he loves his savage life as the

distinguishing mark of his race and repels every advance to civilization, less, perhaps, from hatred of it than from a dread of resembling the Europeans.[1] While he has nothing to oppose to our perfection in the arts but the resources of the wilderness, to our tactics nothing but undisciplined courage, while our well-digested plans are met only by the spontaneous instincts of savage life, who can wonder if he fails in this unequal contest?

The Negro, who earnestly desires to mingle his race with that of the European, cannot do so; while the Indian, who might succeed to a certain extent, disdains to make the attempt. The servility of the one dooms him to slavery, the pride of the other to death.

I remember that while I was traveling through the forests which still cover the state of Alabama, I arrived one day at the log house of a pioneer. I did not wish to penetrate into the dwelling of the American, but retired to rest myself for a while on the margin of a spring, which was not far off, in the woods. While I was in this place (which was in the

[1] The native of North America retains his opinions and the most insignificant of his habits with a degree of tenacity that has no parallel in history. For more than two hundred years the wandering tribes of North America have had daily intercourse with the whites, and they have never derived from them a custom or an idea. Yet the Europeans have exercised a powerful influence over the savages: they have made them more licentious, but not more European. In the summer of 1831 I happened to be beyond Lake Michigan, at a place called Green Bay, which serves as the extreme frontier between the United States and the Indians of the Northwest. Here I became acquainted with an American officer, Major H., who, after talking to me at length about the inflexibility of the Indian character, related the following fact: "I formerly knew a young Indian," said he, "who had been educated at a college in New England, where he had greatly distinguished himself and had acquired the external appearance of a civilized man. When the war broke out between ourselves and the English in 1812, I saw this young man again; he was serving in our army, at the head of the warriors of his tribe; for the Indians were admitted among the ranks of the Americans, on condition only that they would abstain from their horrible custom of scalping their victims. On the evening of the battle of ——, C. came and sat himself down by the fire of our bivouac. I asked him what had been his fortune that day. He related his exploits, and growing warm and animated by the recollection of them, he concluded by suddenly opening the breast of his coat, saying: 'You must not betray me; see here!' And I actually beheld," said the major, "between his body and his shirt, the skin and hair of an English head, still dripping with blood."

neighborhood of the Creek territory), an Indian woman appeared, followed by a Negress, and holding by the hand a little white girl of five or six years, whom I took to be the daughter of the pioneer. A sort of barbarous luxury set off the costume of the Indian; rings of metal were hanging from her nostrils and ears, her hair, which was adorned with glass beads, fell loosely upon her shoulders; and I saw that she was not married, for she still wore that necklace of shells which the bride always deposits on the nuptial couch. The Negress was clad in squalid European garments. All three came and seated themselves upon the banks of the spring; and the young Indian, taking the child in her arms, lavished upon her such fond caresses as mothers give, while the Negress endeavored, by various little artifices, to attract the attention of the young Creole. The child displayed in her slightest gestures a consciousness of superiority that formed a strange contrast with her infantine weakness; as if she received the attentions of her companions with a sort of condescension. The Negress was seated on the ground before her mistress, watching her smallest desires and apparently divided between an almost maternal affection for the child and servile fear; while the savage, in the midst of her tenderness, displayed an air of freedom and pride which was almost ferocious. I had approached the group and was contemplating them in silence, but my curiosity was probably displeasing to the Indian woman, for she suddenly rose, pushed the child roughly from her, and, giving me an angry look, plunged into the thicket.

In the same place I had often chanced to see individuals together who belonged to the three races that people North America. I had perceived from many different traits the preponderance of the whites. But in the picture that I have just been describing there was something peculiarly touching; a bond of affection here united the oppressors with the oppressed, and the effort of Nature to bring them together rendered still more striking the immense distance placed between them by prejudice and the laws.

THE PRESENT AND PROBABLE FUTURE CONDITION OF THE IN-
DIAN TRIBES THAT INHABIT THE TERRITORY POSSESSED BY
THE UNION. *Gradual disappearance of the native tribes
—Manner in which it takes place—Miseries accom-
panying the forced migrations of the Indians—The sav-*

*ages of North America had only two ways of escaping
destruction, war or civilization—They are no longer
able to make war—Reasons why they refused to become
civilized when it was in their power, and why they cannot become so now that they desire it—Instance of the
Creeks and Cherokees—Policy of the particular states
towards these Indians—Policy of the Federal government.*

NONE of the Indian tribes which formerly inhabited the
territory of New England, the Narragansetts, the Mohicans,
the Pequots, have any existence but in the recollection of
man. The Lenapes, who received William Penn a hundred
and fifty years ago upon the banks of the Delaware, have
disappeared; and I myself met with the last of the Iroquois,
who were begging alms. The nations I have mentioned formerly covered the country to the seacoast; but a traveler at
the present day must penetrate more than a hundred leagues
into the interior of the continent to find an Indian. Not only
have these wild tribes receded, but they are destroyed; [2] and
as they give way or perish, an immense and increasing people fill their place. There is no instance upon record of so
prodigious a growth or so rapid a destruction; the manner
in which the latter change takes place is not difficult to
describe.

When the Indians were the sole inhabitants of the wilds
whence they have since been expelled, their wants were few.
Their arms were of their own manufacture, their only drink
was the water of the brook, and their clothes consisted of
the skins of animals, whose flesh furnished them with food.

The Europeans introduced among the savages of North
America firearms, ardent spirits, and iron; they taught them
to exchange for manufactured stuffs the rough garments
that had previously satisfied their untutored simplicity. Having acquired new tastes, without the arts by which they
could be gratified, the Indians were obliged to have recourse
to the workmanship of the whites; but in return for their
productions the savage had nothing to offer except the rich
furs that still abounded in his woods. Hence the chase became necessary, not merely to provide for his subsistence,

[2] In the thirteen original states there are only 6,273 Indians
remaining. (See *Legislative Documents,* 20th Congress, No. 117.
p. 20.)

but to satisfy the frivolous desires of Europeans. He no longer hunted merely to obtain food, but to procure the only objects of barter which he could offer.[3] While the wants of the natives were thus increasing, their resources continued to diminish.

From the moment when a European settlement is formed in the neighborhood of the territory occupied by the Indians, the beasts of chase take the alarm.[4] Thousands of savages, wandering in the forests and destitute of any fixed dwelling, did not disturb them; but as soon as the continuous sounds of European labor are heard in their neighborhood, they begin to flee away and retire to the West, where their instinct teaches them that they will still find deserts of immeasurable extent. "The buffalo is constantly receding," say Messrs. Clarke and Cass in their *Report* of the year 1829; "a few

[3] Messrs. Clarke and Cass, in their *Report to Congress*, of February 4, 1829, p. 23, remarked: "The time when the Indians generally could supply themselves with food and clothing, without any of the articles of civilized life, has long since passed away. The more remote tribes, beyond the Mississippi, who live where immense herds of buffalo are yet to be found, and who follow those animals in their periodical migrations, could more easily than any others recur to the habits of their ancestors, and live without the white man or any of his manufactures. But the buffalo is constantly receding. The smaller animals, the bear, the deer, the beaver, the otter, the musk-rat, etc., principally minister to the comfort and support of the Indians; and these cannot be taken without guns, ammunition, and traps. Among the Northwestern Indians, particularly, the labor of supplying a family with food is excessive. Day after day is spent by the hunter without success, and during this interval his family must exist upon bark or roots, or perish. Want and misery are around them and among them. Many die every winter from actual starvation."

The Indians will not live as Europeans live; and yet they can neither exist without them nor live exactly after the fashion of their fathers. This is demonstrated by a fact which I likewise give upon official authority. Some Indians of a tribe on the banks of Lake Superior had killed a European; the American government prohibited all traffic with the tribe to which the guilty parties belonged until they were delivered up to justice. This measure had the desired effect.

[4] "Five years ago," says Volney in his *Tableau des États-Unis*, p. 370, "in going from Vincennes to Kaskaskia, a territory which now forms part of the state of Illinois, but which at the time I mention was completely wild (1797), you could not cross a prairie without seeing herds of from four to five hundred buffaloes. There is now none remaining; they swam across the Mississippi, to escape from the hunters, and more particularly from the bells of the American cows."

years since they approached the base of the Allegheny; and a few years hence they may even be rare upon the immense plains which extend to the base of the Rocky Mountains." I have been assured that this effect of the approach of the whites is often felt at two hundred leagues' distance from their frontier. Their influence is thus exerted over tribes whose name is unknown to them, and who suffer the evils of usurpation long before they are acquainted with the authors of their distress.[5]

Bold adventurers soon penetrate into the country the Indians have deserted, and when they have advanced about fifteen or twenty leagues from the extreme frontiers of the whites, they begin to build habitations for civilized beings in the midst of the wilderness. This is done without difficulty, as the territory of a hunting nation is ill defined; it is the common property of the tribe and belongs to no one in particular, so that individual interests are not concerned in protecting any part of it.

A few European families, occupying points very remote from one another, soon drive away the wild animals that remain between their places of abode. The Indians, who had previously lived in a sort of abundance, then find it difficult to subsist, and still more difficult to procure the articles of barter that they stand in need of. To drive away their game has the same effect as to render sterile the fields of our agriculturists; deprived of the means of subsistence, they are reduced, like famished wolves, to prowl through the forsaken woods in quest of prey. Their instinctive love of country attaches them to the soil that gave them birth,[6] even

[5] The truth of what I here advance may be easily proved by consulting the tabular statement of Indian tribes inhabiting the United States and their territories. (*Legislative Documents,* 20th Congress, No. 117, pp. 90–105.) It is there shown that the tribes in the center of America are rapidly decreasing, although the Europeans are still at a considerable distance from them.

[6] "The Indians," say Messrs. Clarke and Cass, in their *Report to Congress,* p. 15, "are attached to their country by the same feelings which bind us to ours; and, besides, there are certain superstitious notions connected with the alienation of what the Great Spirit gave to their ancestors, which operate strongly upon the tribes which have made few or no cessions, but which are gradually weakened as our intercourse with them is extended. 'We will not sell the spot which contains the bones of our fathers,' is almost always the first answer to a proposal to buy their land."

after it has ceased to yield anything but misery and death. At length they are compelled to acquiesce and depart; they follow the traces of the elk, the buffalo, and the beaver and are guided by these wild animals in the choice of their future country. Properly speaking, therefore, it is not the Europeans who drive away the natives of America; it is famine, a happy distinction which had escaped the casuists of former times and for which we are indebted to modern discovery!

It is impossible to conceive the frightful sufferings that attend these forced migrations. They are undertaken by a people already exhausted and reduced; and the countries to which the new-comers betake themselves are inhabited by other tribes, which receive them with jealous hostility. Hunger is in the rear, war awaits them, and misery besets them on all sides. To escape from so many enemies, they separate, and each individual endeavors to procure secretly the means of supporting his existence by isolating himself, living in the immensity of the desert like an outcast in civilized society. The social tie, which distress had long since weakened, is then dissolved; they have no longer a country, and soon they will not be a people; their very families are obliterated; their common name is forgotten; their language perishes; and all traces of their origin disappear. Their nation has ceased to exist except in the recollection of the antiquaries of America and a few of the learned of Europe.

I should be sorry to have my reader suppose that I am coloring the picture too highly; I saw with my own eyes many of the miseries that I have just described, and was the witness of sufferings that I have not the power to portray.

At the end of the year 1831, while I was on the left bank of the Mississippi, at a place named by Europeans Memphis, there arrived a numerous band of Choctaws (or Chactas, as they are called by the French in Louisiana). These savages had left their country and were endeavoring to gain the right bank of the Mississippi, where they hoped to find an asylum that had been promised them by the American government. It was then the middle of winter, and the cold was unusually severe; the snow had frozen hard upon the ground, and the river was drifting huge masses of ice. The Indians had their families with them, and they brought in their train the wounded and the sick. with children newly born and old men upon the verge of death. They possessed neither tents nor wagons, but only their arms and some provisions. I saw them embark to pass the mighty river, and never will that solemn spectacle fade from my remembrance. No cry, no sob, was heard among the assembled crowd; all were silent. Their calamities were of ancient date, and they knew them to be irremediable. The Indians had all stepped into the bark that was to carry them across, but their dogs remained upon the bank. As soon as these animals perceived that their masters were finally leaving the shore, they set up a dismal howl and, plunging all together into the icy waters of the Mississippi, swam after the boat.

The expulsion of the Indians often takes place at the present day in a regular and, as it were, a legal manner. When the European population begins to approach the limit of the desert inhabited by a savage tribe, the government of the United States usually sends forward envoys who assemble the Indians in a large plain and, having first eaten and drunk with them, address them thus: "What have you to do in the land of your fathers? Before long, you must dig up their bones in order to live. In what respect is the country you inhabit better than another? Are there no woods, marshes, or prairies except where you dwell? And can you live nowhere but under your own sun? Beyond those mountains which you see at the horizon, beyond the lake which bounds your territory on the west, there lie vast countries where beasts of chase are yet found in great abundance; sell us your lands, then, and go to live happily in those solitudes." After holding this language, they spread before the eyes of the Indians firearms, woolen garments, kegs of brandy, glass necklaces, bracelets of tinsel, ear-rings, and looking-glasses.[7] If, when they have beheld all these riches,

---

[7] See in the *Legislative Documents of Congress* (Doc. 117) the narrative of what takes place on these occasions. This curious passage is from the formerly mentioned *Report* made to Congress by Messrs. Clarke and Cass, February 4, 1829.

"The Indians," says the *Report,* "reach the treaty-ground poor, and almost naked. Large quantities of goods are taken there by the traders, and are seen and examined by the Indians. The women and children become importunate to have their wants supplied, and their influence is soon exerted to induce a sale. Their improvidence is habitual and unconquerable. The gratification of his immediate wants and desires is the ruling passion of an Indian. The expectation of future advantages seldom produces

they still hesitate, it is insinuated that they cannot refuse the required consent and that the government itself will not long have the power of protecting them in their rights. What are they to do? Half convinced and half compelled, they go to inhabit new deserts, where the importunate whites will not let them remain ten years in peace. In this manner do the Americans obtain, at a very low price, whole provinces, which the richest sovereigns of Europe could not purchase.[8]

These are great evils; and it must be added that they appear to me to be irremediable. I believe that the Indian nations of North America are doomed to perish, and that whenever the Europeans shall be established on the shores of the Pacific Ocean, that race of men will have ceased to exist.[9] The Indians had only the alternative of war or

much effect. The experience of the past is lost, and the prospects of the future disregarded. It would be utterly hopeless to demand a cession of land, unless the means were at hand of gratifying their immediate wants; and when their condition and circumstances are fairly considered, it ought not to surprise us that they are so anxious to relieve themselves."

[8] On May 19, 1830 Mr. Edward Everett affirmed before the House of Representatives that the Americans had already acquired by *treaty,* to the east and west of the Mississippi, 230,000,-000 acres. In 1808 the Osages gave up 48,000,000 acres for an annual payment of 1,000 dollars. In 1818 the Quapaws yielded up 20,000,000 acres for 4,000 dollars. They reserved for themselves a territory of 1,000,000 acres for a hunting-ground. A solemn oath was taken that it should be respected, but before long it was invaded like the rest.

Mr. Bell, in his *Report of the Committee on Indian Affairs,* February 24, 1830, has these words: "To pay an Indian tribe what their ancient hunting-grounds are worth to them after the game is fled or destroyed, as a mode of appropriating wild lands claimed by Indians, has been found more convenient, and certainly it is more agreeable to the forms of justice, as well as more merciful, than to assert the possession of them by the sword. Thus the practice of buying Indian titles is only the substitute which humanity and expediency have imposed, in place of the sword, in arriving at the actual enjoyment of property claimed by the right of discovery, and sanctioned by the natural superiority allowed to the claims of civilized communities over those of savage tribes. Up to the present time, so invariable has been the operation of certain causes, first in diminishing the value of forest lands to the Indians, and secondly, in disposing them to sell readily, that the plan of buying their right of occupancy has never threatened to retard, in any perceptible degree, the prosperity of any of the States." (*Legislative Documents,* 21st Congress, No. 227, p. 6.)

[9] This seems, indeed, to be the opinion of almost all American statesmen. "Judging of the future by the past," says Mr. Cass,

civilization; in other words, they must either destroy the Europeans or become their equals.

At the first settlement of the colonies they might have found it possible, by uniting their forces, to deliver themselves from the small bodies of strangers who landed on their continent.[10] They several times attempted to do it, and were on the point of succeeding; but the disproportion of their resources at the present day, when compared with those of the whites, is too great to allow such an enterprise to be thought of. But from time to time among the Indians men of sagacity and energy foresee the final destiny that awaits the native population and exert themselves to unite all the tribes in common hostility to the Europeans; but their efforts are unavailing. The tribes which are in the neighborhood of the whites are too much weakened to offer an effectual resistance; while the others, giving way to that childish carelessness of the morrow which characterizes savage life, wait for the near approach of danger before they prepare to meet it; some are unable, others are unwilling, to act.

It is easy to foresee that the Indians will never civilize themselves, or that it will be too late when they may be inclined to make the experiment.

Civilization is the result of a long social process, which takes place in the same spot and is handed down from one generation to another, each one profiting by the experience of the last. Of all nations, those submit to civilization with the most difficulty who habitually live by the chase. Pastoral tribes, indeed, often change their place of abode; but they follow a regular order in their migrations and often return to their old stations, while the dwelling of the hunter varies with that of the animals he pursues.

Several attempts have been made to diffuse knowledge

"we cannot err in anticipating a progressive diminution of their numbers, and their eventual extinction, unless our border should become stationary, and they be removed beyond it, or unless some radical change should take place in the principles of our intercourse with them, which it is easier to hope for than to expect."

[10] Among other warlike enterprises, there was one of the Wampanoags, and other confederate tribes, under Metacom, in 1675, against the colonists of New England; the English were also engaged in war with them in Virginia in 1622.

among the Indians, leaving unchecked their wandering propensities, by the Jesuits in Canada and by the Puritans in New England;[11] but none of these endeavors have been crowned by any lasting success. Civilization began in the cabin, but soon retired to expire in the woods. The great error of these legislators for the Indians was their failure to understand that in order to succeed in civilizing a people it is first necessary to settle them permanently, which cannot be done without inducing them to cultivate the soil; the Indians ought in the first place to have been accustomed to agriculture. But not only are they destitute of this indispensable preliminary to civilization, they would even have great difficulty in acquiring it. Men who have once abandoned themselves to the restless and adventurous life of the hunter feel an insurmountable disgust for the constant and regular labor that tillage requires. We see this proved even in our own societies; but it is far more visible among races whose partiality for the chase is a part of their national character.

Independently of this general difficulty, there is another, which applies peculiarly to the Indians. They consider labor not merely as an evil, but as a disgrace; so that their pride contends against civilization as obstinately as their indolence.[12]

There is no Indian so wretched as not to retain under his hut of bark a lofty idea of his personal worth; he considers the cares of industry as degrading occupations; he compares the plowman to the ox that traces the furrow; and in each of our handicrafts he can see only the labor of slaves. Not that he is devoid of admiration for the power and intellectual greatness of the whites; but although the result of our efforts surprises him, he despises the means by which we obtain it; and while he acknowledges our ascendancy, he still believes in his own superiority. War and hunting are the only

[11] See the historians of New England, the *Histoire de la Nouvelle France,* by Charlevoix, and the work entitled *Lettres édifiantes.*

[12] "In all the tribes," says Volney, in his *Tableau des États-Unis* (p. 423), "there still exists a generation of old warriors who cannot forbear, when they see their countrymen using the hoe, from exclaiming against the degradation of ancient manners and asserting that the savages owe their decline to these innovations; adding that they have only to return to their primitive habits in order to recover their power and glory."

pursuits that appear to him worthy of a man.[13] The Indian, in the dreary solitudes of his woods, cherishes the same ideas, the same opinions, as the noble of the Middle Ages in his castle; and he only needs to become a conqueror to complete the resemblance. Thus, however strange it may seem, it is in the forests of the New World, and not among the Europeans who people its coasts, that the ancient prejudices of Europe still exist.

More than once in the course of this work I have endeavored to explain the prodigious influence that the social condition appears to exercise upon the laws and the manners of men, and I beg to add a few words on the same subject.

When I perceive the resemblance that exists between the political institutions of our ancestors, the Germans, and the wandering tribes of North America, between the customs described by Tacitus and those of which I have sometimes been a witness, I cannot help thinking that the same cause has brought about the same results in both hemispheres; and that in the midst of the apparent diversity of human affairs certain primary facts may be discovered from which all the others are derived. In what we usually call the German institutions, then, I am inclined to perceive only barbarian habits, and the opinions of savages in what we style feudal principles.

However strongly the vices and prejudices of the North American Indians may be opposed to their becoming agricultural and civilized, necessity sometimes drives them to it.

[13] The following description occurs in an official document: "Until a young man has been engaged with an enemy, and has performed some acts of valor, he gains no consideration, but is regarded nearly as a woman. In their great war-dances, all the warriors in succession strike the post, as it is called, and recount their exploits. On these occasions, their audience consists of the kinsmen, friends, and comrades of the narrator. The profound impression which his discourse produces on them is manifested by the silent attention it receives, and by the loud shouts which hail its termination. The young man who finds himself at such a meeting without anything to recount is very unhappy; and instances have sometimes occurred of young warriors, whose passions had been thus inflamed, quitting the war-dance suddenly, and going off alone to seek for trophies which they might exhibit and adventures by which they might be allowed to glorify themselves."

Several of the Southern tribes, considerably numerous, and among others the Cherokees and the Creeks,[14] found themselves, as it were, surrounded by Europeans, who had landed on the shores of the Atlantic and, either descending the Ohio or proceeding up the Mississippi, arrived simultaneously upon their borders. These tribes had not been driven from place to place like their Northern brethren; but they had been gradually shut up within narrow limits, like game driven into an enclosure before the huntsmen plunge among them. The Indians, who were thus placed between civilization and death, found themselves obliged to live ignominiously by labor, like the whites. They took to agriculture and, without entirely forsaking their old habits or manners, sacrificed only as much as was necessary to their existence.

The Cherokees went further; they created a written language, established a permanent form of government, and, as everything proceeds rapidly in the New World, before they all of them had clothes they set up a newspaper.[15]

The development of European habits has been much accelerated among these Indians by the mixed race which has sprung up.[16] Deriving intelligence from the father's side without entirely losing the savage customs of the mother, the half-blood forms the natural link between civilization and barbarism. Wherever this race has multiplied,

[14] These nations are now swallowed up in the states of Georgia, Tennessee, Alabama, and Mississippi. There were formerly in the South four great nations (remnants of which still exist), the Choctaws, the Chickasaws, the Creeks, and the Cherokees. The remnants of these four nations amounted in 1830 to about 75,-000 individuals. It is computed that there are now remaining in the territory occupied or claimed by the Anglo-American Union about 300,000 Indians. (See *Proceeding of the Indian Board in the City of New York*.) The official documents supplied to Congress make the number amount to 313,130. The reader who is curious to know the names and numerical strength of all the tribes that inhabit the Anglo-American territory should consult the documents I have just referred to. (*Legislative Documents, 20th Congress, No. 117, pp. 90–105*.)

[15] I brought back with me to France one or two copies of this singular publication.

[16] See, in the *Report of the Committee on Indian Affairs*, 21st Congress, No. 227, p. 23, the reasons for the multiplication of Indians of mixed blood among the Cherokees. The principal cause dates from the War of Independence. Many Anglo-Americans of Georgia, having taken the side of England, were obliged to retreat among the Indians, where they married.

the savage state has become modified and a great change has taken place in the manners of the people.[17]

The success of the Cherokees proves that the Indians are capable of civilization, but it does not prove that they will succeed in it. This difficulty that the Indians find in submitting to civilization proceeds from a general cause, the influence of which it is almost impossible for them to escape. An attentive survey of history demonstrates that, in general, barbarous nations have raised themselves to civilization by degrees and by their own efforts. Whenever they derived knowledge from a foreign people, they stood towards them in the relation of conquerors, and not of a conquered nation. When the conquered nation is enlightened and the conquerors are half-savage, as in the invasion of the Roman Empire by the northern nations, or that of China by the Mongols, the power that victory bestows upon the barbarian is sufficient to keep up his importance among civilized men and permit him to rank as their equal until he becomes their rival. The one has might on his side, the other has intelligence; the former admires the knowledge and the arts of the conquered, the latter envies the power of the conquerors.

---

[17] Unhappily, the mixed race has been less numerous and less influential in North America than in any other country. The American continent was peopled by two great nations of Europe, the French and the English. The former were not slow in connecting themselves with the daughters of the natives, but there was an unfortunate affinity between the Indian character and their own: instead of giving the tastes and habits of civilized life to the savages, the French too often grew passionately fond of Indian life. They became the most dangerous inhabitants of the wilderness, and won the friendship of the Indian by exaggerating his vices and his virtues. M. de Senonville, the Governor of Canada, wrote thus to Louis XIV in 1685: "It has long been believed that in order to civilize the savages we ought to draw them nearer to us. But there is every reason to suppose we have been mistaken. Those that have been brought into contact with us have not become French, and the French who have lived among them are changed into savages, affecting to dress and live like them." (*History of New France,* by Charlevoix, Vol. II, p 345.) The Englishman, on the contrary, continuing obstinately attached to the customs and the most insignificant habits of his forefathers, has remained in the midst of the American solitudes just what he was in the heart of European cities; he would not establish any communication with savages whom he despised, and avoided with care the union of his race with theirs. Thus, while the French exercised no salutary influence over the Indians, the English have always remained alien from them.

The barbarians at length admit civilized man into their palaces, and he in turn opens his schools to the barbarians. But when the side on which the physical force lies also possesses an intellectual superiority, the conquered party seldom becomes civilized; it retreats or is destroyed. It may therefore be said, in a general way, that savages go forth in arms to seek knowledge, but do not receive it when it comes to them.

If the Indian tribes that now inhabit the heart of the continent could summon up energy enough to attempt to civilize themselves, they might possibly succeed. Superior already to the barbarous nations that surround them, they would gradually gain strength and experience, and when the Europeans appear upon their borders, they would be in a state, if not to maintain their independence, at least to assert their right to the soil and to incorporate themselves with the conquerors. But it is the misfortune of Indians to be brought into contact with a civilized people, who are also (it must be owned) the most grasping nation on the globe, while they are still semi-barbarian; to find their masters in their instructors, and to receive knowledge and oppression at the same time. Living in the freedom of the woods, the North American Indian was destitute, but he had no feeling of inferiority towards anyone; as soon, however, as he desires to penetrate into the social scale of the whites, he can take only the lowest rank in society, for he enters ignorant and poor within the pale of science and wealth. After having led a life of agitation, beset with evils and dangers, but at the same time filled with proud emotions,[18] he is obliged to

[18] There is in the adventurous life of the hunter a certain irresistible charm, which seizes the heart of man and carries him away in spite of reason and experience. This is plainly shown by the *Memoirs of Tanner*. Tanner was a European who was carried away at the age of six by the Indians and remained thirty years with them in the woods. Nothing can be conceived more appalling than the miseries that he describes. He tells us of tribes without a chief, families without a nation to call their own, men in a state of isolation, wrecks of powerful tribes wandering at random amid the ice and snow and desolate solitudes of Canada. Hunger and cold pursue them; every day their life is in jeopardy. Among these men manners have lost their empire, traditions are without power. They become more and more savage. Tanner shared in all these miseries; he was aware of his European origin; he was not kept away from the whites by force; on the contrary, he came every year to trade with them, entered their

submit to a wearisome, obscure, and degraded state. To gain by hard and ignoble labor the bread that nourishes him is in his eyes the only result of which civilization can boast; and even this he is not always sure to obtain.

When the Indians undertake to imitate their European neighbors, and to till the earth as they do, they are immediately exposed to a formidable competition. The white man is skilled in the craft of agriculture; the Indian is a rough beginner in an art with which he is unacquainted. The former reaps abundant crops without difficulty, the latter meets with a thousand obstacles in raising the fruits of the earth.

The European is placed among a population whose wants he knows and shares. The savage is isolated in the midst of a hostile people, with whose customs, language, and laws he is imperfectly acquainted, but without whose assistance he cannot live. He can procure only the materials of comfort by bartering his commodities for the goods of the European, for the assistance of his countrymen is wholly insufficient to supply his wants. Thus, when the Indian wishes to sell the produce of his labor, he cannot always find a purchaser, while the European readily obtains a market; the former can produce only at considerable cost what the latter sells at

---

dwellings, and witnessed their enjoyments; he knew that whenever he chose to return to civilized life, he was perfectly able to do so, and he remained thirty years in the wilderness. When he came into civilized society, he declared that the rude existence, the miseries of which he described, had a secret charm for him which he could not define; he returned to it again and again, at length he abandoned it with poignant regret; and when he was at length settled among the whites, several of his children refused to share his tranquil and easy situation. I saw Tanner myself at the lower end of Lake Superior: he seemed to me more like a savage than a civilized being. His book is written without either taste or order; but he gives, even unconsciously, a lively picture of the prejudices, the passions, the vices, and, above all, the destitution in the midst of which he lived.

The Viscount Ernest de Blosseville, author of an excellent treatise on the penal colonies of England, has translated the *Memoirs of Tanner*. M. de Blosseville has added to his translation some very interesting notes which will enable the reader to compare the facts related by Tanner with those already recorded by a great number of observers, ancient and modern.

All those who desire to know the present status of the Indians of North America and would foresee their destiny should consult M. de Blosseville's work.

a low rate. Thus the Indian has no sooner escaped those evils to which barbarous nations are exposed than he is subjected to the still greater miseries of civilized communities; and he finds it scarcely less difficult to live in the midst of our abundance than in the depth of his own forest.

He has not yet lost the habits of his erratic life; the traditions of his fathers and his passion for the chase are still alive within him. The wild enjoyments that formerly animated him in the woods painfully excite his troubled imagination; the privations that he endured there appear less keen, his former perils less appalling. He contrasts the independence that he possessed among his equals with the servile position that he occupies in civilized society. On the other hand, the solitudes which were so long his free home are still at hand; a few hours' march will bring him back to them once more. The whites offer him a sum which seems to him considerable for the half-cleared ground whence he obtains sustenance with difficulty. This money of the Europeans may possibly enable him to live a happy and tranquil life far away from them; and he quits the plow, resumes his native arms, and returns to the wilderness forever.[19] The

[19] This destructive influence of highly civilized nations upon others which are less so has been observed among the Europeans themselves. About a century ago the French founded the town of Vincennes on the Wabash, in the middle of the wilderness; and they lived there in great plenty until the arrival of the American settlers, who first ruined the previous inhabitants by their competition and afterwards purchased their lands at a very low rate. At the time when M. de Volney, from whom I borrow these details, passed through Vincennes, the number of the French was reduced to a hundred individuals, most of whom were about to migrate to Louisiana or to Canada. These French settlers were worthy people, but idle and uninstructed; they had contracted many of the habits of savages. The Americans, who were perhaps their inferiors from a moral point of view, were immeasurably superior to them in intelligence: they were industrious, well informed, well off, and accustomed to govern their own community.

I myself saw in Canada, where the intellectual difference between the two races is less striking, that the English are the masters of commerce and manufacture in the Canadian country, that they spread on all sides and confine the French within limits which scarcely suffice to contain them. In like manner in Louisiana almost all activity in commerce and manufacture centers in the hands of the Anglo-Americans.

But the case of Texas is still more striking: the state of Texas is a part of Mexico and is on the frontier between that country and the United States. In the course of the last few years the

condition of the Creeks and Cherokees, to which I have already alluded, sufficiently corroborates the truth of this sad picture.

The Indians, in the little which they have done, have unquestionably displayed as much natural genius as the peoples of Europe in their greatest undertakings; but nations as well as men require time to learn, whatever may be their intelligence and their zeal. While the savages were endeavoring to civilize themselves, the Europeans continued to surround them on every side and to confine them within narrower limits; the two races gradually met, and they are now in immediate contact with each other. The Indian is already superior to his barbarous parent, but he is still far below his white neighbor. With their resources and acquired knowledge, the Europeans soon appropriated to themselves most of the advantages that the natives might have derived from the possession of the soil: they have settled among them, have purchased land at a low rate, or have occupied it by force, and the Indians have been ruined by a competition which they had not the means of sustaining. They were isolated in their own country, and their race constituted only a little colony of troublesome strangers in the midst of a numerous and dominant people.[20]

Anglo-Americans have penetrated into this province, which is still thinly peopled; they purchase land, they produce the commodities of the country, and supplant the original population. It may easily be foreseen that if Mexico takes no steps to check this change, the province of Texas will very shortly cease to belong to that government.

If the differences, comparatively less obvious, which exist in European civilization lead to similar results, it is easy to understand what must happen when the most perfect European civilization comes in contact with Indian barbarism.

[20] See in the *Legislative Documents* (21st Congress, No. 89) instances of excesses of every kind committed by the whites upon the territory of the Indians, either in taking possession of a part of their lands, until compelled to retire by federal troops, or carrying off their cattle, burning their houses, cutting down their corn, and doing violence to their persons.

The Union has a representative agent continually employed to reside among the Indians; and the report of the Cherokee agent, which is among the documents I have referred to, is almost always favorable to the Indians. "The intrusion of whites," he says, "upon the lands of the Cherokees will cause ruin to the poor, helpless, and inoffensive inhabitants." And he further remarks upon the attempt of the state of Georgia to establish a boundary line for the country of the Cherokees that the line, having been

Washington said in one of his messages to Congress: "We are more enlightened and more powerful than the Indian nations; we are therefore bound in honor to treat them with kindness, and even with generosity." But this virtuous and high-minded policy has not been followed. The rapacity of the settlers is usually backed by the tyranny of the government. Although the Cherokees and the Creeks are established upon territory which they inhabited before the arrival of the Europeans, and although the Americans have frequently treated with them as with foreign nations, the surrounding states have not been willing to acknowledge them as an independent people and have undertaken to subject these children of the woods to Anglo-American magistrates, laws, and customs.[21] Destitution had driven these unfortunate Indians to civilization, and oppression now drives them back to barbarism: many of them abandon the soil which they had begun to clear and return to the habits of savage life.

If we consider the tyrannical measures that have been adopted by the legislatures of the Southern states, the conduct of their governors, and the decrees of their courts of justice, we shall be convinced that the entire expulsion of the Indians is the final result to which all the efforts of their policy are directed. The Americans of that part of the Union look with jealousy upon the lands which the natives still possess;[22] they are aware that these tribes have not yet lost

---

made by the whites alone, and entirely upon *ex parte* evidence of their several rights, was of no validity whatever.

[21] In 1829 the state of Alabama divided the Creek territory into counties and subjected the Indian population to European magistrates.

In 1830 the state of Mississippi assimilated the Choctaws and Chickasaws to the white population and declared that any of them who should take the title of chief would be punished by a fine of 1,000 dollars and a year's imprisonment. When these laws were announced to the Choctaws who inhabited that district, the tribe assembled, their chief communicated to them the intentions of the whites and read to them some of the laws to which it was intended that they should submit, and they unanimously declared that it was better at once to retreat again into the wilds. (Mississippi *Papers*.)

[22] The Georgians, who are so much troubled by the proximity of the Indians, inhabit a territory that does not at present contain more than seven inhabitants to the square mile. In France there are one hundred and sixty-two inhabitants in the same extent of country.

the traditions of savage life, and before civilization has permanently fixed them to the soil it is intended to force them to depart by reducing them to despair. The Creeks and Cherokees, oppressed by the several states, have appealed to the central government, which is by no means insensible to their misfortunes and is sincerely desirous of saving the remnant of the natives and of maintaining them in the free possession of that territory which the Union has guaranteed to them.[23] But when it seeks to carry out this plan, the several states set up a tremendous resistance, and so it makes up its mind not to take the easier way, and to let a few savage tribes perish, since they are already half-decimated, in order not to endanger the safety of the American Union.

But the Federal government, which is not able to protect the Indians, would fain mitigate the hardships of their lot; and with this intention it has undertaken to transport them into remote regions at the public cost.

Between the 33rd and 37th degrees of north latitude lies a vast tract of country that has taken the name of Arkansas, from the principal river that waters it. It is bounded on one side by the confines of Mexico, on the other by the Mississippi. Numberless streams cross it in every direction; the climate is mild and the soil productive, and it is inhabited only by a few wandering hordes of savages. The government of the Union wishes to transport the broken remnants of the indigenous population of the South to the portion of this country that is nearest to Mexico and at a great distance from the American settlements.

We were assured, towards the end of the year 1831, that 10,000 Indians had already gone to the shores of the Arkansas, and fresh detachments were constantly following them. But Congress has been unable to create a unanimous determination in those whom it is disposed to protect. Some, indeed, joyfully consent to quit the seat of oppression; but the most enlightened members of the community refuse to abandon their recent dwellings and their growing crops; they are of opinion that the work of civilization, once inter-

[23] In 1818 Congress appointed commissioners to visit the Arkansas territory, accompanied by a deputation of Creeks, Choctaws, and Chickasaws. This expedition was commanded by Messrs. Kennerly, M'Coy, Wash Hood, and John Bell. See the different reports of the commissioners and their journal in the *Documents of Congress*, No. 87, House of Representatives.

rupted, will never be resumed; they fear that those domestic habits which have been so recently contracted may be irrevocably lost in the midst of a country that is still barbarous and where nothing is prepared for the subsistence of an agricultural people; they know that their entrance into those wilds will be opposed by hostile hordes, and that they have lost the energy of barbarians without having yet acquired the resources of civilization to resist their attacks. Moreover, the Indians readily discover that the settlement which is proposed to them is merely temporary. Who can assure them that they will at length be allowed to dwell in peace in their new retreat? The United States pledges itself to maintain them there, but the territory which they now occupy was formerly secured to them by the most solemn oaths.[24] The American government does not indeed now rob them of their lands, but it allows perpetual encroachments on them. In a few years the same white population that now flocks around them will doubtless track them anew to the solitudes of the Arkansas; they will then be exposed to the same evils, without the same remedies; and as the limits of the earth will at last fail them, their only refuge is the grave.

The Union treats the Indians with less cupidity and violence than the several states, but the two governments are alike deficient in good faith. The states extend what they call the benefits of their laws to the Indians, believing that the tribes will recede rather than submit to them; and the central government, which promises a permanent refuge to these unhappy beings in the West, is well aware of its inability to secure it to them.[25] Thus the tyranny of the states

---

[24] One finds in the treaty made with the Creeks in 1790 this clause: "The United States solemnly guarantee to the Creek nation all their land within the limits of the United States."

The treaty concluded in 1791 with the Cherokees states: "The United States solemnly guarantee to the Cherokee nation all their lands not hereby ceded. If any citizen of the United States, or other settler not of the Indian race, establishes himself upon the territory of the Cherokees, the United States declare that they will withdraw their protection from that individual, and give him up to be punished as the Cherokee nation thinks fit." (Art. 8.)

[25] This does not prevent them from promising in the most solemn manner to do so. See the letter of the President addressed to the Creek Indians, March 23, 1829 (*Proceedings of the Indian Board in the City of New York,* p. 5): "Beyond the great river Mississippi, where a part of your nation has gone, your father

obliges the savages to retire; the Union, by its promises and resources, facilitates their retreat; and these measures tend to precisely the same end.[26]

"By the will of our Father in heaven, the Governor of the whole world," said the Cherokees in their petition to Congress,[27] "the red man of America has become small, and the white man great and renowned. When the ancestors of the people of these United States first came to the shores of America, they found the red man strong: though he was ignorant and savage, yet he received them kindly and gave them dry land to rest their weary feet. They met in peace and shook hands in token of friendship. Whatever the white man wanted and asked of the Indian, the latter willingly gave. At that time the Indian was the lord, and the white man the suppliant. But now the scene has changed. The strength of the red man has become weakness. As his neighbors increased in numbers, his power became less and less; and now, of the many and powerful tribes who once covered these United States, only a few are to be seen—a few whom a sweeping pestilence has left. The Northern tribes, who were once so numerous and powerful, are now nearly extinct. Thus it has happened to the red man in America. Shall we, who are remnants, share the same fate?

"The land on which we stand we have received as an in-

---

has provided a country large enough for all of you, and he advises you to remove to it. There your white brothers will not trouble you; they will have no claim to the land, and you can live upon it, you and all your children, as long as the grass grows, or the water runs, in peace and plenty. *It will be yours forever.*"
The Secretary of War in a letter written to the Cherokees, April 18, 1829, declares to them that they cannot expect to retain possession of the lands at that time occupied by them, but gives them the most positive assurance of uninterrupted peace if they would remove beyond the Mississippi (ibid., p. 6); as if the power which could not grant them protection then would be able to afford it to them hereafter!

[26] To obtain a correct idea of the policy pursued by the several states and the Union with respect to the Indians, it is necessary to consult: (1) "The Laws of the Colonial and State Governments relating to the Indian Inhabitants" (see *Legislative Documents,* 21st Congress, No. 319); (2) "The Laws of the Union on the same subject, and especially that of March 30th, 1802" (these laws will be found in the work of Mr. Story entitled *Laws of the United States*); (3) *"The Report of Mr. Cass, Secretary of War,* relative to Indian Affairs, November 29th, 1823."

[27] November 19, 1829. This item is literally translated.

heritance from our fathers, who possessed it from time immemorial, as a gift from our common Father in heaven. They bequeathed it to us as their children, and we have sacredly kept it, as containing the remains of our beloved men. This right of inheritance we have never ceded nor ever forfeited. Permit us to ask what better right can the people have to a country than the right of inheritance and immemorial peaceable possession? We know it is said of late by the state of Georgia and by the Executive of the United States that we have forfeited this right; but we think this is said gratuitously. At what time have we made the forfeit? What great crime have we committed whereby we must forever be divested of our country and rights? Was it when we were hostile to the United States and took part with the King of Great Britain during the struggle for independence? If so, why was not this forfeiture declared in the first treaty of peace between the United States and our beloved men? Why was not such an article as the following inserted in the treaty: 'The United States give peace to the Cherokees, but, for the part they took in the late war, declare them to be but tenants at will, to be removed when the convenience of the states within those chartered limits they live shall require it'? That was the proper time to assume such a possession. But it was not thought of; nor would our forefathers have agreed to any treaty whose tendency was to deprive them of their rights and their country."

Such is the language of the Indians; what they say is true; what they foresee seems inevitable. From whichever side we consider the destinies of the aborigines of North America, their calamities appear irremediable: if they continue barbarous, they are forced to retire; if they attempt to civilize themselves, the contact of a more civilized community subjects them to oppression and destitution. They perish if they continue to wander from waste to waste, and if they attempt to settle they still must perish. The assistance of Europeans is necessary to instruct them, but the approach of Europeans corrupts and repels them into savage life. They refuse to change their habits as long as their solitudes are their own, and it is too late to change them when at last they are forced to submit.

The Spaniards pursued the Indians with bloodhounds,

like wild beasts; they sacked the New World like a city taken by storm, with no discernment or compassion; but destruction must cease at last and frenzy has a limit: the remnant of the Indian population which had escaped the massacre mixed with its conquerors and adopted in the end their religion and their manners.[28] The conduct of the Americans of the United States towards the aborigines is characterized, on the other hand, by a singular attachment to the formalities of law. Provided that the Indians retain their barbarous condition, the Americans take no part in their affairs; they treat them as independent nations and do not possess themselves of their hunting-grounds without a treaty of purchase; and if an Indian nation happens to be so encroached upon as to be unable to subsist upon their territory, they kindly take them by the hand and transport them to a grave far from the land of their fathers.

The Spaniards were unable to exterminate the Indian race by those unparalleled atrocities which brand them with indelible shame, nor did they succeed even in wholly depriving it of its rights; but the Americans of the United States have accomplished this twofold purpose with singular felicity, tranquilly, legally, philanthropically, without shedding blood, and without violating a single great principle of morality in the eyes of the world.[29] It is impossible to destroy men with more respect for the laws of humanity.

[28] The honor of this result, however, is by no means due to the Spaniards. If the Indian tribes had not been tillers of the ground at the time of the arrival of the Europeans, they would unquestionably have been destroyed in South as well as in North America.

[29] See, among other documents, the *Report* made by Mr. Bell in the name of the Committee on Indian Affairs, February 24, 1830, in which it is most logically established and most learnedly proved that "the fundamental principle, that the Indians had no right, by virtue of their ancient possession, either of soil or sovereignty, has never been abandoned either expressly or by implication."

In perusing this *Report*, which is evidently drawn up by a skillful hand, one is astonished at the facility with which the author gets rid of all arguments founded upon reason and natural right, which he designates as abstract and theoretical principles. The more I contemplate the difference between civilized and uncivilized man with regard to the principles of justice, the more I observe that the former contests the foundation of those rights, which the latter simply violates.

SITUATION OF THE BLACK POPULATION IN THE UNITED STATES,[30] AND DANGERS WITH WHICH ITS PRESENCE THREATENS THE WHITES. *Why it is more difficult to abolish slavery, and to efface all vestiges of it among the moderns than it was among the ancients—In the United States the prejudices of the whites against the blacks seem to increase in proportion as slavery is abolished—Situation of the Negroes in the Northern and Southern states— Why the Americans abolish slavery—Servitude, which debases the slave, impoverishes the master—Contrast between the left and the right bank of the Ohio—To what attributable—The black race, as well as slavery, recedes towards the South—Explanation of this fact— Difficulties attendant upon the abolition of slavery in the South—Dangers to come—General anxiety—Foundation of a black colony in Africa—Why the Americans of the South increase the hardships of slavery while they are distressed at its continuance.*

THE Indians will perish in the same isolated condition in which they have lived, but the destiny of the Negroes is in some measure interwoven with that of the Europeans. These two races are fastened to each other without intermingling; and they are alike unable to separate entirely or to combine. The most formidable of all the ills that threaten the future of the Union arises from the presence of a black population upon its territory; and in contemplating the cause of the present embarrassments, or the future dangers of the United States, the observer is invariably led to this as a primary fact.

[30] Before treating of this matter, I would call the reader's attention to a book of which I spoke at the beginning of this work, and which is about to be published. The chief aim of M. Gustave de Beaumont, my traveling-companion, was to inform Frenchmen of the position of the Negroes among the white population in the United States. M. de Beaumont has plumbed the depths of a question which my subject has allowed me merely to touch upon.

His book, the notes to which contain a great number of legislative and historical documents, extremely valuable and heretofore unpublished, furthermore presents pictures the vividness of which is ample proof of their verity. M. de Beaumont's book should be read by all those who would know into what excesses men may be driven when once they attempt to go against natural and human laws.

Generally speaking, men must make great and unceasing efforts before permanent evils are created; but there is one calamity which penetrated furtively into the world, and which was at first scarcely distinguishable amid the ordinary abuses of power: it originated with an individual whose name history has not preserved; it was wafted like some accursed germ upon a portion of the soil; but it afterwards nurtured itself, grew without effort, and spread naturally with the society to which it belonged. This calamity is slavery. Christianity suppressed slavery, but the Christians of the sixteenth century re-established it, as an exception, indeed, to their social system, and restricted to one of the races of mankind; but the wound thus inflicted upon humanity, though less extensive, was far more difficult to cure.

It is important to make an accurate distinction between slavery itself and its consequences. The immediate evils produced by slavery were very nearly the same in antiquity as they are among the moderns, but the consequences of these evils were different. The slave among the ancients belonged to the same race as his master, and was often the superior of the two in education[31] and intelligence. Freedom was the only distinction between them; and when freedom was conferred, they were easily confounded together. The ancients, then, had a very simple means of ridding themselves of slavery and its consequences: that of enfranchisement; and they succeeded as soon as they adopted this measure generally. Not but that in ancient states the vestiges of servitude subsisted for some time after servitude itself was abolished. There is a natural prejudice that prompts men to despise whoever has been their inferior long after he has become their equal; and the real inequality that is produced by fortune or by law is always succeeded by an imaginary inequality that is implanted in the manners of the people. But among the ancients this secondary consequence of slavery had a natural limit; for the freedman bore so entire a resemblance to those born free that it soon became impossible to distinguish him from them.

The greatest difficulty in antiquity was that of altering the

[31] It is well known that several of the most distinguished authors of antiquity, and among them Æsop and Terence, were, or had been, slaves. Slaves were not always taken from barbarous nations; the chances of war reduced highly civilized men to servitude.

law; among the moderns it is that of altering the customs, and as far as we are concerned, the real obstacles begin where those of the ancients left off. This arises from the circumstance that among the moderns the abstract and transient fact of slavery is fatally united with the physical and permanent fact of color. The tradition of slavery dishonors the race, and the peculiarity of the race perpetuates the tradition of slavery. No African has ever voluntarily emigrated to the shores of the New World, whence it follows that all the blacks who are now found there are either slaves or freedmen. Thus the Negro transmits the eternal mark of his ignominy to all his descendants; and although the law may abolish slavery, God alone can obliterate the traces of its existence.

The modern slave differs from his master not only in his condition but in his origin. You may set the Negro free, but you cannot make him otherwise than an alien to the European. Nor is this all; we scarcely acknowledge the common features of humanity in this stranger whom slavery has brought among us. His physiognomy is to our eyes hideous, his understanding weak, his tastes low; and we are almost inclined to look upon him as a being intermediate between man and the brutes.[32] The moderns, then, after they have abolished slavery, have three prejudices to contend against, which are less easy to attack and far less easy to conquer than the mere fact of servitude: the prejudice of the master, the prejudice of the race, and the prejudice of color.

It is difficult for us, who have had the good fortune to be born among men like ourselves by nature and our equals by law, to conceive the irreconcilable differences that separate the Negro from the European in America. But we may derive some faint notion of them from analogy. France was formerly a country in which numerous inequalities existed that had been created by law. Nothing can be more fictitious than a purely legal inferiority, nothing more contrary to the instinct of mankind than these permanent divisions established between beings evidently similar. Yet these divisions existed for ages; they still exist in many places; and

[32] To induce the whites to abandon the opinion they have conceived of the moral and intellectual inferiority of their former slaves, the Negroes must change; but as long as this opinion persists, they cannot change.

everywhere they have left imaginary vestiges, which time alone can efface. If it be so difficult to root out an inequality that originates solely in the law, how are those distinctions to be destroyed which seem to be based upon the immutable laws of Nature herself? When I remember the extreme difficulty with which aristocratic bodies, of whatever nature they may be, are commingled with the mass of the people, and the exceeding care which they take to preserve for ages the ideal boundaries of their caste inviolate, I despair of seeing an aristocracy disappear which is founded upon visible and indelible signs. Those who hope that the Europeans will ever be amalgamated with the Negroes appear to me to delude themselves. I am not led to any such conclusion by my reason or by the evidence of facts. Hitherto wherever the whites have been the most powerful, they have held the blacks in degradation or in slavery; wherever the Negroes have been strongest, they have destroyed the whites: this has been the only balance that has ever taken place between the two races.

I see that in a certain portion of the territory of the United States at the present day the legal barrier which separated the two races is falling away, but not that which exists in the manners of the country; slavery recedes, but the prejudice to which it has given birth is immovable. Whoever has inhabited the United States must have perceived that in those parts of the Union in which the Negroes are no longer slaves they have in no wise drawn nearer to the whites. On the contrary, the prejudice of race appears to be stronger in the states that have abolished slavery than in those where it still exists; and nowhere is it so intolerant as in those states where servitude has never been known.

It is true that in the North of the Union marriages may be legally contracted between Negroes and whites; but public opinion would stigmatize as infamous a man who should connect himself with a Negress, and it would be difficult to cite a single instance of such a union. The electoral franchise has been conferred upon the Negroes in almost all the states in which slavery has been abolished, but if they come forward to vote, their lives are in danger. If oppressed, they may bring an action at law, but they will find none but whites among their judges; and although they may legally serve as jurors, prejudice repels them from that office. The same schools do not receive the children of the black and of the European. In the theaters gold cannot procure a seat for the servile race beside their former masters; in the hospitals they lie apart; and although they are allowed to invoke the same God as the whites, it must be at a different altar and in their own churches, with their own clergy. The gates of heaven are not closed against them, but their inferiority is continued to the very confines of the other world. When the Negro dies, his bones are cast aside, and the distinction of condition prevails even in the equality of death. Thus the Negro is free, but he can share neither the rights, nor the pleasures, nor the labor, nor the afflictions, nor the tomb of him whose equal he has been declared to be; and he cannot meet him upon fair terms in life or in death.

In the South, where slavery still exists, the Negroes are less carefully kept apart; they sometimes share the labors and the recreations of the whites; the whites consent to inter-mix with them to a certain extent, and although legislation treats them more harshly, the habits of the people are more tolerant and compassionate. In the South the master is not afraid to raise his slave to his own standing, because he knows that he can in a moment reduce him to the dust at pleasure. In the North the white no longer distinctly per-ceives the barrier that separates him from the degraded race, and he shuns the Negro with the more pertinacity since he fears lest they should some day be confounded together.

Among the Americans of the South, Nature sometimes reasserts her rights and restores a transient equality between the blacks and the whites; but in the North pride restrains the most imperious of human passions. The American of the Northern states would perhaps allow the Negress to share his licentious pleasures if the laws of his country did not declare that she may aspire to be the legitimate partner of his bed, but he recoils with horror from her who might be-come his wife.

Thus it is in the United States that the prejudice which repels the Negroes seems to increase in proportion as they are emancipated, and inequality is sanctioned by the man-ners while it is effaced from the laws of the country. But if the relative position of the two races that inhabit the United States is such as I have described, why have the Americans abolished slavery in the North of the Union, why do they maintain it in the South, and why do they aggravate its hardships? The answer is easily given. It is not for the good of the Negroes, but for that of the whites, that measures are taken to abolish slavery in the United States.

The first Negroes were imported into Virginia about the year 1621.[33] In America, therefore, as well as in the rest of the globe, slavery originated in the South. Thence it spread from one settlement to another; but the number of slaves diminished towards the Northern states, and the Negro population was always very limited in New England.[34]

A century had scarcely elapsed since the foundation of the colonies when the attention of the planters was struck by the extraordinary fact that the provinces which were comparatively destitute of slaves increased in population, in wealth, and in prosperity more rapidly than those which contained many of them. In the former, however, the inhabitants were obliged to cultivate the soil themselves or by hired laborers; in the latter they were furnished with hands for which they paid no wages. Yet though labor and expense were on the one side and ease with economy on the other, the former had the more advantageous system. This result seemed the more difficult to explain since the settlers, who all belonged to the same European race, had the same habits, the same civilization, the same laws, and their shades of difference were extremely slight.

Time, however, continued to advance, and the Anglo-Americans, spreading beyond the coasts of the Atlantic

[33] See Beverley's *History of Virginia*. See also, in Jefferson's *Memoirs*, some curious details concerning the introduction of Negroes into Virginia, and the first Act that prohibited the importation of them, in 1778.

[34] The number of slaves was less considerable in the North, but the advantages resulting from slavery were not more contested there than in the South. In 1740 the legislature of the state of New York declared that the direct importation of slaves ought to be encouraged as much as possible, and smuggling severely punished, in order not to discourage the fair trader. (Kent's *Commentaries*, Vol. II, p. 206.) Curious researches by Belknap upon slavery in New England are to be found in the *Historical Collections of Massachusetts*, Vol. IV, p. 193. It appears that Negroes were introduced there in 1630, but that the legislation and manners of the people were opposed to slavery from the first. See also, in the same work, the manner in which public opinion, and afterwards the laws, finally put an end to slavery.

Ocean, penetrated farther and farther into the solitudes of the West. They met there with a new soil and an unwonted climate; they had to overcome obstacles of the most various character; their races intermingled, the inhabitants of the South going up towards the North, those of the North descending to the South. But in the midst of all these causes the same result occurred at every step; in general, the colonies in which there were no slaves became more populous and more prosperous than those in which slavery flourished. The farther they went, the more was it shown that slavery, which is so cruel to the slave, is prejudicial to the master.

But this truth was most satisfactorily demonstrated when civilization reached the banks of the Ohio. The stream that the Indians had distinguished by the name of Ohio, or the Beautiful River, waters one of the most magnificent valleys which have ever been made the abode of man. Undulating lands extend upon both shores of the Ohio, whose soil affords inexhaustible treasures to the laborer; on either bank the air is equally wholesome and the climate mild; and each of them forms the extreme frontier of a vast state: that which follows the numerous windings of the Ohio upon the left is called Kentucky; that upon the right bears the name of the river. These two states differ only in a single respect: Kentucky has admitted slavery, but the state of Ohio has prohibited the existence of slaves within its borders.[35] Thus the traveler who floats down the current of the Ohio to the spot where that river falls into the Mississippi may be said to sail between liberty and servitude; and a transient inspection of surrounding objects will convince him which of the two is more favorable to humanity.

Upon the left bank of the stream the population is sparse; from time to time one descries a troop of slaves loitering in the half-desert fields; the primeval forest reappears at every turn; society seems to be asleep, man to be idle, and nature alone offers a scene of activity and life.

From the right bank, on the contrary, a confused hum is heard, which proclaims afar the presence of industry; the fields are covered with abundant harvests; the elegance of the dwellings announces the taste and activity of the labor-

[35] Not only is slavery prohibited in Ohio, but no free Negroes are allowed to enter the territory of that state or to hold property in it. See the statutes of Ohio.

ers; and man appears to be in the enjoyment of that wealth and contentment which is the reward of labor.[36]

The state of Kentucky was founded in 1775, the state of Ohio only twelve years later; but twelve years are more in America than half a century in Europe; and at the present day the population of Ohio exceeds that of Kentucky by two hundred and fifty thousand souls.[37] These different effects of slavery and freedom may readily be understood; and they suffice to explain many of the differences which we notice between the civilization of antiquity and that of our own time.

Upon the left bank of the Ohio labor is confounded with the idea of slavery, while upon the right bank it is identified with that of prosperity and improvement; on the one side it is degraded, on the other it is honored. On the former territory no white laborers can be found, for they would be afraid of assimilating themselves to the Negroes; all the work is done by slaves; on the latter no one is idle, for the white population extend their activity and intelligence to every kind of employment. Thus the men whose task it is to cultivate the rich soil of Kentucky are ignorant and apathetic, while those who are active and enlightened either do nothing or pass over into Ohio, where they may work without shame.

It is true that in Kentucky the planters are not obliged to pay the slaves whom they employ, but they derive small profits from their labor, while the wages paid to free workmen would be returned with interest in the value of their services. The free workman is paid, but he does his work quicker than the slave; and rapidity of execution is one of the great elements of economy. The white sells his services, but they are purchased only when they may be useful; the black can claim no remuneration for his toil, but the expense of his maintenance is perpetual; he must be supported

[36] The activity of Ohio is not confined to individuals, but the undertakings of the state are surprisingly great: a canal has been established between Lake Erie and the Ohio, by means of which the valley of the Mississippi communicates with the river of the North, and the European commodities which arrive at New York may be forwarded by water to New Orleans across five hundred leagues of continent.

[37] The exact numbers given by the census of 1830 were: Kentucky, 688,844; Ohio, 937,679.

in his old age as well as in manhood, in his profitless infancy as well as in the productive years of youth, in sickness as well as in health. Payment must equally be made in order to obtain the services of either class of men: the free workman receives his wages in money; the slave in education, in food, in care, and in clothing. The money which a master spends in the maintenance of his slaves goes gradually and in detail, so that it is scarcely perceived; the salary of the free workman is paid in a round sum and appears to enrich only him who receives it; but in the end the slave has cost more than the free servant, and his labor is less productive.[38]

The influence of slavery extends still further: it affects the character of the master and imparts a peculiar tendency to his ideas and tastes. Upon both banks of the Ohio the character of the inhabitants is enterprising and energetic, but this vigor is very differently exercised in the two states. The white inhabitant of Ohio, obliged to subsist by his own exertions, regards temporal prosperity as the chief aim of his existence; and as the country which he occupies presents inexhaustible resources to his industry, and ever varying lures to his activity, his acquisitive ardor surpasses the ordinary limits of human cupidity: he is tormented by the desire of wealth, and he boldly enters upon every path that fortune opens to him; he becomes a sailor, a pioneer, an artisan, or a cultivator with the same indifference, and supports with equal constancy the fatigues and the dangers incidental to these various professions; the resources of his intelligence are astonishing, and his avidity in the pursuit of gain amounts to a species of heroism.

[38] Independently of these causes, which, wherever free workmen abound, render their labor more productive and more economical than that of slaves, another cause may be pointed out which is peculiar to the United States: sugar-cane has hitherto been cultivated with success only upon the banks of the Mississippi, near the mouth of that river in the Gulf of Mexico. In Louisiana the cultivation of sugar-cane is exceedingly lucrative; nowhere does a laborer earn so much by his work; and as there is always a certain relation between the cost of production and the value of the produce, the price of slaves is very high in Louisiana. But Louisiana is one of the federal states, and slaves may be carried thither from all parts of the Union; the price given for slaves in New Orleans consequently raises the value of slaves in all the other markets. The consequence of this is that in the regions where the land is less productive, the cost of slave labor is still very considerable, which gives an additional advantage to the competition of free labor.

But the Kentuckian scorns not only labor but all the undertakings that labor promotes; as he lives in an idle independence, his tastes are those of an idle man; money has lost a portion of its value in his eyes; he covets wealth much less than pleasure and excitement; and the energy which his neighbor devotes to gain turns with him to a passionate love of field sports and military exercises; he delights in violent bodily exertion, he is familiar with the use of arms, and is accustomed from a very early age to expose his life in single combat. Thus slavery prevents the whites not only from becoming opulent, but even from desiring to become so.

As the same causes have been continually producing opposite effects for the last two centuries in the British colonies of North America, they have at last established a striking difference between the commercial capacity of the inhabitants of the South and those of the North. At the present day it is only the Northern states that are in possession of shipping, manufactures, railroads, and canals. This difference is perceptible not only in comparing the North with the South, but in comparing the several Southern states. Almost all those who carry on commercial operations or endeavor to turn slave labor to account in the most southern districts of the Union have emigrated from the North. The natives of the Northern states are constantly spreading over that portion of the American territory where they have less to fear from competition; they discover resources there which escaped the notice of the inhabitants; and as they comply with a system which they do not approve, they succeed in turning it to better advantage than those who first founded and who still maintain it.

Were I inclined to continue this parallel, I could easily prove that almost all the differences which may be noticed between the characters of the Americans in the Southern and in the Northern states have originated in slavery; but this would divert me from my subject, and my present intention is not to point out all the consequences of servitude, but those effects which it has produced upon the material prosperity of the countries that have admitted it.

The influence of slavery upon the production of wealth must have been very imperfectly known in antiquity, as slavery then obtained throughout the civilized world, and the nations that were unacquainted with it were barbarians.

And, indeed, Christianity abolished slavery only by advocating the claims of the slave; at the present time it may be attacked in the name of the master, and upon this point interest is reconciled with morality.

As these truths became apparent in the United States, slavery receded before the progress of experience. Servitude had begun in the South and had thence spread towards the North, but it now retires again. Freedom, which started from the North, now descends uninterruptedly towards the South. Among the great states, Pennsylvania now constitutes the extreme limit of slavery to the North; but even within those limits the slave system is shaken: Maryland, which is immediately below Pennsylvania, is preparing for its abolition; and Virginia, which comes next to Maryland, is already discussing its utility and its dangers.[39]

No great change takes place in human institutions without involving among its causes the law of inheritance. When the law of primogeniture obtained in the South, each family was represented by a wealthy individual, who was neither compelled nor induced to labor; and he was surrounded, as by parasitic plants, by the other members of his family, who were then excluded by law from sharing the common inheritance, and who led the same kind of life as himself. The same thing then occurred in all the families of the South which still happens in the noble families of some countries in Europe: namely, that the younger sons remain in the same state of idleness as their elder brother, without being as rich as he is. This identical result seems to be produced in Europe and in America by wholly analogous causes. In the South of the United States the whole race of whites formed an aristocratic body, headed by a certain number of privileged individuals, whose wealth was permanent and whose leisure was hereditary. These leaders of the American

[39] A peculiar reason contributes to detach the two last-mentioned states from the cause of slavery. The former wealth of this part of the Union was principally derived from the cultivation of tobacco. This cultivation is specially suited to slave labor; but within the last few years the market price of tobacco has diminished, while the value of the slaves remains the same. Thus the ratio between the cost of production and the value of the produce is changed. The inhabitants of Maryland and Virginia are therefore more disposed than they were thirty years ago to give up slave labor in the cultivation of tobacco, or to give up slavery and tobacco at the same time.

nobility kept alive the traditional prejudices of the white race, in the body of which they were the representatives, and maintained idleness in honor. This aristocracy contained many who were poor, but none who would work; its members preferred want to labor; consequently Negro laborers and slaves met with no competition; and, whatever opinion might be entertained as to the utility of their industry, it was necessary to employ them, since there was no one else to work.

No sooner was the law of primogeniture abolished than fortunes began to diminish and all the families of the country were simultaneously reduced to a state in which labor became necessary to existence; several of them have since entirely disappeared, and all of them learned to look forward to the time when it would be necessary for everyone to provide for his own wants. Wealthy individuals are still to be met with, but they no longer constitute a compact and hereditary body, nor have they been able to adopt a line of conduct in which they could persevere and which they could infuse into all ranks of society. The prejudice that stigmatized labor was, in the first place, abandoned by common consent, the number of needy men was increased, and the needy were allowed to gain a subsistence by labor without blushing for their toil. Thus one of the most immediate consequences of the equal division of estates has been to create a class of free laborers. As soon as competition began between the free laborer and the slave, the inferiority of the latter became manifest and slavery was attacked in its fundamental principle, which is the interest of the master.

As slavery recedes, the black population follows its retrograde course and returns with it towards those tropical regions whence it originally came. However singular this fact may at first appear to be, it may readily be explained. Although the Americans abolish the principle of slavery, they do not set their slaves free. To illustrate this remark, I will quote the example of the state of New York. In 1788 this state prohibited the sale of slaves within its limits, which was an indirect method of prohibiting the importation of them. Thenceforward the number of Negroes could only increase according to the ratio of the natural increase of population. But eight years later, a more decisive measure was taken, and it was enacted that all children born of slave parents after the 4th of July 1799 should be free. No increase could then take place, and although slaves still existed, slavery might be said to be abolished.

As soon as a Northern state thus prohibited the importation, no slaves were brought from the South to be sold in its markets. On the other hand, as the sale of slaves was forbidden in that state, an owner could no longer get rid of his slave (who thus became a burdensome possession) otherwise than by transporting him to the South. But when a Northern state declared that the son of the slave should be born free, the slave lost a large portion of his market value, since his posterity was no longer included in the bargain, and the owner had then a strong interest in transporting him to the South. Thus the same law prevents the slaves of the South from coming North and drives those of the North to the South.

But there is another cause more powerful than any that I have described. The want of free hands is felt in a state in proportion as the number of slaves decreases. But in proportion as labor is performed by free hands, slave labor becomes less productive; and the slave is then a useless or onerous possession, whom it is important to export to the South, where the same competition is not to be feared. Thus the abolition of slavery does not set the slave free, but merely transfers him to another master, and from the North to the South.

The emancipated Negroes and those born after the abolition of slavery do not, indeed, migrate from the North to the South; but their situation with regard to the Europeans is not unlike that of the Indians; they remain half civilized and deprived of their rights in the midst of a population that is far superior to them in wealth and knowledge, where they are exposed to the tyranny of the laws[40] and the intolerance of the people. On some accounts they are still more to be pitied than the Indians, since they are haunted by the reminiscence of slavery, and they cannot claim possession of any

---

[40] The states in which slavery is abolished usually do what they can to render their territory disagreeable to the Negroes as a place of residence; and as a kind of emulation exists between the different states in this respect, the unhappy blacks can only choose the least of the evils that beset them.

part of the soil. Many of them perish miserably,[41] and the rest congregate in the great towns, where they perform the meanest offices and lead a wretched and precarious existence.

If, moreover, the number of Negroes were to continue to grow in the same proportion during the period when they did not have their liberty, yet, with the number of the whites increasing at a double rate after the abolition of slavery, the Negroes would soon be swallowed up in the midst of an alien population.

A district which is cultivated by slaves is in general less populous than a district cultivated by free labor; moreover, America is still a new country, and a state is therefore not half peopled when it abolishes slavery. No sooner is an end put to slavery than the want of free labor is felt, and a crowd of enterprising adventurers immediately arrives from all parts of the country, who hasten to profit by the fresh resources which are then opened to industry. The soil is soon divided among them, and a family of white settlers takes possession of each portion. Besides, European immigration is exclusively directed to the free states; for what would a poor immigrant do who crosses the Atlantic in search of ease and happiness if he were to land in a country where labor is stigmatized as degrading?

Thus the white population grows by its natural increase, and at the same time by the immense influx of immigrants; while the black population receives no immigrants and is upon its decline. The proportion that existed between the two races is soon inverted. The Negroes constitute a scanty remnant, a poor tribe of vagrants, lost in the midst of an immense people who own the land; and the presence of the blacks is only marked by the injustice and the hardships of which they are the victims.

In several of the Western states the Negro race never made its appearance, and in all the Northern states it is

[41] There is a great difference between the mortality of the blacks and of the whites in the states in which slavery is abolished; from 1820 to 1831 only one out of forty-two individuals of the white population died in Philadelphia; but one out of twenty-one of the black population died in the same time. The mortality is by no means so great among the Negroes who are still slaves. (See Emerson's *Medical Statistics*, p. 28.)

rapidly declining. Thus the great question of its future condition is confined within a narrow circle, where it becomes less formidable, though not more easy of solution. The more we descend towards the South, the more difficult it becomes to abolish slavery with advantage; and this arises from several physical causes which it is important to point out.

The first of these causes is the climate: it is well known that, in proportion as Europeans approach the tropics, labor becomes more difficult to them. Many of the Americans even assert that within a certain latitude it is fatal to them, while the Negroes can work there without danger;[42] but I do not think that this opinion, which is so favorable to the indolence of the inhabitants of the South, is confirmed by experience. The southern parts of the Union are not hotter than the south of Italy and of Spain;[43] and it may be asked why the European cannot work as well there as in the latter two countries. If slavery has been abolished in Italy and in Spain without causing the destruction of the masters, why should not the same thing take place in the Union? I cannot believe that nature has prohibited the Europeans in Georgia and the Floridas, under pain of death, from raising the means of subsistence from the soil; but their labor would unquestionably be more irksome and less productive[44] to them than to the inhabitants of New England. As the free workman thus loses a portion of his superiority over the slave in the Southern states, there are fewer inducements to abolish slavery.

All the plants of Europe grow in the northern parts of the Union; the South has special products of its own. It has been observed that slave labor is a very expensive method of cul-

[42] This is true of the places in which rice is cultivated; rice-fields, which are unhealthful in all countries, are particularly dangerous in those regions which are exposed to the rays of a tropical sun. Europeans would not find it easy to cultivate the soil in that part of the New World if they insisted on making it produce rice; but may they not exist without growing rice?

[43] These states are nearer to the equator than Italy and Spain, but the temperature of the continent of America is much lower than that of Europe.

[44] The Spanish government formerly caused a certain number of peasants from the Azores to be transported into a district of Louisiana called Attakapas. Slavery was not introduced among them; it was an experiment. These settlers still cultivate the soil without the assistance of slaves, but their industry is so sluggish as scarcely to supply their most necessary wants.

tivating cereal grain. The farmer of grainland in a country where slavery is unknown habitually retains only a small number of laborers in his service, and at seed-time and harvest he hires additional hands, who live at his cost for only a short period. But the agriculturist in a slave state is obliged to keep a large number of slaves the whole year round in order to sow his fields and to gather in his crops, although their services are required only for a few weeks; for slaves are unable to wait till they are hired and to subsist by their own labor in the meantime, like free laborers; in order to have their services, they must be bought. Slavery, independently of its general disadvantages, is therefore still more inapplicable to countries in which grain is cultivated than to those which produce crops of a different kind. The cultivation of tobacco, of cotton, and especially of sugar-cane demands, on the other hand, unremitting attention; and women and children are employed in it, whose services are of little use in the cultivation of wheat. Thus slavery is naturally more fitted to the countries from which these productions are derived.

Tobacco, cotton, and sugar-cane are exclusively grown in the South, and they form the principal sources of the wealth of those states. If slavery were abolished, the inhabitants of the South would be driven to this alternative: they must either change their system of cultivation, and then they would come into competition with the more active and more experienced inhabitants of the North; or, if they continued to cultivate the same produce without slave labor, they would have to support the competition of the other states of the South, which might still retain their slaves. Thus peculiar reasons for maintaining slavery exist in the South which do not operate in the North.

But there is yet another motive, which is more cogent than all the others: the South might, indeed, rigorously speaking, abolish slavery; but how should it rid its territory of the black population? Slaves and slavery are driven from the North by the same law; but this twofold result cannot be hoped for in the South.

In proving that slavery is more natural and more advantageous in the South than in the North, I have shown that the number of slaves must be far greater in the former. It was to the Southern settlements that the first Africans were brought, and it is there that the greatest number of them have always been imported. As we advance towards the South, the prejudice that sanctions idleness increases in power. In the states nearest to the tropics there is not a single white laborer; the Negroes are consequently much more numerous in the South than in the North. And, as I have already observed, this disproportion increases daily, since the Negroes are transferred to one part of the Union as soon as slavery is abolished in the other. Thus the black population augments in the South, not only by its natural fecundity, but by the compulsory emigration of the Negroes from the North; and the African race has causes of increase in the South very analogous to those which accelerate the growth of the European race in the North.

In the state of Maine there is one Negro in three hundred inhabitants; in Massachusetts, one in one hundred; in New York, two in one hundred; in Pennsylvania, three in the same number; in Maryland, thirty-four; in Virginia, forty-two; and lastly, in South Carolina,[45] fifty-five per cent of the inhabitants are black. Such was the proportion of the black population to the whites in the year 1830. But this proportion is perpetually changing, as it constantly decreases in the North and augments in the South.

It is evident that the most southern states of the Union cannot abolish slavery without incurring great dangers, which the North had no reason to apprehend when it emancipated its black population. I have already shown how the Northern states made the transition from slavery to freedom, by keeping the present generation in chains and setting their descendants free; by this means the Negroes are only gradually introduced into society; and while the men who

[45] We find it asserted in an American work entitled *Letters on the Colonization Society,* by Mr. Carey (1833): "That for the last forty years, the black race has increased more rapidly than the white race in the State of South Carolina; and that, if we take the average population of the five States of the South into which slaves were first introduced, viz. Maryland, Virginia, South Carolina, North Carolina, and Georgia, we shall find that from 1790 to 1830 the whites have augmented in the proportion of 80 to 100, and the blacks in that of 100 to 112."

In the United States in 1830 the population of the two races stood as follows: States where slavery is abolished, 6,565,434 whites; 120,520 blacks. Slave States, 3,960,814 whites; 2,208,102 blacks.

might abuse their freedom are kept in servitude, those who are emancipated may learn the art of being free before they become their own masters. But it would be difficult to apply this method in the South. To declare that all the Negroes born after a certain period shall be free is to introduce the principle and the notion of liberty into the heart of slavery; the blacks whom the law thus maintains in a state of slavery from which their children are delivered are astonished at so unequal a fate, and their astonishment is only the prelude to their impatience and irritation. Thenceforward slavery loses, in their eyes, that kind of moral power which it derived from time and habit; it is reduced to a mere palpable abuse of force. The Northern states had nothing to fear from the contrast, because in them the blacks were few in number, and the white population was very considerable. But if this faint dawn of freedom were to show two millions of men their true position, the oppressors would have reason to tremble. After having enfranchised the children of their slaves, the Europeans of the Southern states would very shortly be obliged to extend the same benefit to the whole black population.

In the North, as I have already remarked, a twofold migration ensues upon the abolition of slavery, or even precedes that event when circumstances have rendered it probable: the slaves quit the country to be transported southwards; and the whites of the Northern states, as well as the immigrants from Europe, hasten to fill their place. But these two causes cannot operate in the same manner in the Southern states. On the one hand, the mass of slaves is too great to allow any expectation of their being removed from the country; and on the other hand, the Europeans and Anglo-Americans of the North are afraid to come to inhabit a country in which labor has not yet been reinstated in its rightful honors. Besides, they very justly look upon the states in which the number of the Negroes equals or exceeds that of the whites as exposed to very great dangers; and they refrain from turning their activity in that direction.

Thus the inhabitants of the South, while abolishing slavery, would not be able, like their Northern countrymen, to initiate the slaves gradually into a state of freedom; they have no means of perceptibly diminishing the black population, and they would remain unsupported to repress its excesses. Thus in the course of a few years a great people of free Negroes would exist in the heart of a white nation of equal size.

The same abuses of power that now maintain slavery would then become the source of the most alarming perils to the white population of the South. At the present time the descendants of the Europeans are the sole owners of the land and the absolute masters of all labor; they alone possess wealth, knowledge, and arms. The black is destitute of all these advantages, but can subsist without them because he is a slave. If he were free, and obliged to provide for his own subsistence, would it be possible for him to remain without these things and to support life? Or would not the very instruments of the present superiority of the white while slavery exists expose him to a thousand dangers if it were abolished?

As long as the Negro remains a slave, he may be kept in a condition not far removed from that of the brutes; but with his liberty he cannot but acquire a degree of instruction that will enable him to appreciate his misfortunes and to discern a remedy for them. Moreover, there exists a singular principle of relative justice which is firmly implanted in the human heart. Men are much more forcibly struck by those inequalities which exist within the same class than by those which may be noted between different classes. One can understand slavery, but how allow several millions of citizens to exist under a load of eternal infamy and hereditary wretchedness? In the North the population of freed Negroes feels these hardships and indignities, but its numbers and its powers are small, while in the South it would be numerous and strong.

As soon as it is admitted that the whites and the emancipated blacks are placed upon the same territory in the situation of two foreign communities, it will readily be understood that there are but two chances for the future: the Negroes and the whites must either wholly part or wholly mingle. I have already expressed my conviction as to the latter event.[46] I do not believe that the white and black races

---

[46] This opinion is sanctioned by authorities infinitely weightier than anything that I can say. Thus, for instance, it is stated in the *Memoirs* of Jefferson: "Nothing is more clearly written in the book of destiny than the emancipation of the blacks; and it is

will ever live in any country upon an equal footing. But I believe the difficulty to be still greater in the United States than elsewhere. An isolated individual may surmount the prejudices of religion, of his country, or of his race; and if this individual is a king, he may effect surprising changes in society; but a whole people cannot rise, as it were, above itself. A despot who should subject the Americans and their former slaves to the same yoke might perhaps succeed in commingling their races; but as long as the American democracy remains at the head of affairs, no one will undertake so difficult a task; and it may be foreseen that the freer the white population of the United States becomes, the more isolated will it remain.[47]

I have previously observed that the mixed race is the true bond of union between the Europeans and the Indians; just so, the mulattoes are the true means of transition between the white and the Negro; so that wherever mulattoes abound, the intermixture of the two races is not impossible. In some parts of America the European and the Negro races are so crossed with one another that it is rare to meet with a man who is entirely black or entirely white; when they have arrived at this point, the two races may really be said to be combined, or, rather, to have been absorbed in a third race, which is connected with both without being identical with either.

Of all Europeans, the English are those who have mixed least with the Negroes. More mulattoes are to be seen in the South of the Union than in the North, but infinitely fewer than in any other European colony. Mulattoes are by no means numerous in the United States; they have no force peculiar to themselves, and when quarrels originating in differences of color take place, they generally side with the whites, just as the lackeys of the great in Europe assume the contemptuous airs of nobility towards the lower orders.

The pride of origin, which is natural to the English, is

equally certain, that the two races will never live in a state of equal freedom under the same government, so insurmountable are the barriers which nature, habit, and opinion have established between them." (See *Extracts from the Memoirs of Jefferson*, by M. Conseil.)

[47] If the British West India planters had governed themselves, they would assuredly not have passed the Slave Emancipation Bill which the mother country has recently imposed upon them.

singularly augmented by the personal pride that democratic liberty fosters among the Americans: the white citizen of the United States is proud of his race and proud of himself. But if the whites and the Negroes do not intermingle in the North of the Union, how should they mix in the South? Can it be supposed for an instant that an American of the Southern states, placed, as he must forever be, between the white man, with all his physical and moral superiority, and the Negro, will ever think of being confounded with the latter? The Americans of the Southern states have two powerful passions which will always keep them aloof: the first is the fear of being assimilated to the Negroes, their former slaves; and the second, the dread of sinking below the whites, their neighbors.

If I were called upon to predict the future, I should say that the abolition of slavery in the South will, in the common course of things, increase the repugnance of the white population for the blacks. I base this opinion upon the analogous observation I have already made in the North. I have remarked that the white inhabitants of the North avoid the Negroes with increasing care in proportion as the legal barriers of separation are removed by the legislature; and why should not the same result take place in the South? In the North the whites are deterred from intermingling with the blacks by an imaginary danger; in the South, where the danger would be real, I cannot believe that the fear would be less.

If, on the one hand, it be admitted (and the fact is unquestionable) that the colored population perpetually accumulate in the extreme South and increase more rapidly than the whites; and if, on the other hand, it be allowed that it is impossible to foresee a time at which the whites and the blacks will be so intermingled as to derive the same benefits from society, must it not be inferred that the blacks and the whites will, sooner or later, come to open strife in the Southern states? But if it be asked what the issue of the struggle is likely to be, it will readily be understood that we are here left to vague conjectures. The human mind may succeed in tracing a wide circle, as it were, which includes the future; but within that circle chance rules, and eludes all our foresight. In every picture of the future there is a dim spot which the eye of the understanding cannot penetrate. It appears, however, extremely probable that in the West Indies islands the white race is destined to be subdued, and upon the continent the blacks.

In the West Indies the white planters are isolated amid an immense black population; on the continent the blacks are placed between the ocean and an innumerable people, who already extend above them, in a compact mass, from the icy confines of Canada to the frontiers of Virginia, and from the banks of the Missouri to the shores of the Atlantic. If the white citizens of North America remain united, it is difficult to believe that the Negroes will escape the destruction which menaces them; they must be subdued by want or by the sword. But the black population accumulated along the coast of the Gulf of Mexico have a chance of success if the American Union should be dissolved when the struggle between the two races begins. The Federal tie once broken, the people of the South could not rely upon any lasting succor from their Northern countrymen. The latter are well aware that the danger can never reach them; and unless they are constrained to march to the assistance of the South by a positive obligation, it may be foreseen that the sympathy of race will be powerless.

Yet, at whatever period the strife may break out, the whites of the South, even if they are abandoned to their own resources, will enter the lists with an immense superiority of knowledge and the means of warfare; but the blacks will have numerical strength and the energy of despair upon their side, and these are powerful resources to men who have taken up arms. The fate of the white population of the Southern states will perhaps be similar to that of the Moors in Spain. After having occupied the land for centuries, it will perhaps retire by degrees to the country whence its ancestors came and abandon to the Negroes the possession of a territory which Providence seems to have destined for them, since they can subsist and labor in it more easily than the whites.

The danger of a conflict between the white and the black inhabitants of the Southern states of the Union (a danger which, however remote it may be, is inevitable) perpetually haunts the imagination of the Americans, like a painful dream. The inhabitants of the North make it a common topic of conversation, although directly they have nothing to fear from it; but they vainly endeavor to devise some means of obviating the misfortunes which they foresee. In the Southern states the subject is not discussed: the planter does not allude to the future in conversing with strangers; he does not communicate his apprehensions to his friends; he seeks to conceal them from himself. But there is something more alarming in the tacit forebodings of the South than in the clamorous fears of the North.

This all-pervading disquietude has given birth to an undertaking as yet but little known, which, however, may change the fate of a portion of the human race. From apprehension of the dangers that I have just described, some American citizens have formed a society for the purpose of exporting to the coast of Guinea, at their own expense, such free Negroes as may be willing to escape from the oppression to which they are subject.[48]

In 1820 the society to which I allude formed a settlement in Africa, on the seventh degree of north latitude, which bears the name of Liberia. The most recent intelligence informs us that two thousand five hundred Negroes are collected there. They have introduced the democratic institutions of America into the country of their forefathers. Liberia has a representative system of government, Negro jurymen, Negro magistrates, and Negro priests; churches have been built, newspapers established, and, by a singular turn in the vicissitudes of the world, white men are prohibited from establishing themselves within the settlement.[49]

This is indeed a strange caprice of fortune. Two hundred years have now elapsed since the inhabitants of Europe

[48] This society assumed the name of "The Society for the Colonization of the Blacks." See its *Annual Reports* and more particularly the fifteenth. See also the pamphlet, to which allusion has already been made, entitled: *Letters on the Colonization Society, and on Its Probable Results,* by Mr. Carey (Philadelphia, April 1833).

[49] This last regulation was laid down by the founders of the settlement; they believed that a state of things might arise in Africa similar to that which exists on the frontiers of the United States, and that if the Negroes, like the Indians, were brought into collision with a people more enlightened than themselves, they would be destroyed before they could be civilized.

undertook to tear the Negro from his family and his home in order to transport him to the shores of North America. Now the European settlers are engaged in sending back the descendants of those very Negroes to the continent whence they were originally taken: the barbarous Africans have learned civilization in the midst of bondage and have become acquainted with free political institutions in slavery. Up to the present time Africa has been closed against the arts and sciences of the whites, but the inventions of Europe will perhaps penetrate into those regions now that they are introduced by Africans themselves. The settlement of Liberia is founded upon a lofty and fruitful idea; but, whatever may be its results with regard to Africa, it can afford no remedy to the New World.

In twelve years the Colonization Society has transported two thousand five hundred Negroes to Africa; in the same space of time about seven hundred thousand blacks were born in the United States. If the colony of Liberia were able to receive thousands of new inhabitants every year, and if the Negroes were in a state to be sent thither with advantage; if the Union were to supply the society with annual subsidies,[50] and to transport the Negroes to Africa in government vessels, it would still be unable to counterpoise the natural increase of population among the blacks; and as it could not remove as many men in a year as are born upon its territory within that time, it could not prevent the growth of the evil which is daily increasing in the states.[51] The Negro race will never leave those shores of the American continent to which it was brought by the passions and the vices of Europeans; and it will not disappear from the New

[50] Nor would these be the only difficulties attendant upon the undertaking; if the Union undertook to buy up the Negroes now in America in order to transport them to Africa, the price of slaves, increasing with their scarcity, would soon become enormous; and the states of the North would never consent to expend such great sums for a purpose that would profit them but little. If the Union took possession of the slaves in the Southern states by force, or at a rate determined by law, an insurmountable resistance would arise in that part of the country. Both courses are equally impossible.

[51] In 1830 there were in the United States 2,010,327 slaves and 319,439 free blacks, in all 2,329,766 Negroes, who formed about one fifth of the total population of the United States at that time.

World as long as it continues to exist. The inhabitants of the United States may retard the calamities which they apprehend, but they cannot now destroy their efficient cause.

I am obliged to confess that I do not regard the abolition of slavery as a means of warding off the struggle of the two races in the Southern states. The Negroes may long remain slaves without complaining; but if they are once raised to the level of freemen, they will soon revolt at being deprived of almost all their civil rights; and as they cannot become the equals of the whites, they will speedily show themselves as enemies. In the North everything facilitated the emancipation of the slaves, and slavery was abolished without rendering the free Negroes formidable, since their number was too small for them ever to claim their rights. But such is not the case in the South. The question of slavery was a commercial and manufacturing question for the slaveowners in the North; for those of the South it is a question of life and death. God forbid that I should seek to justify the principle of Negro slavery, as has been done by some American writers! I say only that all the countries which formerly adopted that execrable principle are not equally able to abandon it at the present time.

When I contemplate the condition of the South, I can discover only two modes of action for the white inhabitants of those States: namely, either to emancipate the Negroes and to intermingle with them, or, remaining isolated from them, to keep them in slavery as long as possible. All intermediate measures seem to me likely to terminate, and that shortly, in the most horrible of civil wars and perhaps in the extirpation of one or the other of the two races. Such is the view that the Americans of the South take of the question, and they act consistently with it. As they are determined not to mingle with the Negroes, they refuse to emancipate them.

Not that the inhabitants of the South regard slavery as necessary to the wealth of the planter; on this point many of them agree with their Northern countrymen, in freely admitting that slavery is prejudicial to their interests; but they are convinced that the removal of this evil would imperil their own existence. The instruction which is now diffused in the South has convinced the inhabitants that slavery is injurious to the slave-owner, but it has also shown them, more clearly than before, that it is almost an impossibility to get rid of it. Hence arises a singular contrast: the more the utility of slavery is contested, the more firmly is it established in the laws; and while its principle is gradually abolished in the North, that selfsame principle gives rise to more and more rigorous consequences in the South.

The legislation of the Southern states with regard to slaves presents at the present day such unparalleled atrocities as suffice to show that the laws of humanity have been totally perverted, and to betray the desperate position of the community in which that legislation has been promulgated. The Americans of this portion of the Union have not, indeed, augmented the hardships of slavery; on the contrary, they have bettered the physical condition of the slaves. The only means by which the ancients maintained slavery were fetters and death; the Americans of the South of the Union have discovered more intellectual securities for the duration of their power. They have employed their despotism and their violence against the human mind. In antiquity precautions were taken to prevent the slave from breaking his chains; at the present day measures are adopted to deprive him even of the desire for freedom. The ancients kept the bodies of their slaves in bondage, but placed no restraint upon the mind and no check upon education; and they acted consistently with their established principle, since a natural termination of slavery then existed, and one day or other the slave might be set free and become the equal of his master. But the Americans of the South, who do not admit that the Negroes can ever be commingled with themselves, have forbidden them, under severe penalties, to be taught to read or write; and as they will not raise them to their own level, they sink them as nearly as possible to that of the brutes.

The hope of liberty had always been allowed to the slave, to cheer the hardships of his condition. But the Americans of the South are well aware that emancipation cannot but be dangerous when the freed man can never be assimilated to his former master. To give a man his freedom and to leave him in wretchedness and ignominy is nothing less than to prepare a future chief for a revolt of the slaves. Moreover, it has long been remarked that the presence of a free Negro vaguely agitates the minds of his less fortunate brethren, and conveys to them a dim notion of their rights. The Americans of the South have consequently taken away from slave-owners the right of emancipating their slaves in most cases.[52]

I happened to meet an old man, in the South of the Union, who had lived in illicit intercourse with one of his Negresses and had had several children by her, who were born the slaves of their father. He had, indeed, frequently thought of bequeathing to them at least their liberty; but years had elapsed before he could surmount the legal obstacles to their emancipation, and meanwhile his old age had come and he was about to die. He pictured to himself his sons dragged from market to market and passing from the authority of a parent to the rod of the stranger, until these horrid anticipations worked his expiring imagination into frenzy. When I saw him, he was a prey to all the anguish of despair; and I then understood how awful is the retribution of Nature upon those who have broken her laws.

These evils are unquestionably great, but they are the necessary and foreseen consequences of the very principle of modern slavery. When the Europeans chose their slaves from a race differing from their own, which many of them considered as inferior to the other races of mankind, and any notion of intimate union with which they all repelled with horror, they must have believed that slavery would last forever, since there is no intermediate state that can be durable between the excessive inequality produced by servitude and the complete equality that originates in independence. The Europeans did imperfectly feel this truth, but without acknowledging it even to themselves. Whenever they have had to do with Negroes, their conduct has been dictated either by their interest and their pride or by their compassion. They first violated every right of humanity by their treatment of the Negro, and they afterwards informed him that those rights were precious and inviolable. They opened their ranks to their slaves, and when the latter tried to come in, they drove them forth in scorn. Desiring slavery, they have allowed themselves unconsciously to be swayed in spite of themselves towards liberty, without having the courage to be either completely iniquitous or completely just.

If it is impossible to anticipate a period at which the Americans of the South will mingle their blood with that of

[52] Emancipation is not prohibited, but surrounded with such formalities as to render it difficult.

the Negroes, can they allow their slaves to become free without compromising their own security? And if they are obliged to keep that race in bondage in order to save their own families, may they not be excused for availing themselves of the means best adapted to that end? The events that are taking place in the Southern states appear to me to be at once the most horrible and the most natural results of slavery. When I see the order of nature overthrown, and when I hear the cry of humanity in its vain struggle against the laws, my indignation does not light upon the men of our own time who are the instruments of these outrages; but I reserve my execration for those who, after a thousand years of freedom, brought back slavery into the world once more.

Whatever may be the efforts of the Americans of the South to maintain slavery, they will not always succeed. Slavery, now confined to a single tract of the civilized earth, attacked by Christianity as unjust and by political economy as prejudicial, and now contrasted with democratic liberty and the intelligence of our age, cannot survive. By the act of the master, or by the will of the slave, it will cease; and in either case great calamities may be expected to ensue. If liberty be refused to the Negroes of the South, they will in the end forcibly seize it for themselves; if it be given, they will before long abuse it.

WHAT ARE THE CHANCES OF DURATION OF THE AMERICAN UNION, AND WHAT DANGERS THREATEN IT. *What makes the preponderant force lie in the states rather than in the Union—The Union will last only as long as all the states choose to belong to it—Causes that tend to keep them united—Utility of the Union to resist foreign enemies and to exclude foreigners from America—No natural barriers between the several states—No conflicting interests to divide them—Reciprocal interests of the Northern, Southern, and Western states—Intellectual ties of Union—Uniformity of opinions—Dangers of the Union resulting from the different characters and the passions of its citizens—Character of the citizens in the South and in the North—The rapid growth of the Union one of its greatest dangers—Progress of the population to the northwest—Power gravitates in the same direction—Passions originating from sudden turns of fortune—Whether the existing government of the Union tends to gain strength or to lose it—Various signs of its decrease—Internal improvements—Wastelands—Indians —The bank—The tariff—General Jackson.*

THE MAINTENANCE of the existing institutions of the several states depends in part upon the maintenance of the Union itself. We must therefore first inquire into the probable fate of the Union. One point may be assumed at once: if the present confederation were dissolved, it appears to me to be incontestable that the states of which it is now composed would not return to their original isolated condition, but that several unions would then be formed in the place of one. It is not my intention to inquire into the principles upon which these new unions would probably be established, but merely to show what the causes are which may effect the dismemberment of the existing confederation.

With this object, I shall be obliged to retrace some of the steps that I have already taken and to revert to topics that I have before discussed. I am aware that the reader may accuse me of repetition, but the importance of the matter which still remains to be treated is my excuse: I had rather say too much than not be thoroughly understood; and I prefer injuring the author to slighting the subject.

The legislators who formed the Constitution of 1789 endeavored to confer a separate existence and superior strength upon the Federal power. But they were confined by the conditions of the task which they had undertaken to perform. They were not appointed to constitute the government of a single people, but to regulate the association of several states; and, whatever their inclinations might be, they could not but divide the exercise of sovereignty.

In order to understand the consequences of this division it is necessary to make a short distinction between the functions of government. There are some objects which are national by their very nature; that is to say, which affect the nation as a whole, and can be entrusted only to the man or the assembly of men who most completely represent the entire nation. Among these may be reckoned war and diplomacy. There are other objects which are provincial by their very nature; that is to say, which affect only certain localities and which can be properly treated only in that locality.

Such, for instance, is the budget of a municipality. Lastly, there are objects of a mixed nature, which are national inasmuch as they affect all the citizens who compose the nation, and which are provincial inasmuch as it is not necessary that the nation itself should provide for them all. Such are the rights that regulate the civil and political condition of the citizens. No society can exist without civil and political rights. These rights, therefore, interest all the citizens alike; but it is not always necessary to the existence and the prosperity of the nation that these rights should be uniform, nor, consequently, that they should be regarded by the central authority.

There are, then, two distinct categories of objects which are submitted to the sovereign power; and these are found in all well-constituted communities, whatever may be the basis of the political constitution. Between these two extremes the objects which I have termed mixed may be considered to lie. As these are neither exclusively national nor entirely provincial, the care of them may be given to a national or a provincial government, according to the agreement of the contracting parties, without in any way impairing the object of association.

The sovereign power is usually formed by the union of individuals, who compose a people; and individual powers or collective forces, each representing a small fraction of the sovereign, are the only elements that are found under the general government. In this case the general government is more naturally called upon to regulate not only those affairs which are essentially national, but most of those which I have called mixed; and the local governments are reduced to that small share of sovereign authority which is indispensable to their well-being.

But sometimes the sovereign authority is composed of preorganized political bodies, by virtue of circumstances anterior to their union; and in this case the state governments assume the control not only of those affairs which more peculiarly belong to them, but of all or a part of the mixed objects in question. For the confederate nations, which were independent sovereignties before their union, and which still represent a considerable share of the sovereign power, have consented to cede to the general government the exercise only of those rights which are indispensable to the Union.

When the national government, independently of the prerogatives inherent in its nature, is invested with the right of regulating the mixed objects of sovereignty, it possesses a preponderant influence. Not only are its own rights extensive, but all the rights which it does not possess exist by its sufferance; and it is to be feared that the provincial governments may be deprived by it of their natural and necessary prerogatives.

When, on the other hand, the provincial governments are invested with the power of regulating those same affairs of mixed interest, an opposite tendency prevails in society. The preponderant force resides in the province, not in the nation; and it may be apprehended that the national government may, in the end, be stripped of the privileges that are necessary to its existence.

Single nations have therefore a natural tendency to centralization, and confederations to dismemberment.

It now remains to apply these general principles to the American Union. The several states necessarily retained the right of regulating all purely local affairs. Moreover, these same states kept the rights of determining the civil and political competency of the citizens, of regulating the reciprocal relations of the members of the community, and of dispensing justice—rights which are general in their nature, but do not necessarily appertain to the national government. We have seen that the government of the Union is invested with the power of acting in the name of the whole nation in those cases in which the nation has to appear as a single and undivided power; as, for instance, in foreign relations, and in offering a common resistance to a common enemy; in short, in conducting those affairs which I have styled exclusively national.

In this division of the rights of sovereignty the share of the Union seems at first sight more considerable than that of the states, but a more attentive investigation shows it to be less so. The undertakings of the government of the Union are more vast, but it has less frequent occasion to act at all. Those of the state governments are comparatively small, but they are incessant and they keep alive the authority which they represent. The government of the Union watches over the general interests of the country; but the general interests of a people have but a questionable influence upon individual happiness, while state interests produce an immediate effect upon the welfare of the inhabitants. The Union secures the independence and the greatness of the nation, which do not immediately affect private citizens; but the several states maintain the liberty, regulate the rights, protect the fortune, and secure the life and the whole future prosperity of every citizen.

The Federal government is far removed from its subjects, while the state governments are within the reach of them all and are ready to attend to the smallest appeal. The central government has on its side the passions of a few superior men who aspire to conduct it; but on the side of the state governments are the interests of all those second-rate individuals who can only hope to obtain power within their own state, and who nevertheless exercise more authority over the people because they are nearer to them.

The Americans have, therefore, much more to hope and to fear from the states than from the Union; and, according to the natural tendency of the human mind, they are more likely to attach themselves strongly to the former than to the latter. In this respect their habits and feelings harmonize with their interests.

When a compact nation divides its sovereignty and adopts a confederate form of government, the traditions, the customs, and the usages of the people for a long time struggle against the laws and give an influence to the central government which the laws forbid. But when a number of confederate states unite to form a single nation, the same causes operate in an opposite direction. I have no doubt that if France were to become a confederate republic like that of the United States, the government would at first be more energetic than that of the Union; and if the Union were to alter its constitution to a monarchy like that of France, I think that the American government would long remain weaker than the French. When the national existence of the Anglo-Americans began, their colonial existence was already of long standing; necessary relations were established between the townships and the individual citizens of the same states; and they were accustomed to consider some objects as common to them all, and to conduct other affairs as exclusively relating to their own special interests.

The Union is a vast body, which presents no definite object to patriotic feeling. The forms and limits of the state are distinct and circumscribed, since it represents a certain number of objects that are familiar to the citizens and dear to them all. It is identified with the soil; with the right of property and the domestic affections; with the recollections of the past, the labors of the present, and the hopes of the future. Patriotism, then, which is frequently a mere extension of individual selfishness, is still directed to the state and has not passed over to the Union. Thus the tendency of the interests, the habits, and the feelings of the people is to center political activity in the states in preference to the Union.

It is easy to estimate the different strength of the two governments by noting the manner in which they exercise their respective powers. Whenever the government of a state addresses an individual or an assembly of individuals, its language is clear and imperative, and such is also the tone of the Federal government when it speaks to individuals; but no sooner has it anything to do with a state than it begins to parley, to explain its motives and justify its conduct, to argue, to advise, and, in short, anything but to command. If doubts are raised as to limits of the constitutional powers of either government, the state government prefers its claim with boldness and takes prompt and energetic steps to support it. Meanwhile the government of the Union reasons; it appeals to the interests, the good sense, the glory of the nation; it temporizes, it negotiates, and does not consent to act until it is reduced to the last extremity. At first sight it might readily be imagined that it is the state government which is armed with the authority of the nation and that Congress represents a single state.

The Federal government is, therefore, notwithstanding the precautions of those who founded it, naturally so weak that, more than any other, it requires the free consent of the governed to enable it to exist. It is easy to perceive that its object is to enable the states to realize with facility their determination of remaining united; and as long as this preliminary condition exists, it is wise, strong, and active. The Constitution fits the government to control individuals and easily to surmount such obstacles as they may be inclined to offer, but it was by no means established with a view to the possible voluntary separation of one or more of the states from the Union.

If the sovereignty of the Union were to engage in a struggle with that of the states at the present day, its defeat may be confidently predicted; and it is not probable that such a struggle would be seriously undertaken. As often as a steady resistance is offered to the Federal government, it will be found to yield. Experience has hitherto shown that whenever a state has demanded anything with perseverance and resolution, it has invariably succeeded; and that if it has distinctly refused to act, it was left to do as it thought fit.[53]

But even if the government of the Union had any strength inherent in itself, the physical situation of the country would render the exercise of that strength very difficult.[54] The United States covers an immense territory, the individual states are separated from each other by great distances, and the population is disseminated over the surface of a country which is still half a wilderness. If the Union were to undertake to enforce by arms the allegiance of the federated states, it would be in a position very analogous to that of England at the time of the War of Independence.

However strong a government may be, it cannot easily escape from the consequences of a principle which it has once admitted as the foundation of its constitution. The Union was formed by the voluntary agreement of the states; and these, in uniting together, have not forfeited their sovereignty, nor have they been reduced to the condition of one and the same people. If one of the states chose to withdraw its name from the contract, it would be difficult to disprove its right of doing so, and the Federal government would have no means of maintaining its claims directly, either by force or by right. In order to enable the Federal government easily to conquer the resistance that may be offered to it by any of its subjects, it would be necessary that one or more of them should be specially interested

---

[53] See the conduct of the Northern states in the War of 1812. "During that war," says Jefferson in a letter of March 17, 1817, to General Lafayette, "four of the Eastern States were only attached to the Union like so many inanimate bodies to living men." (*Correspondence of Jefferson,* published by M. Conseil.)

[54] The state of peace of the Union affords no pretext for a standing army, and without a standing army a government is not prepared to profit by a favorable opportunity to conquer resistance and seize the sovereign power by surprise.

in the existence of the Union, as has frequently been the case in the history of confederations.

If it be supposed that among the states that are united by the federal tie there are some which exclusively enjoy the principal advantages of union, or whose prosperity entirely depends on the duration of that union, it is unquestionable that they will always be ready to support the central government in enforcing the obedience of the others. But the government would then be exerting a force not derived from itself, but from a principle contrary to its nature. States form confederations in order to derive equal advantages from their union; and in the case just alluded to, the Federal government would derive its power from the unequal distribution of those benefits among the states.

If one of the federated states acquires a preponderance sufficiently great to enable it to take exclusive possession of the central authority, it will consider the other states as subject provinces and will cause its own supremacy to be respected under the borrowed name of the sovereignty of the Union. Great things may then be done in the name of the Federal government, but in reality that government will have ceased to exist.[55] In both these cases the power that acts in the name of the confederation becomes stronger the more it abandons the natural state and the acknowledged principles of confederations.

In America the existing Union is advantageous to all the states, but it is not indispensable to any one of them. Several of them might break the Federal tie without compromising the welfare of the others, although the sum of their joint prosperity would be less. As the existence and the happiness of none of the states are wholly dependent on the present Constitution, none of them would be disposed to make great personal sacrifices to maintain it. On the other hand, there is no state which seems hitherto to have been by its ambition much interested in the maintenance of the existing Union. They certainly do not all exercise the same influence in the Federal councils; but no one can hope to

[55] Thus the province of Holland, in the republic of the Low Countries, and the Emperor in the Germanic Confederation, have sometimes put themselves in the place of the Union and have employed the federal authority to their own advantage.

domineer over the rest or to treat them as its inferiors or as its subjects.

It appears to me unquestionable that if any portion of the Union seriously desired to separate itself from the other states, they would not be able, nor indeed would they attempt, to prevent it; and that the present Union will last only as long as the states which compose it choose to continue members of the confederation. If this point be admitted, the question becomes less difficult; and our object is, not to inquire whether the states of the existing Union are capable of separating, but whether they will choose to remain united.

Among the various reasons that tend to render the existing Union useful to the Americans, two principal ones are especially evident to the observer. Although the Americans are, as it were, alone upon their continent, commerce gives them for neighbors all the nations with which they trade. Notwithstanding their apparent isolation, then, the Americans need to be strong, and they can be strong only by remaining united. If the states were to split, not only would they diminish the strength that they now have against foreigners, but they would soon create foreign powers upon their own territory. A system of inland custom-houses would then be established; the valleys would be divided by imaginary boundary lines; the courses of the rivers would be impeded, and a multitude of hindrances would prevent the Americans from using that vast continent which Providence has given them for a dominion. At present they have no invasion to fear, and consequently no standing armies to maintain, no taxes to levy. If the Union were dissolved, all these burdensome things would before long be required. The Americans are, then, most deeply interested in the maintenance of their Union. On the other hand, it is almost impossible to discover any private interest that might now tempt a portion of the Union to separate from the other states.

When we cast our eyes on the map of the United States, we perceive the chain of the Allegheny Mountains, running from the northeast to the southwest, and crossing nearly one thousand miles of country; and we are led to imagine that the design of Providence was to raise between the valley

of the Mississippi and the coasts of the Atlantic Ocean one of
those natural barriers which break the mutual intercourse
of men and form the necessary limits of different states. But
the average height of the Alleghenies does not exceed 800
meters.[56] Their rounded summits, and the spacious valleys
which they enclose within their passes, are of easy access in
several directions. Besides, the principal rivers that fall into
the Atlantic Ocean, the Hudson, the Susquehanna, and the
Potomac, take their rise beyond the Alleghenies, in an open
elevated plain, which borders on the valley of the Mississippi. These streams quit this region,[57] make their way
through the barrier which would seem to turn them westward, and, as they wind through the mountains, open an
easy and natural passage to man.

No natural barrier divides the regions that are now inhabited by the Anglo-Americans; the Alleghenies are so far
from separating nations that they do not even divide different states. New York, Pennsylvania, and Virginia comprise
them within their borders and extend as much to the west as
to the east of these mountains.[58]

The territory now occupied by the twenty-four states of
the Union, and the three great districts which have not yet
acquired the rank of states, although they already contain
inhabitants, cover a surface of 131,144 square leagues,[59]
which is about equal to five times the extent of France.
Within these limits the quality of the soil, the temperature,
and the produce of the country are extremely various. The
vast extent of territory occupied by the Anglo-American
republics has given rise to doubts as to the maintenance of
their Union. Here a distinction must be made; contrary interests sometimes arise in the different provinces of a vast

[56] Average height of the Alleghenies, following Volney (*Atlas
of the United States,* p. 33), 700–800 meters; following Darby,
500–6,000 feet. The highest point of the Vosges is 1,400 meters
above sea level.

[57] See *View of the United States,* by Darby, pp. 64 and 79.

[58] The chain of the Alleghenies is not so high as that of the
Vosges and does not offer as many obstacles as the latter to the
efforts of human industry. The regions lying on the eastern slopes
of the Alleghenies are as naturally attached to the Mississippi
Valley as Franche-Comté, Upper Burgundy, and Alsace are to
France.

[59] 1,002,600 square miles. See Darby's *View of the United
States,* p. 435.

empire, which often terminate in open dissensions; and the extent of the country is then most prejudicial to the duration of the state. But if the inhabitants of these vast regions are not divided by contrary interests, the extent of the territory is favorable to their prosperity; for the unity of the government promotes the interchange of the different products of the soil and increases their value by facilitating their sale.

It is indeed easy to discover different interests in the different parts of the Union, but I am unacquainted with any that are hostile to one another. The Southern states are almost exclusively agricultural. The Northern states are more peculiarly commercial and manufacturing. The states of the West are at the same time agricultural and manufacturing. In the South the crops consist of tobacco, rice, cotton, and sugar; in the North and the West, of wheat and corn. These are different sources of wealth, but union is the means by which these sources are opened and rendered equally advantageous to all.

The North, which ships the produce of the Anglo-Americans to all parts of the world and brings back the produce of the globe to the Union, is evidently interested in maintaining the confederation in its present condition, in order that the number of American producers and consumers may remain as large as possible. The North is the most natural agent of communication between the South and the West of the Union on the one hand, and the rest of the world on the other; the North is therefore interested in the union and prosperity of the South and the West, in order that they may continue to furnish raw materials for its manufactures, and cargoes for its shipping.

The South and the West, on their side, are still more directly interested in the preservation of the Union and the prosperity of the North. The produce of the South is, for the most part, exported beyond seas; the South and the West consequently stand in need of the commercial resources of the North. They are likewise interested in the maintenance of a powerful fleet by the Union, to protect them efficaciously. The South and the West have no vessels, but willingly contribute to the expense of a navy, for if the fleets of Europe were to blockade the ports of the South and the delta of the Mississippi, what would become of the rice of the Carolinas, the tobacco of Virginia, and the sugar and cotton that grow in the valley of the Mississippi? Every portion of the Federal budget does, therefore, contribute to the maintenance of material interests that are common to all the federated states.

Independently of this commercial utility, the South and the West derive great political advantages from their union with each other and with the North. The South contains an enormous slave population, a population which is already alarming and still more formidable for the future. The states of the West occupy a single valley; the rivers that intersect their territory rise in the Rocky Mountains or in the Alleghenies, and fall into the Mississippi, which bears them onwards to the Gulf of Mexico. The Western states are consequently entirely cut off, by their position, from the traditions of Europe and the civilization of the Old World. The inhabitants of the South, then, are induced to support the Union in order to avail themselves of its protection against the blacks; and the inhabitants of the West, in order not to be excluded from a free communication with the rest of the globe and shut up in the wilds of central America. The North cannot but desire the maintenance of the Union in order to remain, as it now is, the connecting link between that vast body and the other parts of the world.

The material interests of all the parts of the Union are, then, intimately connected; and the same assertion holds true respecting those opinions and sentiments that may be termed the immaterial interests of men.

The inhabitants of the United States talk much of their attachment to their country; but I confess that I do not rely upon that calculating patriotism which is founded upon interest and which a change in the interests may destroy. Nor do I attach much importance to the language of the Americans when they manifest, in their daily conversation, the intention of maintaining the Federal system adopted by their forefathers. A government retains its sway over a great number of citizens far less by the voluntary and rational consent of the multitude than by that instinctive, and to a certain extent involuntary, agreement which results from similarity of feelings and resemblances of opinion. I will never admit that men constitute a social body simply because they obey the same head and the same laws. Society can exist only when a great number of men consider a great number of things under the same aspect, when they hold the same opinions upon many subjects, and when the same occurrences suggest the same thoughts and impressions to their minds.

The observer who examines what is passing in the United States upon this principle will readily discover that their inhabitants, though divided into twenty-four distinct sovereignties, still constitute a single people; and he may perhaps be led to think that the Anglo-American Union is more truly a united society than some nations of Europe which live under the same legislation and the same prince.

Although the Anglo-Americans have several religious sects, they all regard religion in the same manner. They are not always agreed upon the measures that are most conducive to good government, and they vary upon some of the forms of government which it is expedient to adopt; but they are unanimous upon the general principles that ought to rule human society. From Maine to the Floridas, and from the Missouri to the Atlantic Ocean, the people are held to be the source of all legitimate power. The same notions are entertained respecting liberty and equality, the liberty of the press, the right of association, the jury, and the responsibility of the agents of government.

If we turn from their political and religious opinions to the moral and philosophical principles that regulate the daily actions of life and govern their conduct, we still find the same uniformity. The Anglo-Americans[60] acknowledge the moral authority of the reason of the community as they acknowledge the political authority of the mass of citizens; and they hold that public opinion is the surest arbiter of what is lawful or forbidden, true or false. The majority of them believe that a man by following his own interest, rightly understood, will be led to do what is just and good. They hold that every man is born in possession of the right of self-government, and that no one has the right of constraining his fellow creatures to be happy. They have all a lively faith in the perfectibility of man, they judge that the diffusion of knowledge must necessarily be advantageous,

[60] It is scarcely necessary for me to observe that by the expression Anglo-Americans I mean to designate only the great majority of the nation. Some isolated individuals, of course, hold very different opinions.

and the consequences of ignorance fatal; they all consider society as a body in a state of improvement, humanity as a changing scene, in which nothing is, or ought to be, permanent; and they admit that what appears to them today to be good, may be superseded by something better tomorrow. I do not give all these opinions as true, but as American opinions.

Not only are the Anglo-Americans united by these common opinions, but they are separated from all other nations by a feeling of pride. For the last fifty years no pains have been spared to convince the inhabitants of the United States that they are the only religious, enlightened, and free people. They perceive that, for the present, their own democratic institutions prosper, while those of other countries fail; hence they conceive a high opinion of their superiority and are not very remote from believing themselves to be a distinct species of mankind.

Thus the dangers that threaten the American Union do not originate in diversity of interests or of opinions, but in the various characters and passions of the Americans. The men who inhabit the vast territory of the United States are almost all the issue of a common stock; but climate, and more especially slavery, have gradually introduced marked differences between the British settler of the Southern states and the British settler of the North. In Europe it is generally believed that slavery has rendered the interests of one part of the Union contrary to those of the other, but I have not found this to be the case. Slavery has not created interests in the South contrary to those of the North, but it has modified the character and changed the habits of the natives of the South.

I have already explained the influence of slavery upon the commercial ability of the Americans in the South; and this same influence equally extends to their manners. The slave is a servant who never remonstrates and who submits to everything without complaint. He may sometimes assassinate his master, but he never withstands him. In the South there are no families so poor as not to have slaves. The citizen of the Southern states becomes a sort of domestic dictator from infancy; the first notion he acquires in life is that he is born to command, and the first habit which he contracts is that of ruling without resistance. His education tends, then, to give him the character of a haughty and hasty man, irascible, violent, ardent in his desires, impatient of obstacles, but easily discouraged if he cannot succeed upon his first attempt.

The American of the North sees no slaves around him in his childhood; he is even unattended by free servants, for he is usually obliged to provide for his own wants. As soon as he enters the world, the idea of necessity assails him on every side; he soon learns to know exactly the natural limits of his power; he never expects to subdue by force those who withstand him; and he knows that the surest means of obtaining the support of his fellow creatures is to win their favor. He therefore becomes patient, reflecting, tolerant, slow to act, and persevering in his designs.

In the Southern states the more pressing wants of life are always supplied; the inhabitants, therefore, are not occupied with the material cares of life, from which they are relieved by others; and their imagination is diverted to more captivating and less definite objects. The American of the South is fond of grandeur, luxury, and renown, of gayety, pleasure, and, above all, of idleness; nothing obliges him to exert himself in order to subsist; and as he has no necessary occupations, he gives way to indolence and does not even attempt what would be useful.

But the equality of fortunes and the absence of slavery in the North plunge the inhabitants in those material cares which are disdained by the white population of the South. They are taught from infancy to combat want and to place wealth above all the pleasures of the intellect or the heart. The imagination is extinguished by the trivial details of life, and the ideas become less numerous and less general, but far more practical, clearer, and more precise. As prosperity is the sole aim of exertion, it is excellently well attained; nature and men are turned to the best pecuniary advantage; and society is dexterously made to contribute to the welfare of each of its members, while individual selfishness is the source of general happiness.

The American of the North has not only experience but knowledge; yet he values science not as an enjoyment, but as a means, and is only anxious to seize its useful applications. The American of the South is more given to act upon impulse; he is more clever, more frank, more generous, more intellectual, and more brilliant. The former, with a greater degree of activity, common sense, information, and general aptitude, has the characteristic good and evil qualities of the middle classes. The latter has the tastes, the prejudices, the weaknesses, and the magnanimity of all aristocracies.

If two men are united in society who have the same interests, and, to a certain extent, the same opinions, but different characters, different acquirements, and a different style of civilization, it is most probable that these men will not agree. The same remark is applicable to a society of nations.

Slavery, then, does not attack the American Union directly in its interests, but indirectly in its manners.

The states that gave their assent to the Federal contract in 1790 were thirteen in number; the Union now consists of twenty-four members. The population, which amounted to nearly four millions in 1790, had more than tripled in the space of forty years; in 1830 it amounted to nearly thirteen millions.[61] Changes of such magnitude cannot take place without danger.

A society of nations, as well as a society of individuals, has three principal chances of duration: namely, the wisdom of its members, their individual weakness, and their limited number. The Americans who quit the coasts of the Atlantic Ocean to plunge into the Western wilderness are adventurers, impatient of restraint, greedy of wealth, and frequently men expelled from the states in which they were born. When they arrive in the wilderness, they are unknown to one another; they have neither traditions, family feeling, nor the force of example to check their excesses. The authority of the laws is feeble among them; that of morality is still weaker. The settlers who are constantly peopling the valley of the Mississippi are, then, in every respect, inferior to the Americans who inhabit the older parts of the Union. But they already exercise a great influence in its councils; and they arrive at the government of the commonwealth before they have learned to govern themselves.[62]

[61] Census of 1790   3,929,328
Census of 1830   12,856,165

[62] This indeed is only a temporary danger. I have no doubt that in time society will assume as much stability and regularity in the West as it has already done upon the Atlantic coast.

The greater the individual weakness of the contracting parties, the greater are the chances of the duration of the contract; for their safety is then dependent upon their union. When, in 1790, the most populous of the American republics did not contain 500,000 inhabitants,[63] each of them felt its own insignificance as an independent people, and this feeling rendered compliance with the Federal authority more easy. But when one of the federated states reckons, like the state of New York, two million inhabitants and covers an extent of territory equal to a quarter of France,[64] it feels its own strength; and although it may still support the Union as useful to its prosperity, it no longer regards it as necessary to its existence; and while consenting to continue in it, it aims at preponderance in the federal councils. The mere increase in number of the states weakens the tie that holds them together. All men who are placed at the same point of view do not look at the same objects in the same manner. Still less do they do so when the point of view is different. In proportion, then, as the American republics become more numerous, there is less chance of their unanimity in matters of legislation. At present the interests of the different parts of the Union are not at variance, but who can foresee the various changes of the future in a country in which new towns are founded every day and new states almost every year?

Since the first settlement of the British colonies the number of inhabitants has about doubled every twenty-two years. I perceive no causes that are likely to check this ratio of increase of the Anglo-American population for the next hundred years; and before that time has elapsed, I believe that the territories and dependencies of the United States will be covered by more than a hundred millions of inhabitants and divided into forty states.[65] I admit that these hun-

[63] Pennsylvania contained 431,373 inhabitants in 1790.
[64] The area of the state of New York is about 6,213 square leagues (500 [sic; actually about 50,000] square miles). See *View of the United States*, by Darby, p. 435.
[65] If the population continues to double every twenty-two years, as it has done for the last two hundred years, the number of inhabitants in the United States in 1852 will be twenty-four million; in 1874, forty-eight million; and in 1896, ninety-six million. This may still be the case even if the lands on the eastern slope of the Rocky Mountains should be found unfit for cultivation. The territory that is already occupied can easily contain this

dred millions of men have no different interests. I suppose, on the contrary, that they are all equally interested in the maintenance of the Union; but I still say that, for the very reason that they are a hundred millions, forming forty distinct nations unequally strong, the continuance of the Federal government can be only a fortunate accident.

Whatever faith I may have in the perfectibility of man, until human nature is altered and men wholly transformed I shall refuse to believe in the duration of a government that is called upon to hold together forty different nations spread over a territory equal to one half of Europe,[66] to avoid all rivalry, ambition, and struggles between them, and to direct their independent activity to the accomplishment of the same designs.

But the greatest peril to which the Union is exposed by its increase arises from the continual displacement of its internal forces. The distance from Lake Superior to the Gulf of Mexico is more than twelve hundred miles as the crow flies. The frontier of the United States winds along the whole of this immense line; sometimes falling within its limits, but more frequently extending far beyond it, into the waste. It has been calculated that the whites advance every year a mean distance of seventeen miles along the whole of this vast boundary.[67] Obstacles such as an unproductive district, a lake, or an Indian nation are from time to time encountered. The advancing column then halts for a while; its two extremities curve round upon themselves, and as soon as they are reunited, they proceed onwards. This gradual and continuous progress of the European race towards the Rocky Mountains has the solemnity of a providential event; it is like a deluge of men rising unabatedly, and daily driven onwards by the hand of God.

number of inhabitants. One hundred million men spread over the surface of the twenty-four states and the three dependencies which now constitute the Union would give only 762 inhabitants to the square league; this would be far below the mean population of France, which is 1,006 to the square league; or of England, which is 1,457; and it would even be below the population of Switzerland, for that country, notwithstanding its lakes and mountains, contains 783 inhabitants to the square league. See Malte-Brun, Vol. VI, p. 92.

[66] The area of the United States is 295,000 square leagues, that of Europe, following Malte-Brun (Vol. VI, p. 4), is 500,000.

[67] See *Legislative Documents,* 20th Congress, No. 117, p. 105.

Within this front line of conquering settlers, towns are built and vast states founded. In 1790 there were only a few thousand pioneers sprinkled along the valleys of the Mississippi; at the present day these valleys contain as many inhabitants as were to be found in the whole Union in 1790. Their population amounts to nearly four million.[68] The city of Washington was founded in 1800, in the very center of the Union; but such are the changes which have taken place that it now stands at one of the extremities; and the delegates of the most remote Western states, in order to take their seats in Congress, are already obliged to perform a journey as long as that from Vienna to Paris.[69]

All the states of the Union are carried forward at the same time towards prosperity, but all cannot grow and prosper at the same rate. In the North of the Union the detached branches of the Allegheny chain, extending as far as the Atlantic Ocean, form spacious roads and ports, constantly accessible to the largest vessels. But from the Potomac, following the shore, to the mouth of the Mississippi, the coast is sandy and flat. In this part of the Union the mouths of almost all the rivers are obstructed; and the few harbors that exist among these inlets do not offer the same depth to vessels and present, for commerce, facilities less extensive than those of the North.

The first and natural cause of inferiority is united to another cause proceeding from the laws. We have seen that slavery, which is abolished in the North, still exists in the South; and I have pointed out its fatal consequences upon the prosperity of the planter himself.

The North is therefore superior to the South both in commerce[70] and in manufacture, the natural consequence

---

[68] 3,672,317, census of 1830.

[69] The distance from Jefferson, the capital of the state of Missouri, to Washington is 1,019 miles or 420 leagues. (*American Almanac*, 1831, p. 48.)

[70] The following statements will show the difference between the commercial activity of the South and of the North.
In 1829 the tonnage of all the merchant vessels belonging to Virginia, the two Carolinas, and Georgia (the four great Southern states) amounted to only 5,243 tons. In the same year the tonnage of the vessels of the state of Massachusetts alone amounted to 17,322 tons. (See *Legislative Documents*, 21st Congress, 2nd Session, No. 140, p. 244.) Thus Massachusetts alone had three times as much shipping as the four above-mentioned states. Nevertheless, the area of the state of Massachusetts is only

of which is the more rapid increase of population and wealth within its borders. The states on the shores of the Atlantic Ocean are already half people. Most of the land is held by an owner, and they cannot therefore receive so many immigrants as the Western states, where a boundless field is still open to industry. The valley of the Mississippi is far more fertile than the coast of the Atlantic Ocean. This reason, added to all the others, contributes to drive the Europeans westward, a fact which may be rigorously demonstrated by figures. It is found that the sum total of the population of all the United States has about tripled in the course of forty years. But in the new states adjacent to the Mississippi the population[71] has increased thirty-one-fold within the same time.[72]

The center of the federal power is continually displaced. Forty years ago the majority of the citizens of the Union were established upon the coast of the Atlantic, in the environs of the spot where Washington now stands; but the great body of the people is now advancing inland and to the North, so that in twenty years the majority will unquestionably be on the western side of the Alleghenies. If the Union continues, the basin of the Mississippi is evidently marked out, by its fertility and its extent, to be the permanent center of the Federal government. In thirty or forty years that tract of country will have assumed its natural rank. It is

---

959 square leagues (7,335 square miles), and its population amounts to 610,014 inhabitants; while the area of the four other states I have quoted is 27,204 square leagues (210,000 square miles), and their population 3,047,767. Thus the area of the state of Massachusetts forms only one thirtieth part of the area of the four states, and its population is but one fifth of theirs. (*View of the United States,* by Darby.) Slavery is prejudicial to the commercial prosperity of the South in several different ways, by diminishing the spirit of enterprise among the whites and by preventing them from obtaining the sailors whom they require. Sailors are usually taken only from the lowest ranks of the population; but in the Southern states, these lowest ranks are composed of slaves, and it is very difficult to employ them at sea. They are unable to serve as well as a white crew, and fears would always be entertained of their mutinying in the middle of the ocean or of their escaping in the foreign countries at which they might touch.

[71] *View of the United States,* by Darby, p. 444.

[72] Note that when I speak of the basin of the Mississippi, I do not include that portion of the states of New York, Pennsylvania, and Virginia situated west of the Alleghenies, which should, however, be considered as also comprising a part of it.

easy to calculate that its population, compared with that of the coast of the Atlantic, will then be, in round numbers, as 40 to 11. In a few years the states that founded the Union will lose the direction of its policy, and the population of the valley of the Mississippi will preponderate in the Federal assemblies.

This constant gravitation of the Federal power and influence towards the northwest is shown every ten years, when a general census of the population is made and the number of delegates that each state sends to Congress is settled anew.[73] In 1790 Virginia had nineteen representatives in Congress. This number continued to increase until 1813, when it reached twenty-three; from that time it began to decrease, and in 1833 Virginia elected only twenty-one.[74] During the same period the state of New York followed the

[73] It may be seen that in the course of the last ten years the population of one district, as, for instance, the state of Delaware, has increased in the proportion of 5 per cent; while that of another, like the territory of Michigan, has increased 250 per cent. Thus the population of Virginia had augmented 13 per cent, and that of the border state of Ohio 61 per cent, in the same time. The general table of these changes, which is given in the *National Calendar,* is a striking picture of the unequal fortunes of the different states.

[74] It has been said that in the course of the last period the population of Virginia has increased 13 per cent; and it is necessary to explain how the number of representatives for a state may decrease when the population of that state, far from diminishing, is actually increasing. I take the state of Virginia, to which I have already alluded, as the basis of my comparison. The number of representatives of Virginia in 1823 was proportionate to the total number of the representatives of the Union and to the relation which its population bore to that of the whole Union; in 1833 the number of representatives of Virginia was likewise proportionate to the total number of the representatives of the Union and to the relation which its population, increased in the course of ten years, bore to the increased population of the Union in the same space of time. The new number of Virginian representatives will then be to the old number, on the one hand, as the new number of all the representatives is to the old number; and, on the other hand, as the increase of the population of Virginia is to that of the whole population of the country. Thus if the increase of the population of the lesser region be to that of the greater in an exact inverse ratio of the proportion between the new and the old numbers of all the representatives, the number of the representatives of Virginia will remain stationary; and if the increase of the Virginia population be to that of the whole Union in a smaller ratio than the new number of representatives of the Union to the old number, the number of the representatives of Virginia must decrease.

contrary direction: in 1790 it had ten representatives in Congress; in 1813, twenty-seven; in 1823, thirty-four; and in 1833, forty. The state of Ohio had only one representative in 1803; and in 1833 it already had nineteen.

It is difficult to imagine a durable union of a nation that is rich and strong with one that is poor and weak, even if it were proved that the strength and wealth of the one are not the causes of the weakness and poverty of the other. But union is still more difficult to maintain at a time when one party is losing strength and the other is gaining it. This rapid and disproportionate increase of certain states threatens the independence of the others. New York might perhaps succeed, with its two million inhabitants and its forty representatives, in dictating to the other states in Congress. But even if the more powerful states make no attempt to oppress the smaller ones, the danger still exists; for there is almost as much in the possibility of the act as in the act itself. The weak generally mistrust the justice and the reason of the strong. The states that increase less rapidly than the others look upon those that are more favored by fortune with envy and suspicion. Hence arise the deep-seated uneasiness and ill-defined agitation which are observable in the South and which form so striking a contrast to the confidence and prosperity which are common to other parts of the Union. I am inclined to think that the hostile attitude taken by the South recently is attributable to no other cause. The inhabitants of the Southern states are, of all the Americans, those who are most interested in the maintenance of the Union; they would assuredly suffer most from being left to themselves; and yet they are the only ones who threaten to break the tie of confederation. It is easy to perceive that the South, which has given four Presidents to the Union,[75] which perceives that it is losing its federal influence and that the number of its representatives in Congress is diminishing from year to year, while those of the Northern and Western states are increasing, the South, which is peopled with ardent and irascible men, is becoming more and more irritated and alarmed. Its inhabitants reflect upon their present position and remember their past influence, with the melancholy uneasiness of men who suspect oppression. If they discover a law of the Union that is not unequivocally favorable to

[75] Washington, Jefferson, Madison, and Monroe.

their interests, they protest against it as an abuse of force; and if their ardent remonstrances are not listened to, they threaten to quit an association that loads them with burdens while it deprives them of the profits. "The Tariff," said the inhabitants of Carolina in 1832, "enriches the North and ruins the South; for, if this were not the case, to what can we attribute the continually increasing power and wealth of the North, with its inclement skies and arid soil; while the South, which may be styled the garden of America, is rapidly declining." [76]

If the changes which I have described were gradual, so that each generation at least might have time to disappear with the order of things under which it had lived, the danger would be less; but the progress of society in America is precipitate and almost revolutionary. The same citizen may have lived to see his state take the lead in the Union and afterwards become powerless in the Federal assemblies; and an Anglo-American republic has been known to grow as rapidly as a man, passing from birth and infancy to maturity in the course of thirty years. It must not be imagined, however, that the states that lose their preponderance also lose their population or their riches; no stop is put to their prosperity, and they even go on to increase more rapidly than any kingdom in Europe.[77] But they believe themselves to be impoverished because their wealth does not augment as rapidly as that of their neighbors; and they think that their power is lost because they suddenly come in contact with a power greater than their own.[78] Thus they

[76] See the report of its committee to the convention that proclaimed nullification in South Carolina.

[77] The population of a country assuredly constitutes the first element of its wealth. During this same period, from 1820 to 1832, in which Virginia lost two of its representatives in Congress, its population increased in the proportion of 13.7 per cent; that of Carolina in the proportion of 15 per cent; and that of Georgia 15.5 per cent. (See *American Almanac*, 1832, p. 162.) But the population of Russia, which increases more rapidly than that of any other European country, only augments in ten years at the rate of 9.5 per cent; of France at the rate of 7 per cent; and of Europe all together at the rate of 4.7 per cent. (See Malte-Brun, Vol. VI, p. 95.)

[78] It must be admitted, however, that the depreciation that has taken place in the value of tobacco during the last fifty years has notably diminished the opulence of the Southern planters: but this circumstance is as independent of the will of their Northern brethren as it is of their own.

are more hurt in their feelings and their passions than in their interests. But this is amply sufficient to endanger the maintenance of the Union. If kings and peoples had only had their true interests in view ever since the beginning of the world, war would scarcely be known among mankind.

Thus the prosperity of the United States is the source of their most serious dangers, since it tends to create in some of the federal states that intoxication which accompanies a rapid increase of fortune, and to awaken in others those feelings of envy, mistrust, and regret which usually attend the loss of it. The Americans contemplate this extraordinary progress with exultation; but they would be wiser to consider it with sorrow and alarm. The Americans of the United States must inevitably become one of the greatest nations in the world; their offspring will cover almost the whole of North America; the continent that they inhabit is their dominion, and it cannot escape them. What urges them to take possession of it so soon? Riches, power, and renown cannot fail to be theirs at some future time, but they rush upon this immense fortune as if but a moment remained for them to make it their own.

I think that I have demonstrated that the existence of the present confederation depends entirely on the continued assent of all the confederates; and starting from this principle, I have inquired into the causes that may induce some of the states to separate from the others. The Union may, however, perish in two different ways: one of the federated states may choose to retire from the compact, and so forcibly to sever the Federal tie; and it is to this supposition that most of the remarks that I have made apply; or the authority of the Federal government may be gradually lost by the simultaneous tendency of the united republics to resume their independence. The central power, successively stripped of all its prerogatives and reduced to impotence by tacit consent, would become incompetent to fulfill its purpose, and the second union would perish, like the first, by a sort of senile imbecility. The gradual weakening of the Federal tie, which may finally lead to the dissolution of the Union, is a distinct circumstance that may produce a variety of minor consequences before it operates so violent a change. The confederation might still exist although its government were reduced to such a degree of inanition as to paralyze the nation, to cause internal anarchy, and to check the general prosperity of the country.

After having investigated the causes that may induce the Anglo-Americans to disunite, it is important to inquire whether, if the Union continues to survive, their government will extend or contract its sphere of action, and whether it will become more energetic or more weak.

The Americans are evidently disposed to look upon their condition with alarm. They perceive that in most of the nations of the world the exercise of the rights of sovereignty tends to fall into a few hands, and they are dismayed by the idea that it may be so in their own country. Even the statesmen feel, or affect to feel, these fears; for in America centralization is by no means popular, and there is no surer means of courting the majority than by inveighing against the encroachments of the central power. The Americans do not perceive that the countries in which this alarming tendency to centralization exists are inhabited by a single people, while the Union is composed of different communities, a fact that is sufficient to baffle all the inferences which might be drawn from analogy. I confess that I am inclined to consider these fears of a great number of Americans as purely imaginary. Far from participating in their dread of the consolidation of power in the hands of the Union, I think that the Federal government is visibly losing strength. To prove this assertion, I shall not have recourse to any remote occurrences, but to circumstances which I have myself witnessed and which belong to our own time.

An attentive examination of what is going on in the United States will easily convince us that two opposite tendencies exist there, like two currents flowing in contrary directions in the same channel. The Union has now existed for forty-five years, and time has done away with many provincial prejudices which were at first hostile to its power. The patriotic feeling that attached each of the Americans to his own state has become less exclusive, and the different parts of the Union have become more amicable as they have become better acquainted with each other. The post, that great instrument of intercourse, now reaches into the backwoods; [79] and steamboats have established daily means of

[79] In 1832 the district of Michigan, which had only 31,639 inhabitants and was hardly more than a wilderness, had developed

communication between the different points of the coast. An inland navigation of unexampled rapidity conveys commodities up and down the rivers of the country.[80] And to these facilities of nature and art may be added those restless cravings, that busy-mindedness and love of pelf, which are constantly urging the American into active life and bringing him into contact with his fellow citizens. He crosses the country in every direction; he visits all the various populations of the land. There is not a province in France in which the natives are so well known to one another as the thirteen millions of men who cover the territory of the United States.

While the Americans intermingle, they assimilate; the differences resulting from their climate, their origin, and their institutions diminish; and they all draw nearer and nearer to the common type. Every year thousands of men leave the North to settle in different parts of the Union; they bring with them their faith, their opinions, and their manners, and as they are more enlightened than the men among whom they are about to dwell, they soon rise to the head of affairs and adapt society to their own advantage. This continual emigration of the North to the South is peculiarly favorable to the fusion of all the different provincial characters into one national character. The civilization of the North appears to be the common standard, to which the whole nation will one day be assimilated.

The commercial ties that unite the federated states are strengthened by the increasing manufactures of the Americans, and the union which began in their opinions gradually forms a part of their habits; the course of time has swept away the bugbear thoughts that haunted the imaginations of the citizens in 1789. The Federal power has not become oppressive; it has not destroyed the independence of the states; it has not subjected the confederates to mo-

---

940 miles of post roads. The almost entirely unsettled territory of Arkansas was already covered by 1,938 miles of post roads. See the *Report of the Postmaster General,* November 30, 1833. The carriage of newspapers alone throughout the Union brought in $254,796 annually.

[80] In the course of ten years, from 1821 to 1831, 271 steamboats were launched on the rivers flowing through the Mississippi Valley. In 1829 there were 256 steamboats in the United States. See *Legislative Documents,* No. 140, p. 274.

narchical institutions; and the Union has not rendered the lesser states dependent upon the larger ones. The confederation has continued to increase in population, in wealth, and in power. I am therefore convinced that the natural obstacles to the continuance of the American Union are not so powerful as they were in 1789, and that the enemies of the Union are not so numerous.

And yet a careful examination of the history of the United States for the last forty-five years will readily convince us that the Federal power is declining; nor is it difficult to explain the causes of this phenomenon. When the Constitution of 1789 was promulgated, the nation was a prey to anarchy; the Union which succeeded this confusion excited much dread and hatred, but it was warmly supported because it satisfied an imperious want. Although it was then more attacked than it is now, the Federal power soon reached the maximum of its authority, as is usually the case with a government that triumphs after having braced its strength by the struggle. At that time the interpretation of the Constitution seemed to extend rather than to repress the Federal sovereignty; and the Union offered, in several respects, the appearance of a single and undivided people, directed in its foreign and internal policy by a single government. But to attain this point the people had risen, to some extent, above itself.

The Constitution had not destroyed the individuality of the states, and all communities, of whatever nature they may be, are impelled by a secret instinct towards independence. This propensity is still more decided in a country like America, in which every village forms a sort of republic, accustomed to govern itself. It therefore cost the states an effort to submit to the Federal supremacy; and all efforts, however successful, necessarily subside with the causes in which they originated.

As the Federal government consolidated its authority, America resumed its rank among the nations, peace returned to its frontiers, and public credit was restored; confusion was succeeded by a fixed state of things, which permitted the full and free exercise of industrious enterprise. It was this very prosperity that made the Americans forget the cause which had produced it; and when once the danger was passed, the energy and the patriotism that had enabled them to brave it disappeared from among them. Delivered from the cares that oppressed them, they easily returned to their ordinary habits and gave themselves up without resistance to their natural inclinations. When a powerful government no longer appeared to be necessary, they once more began to think it irksome. Everything prospered under the Union, and the states were not inclined to abandon the Union; but they desired to render the action of the power which represented it as light as possible. The general principle of union was adopted, but in every minor detail there was a tendency to independence. The principle of confederation was every day more easily admitted and more rarely applied, so that the Federal government, by creating order and peace, brought about its own decline.

As soon as this tendency of public opinion began to be manifested externally, the leaders of parties, who live by the passions of the people, began to work it to their own advantage. The position of the Federal government then became exceedingly critical. Its enemies were in possession of the popular favor, and they obtained the right of conducting its policy by pledging themselves to lessen its influence. From that time forwards the government of the Union, as often as it has entered the lists with the governments of the states, has almost invariably been obliged to recede. And whenever an interpretation of the terms of the Federal Constitution has been pronounced, that interpretation has generally been opposed to the Union and favorable to the states.

The Constitution gave to the Federal government the right of providing for the national interests; and it had been held that no other authority was so fit to superintend the internal improvements that affected the prosperity of the whole Union, such, for instance, as the cutting of canals. But the states were alarmed at a power that could thus dispose of a portion of their territory; they were afraid that the central government would by this means acquire a formidable patronage within their own limits, and exercise influence which they wished to reserve exclusively to their own agents. The Democratic Party, which has constantly opposed the increase of the Federal authority, accused Congress of usurpation, and the chief magistrate of ambition. The central government was intimidated by these clamors, and it finally acknowledged its error, promising to confine

its influence for the future within the circle that was prescribed to it.

The Constitution confers upon the Union the right of
treating with foreign nations. The Indian tribes which
border upon the frontiers of the United States had usually
been regarded in this light. As long as these savages consented to retire before the civilized settlers, the Federal right
was not contested; but as soon as an Indian tribe attempted
to fix its residence upon a given spot, the adjacent states
claimed possession of the lands and a right of sovereignty
over the natives. The central government soon recognized
both these claims; and after it had concluded treaties with
the Indians as independent nations, it gave them up as subjects to the legislative tyranny of the states.[81]

Some of the states which had been founded on the Atlantic coast extended indefinitely to the West, into wild
regions where no European had yet penetrated. The states
whose confines were irrevocably fixed looked with a jealous
eye upon the unbounded regions that were thus opened to
their neighbors. The latter, with a view to conciliate the
others and to facilitate the act of union, then agreed to lay
down their own boundaries and to abandon all the territory
that lay beyond them to the confederation at large.[82]
Thenceforward the Federal government became the owner
of all the uncultivated lands that lie beyond the borders of
the thirteen states first confederated. It had the right of
parceling and selling them, and the sums derived from this
source were paid into the public treasury to furnish the
means of purchasing tracts of land from the Indians, opening roads to the remote settlements, and accelerating the advance of civilization. New states have been formed in the
course of time in the midst of those wilds which were
formerly ceded by the Atlantic states. Congress has gone on
to sell, for the profit of the nation at large, the uncultivated
lands which those new states contained. But the latter at

[81] See, in the legislative documents already quoted in speaking
of the Indians, the letter of the President of the United States to
the Cherokees, his correspondence on this subject with his agents,
and his messages to Congress.

[82] The first act of cession was made by the state of New York
in 1780; Virginia, Massachusetts, Connecticut, South and North
Carolina followed this example at different times, Georgia making the last; its act of cession was not completed till 1802.

length asserted that, as they were now fully constituted, they ought to have the right of converting the produce of these sales exclusively to their own use. As their remonstrances became more and more threatening, Congress thought fit to deprive the Union of a portion of the privileges that it had hitherto enjoyed; and at the end of 1832 it passed a law by which the greatest part of the revenue derived from the sale of lands was made over to the new Western republics, although the lands themselves were not ceded to them.[83]

The slightest observation in the United States enables one to appreciate the advantages that the country derives from the Bank of the United States. These advantages are of several kinds, but one of them is peculiarly striking to the stranger. The notes of the bank are taken upon the borders of the wilderness for the same value as at Philadelphia, where the bank conducts its operations.[84]

But the Bank of the United States is the object of great animosity. Its directors proclaimed their hostility to the President, and they were accused, not without probability, of having abused their influence to thwart his election. The President therefore attacked the establishment with all the warmth of personal enmity; and he was encouraged in the pursuit of his revenge by the conviction that he was supported by the secret inclinations of the majority. The bank may be regarded as the great monetary tie of the Union, just as Congress is the great legislative tie; and the same passions that tend to render the states independent of the central power contributed to the overthrow of the bank.

The Bank of the United States always held a great number of the notes issued by the state banks, which it can at any time oblige them to convert into cash. It has itself nothing to fear from a similar demand, as the extent of its resources enables it to meet all claims. But the existence of the provincial banks is thus threatened and their operations

[83] It is true that the President refused his assent to this law; but he completely adopted it in principle. See Message of December 8, 1833.

[84] The Bank of the United States was established in 1816, with a capital of 35,000,000 dollars (185,500,000 fr.); its charter expired in 1836. In 1832 Congress passed a law to renew it, but the President vetoed the bill. The struggle continues with great violence on either side, and it is easy to forecast the speedy fall of the bank.

are restricted, since they are able to issue only a quantity of notes duly proportioned to their capital. They submitted with impatience to this salutary control. The newspapers that they bought over, and the President, whose interest rendered him their instrument, attacked the bank with the greatest vehemence. They roused the local passions and the blind democratic instinct of the country to aid their cause; and they asserted that the bank directors formed a permanent aristocratic body, whose influence would ultimately be felt in the government and affect those principles of equality upon which society rests in America.

The contest between the bank and its opponents was only an incident in the great struggle which is going on in America between the states and the central power, between the spirit of democratic independence and that of a proper distribution and subordination of power. I do not mean that the enemies of the bank were identically the same individuals who on other points attacked the Federal government, but I assert that the attacks directed against the Bank of the United States originated in the same propensities that militate against the Federal government, and that the very numerous opponents of the former afford a deplorable symptom of the decreasing strength of the latter.

But the Union has never shown so much weakness as on the celebrated question of the tariff.[85] The wars of the French Revolution and of 1812 had created manufacturing establishments in the North of the Union, by cutting off free communication between America and Europe. When peace was concluded and the channel of intercourse reopened by which the produce of Europe was transmitted to the New World, the Americans thought fit to establish a system of import duties for the twofold purpose of protecting their incipient manufactures and of paying off the amount of the debt contracted during the war. The Southern states, which have no manufactures to encourage and which are exclusively agricultural, soon complained of this measure. I do not pretend to examine here whether their complaints were well or ill founded, but only to recite the facts.

As early as 1820 South Carolina declared in a petition to Congress that the tariff was "unconstitutional, oppressive,

[85] See principally, for the details of this affair, *Legislative Documents,* 22nd Congress, 2nd Session, No. 30.

and unjust." And the states of Georgia, Virginia, North Carolina, Alabama, and Mississippi subsequently remonstrated against it with more or less vigor. But Congress, far from lending an ear to these complaints, raised the scale of tariff duties in the years 1824 and 1828 and recognized anew the principle on which it was founded. A doctrine was then proclaimed, or rather revived, in the South, which took the name of Nullification.

I have shown in the proper place that the object of the Federal Constitution was not to form a league, but to create a national government. The Americans of the United States form one and the same people, in all the cases which are specified by that Constitution; and upon these points the will of the nation is expressed, as it is in all constitutional nations, by the voice of the majority. When the majority has once spoken, it is the duty of the minority to submit. Such is the sound legal doctrine, and the only one that agrees with the text of the Constitution and the known intention of those who framed it.

The partisans of Nullification in the South maintain, on the contrary, that the intention of the Americans in uniting was not to combine themselves into one and the same people, but that they meant only to form a league of independent states; and that each state, consequently, retains its entire sovereignty, if not *de facto*, at least *de jure*, and has the right of putting its own construction upon the laws of Congress and of suspending their execution within the limits of its own territory if they seem unconstitutional and unjust.

The entire doctrine of Nullification is comprised in a sentence uttered by Vice President Calhoun, the head of that party in the South, before the Senate of the United States, in 1833: "The Constitution is a compact to which the States were parties in their sovereign capacity: now, whenever a compact is entered into by parties which acknowledge no common arbiter to decide in the last resort, each of them has a right to judge for itself in relation to the nature, extent, and obligations of the instrument." It is evident that such a doctrine destroys the very basis of the Federal Constitution and brings back the anarchy from which the Americans were delivered by the act of 1789.

When South Carolina perceived that Congress turned a deaf ear to its remonstrances, it threatened to apply the doctrine of Nullification to the Federal tariff law. Congress persisted in its system, and at length the storm broke out. In the course of 1832 the people of South Carolina[86] named a national convention to consult upon the extraordinary measures that remained to be taken; and on the 24th of November of the same year this convention promulgated a law, under the form of a decree, which annulled the Federal tariff law, forbade the levy of the duties which that law commands, and refused to recognize the appeal that might be made to the Federal courts of law.[87] This decree was only to be put in execution in the ensuing month of February; and it was intimated that if Congress modified the tariff before that period, South Carolina might be induced to proceed no further with her menaces; and a vague desire was afterwards expressed of submitting the question to an extraordinary assembly of all the federated states. In the meantime South Carolina armed her militia and prepared for war.

But Congress, which had slighted its suppliant subjects, listened to their complaints as soon as they appeared with arms in their hands.[88] A law was passed [89] by which the tariff duties were to be gradually reduced for ten years, until

[86] That is to say, the majority of the people; for the opposite party, called the Union Party, always formed a very strong and active minority. Carolina may contain about 47,000 voters; 30,-000 were in favor of nullification, and 17,000 opposed to it.

[87] This decree was preceded by a *Report* of the committee by which it was framed, containing the explanation of the motives and object of the law. The following passage occurs in it (p. 34): "When the rights reserved by the Constitution to the different States are deliberately violated, it is the duty and the right of those States to interfere, in order to check the progress of the evil; to resist usurpation, and to maintain, within their respective limits, those powers and privileges which belong to them as *independent, sovereign States*. If they were destitute of this right, they would not be sovereign. South Carolina declares that she acknowledges no tribunal upon earth above her authority. She has indeed entered into a solemn compact of union with the other States; but she demands, and will exercise, the right of putting her own construction upon it; and when this compact is violated by her sister States, and by the government which they have created, she is determined to avail herself of the unquestionable right of judging what is the extent of the infraction, and what are the measures best fitted to obtain justice."

[88] Congress was finally persuaded to take this step by the conduct of the powerful state of Virginia, whose legislature offered to serve as a mediator between the Union and South Carolina. Hitherto the latter state had appeared to be entirely abandoned, even by the states that had joined in her remonstrances.

[89] Law of March 2, 1833.

they were brought so low as not to exceed the supplies necessary to the government. Thus Congress completely abandoned the principle of the tariff and substituted a mere fiscal impost for a system of protective duties.[90] The government of the Union, to conceal its defeat, had recourse to an expedient that is much in vogue with feeble governments. It yielded the point *de facto,* but remained inflexible upon the principles; and while it was altering the tariff law, it passed another bill by which the President was invested with extraordinary powers enabling him to overcome by force a resistance which was then no longer to be feared.

But South Carolina did not consent to leave the Union in the enjoyment of these scanty appearances of success: the same national convention that had annulled the tariff bill met again and accepted the proffered concession; but at the same time it declared its unabated perseverance in the doctrine of Nullification; and to prove what it said, it annulled the law investing the President with extraordinary powers, although it was very certain that the law would never be carried into effect.

Almost all the controversies of which I have been speaking have taken place under the Presidency of General Jackson; and it cannot be denied that in the question of the tariff he has supported the rights of the Union with energy and skill. I think, however, that the conduct of this President of the Federal government may be reckoned as one of the dangers that threaten its continuance.

Some persons in Europe have formed an opinion of the influence of General Jackson upon the affairs of his country which appears highly extravagant to those who have seen the subject nearer at hand. We have been told that General Jackson has won battles; that he is an energetic man, prone by nature and habit to the use of force, covetous of power, and a despot by inclination. All this may be true; but the inferences which have been drawn from these truths are very erroneous. It has been imagined that General Jackson is bent on establishing a dictatorship in America, introducing a military spirit, and giving a degree of influence to the central authority that cannot but be dangerous to provincial liberties. But in America the time for similar undertakings,

[90] This bill was brought in by Mr. Clay, and it passed, in four days, through both houses of Congress, by an immense majority.

and the age for men of this kind, has not yet come; if General Jackson had thought of exercising his authority in this manner, he would infallibly have forfeited his political station and compromised his life; he has not been so imprudent as to attempt anything of the kind.

Far from wishing to extend the Federal power, the President belongs to the party which is desirous of limiting that power to the clear and precise letter of the Constitution, and which never puts a construction upon that act favorable to the government of the Union; far from standing forth as the champion of centralization, General Jackson is the agent of the state jealousies; and he was placed in his lofty station by the passions that are most opposed to the central government. It is by perpetually flattering these passions that he maintains his station and his popularity. General Jackson is the slave of the majority: he yields to its wishes, its propensities, and its demands—say, rather, anticipates and forestalls them.

Whenever the governments of the states come into collision with that of the Union, the President is generally the first to question his own rights; he almost always outstrips the legislature; and when the extent of the Federal power is controverted, he takes part, as it were, against himself; he conceals his official interests, and labors to diminish his own dignity. Not, indeed, that he is naturally weak or hostile to the Union; for when the majority decided against the claims of Nullification, he put himself at their head, asserted distinctly and energetically the doctrines which the nation held, and was the first to recommend force; but General Jackson appears to me, if I may use the American expression, to be a Federalist by taste and a Republican by calculation.

General Jackson stoops to gain the favor of the majority; but when he feels that his popularity is secure, he overthrows all obstacles in the pursuit of the objects which the community approves or of those which it does not regard with jealousy. Supported by a power that his predecessors never had, he tramples on his personal enemies, whenever they cross his path, with a facility without example; he takes upon himself the responsibility of measures that no one before him would have ventured to attempt. He even treats the national representatives with a disdain approaching to insult; he puts his veto on the laws of Congress and frequently neglects even to reply to that powerful body. He is a favorite who sometimes treats his master roughly. The power of General Jackson perpetually increases, but that of the President declines; in his hands the Federal government is strong, but it will pass enfeebled into the hands of his successor.

I am strangely mistaken if the Federal government of the United States is not constantly losing strength, retiring gradually from public affairs, and narrowing its circle of action. It is naturally feeble, but it now abandons even the appearance of strength. On the other hand, I thought that I noticed a more lively sense of independence and a more decided attachment to their separate governments in the states. The Union is desired, but only as a shadow; they wish it to be strong in certain cases and weak in all others; in time of warfare it is to be able to concentrate all the forces of the nation and all the resources of the country in its hands, and in time of peace its existence is to be scarcely perceptible, as if this alternate debility and vigor were natural or possible.

I do not see anything for the present that can check this general tendency of opinion; the causes in which it originated do not cease to operate in the same direction. The change will therefore go on, and it may be predicted that unless some extraordinary event occurs, the government of the Union will grow weaker and weaker every day.

I think, however, that the period is still remote at which the Federal power will be entirely extinguished by its inability to protect itself and to maintain peace in the country. The Union is sanctioned by the manners and desires of the people; its results are palpable, its benefits visible. When it is perceived that the weakness of the Federal government compromises the existence of the Union, I do not doubt that a reaction will take place with a view to increase its strength.

The government of the United States is, of all the federal governments which have hitherto been established, the one that is most naturally destined to act. As long as it is only indirectly assailed by the interpretation of its laws and as long as its substance is not seriously impaired, a change of opinion, an internal crisis, or a war may restore all the vigor that it requires. What I have been most anxious to establish is simply this: Many people in France imagine that a change of opinion is going on in the United States which is favorable to a centralization of power in the hands of the President and the Congress. I hold that a contrary tendency may distinctly be observed. So far is the Federal government, as it grows old, from acquiring strength and from threatening the sovereignty of the states that I maintain it to be growing weaker and the sovereignty of the Union alone to be in danger. Such are the facts that the present time discloses. The future conceals the final result of this tendency and the events which may check, retard, or accelerate the changes I have described; I do not pretend to be able to remove the veil that hides them.

OF THE REPUBLICAN INSTITUTIONS OF THE UNITED STATES, AND WHAT THEIR CHANCES OF DURATION ARE. *The Union is only an accident—Republican institutions have more permanence—A republic for the present is the natural state of the Anglo-Americans—Reason for this—In order to destroy it, all the laws must be changed at the same time, and a great alteration take place in manners—Difficulties which the Americans would experience in creating an aristocracy.*

THE DISMEMBERMENT of the Union, by introducing war into the heart of those states which are now federated, with standing armies, a dictatorship, and heavy taxation, might eventually compromise the fate of republican institutions. But we ought not to confound the future prospects of the republic with those of the Union. The Union is an accident, which will last only as long as circumstances favor it; but a republican form of government seems to me the natural state of the Americans, which nothing but the continued action of hostile causes, always acting in the same direction, could change into a monarchy. The Union exists principally in the law which formed it; one revolution, one change in public opinion, might destroy it forever; but the republic has a deeper foundation to rest upon.

What is understood by a republican government in the United States is the slow and quiet action of society upon itself. It is a regular state of things really founded upon the enlightened will of the people. It is a conciliatory government, under which resolutions are allowed time to ripen, and in which they are deliberately discussed, and are exe-

:uted only when mature. The republicans in the United States set a high value upon morality, respect religious belief, and acknowledge the existence of rights. They profess to think that a people ought to be moral, religious, and temperate in proportion as it is free. What is called the republic in the United States is the tranquil rule of the majority, which, after having had time to examine itself and to give proof of its existence, is the common source of all the powers of the state. But the power of the majority itself is not unlimited. Above it in the moral world are humanity, justice, and reason; and in the political world, vested rights. The majority recognizes these two barriers; and if it now and then oversteps them, it is because, like individuals, it has passions and, like them, it is prone to do what is wrong, while it discerns what is right.

But the demagogues of Europe have made strange discoveries. According to them, a republic is not the rule of the majority, as has hitherto been thought, but the rule of those who are strenuous partisans of the majority. It is not the people who preponderate in this kind of government, but those who know what is good for the people, a happy distinction which allows men to act in the name of nations without consulting them and to claim their gratitude while their rights are trampled underfoot. A republican government, they hold, moreover, is the only one that has the right of doing whatever it chooses and despising what men have hitherto respected, from the highest moral laws to the vulgar rules of common sense. Until our time it had been supposed that despotism was odious, under whatever form it appeared. But it is a discovery of modern days that there are such things as legitimate tyranny and holy injustice, provided they are exercised in the name of the people.

The ideas that the Americans have adopted respecting the republic render it easy for them to live under it and ensure its duration. With them, if the republic is often bad practically, at least it is good theoretically; and in the end the people always act in conformity to it.

It was impossible at the foundation of the states, and it would still be difficult, to establish a central administration in America. The inhabitants are dispersed over too great a space and separated by too many natural obstacles for one man to undertake to direct the details of their existence.

America is therefore pre-eminently the country of state and municipal government. To this cause, which was plainly felt by all the Europeans of the New World, the Anglo-Americans added several others peculiar to themselves.

At the time of the settlement of the North American colonies municipal liberty had already penetrated into the laws as well as the customs of the English, and the immigrants adopted it, not only as a necessary thing, but as a benefit which they knew how to appreciate. We have already seen how the colonies were founded: every colony and almost every district was peopled separately by men who were strangers to one another or were associated with very different purposes. The English settlers in the United States, therefore, early perceived that they were divided into a great number of small and distinct communities, which belonged to no common center; and that each of these little communities must take care of its own affairs, since there was not any central authority that was naturally bound and easily enabled to provide for them. Thus the nature of the country, the manner in which the British colonies were founded, the habits of the first immigrants—in short, everything—united to promote in an extraordinary degree municipal and state liberties.

In the United States, therefore, the mass of the institutions of the country is essentially republican; and in order permanently to destroy the laws which form the basis of the republic, it would be necessary to abolish all the laws at once. At the present day it would be even more difficult for a party to found a monarchy in the United States than for a set of men to convert France into a republic. Royalty would not find a system of legislation prepared for it beforehand; and a monarchy would then really exist surrounded by republican institutions. The monarchical principle would likewise have great difficulty in penetrating into the customs of the Americans.

In the United States the sovereignty of the people is not an isolated doctrine, bearing no relation to the prevailing habits and ideas of the people; it may, on the contrary, be regarded as the last link of a chain of opinions which binds the whole Anglo-American world. That Providence has given to every human being the degree of reason necessary to direct himself in the affairs that interest him exclusively is the grand maxim upon which civil and political society rests in the United States. The father of a family applies it to his children, the master to his servants, the township to its officers, the county to its townships, the state to the counties, the Union to the states; and when extended to the nation, it becomes the doctrine of the sovereignty of the people.

Thus in the United States the fundamental principle of the republic is the same which governs the greater part of human actions; republican notions insinuate themselves into all the ideas, opinions, and habits of the Americans and are formally recognized by the laws; and before the laws could be altered, the whole community must be revolutionized. In the United States even the religion of most of the citizens is republican, since it submits the truths of the other world to private judgment, as in politics the care of their temporal interests is abandoned to the good sense of the people. Thus every man is allowed freely to take that road which he thinks will lead him to heaven, just as the law permits every citizen to have the right of choosing his own government.

It is evident that nothing but a long series of events, all having the same tendency, could substitute for this combination of laws, opinions, and manners a mass of opposite opinions, manners, and laws.

If republican principles are to perish in America, they can yield only after a laborious social process, often interrupted and as often resumed; they will have many apparent revivals and will not become totally extinct until an entirely new people have succeeded to those who now exist. There is no symptom or presage of the approach of such a revolution. There is nothing more striking to a person newly arrived in the United States than the kind of tumultuous agitation in which he finds political society. The laws are incessantly changing, and at first sight it seems impossible that a people so fickle in its desires should avoid adopting, within a short space of time, a completely new form of government. But such apprehensions are premature; the instability that affects political institutions is of two kinds, which ought not to be confounded. The first, which modifies secondary laws, is not incompatible with a very settled state of society. The other shakes the very foundations of the constitution and attacks the fundamental principles of legislation; this species of instability is always followed by troubles and revolutions, and the nation that suffers under it is in a violent and transitory state.

Experience shows that these two kinds of legislative instability have no necessary connection, for they have been found united or separate, according to times and circumstances. The first is common in the United States, but not the second: the Americans often change their laws, but the foundations of the Constitution are respected.

In our days the republican principle rules in America, as the monarchical principle did in France under Louis XIV. The French of that period not only were friends of the monarchy, but thought it impossible to put anything in its place; they received it as we receive the rays of the sun and the return of the seasons. Among them the royal power had neither advocates nor opponents. In like manner the republican government exists in America, without contention or opposition, without proofs or arguments, by a tacit agreement, a sort of *consensus universalis*.

It is my opinion, however, that by changing their administrative forms as often as they do, the inhabitants of the United States compromise the stability of their government. It may be apprehended that men perpetually thwarted in their designs by the mutability of legislation will learn to look on the republic as an inconvenient form of society; the evil resulting from the instability of the secondary enactments might then raise a doubt as to the nature of the fundamental principles of the Constitution and indirectly bring about a revolution; but this epoch is still very remote.

It may be foreseen even now that when the Americans lose their republican institutions they will speedily arrive at a despotic government, without a long interval of limited monarchy. Montesquieu remarked that nothing is more absolute than the authority of a prince who immediately succeeds a republic, since the indefinite powers that had fearlessly been entrusted to an elected magistrate are then transferred to a hereditary sovereign. This is true in general, but it is more peculiarly applicable to a democratic republic. In the United States the magistrates are not elected by a particular class of citizens, but by the majority of the nation; as they are the immediate representatives of the passions of the multitude and are wholly dependent upon its pleasure, they excite neither hatred nor fear; hence, as I have already shown, very little care has been taken to limit their authority, and they are left in possession of a vast amount of arbitrary power. This state of things has created habits that would outlive itself; the American magistrate would retain his indefinite power, but would cease to be responsible for it; and it is impossible to say what bounds could then be set to tyranny.

Some of our European politicians expect to see an aristocracy arise in America, and already predict the exact period at which it will assume the reins of government. I have previously observed, and I repeat it, that the present tendency of American society appears to me to become more and more democratic. Nevertheless, I do not assert that the Americans will not at some future time restrict the circle of political rights, or confiscate those rights to the advantage of a single man; but I cannot believe that they will ever give the exclusive use of them to a privileged class of citizens or, in other words, that they will ever found an aristocracy.

An aristocratic body is composed of a certain number of citizens who, without being very far removed from the mass of the people, are nevertheless permanently stationed above them; a body which it is easy to touch, and difficult to strike, with which the people are in daily contact, but with which they can never combine. Nothing can be imagined more contrary to nature and to the secret instincts of the human heart than a subjection of this kind; and men who are left follow their own bent will always prefer the arbitrary power of a king to the regular administration of an aristocracy. Aristocratic institutions cannot exist without laying down the inequality of men as a fundamental principle, legalizing it beforehand and introducing it into the family as well as into society; but these are things so repugnant to natural equity that they can only be extorted from men by force.

I do not think a single people can be quoted, since human society began to exist, which has, by its own free will and its own exertions, created an aristocracy within its own bosom. All the aristocracies of the Middle Ages were founded by military conquest; the conqueror was the noble, the vanquished became the serf. Inequality was then imposed by force; and after it had once been introduced into the manners of the country, it maintained itself and passed naturally into the laws. Communities have existed which were aristocratic from their earliest origin, owing to circumstances anterior to that event, and which became more democratic in each succeeding age. Such was the lot of the Romans, and of the barbarians after them. But a people, having taken its rise in civilization and democracy, which should gradually establish inequality of condition, until it arrived at inviolable privileges and exclusive castes, would be a novelty in the world; and nothing indicates that America is likely to be the first to furnish such an example.

SOME CONSIDERATIONS ON THE CAUSES OF THE COMMERCIAL PROSPERITY OF THE UNITED STATES. *The Americans destined by nature to be a great maritime people—Extent of their coasts—Depth of their ports—Size of their rivers—The commercial superiority of the Anglo-Americans less attributable, however, to physical circumstances than to moral and intellectual causes—Reason for this opinion—Future of the Anglo-Americans as a commercial nation—The dissolution of the Union would not check the maritime vigor of the states—Reason for this—Anglo-Americans will naturally supply the wants of the inhabitants of South America—They will become, like the English, the commercial agents of a great portion of the world.*

THE COAST of the United States, from the Bay of Fundy to the Sabine River in the Gulf of Mexico, is more than two thousand miles in extent. These shores form an unbroken line, and are all subject to the same government. No nation in the world possesses vaster, deeper, or more secure ports for commerce than the Americans.

The inhabitants of the United States constitute a great civilized people, which fortune has placed in the midst of an uncultivated country, at a distance of three thousand miles from the central point of civilization. America consequently stands in daily need of Europe. The Americans will no doubt ultimately succeed in producing or manufacturing at home most of the articles that they require; but the two continents can never be independent of each other, so numerous are the natural ties between their wants, their ideas, their habits, and their manners.

The Union has peculiar commodities which have now become necessary to us, as they cannot be cultivated or can be raised only at an enormous expense upon the soil of Europe. The Americans consume only a small portion of this produce, and they are willing to sell us the rest. Europe is therefore the market of America, as America is the market of Europe; and maritime commerce is no less necessary to enable the inhabitants of the United States to transport their raw materials to the ports of Europe than it is to enable us to supply them with our manufactured produce. The United States must therefore either furnish much business to other maritime nations, even if they should themselves renounce commerce, as the Spaniards of Mexico have hitherto done, or they must become one of the foremost maritime powers of the globe.

The Anglo-Americans have always displayed a decided taste for the sea. The Declaration of Independence, by breaking the commercial bonds that united them to England, gave a fresh and powerful stimulus to their maritime genius. Ever since that time the shipping of the Union has increased almost as rapidly as the number of its inhabitants. The Americans themselves now transport to their own shores nine tenths of the European produce which they consume.[91] And they also bring three quarters of the exports of the New World to the European consumer.[92] The ships of the United States fill the docks of Havre and of Liverpool, while the number of English and French vessels at New York is comparatively small.[93]

Thus not only does the American merchant brave compe-

[91] The total value of imports for the year ending September 30, 1832 was $101,129,266. The imports carried in foreign vessels amounted to only $10,731,039, or approximately one tenth.

[92] The total value of exports during the same year was $87,176,945. The exports carried in foreign vessels was $21,036,183, or approximately one fourth. (Williams's *Register,* 1833, p. 398.)

[93] During the years 1829, 1830, and 1831, vessels of the tonnage of 3,307,719 entered the ports of the Union. Foreign vessels accounted for a total of only 544,571 tons. The latter were approximately in the proportion of 16 to 100. (*National Calendar,* 1833, p. 304.) During the years 1820, 1826, and 1831 the English vessels entering the ports of London, Liverpool, and Hull amounted to a tonnage of 443,800. Foreign vessels entering the same ports during the same years amounted to a tonnage of 159,431. The relation between the two was approximately 36 to 100. (*Companion to the Almanac,* 1834, p. 169.) In 1832, the proportion of foreign to English vessels entering British ports was 29 to 100.

tition on his own ground, but he even successfully supports that of foreign nations in their own ports. This is readily explained by the fact that the vessels of the United States cross the seas at a cheaper rate. As long as the mercantile shipping of the United States preserves this superiority, it will not only retain what it has acquired, but will constantly increase in prosperity.

It is difficult to say for what reason the Americans can navigate at a lower rate than other nations; one is at first led to attribute this superiority to the physical advantages that nature gives them; but it is not so. The American vessels cost almost as much to build as our own;[94] they are not better built, and they generally last a shorter time. The pay of the American sailor is higher than the pay on board European ships, as is proved by the great number of Europeans who are to be found in the merchant vessels of the United States. How does it happen, then, that the Americans sail their vessels at a cheaper rate than we can ours? I am of the opinion that the true cause of their superiority must not be sought for in physical advantages, but that it is wholly attributable to moral and intellectual qualities.

The following comparison will illustrate my meaning. During the campaigns of the Revolution the French introduced a new system of tactics into the art of war, which perplexed the oldest generals and very nearly destroyed the most ancient monarchies of Europe. They first undertook to make shift without a number of things that had always been held to be indispensable in warfare; they required novel exertions of their troops which no civilized nations had ever thought of; they achieved great actions in an incredibly short time and risked human life without hesitation to obtain the object in view. The French had less money and fewer men than their enemies; their resources were infinitely inferior; nevertheless, they were constantly victorious until their adversaries chose to imitate their example.

The Americans have introduced a similar system into commerce: they do for cheapness what the French did for conquest. The European sailor navigates with prudence; he sets sail only when the weather is favorable; if an unforeseen accident befalls him, he puts into port; at night he furls a

[94] Materials are, generally speaking, less expensive in America than in Europe. but the price of labor is much higher.

portion of his canvas; and when the whitening billows intimate the vicinity of land, he checks his course and takes an
observation of the sun. The American neglects these precautions and braves these dangers. He weighs anchor before the
tempest is over; by night and by day he spreads his sails to
the wind; such damage as his vessel may have sustained
from the storm, he repairs as he goes along; and when he at
last approaches the end of his voyage, he darts onward to
the shore as if he already descried a port. The Americans
are often shipwrecked, but no trader crosses the seas so rapidly. And as they perform the same distance in a shorter
time, they can perform it at a cheaper rate.

The European navigator touches at different ports in the
course of a long voyage; he loses precious time in making
the harbor or in waiting for a favorable wind to leave it;
and he pays daily dues to be allowed to remain there. The
American starts from Boston to purchase tea in China; he
arrives at Canton, stays there a few days, and then returns.
In less than two years he has sailed as far as the entire cir-
cumference of the globe and has seen land but once. It is
true that during a voyage of eight or ten months he has
drunk brackish water and lived on salt meat; that he has
been in a continual contest with the sea, with disease, and
with weariness; but upon his return he can sell a pound of
his tea for a halfpenny less than the English merchant, and
his purpose is accomplished.

I cannot better explain my meaning than by saying that
the Americans show a sort of heroism in their manner of
trading. The European merchant will always find it difficult
to imitate his American competitor, who, in adopting the
system that I have just described, does not follow calculation, but an impulse of his nature.

The inhabitants of the United States experience all the
wants and all the desires that result from an advanced civilization; and as they are not surrounded, as in Europe, by a
community skillfully organized to satisfy them, they are
often obliged to procure for themselves the various articles
that education and habit have rendered necessaries. In
America it sometimes happens that the same person tills his
field, builds his dwelling, fashions his tools, makes his shoes,
and weaves the coarse stuff of which his clothes are composed. This is prejudicial to the excellence of the work, but

it powerfully contributes to awaken the intelligence of the workman. Nothing tends to materialize man and to deprive his work of the faintest trace of mind more than the extreme division of labor. In a country like America, where men devoted to special occupations are rare, a long apprenticeship cannot be required from anyone who embraces a profession. The Americans therefore change their means of gaining a livelihood very readily, and they suit their occupations to the exigencies of the moment. Men are to be met with who have successively been lawyers, farmers, merchants, ministers of the Gospel, and physicians. If the American is less perfect in each craft than the European, at least there is scarcely any trade with which he is utterly unacquainted. His capacity is more general, and the circle of his intelligence is greater.

The inhabitants of the United States are never fettered by the axioms of their profession; they escape from all the prejudices of their present station; they are not more attached to one line of operation than to another; they are not more prone to employ an old method than a new one; they have no rooted habits, and they easily shake off the influence that the habits of other nations might exercise upon them, from a conviction that their country is unlike any other and that its situation is without a precedent in the world. America is a land of wonders, in which everything is in constant motion and every change seems an improvement. The idea of novelty is there indissolubly connected with the idea of amelioration. No natural boundary seems to be set to the efforts of man; and in his eyes what is not yet done is only what he has not yet attempted to do.

This perpetual change which goes on in the United States, these frequent vicissitudes of fortune, these unforeseen fluctuations in private and public wealth, serve to keep the minds of the people in a perpetual feverish agitation, which admirably invigorates their exertions and keeps them, so to speak, above the ordinary level of humanity. The whole life of an American is passed like a game of chance, a revolutionary crisis, or a battle. As the same causes are continually in operation throughout the country, they ultimately impart an irresistible impulse to the national character. The American, taken as a chance specimen of his countrymen, must then be a man of singular warmth in his desires, enterprising, fond of adventure and, above all, of novelty. The same bent is manifest in all that he does: he introduces it into his political laws, his religious doctrines, his theories of social economy, and his domestic occupations; he bears it with him in the depth of the backwoods as well as in the business of the city. It is this same passion, applied to maritime commerce, that makes him the cheapest and the quickest trader in the world.

As long as the sailors of the United States retain these mental advantages, and the practical superiority which they derive from them, they not only will continue to supply the wants of the producers and consumers of their own country, but will tend more and more to become, like the English,[95] the commercial agents of other nations. This prediction has already begun to be realized; we perceive that the American traders are introducing themselves as intermediate agents in the commerce of several European nations,[96] and America will offer a still wider field to their enterprise.

The great colonies that were founded in South America by the Spaniards and the Portuguese have since become empires. Civil war and oppression now lay waste those extensive regions. Population does not increase, and the thinly scattered inhabitants are too much absorbed in the cares of self-defense even to attempt any amelioration of their condition. But it will not always be so. Europe has succeeded by her own efforts in piercing the gloom of the Middle Ages. South America has the same Christian laws and usages as we have; she contains all the germs of civilization that have grown amid the nations of Europe or their offshoots added to the advantages to be derived from our example: why, then, should she always remain uncivilized? It is clear that the question is simply one of time; at some future period, which may be more or less remote, the inhabitants of South America will form flourishing and enlightened nations.

[95] It must not be supposed that English vessels are exclusively employed in transporting foreign produce into England, or British produce to foreign countries; at the present day the merchant shipping of England may be regarded in the light of a vast system of public conveyances, ready to serve all the producers of the world, and to open communications between all nations. The maritime genius of the Americans prompts them to enter into competition with the English.

[96] Part of the commerce of the Mediterranean is already carried on by American vessels.

But when the Spaniards and Portuguese of South America begin to feel the wants common to all civilized nations, they will still be unable to satisfy those wants for themselves; as the youngest children of civilization they must perforce admit the superiority of their elder brothers. They will be agriculturists long before they succeed in manufactures or commerce; and they will require the mediation of strangers to exchange their produce beyond seas for those articles for which a demand will begin to be felt.

It is unquestionable that the North Americans will one day be called upon to supply the wants of the South Americans. Nature has placed them in contiguity and has furnished the former with every means of knowing and appreciating those demands, of establishing permanent relations with those states and gradually filling their markets. The merchant of the United States could only forfeit these natural advantages if he were very inferior to the European merchant; but he is superior to him in several respects. The Americans of the United States already exercise a great moral influence upon all the nations of the New World. They are the source of intelligence, and all those who inhabit the same continent are already accustomed to consider them as the most enlightened, the most powerful, and the most wealthy members of the great American family. All eyes are therefore turned towards the United States: these are the models which the other communities try to imitate to the best of their power; it is from the Union that they borrow their political principles and their laws.

The Americans of the United States stand in precisely the same position with regard to the South Americans as their fathers, the English, occupy with regard to the Italians, the Spaniards, the Portuguese, and all those nations of Europe that receive their articles of daily consumption from England because they are less advanced in civilization and trade. England is at this time the natural emporium of almost all the nations that are within its reach; the American Union will perform the same part in the other hemisphere, and every community which is founded or which prospers in the New World is founded and prospers to the advantage of the Anglo-Americans.

If the Union were to be dissolved, the commerce of the states that now compose it would undoubtedly be checked for a time, but less than one would think. It is evident that, whatever may happen, the commercial states will remain united. They are contiguous, they have the same opinions, interests, and manners, and they alone form a great maritime power. Even if the South of the Union were to become independent of the North, it would still require the services of those states. I have already observed that the South is not a commercial country, and nothing indicates that it will become so. The Americans of the South of the United States will therefore long be obliged to have recourse to strangers to export their produce and supply them with the commodities which satisfy their wants. But the Northern states are undoubtedly able to act as their intermediate agents more cheaply than any other merchants. They will therefore retain that employment, for cheapness is the sovereign law of commerce. Sovereign will and national prejudices cannot long resist the influence of cheapness. Nothing can be more virulent than the hatred that exists between the Americans of the United States and the English. But in spite of these hostile feelings the Americans derive most of their manufactured commodities from England, because England supplies them at a cheaper rate than any other nation. Thus the increasing prosperity of America turns, notwithstanding the grudge of the Americans, to the advantage of British manufactures.

Reason and experience prove that no commercial prosperity can be durable if it cannot be united, in case of need, to naval force. This truth is as well understood in the United States as anywhere else: the Americans are already able to make their flag respected; in a few years they will make it feared. I am convinced that the dismemberment of the Union would not have the effect of diminishing the naval power of the Americans, but would powerfully contribute to increase it. At present the commercial states are connected with others that are not commercial and that unwillingly see the increase of a maritime power by which they are only indirectly benefited. If, on the contrary, the commercial states of the Union formed one and the same nation, commerce would become the foremost of their national interests; they would consequently be willing to make great sacrifices to protect their shipping, and nothing would prevent them from pursuing their desires on this point.

Nations as well as men almost always betray the prominent features of their future destiny in their earliest years. When I contemplate the ardor with which the Anglo-Americans prosecute commerce, the advantages which aid them, and the success of their undertakings, I cannot help believing that they will one day become the foremost maritime power of the globe. They are born to rule the seas, as the Romans were to conquer the world.

CONCLUSION

I AM approaching the close of my inquiry; hitherto, in speaking of the future destiny of the United States, I have endeavored to divide my subject into distinct portions in order to study each of them with more attention. My present object is to embrace the whole from one point of view; the remarks I shall make will be less detailed, but they will be more sure. I shall perceive each object less distinctly, but I shall descry the principal facts with more certainty. A traveler who has just left a vast city climbs the neighboring hill; as he goes farther off, he loses sight of the men whom he has just quitted; their dwellings are confused in a dense mass; he can no longer distinguish the public squares and can scarcely trace out the great thoroughfares; but his eye has less difficulty in following the boundaries of the city, and for the first time he sees the shape of the whole. Such is the future destiny of the British race in North America to my eye; the details of the immense picture are lost in the shade, but I conceive a clear idea of the entire subject.

The territory now occupied or possessed by the United States of America forms about one twentieth of the habitable earth. But extensive as these bounds are, it must not be supposed that the Anglo-American race will always remain within them; indeed, it has already gone far beyond them.

There was a time when we also might have created a great French nation in the American wilds, to counterbalance the influence of the English on the destinies of the New World. France formerly possessed a territory in North America scarcely less extensive than the whole of Europe. The three greatest rivers of that continent then flowed within her dominions. The Indian tribes that dwelt between the mouth of the St. Lawrence and the delta of the Mississippi were unaccustomed to any other tongue than ours; and all the European settlements scattered over that immense region recalled the traditions of our country. Louisburg, Montmorency, Duquesne, St. Louis, Vincennes, New Orleans (for such were the names they bore) are words dear to France and familiar to our ears.

But a course of circumstances which it would be tedious to enumerate[97] has deprived us of this magnificent inheritance. Wherever the French settlers were numerically weak and partially established, they have disappeared; those who remain are collected on a small extent of country and are now subject to other laws. The 400,000 French inhabitants of Lower Canada constitute at the present time the remnant of an old nation lost in the midst of a new people. A foreign population is increasing around them unceasingly and on all sides, who already penetrate among the former masters of the country, predominate in their cities, and corrupt their language. This population is identical with that of the United States; it is therefore with truth that I asserted that the British race is not confined within the frontiers of the Union, since it already extends to the northeast.

To the northwest nothing is to be met with but a few insignificant Russian settlements; but to the southwest Mexico presents a barrier to the Anglo-Americans. Thus the Spaniards and the Anglo-Americans are, properly speaking, the two races that divide the possession of the New World. The limits of separation between them have been settled by treaty; but although the conditions of that treaty are favorable to the Anglo-Americans, I do not doubt that they will shortly infringe it. Vast provinces extending beyond the frontiers of the Union towards Mexico are still destitute of inhabitants. The natives of the United States will people these solitary regions before their rightful occupants. They will take possession of the soil and establish social institutions, so that when the legal owner at length arrives, he will find the wilderness under cultivation, and strangers quietly settled in the midst of his inheritance.

The lands of the New World belong to the first occupant; they are the natural reward of the swiftest pioneer. Even the

[97] The foremost of these circumstances is that nations which are accustomed to township institutions and municipal government are better able than any others to establish prosperous colonies. The habit of thinking and governing for oneself is indispensable in a new country, where success necessarily depends in a great measure upon the individual exertions of the settlers.

countries that are already peopled will have some difficulty in securing themselves from this invasion. I have already alluded to what is taking place in the province of Texas. The inhabitants of the United States are perpetually migrating to Texas, where they purchase land; and although they conform to the laws of the country, they are gradually founding the empire of their own language and their own manners. The province of Texas is still part of the Mexican dominions, but it will soon contain no Mexicans; the same thing has occurred wherever the Anglo-Americans have come in contact with a people of a different origin.

It cannot be denied that the British race has acquired an amazing preponderance over all other European races in the New World; and it is very superior to them in civilization, industry, and power. As long as it is surrounded only by wilderness or thinly peopled countries, as long as it encounters on its route no dense population through which it cannot work its way, it will assuredly continue to spread. The lines marked out by treaties will not stop it, but it will everywhere overleap these imaginary barriers.

The geographical position of the British race in the New World is peculiarly favorable to its rapid increase. Above its northern frontiers the icy regions of the Pole extend; and a few degrees below its southern confines lies the burning climate of the Equator. The Anglo-Americans are therefore placed in the most temperate and habitable zone of the continent.

It is generally supposed that the prodigious increase of population in the United States is posterior to their Declaration of Independence, but this is an error. The population increased as rapidly under the colonial system as at the present day; that is to say, it doubled in about twenty-two years. But this proportion, which is now applied to millions of inhabitants, was then applied to thousands; and the same fact which was scarcely noticeable a century ago is now evident to every observer.

The English in Canada, who are dependent on a king, augment and spread almost as rapidly as the British settlers of the United States, who live under a republican government. During the War of Independence, which lasted eight years, the population continued to increase without intermission in the same ratio. Although powerful Indian nations allied with the English existed at that time on the western frontiers, the emigration westward was never checked. While the enemy laid waste the shores of the Atlantic, Kentucky, the western parts of Pennsylvania, and the states of Vermont and of Maine were filling with inhabitants. Nor did the unsettled state of things which succeeded the war prevent the increase of the population or stop its progress across the wilds. Thus the difference of laws, the various conditions of peace and war, of order or anarchy, have exercised no perceptible influence upon the continued development of the Anglo-Americans. This may be readily understood, for no causes are sufficiently general to exercise a simultaneous influence over the whole of so extensive a territory. One portion of the country always offers a sure retreat from the calamities that afflict another part; and however great may be the evil, the remedy that is at hand is greater still.

It must not, then, be imagined that the impulse of the British race in the New World can be arrested. The dismemberment of the Union and the hostilities that might ensue, the abolition of republican institutions and the tyrannical government that might succeed, may retard this impulse, but they cannot prevent the people from ultimately fulfilling their destinies. No power on earth can shut out the immigrants from that fertile wilderness which offers resources to all industry and a refuge from all want. Future events, whatever they may be, will not deprive the Americans of their climate or their inland seas, their great rivers or their exuberant soil. Nor will bad laws, revolutions, and anarchy be able to obliterate that love of prosperity and spirit of enterprise which seem to be the distinctive characteristics of their race or extinguish altogether the knowledge that guides them on their way.

Thus in the midst of the uncertain future one event at least is sure. At a period that may be said to be near, for we are speaking of the life of a nation, the Anglo-Americans alone will cover the immense space contained between the polar regions and the tropics, extending from the coasts of the Atlantic to those of the Pacific Ocean. The territory that will probably be occupied by the Anglo-Americans may perhaps equal three quarters of Europe in extent.[98] The climate

[98] The United States alone cover an area equal to one half of Europe. The area of Europe is 500,000 square leagues; its population is 205,000,000. (Malte-Brun, Vol. VI, Bk. 114, p. 4.)

of the Union is, on the whole, preferable to that of Europe, and its natural advantages are as great; it is therefore evident that its population will at some future time be proportionate to our own. Europe, divided as it is between so many nations and torn as it has been by incessant wars growing out of the barbarous manners of the Middle Ages, has yet attained a population of 410 inhabitants to the square league.[99] What cause can prevent the United States from having as numerous a population in time?

Many ages must elapse before the different offshoots of the British race in America will cease to present the same physiognomy; and the time cannot be foreseen at which a permanent inequality of condition can be established in the New World. Whatever differences may arise, from peace or war, freedom or oppression, prosperity or want, between the destinies of the different descendants of the great Anglo-American family, they will all preserve at least a similar social condition and will hold in common the customs and opinions to which that social condition has given birth.

In the Middle Ages the tie of religion was sufficiently powerful to unite all the different populations of Europe in the same civilization. The British of the New World have a thousand other reciprocal ties; and they live at a time when the tendency to equality is general among mankind. The Middle Ages were a period when everything was broken up, when each people, each province, each city, and each family tended strongly to maintain its distinct individuality. At the present time an opposite tendency seems to prevail, and the nations seem to be advancing to unity. Our means of intellectual intercourse unite the remotest parts of the earth; and men cannot remain strangers to one another or be ignorant of what is taking place in any corner of the globe. The consequence is that there is less difference at the present day between the Europeans and their descendants in the New World, in spite of the ocean that divides them, than there was in the thirteenth century between certain towns that were separated only by a river. If this tendency to assimilation brings foreign nations closer to each other, it must *a fortiori* prevent the descendants of the same people from becoming aliens to one another.

The time will therefore come when one hundred and fifty

[99] See Malte-Brun, Vol. VI, Bk. 116, p. 92.

million men will be living in North America,[100] equal in condition, all belonging to one family, owing their origin to the same cause, and preserving the same civilization, the same language, the same religion, the same habits, the same manners, and imbued with the same opinions, propagated under the same forms. The rest is uncertain, but this is certain; and it is a fact new to the world, a fact that the imagination strives in vain to grasp.

There are at the present time two great nations in the world, which started from different points, but seem to tend towards the same end. I allude to the Russians and the Americans. Both of them have grown up unnoticed; and while the attention of mankind was directed elsewhere, they have suddenly placed themselves in the front rank among the nations, and the world learned their existence and their greatness at almost the same time.

All other nations seem to have nearly reached their natural limits, and they have only to maintain their power; but these are still in the act of growth.[101] All the others have stopped, or continue to advance with extreme difficulty; these alone are proceeding with ease and celerity along a path to which no limit can be perceived. The American struggles against the obstacles that nature opposes to him; the adversaries of the Russian are men. The former combats the wilderness and savage life; the latter, civilization with all its arms. The conquests of the American are therefore gained by the plowshare; those of the Russian by the sword. The Anglo-American relies upon personal interest to accomplish his ends and gives free scope to the unguided strength and common sense of the people; the Russian centers all the authority of society in a single arm. The principal instrument of the former is freedom; of the latter, servitude. Their starting-point is different and their courses are not the same; yet each of them seems marked out by the will of Heaven to sway the destinies of half the globe.

[100] This would be a population proportionate to that of Europe, taken at a mean rate of 410 inhabitants to the square league.

[101] The population of Russia increases proportionately more rapidly than that of any other country in the Old World.